KEN WILBER

SUNY series in

TRANSPERSONAL AND HUMANISTIC PSYCHOLOGY

Richard D. Mann, *editor*

KEN WILBER

thought as

passion

Frank Visser

STATE UNIVERSITY OF NEW YORK PRESS

Excerpts from the following books are reprinted by arrangement with
Shambhala Publications, Inc. (www.shambhala.com)

The Holographic Paradigm and Other Paradoxes, © 1982 Ken Wilber
Eye to Eye, © 1983, 1990, 1996 Ken Wilber
A Sociable God, © 1983, 1984 Ken Wilber
Quantum Questions, © 1984, 2001 Ken Wilber
Transformations of Consciousness, © 1986 Ken Wilber
Grace and Grit, © 1991, 2000 Ken Wilber
Sex, Ecology, Spirituality, © 1995, 2000 Ken Wilber
A Brief History of Everything, © 1996, 2000 Ken Wilber
The Eye of Spirit, © 1997, 2001 Ken Wilber
One Taste, © 1999, 2000 Ken Wilber
Integral Psychology, © 2000 Ken Wilber
A Theory of Everything, © 2000 Ken Wilber
Boomeritis, © 2002 Ken Wilber

Grateful acknowledgement is made to Shambhala Publications, Inc.
for quotations from the books by Ken Wilber they have published.

Read more about Ken Wilber, this book, and the author on:
www.worldofkenwilber.com

Originally published as *Ken Wilber: Denken als passie*,
Rotterdam, The Netherlands, Lemniscaat, 2001.

Translated from the Dutch language by Rachel Horner.

Published by
STATE UNIVERSITY OF NEW YORK PRESS, ALBANY

For information, address State University of New York Press,
90 State Street, Suite 700, Albany, NY 12207

Production, Laurie Searl
Marketing, Fran Keneston

Library of Congress Cataloging-in-Publication Data

Visser, Frank, 1958–
[Ken Wilber. English]
Ken Wilber : thought as passion / Frank Visser.
p. cm. — (SUNY series in transpersonal and humanistic psychology)
Includes bibliographical references (p.) and index.
ISBN 0-7914-5815-6 (alk. paper) — ISBN 0-7914-5816-4 (pbk. : alk. paper)
1. Wilber, Ken. I. Title. II. Series.

BF109.W54V5713 2003
191—dc21   2003042554

10 9 8 7 6 5 4 3 2 1

The essence of my work is: God, or the absolute Spirit, exists—and can be proven—and there is a ladder that reaches to that summit, a ladder that you can be shown how to climb, a ladder that leads from time to eternity, and from death to immortality. And all philosophy and psychology swings into a remarkable synthesis around that ladder.
—Ken Wilber, *The Great Chain of Being,*
1987 (unpublished manuscript)

Is the outlook for the psychology of mysticism therefore bleak? On the contrary, it seems very promising. I would therefore not be surprised if the study of mysticism would one day be considered as a branch of psych-ology. This does not mean that mysticism would be reduced to what most present-day psychologists seem to spend most of their time on. Rather, it means that psychology would be deepened and widened so as to be in a position to take account of these particular aspects of the mind.
—Frits Staal, *Exploring Mysticism,* 1975

Nothing so practical as a good theory.
—Kurt Lewin

CONTENTS

FOREWORD

KEN WILBER

It is a pleasure to introduce my friend Frank Visser's book *Ken Wilber: Thought as Passion*. Since I seem to be related to the subject of the book, sometimes intimately, perhaps I will be forgiven if I open with a self-serving comment. I very much appreciate the subtitle, *Thought as Passion*. In 1983, when I first moved to California and stayed with Roger Walsh and Frances Vaughan in their lovely home in Tiburon, I became good friends with Rollo May, who at that time was seventy-five years old, but still vibrant, sharp, luminous. Rollo was a true hero of mine, for many reasons. First, he was a student and friend of Paul Tillich's, and Tillich was one of the truly great existentialists, as well as one of the two or three finest theologians of the twentieth century. Second, Rollo May was the major interpreter of existentialism for America, and especially of existential psychology. Rollo was a living connection to the great European philosophers who have been formative for me. (I have often described myself as a northern European thinker with a southern European lifestyle who practices Eastern religion—or something like that. But I do not particularly think of myself as American, although, annoyingly, that is how Europeans think of me, which shows how hard it is to shake cultural embeddedness. But really, Anglo-Saxon empiricism and cowboy pragmatism: who needs it?) Third, Rollo was a wonderful human being, warm and witty and wise.

Here's the self-serving comment. On the cover of one of my books, *Up from Eden*, was a quote from Rollo: "Ken Wilber is the most passionate philosopher I know." Every now and then somebody has said something kind about my work, but that is still my favorite, especially since it came from Rollo, who, as a true existentialist, believed that passion and truth are close to identical. I mention it now because Frank's subtitle reminded me of that comment and how much it meant to me. To have any meaning at all, philosophy must sizzle with passion, boil your brain, fry your eyeballs, or you're just not doing it right. And that applies to the other end of the spectrum of feelings as well. Real philosophy is as gentle as fog and as quiet as tears; it holds the world as if it were a delicate infant, raw and open and vulnerable. I sincerely hope that if I have brought anything to this field, it is a bit of passion.

Although it purports to be about me and my work, the following book is actually about an integral approach to philosophy, spirituality—to the human condition on the whole. It is true that this book is a chronicle of my own journey to what I hope are increasingly integral stances, but I believe that the only enduring parts of that journey are the ideas themselves, not the bearer of those ideas.

In this volume, Frank presents a summary of some of the phases of my work and his commentary on them. Allow me to get the standard disclaimer out of the way, which is that, in fairness to other treatments of my work, I cannot endorse any of them, including this one. I have not read this book for accuracy (except some of the biographical material), and thus I cannot vouch for its soundness, nor can I respond to critics who use the interpretations given in this book. Having said that, Frank Visser has certainly studied this material as carefully as anybody, and I am deeply appreciative of his efforts to make an integral approach more available to the public. Whether or not this book represents my ideas accurately, it definitely represents ideas that need to be a part of any integral conversation, and for that reason alone, this is an invaluable contribution to the ongoing integral dialogue. I myself have some friendly disagreements with Frank about many of these topics, but I always learn something important from him in our exchanges, and I believe you will, too.

The word *integral* means comprehensive, inclusive, nonmarginalizing, embracing. Integral approaches to any field attempt to be exactly that— they include as many perspectives, styles, and methodologies as possible within a coherent view of the topic. In a certain sense, integral approaches are "meta-paradigms," or ways to draw together an already existing number of separate paradigms into a network of interrelated, mutually enriching perspectives. In consciousness studies, for example, there are at least a dozen different schools, but an integral approach insists that all twelve of them have important if partial truths that need to be included in any comprehensive account. The same is true for the many schools of psychology, sociology, philosophy, anthropology, spirituality: they all have important pieces of the integral puzzle, and all of them need to be honored and included in a more comprehensive or integral approach.

I am often asked which of my own books I would recommend as an introduction; I still believe *A Brief History of Everything* is perhaps the best (although *A Theory of Everything* is probably the shortest and simplest). *Brief History* was written as a popular or more accessible version of *Sex, Ecology, Spirituality (SES),* which was the first major statement of my own integral view. The books prior to *SES* are preliminary explorations in integral studies, and, although many of them present what I hope are important pieces of an integral view, were I to summarize my work, I would not start before *Sex, Ecology, Spirituality.* As I said, *SES* was the first book to outline my own version of integral studies (which is sometimes called "AQAL," short for "all quadrants, all levels, all lines, all states, all types"). After presenting *SES,* I would discuss the earlier books only as they were useful in forming the subcomponents of a more integral theory. The problem with chronological accounts of my work is that, in reliving earlier debates and dialogues, many of the terms as I now use them become irreversibly contaminated with the distortions of critics who at the time misunderstood what was being said. I personally do not believe that those debates are of much historical interest because they are more about distortion than facts. At the same time, as a story, the chronology is intriguing enough and has merit as a study in paradigm clashes, where all sides in the discussions (including me) had their fair share of misunderstandings.

The events leading up to *SES,* which was published in 1995, may be of interest. I had not written or published much for almost a decade, a decade largely devoted to caring for a wife who was diagnosed with cancer shortly after we were married; we hadn't had a honeymoon when the shocking news arrived. Treya and I were married in 1983; she died in 1989. At her request, I wrote of our ordeal in *Grace and Grit.* Apart from that, I had written little in ten years. The events with Treya changed me deeply, profoundly, irrevocably. I believe that *SES* represented, in part, the results of the combined growth that Treya and I did for each other. We grew up together, we were enlightened together, and we died together. All of my books up to *SES* always had a dedication. Starting with *SES,* none of my books have had a dedication because all of them have been dedicated to her.

Whatever it was that happened, it was as if all the books I had written previously—some ten or eleven of them—were merely preparations, preliminary glimpses, or parts of an integral embrace still struggling to emerge. It was as if the events that transpired with Treya allowed a growth in spirit, given by grace, that finally made enough room for me to even be able to see some of the integral horizons involved. In any event, I know that all of the work I have done subsequently came out of a Heart that I alone did not discover.

My work is sometimes divided into four phases, with the latest (phase-4) being dated with *SES* and six or seven subsequent books. I am often asked if there is a "phase-5" on the horizon, and I'm not sure exactly what to say about that. As Frank reports, I have in the last year written around 2,000 pages, and I suppose some of that, which seems to be fairly novel, might qualify. Since much of this material will be released only after Frank's book is out, interested readers can see some of it posted at *wilber.shambhala.com* and *integralinstitute.org,* and you can decide for yourself whether it merits a high-sounding "phase-5" name or is simply rambling repetitions of earlier material. Part of it does seem definitely new—an integral semiotics, as well as an integral calculus, a form of mathematics that replaces variables with perspectives. But who knows?

The one thing I do know, and that I would like to emphasize, is that any integral theory is just that—a mere theory. I am always surprised, or rather shocked, at the common perception that I am recommending an intellectual approach to spirituality, when that is the opposite of my view. Just because an author writes, say, a history of dancing, does not mean that the author is advocating that people stop dancing and merely read about it instead. I have written academic treatises that cover areas such as spirituality and its relation to a larger scheme of things, but my recommendation is always that people take up an actual spiritual practice, not merely read about it. An integral approach to dancing says, take up dancing itself, and sure, read a book about it, too. Do both, but in any event, don't merely read the book. That's like taking a vacation to Bermuda by sitting at home and looking through a book of maps. My books are maps, but please, go to Bermuda and see for yourself.

See for yourself if, in the depths of your own awareness, right here and now, you can find the entire Kosmos, because that is where it resides. Birds are singing—in your awareness. Ocean waves are crashing—in your awareness. Clouds are floating by—in the sky of your own awareness. What is this awareness of yours, that holds the entire universe in its embrace and knows the secrets even of God? In the still point of the turning world, in the secret center of the known universe, in the eyes of the very one reading this page, at the very source of thought itself, watch the entire Kosmos emerge, dancing wildly with a passion philosophy tries to capture, crowned with a glory and sealed with a wonder lovers seek to share, rushing through a radiant world of time that is but eternity's bid to be seen. What is this Self of yours?

An integral approach is merely an attempt to categorize, in conceptual terms, some of this glory as it manifests itself. But it is no more than that. Every one of my books has at least one sentence, usually buried, that says the following (this is the version found in *The Atman Project*): "There follows, then, the story of the Atman project. It is a sharing of what I have seen; it is a small offering of what I have remembered; it is also the Zen dust you should shake from your sandals; and it is finally a lie in the face of that Mystery which only alone is."

In other words, all of my books are lies. They are simply maps of a territory, shadows of a reality, gray symbols dragging their bellies across the dead page, suffocated signs full of muffled sound and faded glory, signifying absolutely nothing. And it is the nothing, the Mystery, the Emptiness alone that needs to be realized: not known but felt, not thought but breathed, not an object but an atmosphere, not a lesson but a life.

There follows a book of maps; hopefully more comprehensive maps, but maps nonetheless. Please use them only as a reminder to take up dancing itself, to inquire into this Self of yours, this Self that holds this page and this Kosmos all in a single glance. And then express that glory in integral maps, and sing with passion of the sights you have seen, the sounds that the tender Heart has whispered only to you in the late hours of the quiet night, and come and join us and tell us what you have heard, in your own trip to Bermuda, in the vibrant Silence that you alone own, and the radiant Heart that we alone, together, can discover.

K. W.
Denver, Colorado
December 2002

INTRODUCTION

KEN WILBER: THE PERSON AND HIS WORK

Without holding any kind of degree in psychology, American autodidact Ken Wilber has managed to evolve into a leading theorist in the field. In particular, Wilber started as an exponent of transpersonal psychology—a school of religious psychology set up at the end of the sixties which endeavors to study the field of mystical spirituality in a scientifically sound way. Wilber himself studied biochemistry for a few years and for a time it looked as if he would continue and possibly excel in that direction. Yet during those early years at college Wilber was already starting to explore Eastern philosophy and Western psychology. He came to realize that his calling lay in bringing these two worlds together. Within a few years— he was still only twenty-three years old—he wrote up the results of his private studies in a book entitled *The Spectrum of Consciousness*, a book that would prove to be the first of a commanding oeuvre. *The Spectrum of Consciousness* sets out the basic principles of a vision of the individual and reality that incorporates and does justice to the insights of both East and West—not only the insights of the proverbial Freud and Buddha, but also those of Piaget and Patanjali, Kohlberg and Confucius, Skinner and Shankara, Neumann and Nagarjuna, Bowlby and Bodhidharma, Plato and Padmasambhava, to mention but a few illustrious names. Wilber's work as a whole is motivated by the effort to arrive at a world philosophy.[1] Inclusivity is the dominant hallmark of his vision.

Wilber's influence has since extended far beyond the realm of psychology. While his early works focused primarily on psychology, in his more recent work Wilber has emerged as a cultural philosopher who strives to place contemporary developments in the spheres of religion and politics within the context of the wisdom of the ages. What is particularly striking is that in doing so Wilber is not only critical of the rationalist and materialist mainstream of Western culture, which either shows no interest in spirituality or entertains caricatures in this respect, he is also critical of the highly irrationally tinged counterculture of the New Age and so-called holism, which he accuses of gross superficiality, among other things. Wilber's main objection to New Age thinking is that it frequently equates spirituality with magical thinking, mythological fables, and a narcissistic concern with one's own spiritual well-being.[2] Time and time again Wilber points in his books to the depth and detail of the worldview expounded by the spiritual traditions—precisely what the contemporary alternative culture is in danger of losing sight of.

In the alternative world of the New Age Wilber has always been an outsider, if not an awkward customer, to put it mildly. Many today are extremely taken with Jung—Wilber isn't. Many have taken up with Freud—Wilber hasn't. Many place their hope in holism—Wilber doesn't. Many would see the intellect as the villain of the drama—Wilber won't. He even dares to openly object to such popular conceptions as "there's no such thing as chance," "we create our own reality," "we cause our own illnesses (and are also capable of healing ourselves)," "we need to be less in the mind and more in the body," statements that have come to acquire the status of religious dogmas in the world of the New Age. Wilber sees these notions as twisted interpretations of the profound insights of the spiritual traditions, distortions that urgently need to be corrected. In this respect Wilber sides entirely with the critics of the New Age who see these notions as being symptomatic of the "me" decade. However, though Wilber ardently defends reason as being superior to prerational forms of expression such as magical and mythic thinking, he is fiercely critical of the Western dogma that contends that reason is man's highest possible attainment and that everything needs to be assessed in the light of reason. Wilber differs from those who hold this point of view in that he looks for ways to introduce authentic mystic spirituality into Western culture. Ultimately Wilber is concerned with mystic spirituality as a way of life.[3]

Wilber also differs from most authors who are preoccupied with religion and spirituality in that he attaches a great deal of value to typical Western attainments such as the ability to reason, the sense of individuality, and the drive towards emancipation. At the same time he denounces the materialism of Western philosophers who are only willing to study those aspects of reality that are visible and tangible, an approach which leads to the entire sphere of subjectivity being disregarded and carelessly discarded as unscientific. Yet Wilber also has certain reservations regarding the Eastern way of thinking. While some of the most profound spiritual systems that humanity has ever known have emerged from the East, Wilber is certainly not oblivious to the fact that much of what comes from the East is primitive, magical, or dogmatic. Thus—as is likely to be clear by now—it is difficult to place Wilber in a certain category.

The nineteen books that Wilber has either authored or edited have been translated in more than thirty languages.[4] This makes Wilber the most translated American author of academic books. The fact that all of these books have been in print continuously, in some cases for more than twenty years, is not only remarkable, particularly given the volatile nature of the book market, but it also testifies to the existence of a broadly based and continuous interest in Wilber's work. Although Wilber's books are highly academic in tone, as yet he has received little recognition from the world of academia (though there are signs that this is changing, at least in the United States). This may have something to do with the fact that his books have been published by two rather 'suspect' publishing houses: most of his books have been launched by the Buddhist publisher Shambhala, and several others have issued from the theosophical publisher Quest Books. By way of comparison, the works of two of Wilber's main opponents in the field of transpersonal psychology—Stanislav Grof and Michael Washburn, who we will hear more about in Chapter 7—are published by the State University of New York Press. Only one of Wilber's most recent works, *The Marriage of Sense and Soul*, which came out in 1998, was published by a large general publisher, Random House.[5] All of this points to the fact that Wilber is a long way from the academic and scientific establishment in his thinking. For instance, while most of his opponents are still working within the framework of depth psychology—which is now acknowledged to some extent within academic circles—by basing their work on Freud, Jung, or other distinguished depth psychologists, Wilber has chosen a very different tack. His approach might best be described as "height psychology," particularly when it comes to his attempt to chart the field of mystic spirituality.

Thus Ken Wilber occupies a precarious position between the worlds of academia and esoteric religion, which makes it less likely that he will be accepted by either. Anyone who claims to be able to integrate the diverse and contradictory spheres of science and religion runs a huge risk of being taken seriously by neither. For as far as scientists are concerned, Wilber's work is too lyrical—they readily suspect him of smuggling religion into the world of science. On the other hand, those with a spiritual orientation are inclined to find Wilber too abstract and too scientific—they are not convinced that the field of spirituality needs to be subjected to critical examination nor that it needs to be aligned with recent developments in clinical psychology or movements such as postmodernism. Even the interested layperson who attempts to follow the developments in both worlds as closely as possible is likely to find Wilber hard going. He or she may well be aware of Wilber's reputation but will often not be familiar with his main ideas, to say nothing of the way in which Wilber's vision has developed over the course of more than two decades. Thus while many may have read his book *No Boundary* published in 1979, they may not know that Wilber no longer fully subscribes to the ideas presented in this early work. (However, since even the faux pas of a genius are interesting, a separate chapter covers Wilber's earliest work in some detail.) And even though in another book, *The Holographic Paradigm*, Wilber criticizes the currently fashionable line of thinking which contends that the findings of modern physics support the worldview expounded by the mystics, rumor has it that Wilber also subscribes to the idea that modern physics and mysticism amount to the same thing.

Added to all this is the fact that Wiber's oeuvre is by no means complete.[6] Almost like clockwork, thus far Wilber has come up with a new book virtually every year. This in itself is likely to make it difficult for the average reader to maintain an overview of his work. Even those who are extremely impressed with his work can be heard to sigh that a concise summary of his vision would be most welcome. And the many thousands of people who have read the odd book without studying Wilber's work in any depth, yet who are interested in the essence of his vision, may well find the summary presented in this book to be of interest. In particular, this book has been written for the large group of readers in the latter category.

One of Wilber's fundamental postulates—and in this respect Wilber is close to the postmodernists—is that everything exists within a context and that nothing can be understood independently of its context. And naturally, this is also true of Wilber's way of thinking. Thus in addition to presenting a brief overview of Wilber's work as a whole, this book also attempts to view his oeuvre from the point of view of a broader perspective. After the first six chapters have examined Ken Wilber and his work in some depth, the last chapter adopts a more distant stance with a view to providing for this wider context. What were and are Wilber's greatest sources of inspiration? And where does his own originality lie? Given that Wilber cites so many other writers both in positive and in negative senses, this is a question that needs to be asked. Does Wilber do anything more than present the common denominators in the works of the greatest thinkers of East and West? Would the world be any different if Wilber had never put pen to paper? Who is it that year in and year out tirelessly persists in writing difficult, and occasionally somewhat less difficult but always intractable, books about science and spirituality? Besides giving an account of Wilber's books, this book also reveals the story *behind* his books—his career to date, the motives behind his choice of subjects, his theoretical and personal struggles, his philosophical vision, and, not least of all, his own spiritual experiences. As such this book is based not only on my own thorough study of Wilber's works—two of which I have translated into Dutch[7]—but also on the few details that Wilber has revealed in this respect, on the odd interview that he has given over the years,[8] and, above all, on hours of conversation I had with him at his home in 1997.[9]

For the last ten years Ken Wilber has been living and working virtually in isolation high in the Rocky Mountains in Boulder, Colorado. He doesn't attend conferences on principle—not even those devoted entirely to his own work. He rarely, if ever, grants interviews, though there does seem to have been a change in this respect in recent years. All of this has led to the creation of a remarkable vacuum that leaves people free rein to form their own opinions of the man behind the books.[10] Thus Wilber is accused of shutting himself off from criticism, of feeling himself to be literally and figuratively above the world, and of avoiding any confrontation beyond that of the written word. In this respect Ken Wilber clearly has an image problem. Yet the few people who have come to know him personally present a completely different picture. Wilber emerges as an engaging, even jovial individual and also as a highly impassioned thinker, committed to seeking truth above all else—and writing about it.

THE STRUCTURE OF THIS BOOK

Anyone who attempts to convey the ideological world of someone like Ken Wilber in an intelligible way is rapidly faced with a dilemma. Which is likely to be more appropriate, a thematic approach or a chronological approach? From an intellectual point of view a description which confines itself to the theoretical system as such might well prove to be more satisfying, yet this is offset by the fact that in focusing solely on the theoretical system, we lose sight of the person who elaborated the system. The chronological method offers the advantage that the events of the author's life can be readily interwoven with descriptions of the books as they were written and published over the years—though this approach runs the risk of becoming somewhat monotonous as we review one book after another. Bearing this in mind, I hope to have reduced any such monotony to a minimum by occasionally deviating from the chronological to recount an episode in Wilber's life or to offer my own reflections on the material discussed.

Actually, in Wilber's case there is another reason why a strictly thematic approach is virtually impossible. During the course of his intellectual development Wilber has evolved through a series of phases, occasionally confusing his critics in the process. In a recent book, *The Eye of Spirit* published in 1997, Wilber divides his oeuvre, which now stretches back some twenty years, into four different periods. For the sake of brevity he refers to these periods as Wilber 1, Wilber 2, Wilber 3, and Wilber 4 (and Wilber 4 is highly unlikely to be the last).[11] These four phases in Wilber's intellectual development deserve to be described in some detail. This being the case, I have deliberately devoted a separate chapter to each of these phases, and these four chapters form the basic framework around which this book is structured. Besides creating a context for Wilber's present vision, this approach also reveals how Wilber actually arrived at it.

Though I have made no attempt to hide my enthusiasm for Ken Wilber's work, this book is certainly not intended to be a hagiography. It might best be described as an intellectual biography or a personalized bibliography—if such a genre exists. In other words, while it centers primarily on the essential content and development of Wilber's work, the book also pays due respect to the person behind it. Given the quality and extent of Wilber's oeuvre, it is quite remarkable that there has not been a single monograph published on Wilber during the past two decades. Apparently no one has yet dared to hazard a summary and assessment of his work in book form. And it is easy to speculate why. It would virtually require a second Wilber to be able to fathom Wilber's work in its totality. Having broached so many different academic subjects in so many books, Wilber presents a sizeable challenge for anyone who hopes to present a comprehensive and comprehensible overview of his work. The many quotes included in this book will help to give the reader a clear impression of Wilber's characteristic style, which is both abstract and passionate at the same time. I am certainly not under any illusion that I can surpass or even equal Wilber in this respect. My aim in writing this book is of a far more modest nature. If, after having read this book, the reader has a clearer idea of Wilber's thought and is able to form his or her own opinion of Wilber's work, my efforts will have been amply rewarded.

Chapter 1 introduces Ken Wilber as a person. How did Wilber spend his youth? What were his school years like? How was it that he came to abandon his college studies in order to be able to devote himself to his own self-devised program of study? How did he learn to deal with the fame that came his way at such an early age? Why has he opted for the relatively lonely existence of a writer, when deep down he might have preferred to live in a seething city like San Francisco? Is he really the otherworldly hermit that many take him to be? Is his wisdom derived mainly from books (he claims to read three books a day), or do his own experiences within the realms of meditation also play a part? And how does he see his function as a writer within a broader cultural and religious context? Wilber has often compared himself with the Indian figure of the pandit, who in Indian culture performs the function of a 'spiritual intellectual'—a person who is able to express and defend the truths of the spiritual traditions in a contemporary idiom and a person for whom there seems to be no equivalent in the West.

Chapter 2 looks at the period of Wilber 1. Wilber became a famous author with his debut work *The Spectrum of Consciousness*. Like many other authors in the field of spiritual psychology, in his first book Wilber subscribes very largely to the principles of depth psychology—an approach he now describes as "romantic Jungian."[12] Given that many of Wilber's opponents choose to adopt a similar standpoint, a detailed examination of Wilber's thinking during this period helps to clarify the debate currently raging within the field of transpersonal psychology. In this chapter we see Wilber as he first attempts to integrate not only the worlds of Western and Eastern psychology and philosophy, but also the numerous schools that come under the heading of Western psychology and psychotherapy. In its essential concern with the theory of human consciousness, Eastern philosophy also includes a great deal of psychology, though the language it uses differs from the language evolved by Western psychology. What Wilber tries to do in his first two books is to *translate* the insights that have emerged from the East into scientific psychological terminology with a view to revealing what Eastern philosophy can actually contribute to Western science. In doing so, rather than simply ushering Eastern knowledge into the horizon of Western psychology, he sought to *expand* this horizon so that the world of mystical experience mapped out by Eastern philosophy was also included within the domain of psychology. This field of tension between psychology and spirituality—with all of the promises and pitfalls that it entails—is the territory of the relatively new discipline of transpersonal psychology.

In Chapter 3, which covers Wilber 2, a particularly important period in the development of Wilber's vision, we look at the radical reversal Wilber underwent in his thinking—a fundamental change that has escaped a good many of his readers. After he had written his debut work *The Spectrum of Consciousness* and a popularized version entitled *No Boundary*, despite the fact that his colleagues had attempted to outdo one another in thinking up superlatives to describe these books ("the Einstein of consciousness research" being the most expressive), Wilber was haunted by the uncomfortable feeling that there was something definitely wrong with what he had written. It testifies to Wilber's integrity that even after his first two books had been so successful, he had no qualms about revising the system he had elaborated. On closer examination, Wilber started to doubt the line of thinking expounded by depth psychology, that during the first half of life the individual wrests himself from the unconscious (read "spiritual dimension") only to have to turn around and reenter the unconscious in the second half of life in order to be able to regain the spiritual dimension. Wilbur grew to believe that line of thinking, also referred to as the "spiral model," was untenable. He found a new basis for his vision in developmental psychology, concluding that in growing up and becoming an adult, rather than distancing ourselves from God, we actually move closer and closer to It. The way Wilber now saw it, the entire process of human development was a fundamentally spiritual process in which consciousness becomes clearer and more expanded until ultimately—but by no means in all cases—it unites with the spiritual dimension. Seen from this point of view, spirituality is not something that is lost and has to be regained, but something that is continually approached step by step. For this reason Wilber's model is also known as the "ladder model." And Wilber also came to the same conclusion from an evolutionary point of view. Rather than having *fallen* out of paradise, as many authors in the field of mythology are inclined to claim, though we may not always realize it, we are actually on our way *towards* paradise. Thus Wilber had the effrontery not to reject the idea of the progress of humanity out of hand as an absurd idea. And while his critics might claim otherwise, far from implying that Wilber is a naive progressionist, the fact that he endorses the idea of progress simply indicates that he considers the concept of development to be all-inclusive. And though as far as Wilber is concerned we pay a high price for this individual and cultural development, as we shall see, the pay-off is always greater because there is absolutely no call to indulge in nostalgic dreams of a lost paradise or an idyllic childhood.

Chapter 4 looks at the period of Wilber 3. At this point Wilber further elaborates his view of development, adding a number of important distinctions. Initially he had assumed that human development was a relatively uniform process—the self evolves through a number of different stages, each of which is characterized by its own vision of reality. The world of the magical man of antiquity was very different from the world of today's rational man—as most cultural philosophers and religious scholars will agree. However, an in-depth study of the various schools of thought within the field of developmental psychology led Wilber to see that this approach was too simplistic. As has been well documented, a person may have a highly developed intellect, for example, yet be emotionally or morally naive. Thus there appear to be different dimension or lines of development which operate more or less independently of one another. And if this is really the case, how are we to understand development? How important is cognitive (or intellectual) development within the context of development as a whole? Is intellectual development a basic prerequisite for development in other social, emotional, moral, or spiritual dimensions, as orthodox developmental psychologists have always claimed, or is intellectual development more properly to be regarded as one of many possible lines of development? In other words, is it possible for someone to become spiritually mature without ever displaying any appreciable intellectual capacities? In this respect Eastern philosophy is helpful in view of the fact that it has always acknowledged that there are several different forms of yoga or paths to God—such as the intellectual path or jnana yoga, the emotional path or bhakti yoga, and the path of action or karma yoga. Thus Chapter 4 touches upon the core questions addressed by developmental psychology and attempts to identify Wilber's contribution in this respect. (Wilber has recently returned to these same questions.[13])

In a certain sense Wilber's model of human development reached completion during this period. By the middle of the eighties he had charted in detail a vision of development consisting of a conventional phase (the development from child to adult as described by Western cognitive and psychoanalytical psychology) and a contemplative phase (the development from adulthood to enlightenment, as described in the psychological systems of Buddhism and Hinduism). Thus, in essence, Wilber can be said to regard spirituality as a process of continued development.

In Chapter 5 we enter a period of Wilber's life in which his challenges were not so much intellectual as personal and emotional. In 1983

Wilber met the woman who was to become his second wife, Terry Killam, and within a few weeks he had proposed to her. Just before the couple got married, a routine medical examination revealed that Terry had a highly aggressive form of breast cancer. From one day to the next Wilber gave up his writing in order to be able to support his wife in her battle against cancer—a battle that would go on for some years. Understandably enough, during this emotionally charged period Wilber was unable to write and his views were put to the test in no uncertain terms. Was the vision he had evolved able to withstand the challenges of love, illness, and death? Because this period also influenced Wilber's subsequent thinking with regard to spirituality, particularly in terms of the question as to whether there are male and female variants of spirituality (it turns out that Wilber's thinking up until this point had been almost exclusively male), I have chosen to cover this period in Wilber's life, albeit with some reluctance. Although this chapter is very different in tone from the preceding chapters, Wilber's more recent work can only really be understood in the light of this phase in his life. After Terry died in 1989, it was several years before Wilber was able to pick up the thread of his theoretical work. In 1991 he published *Grace and Grit*, a very personal work based on the diaries Terry—who just before she died changed her name to Treya— wrote during her illness. These diary entries are interwoven with Wilber's thoughts on illness, death, and rebirth. In publishing *Grace and Grit,* Wilber succeeded in attracting an entirely new group of readers.

Chapter 6 discusses the period of Wilber 4, the period during which Wilber's most recent works have been written. These works differ considerably from his previous work in that he now refers to two basic forms of spirituality—the ascending or masculine, and the descending or feminine. He also places his model of individual development within the context of culture and society far more clearly than ever before. Admittedly, this was a theme he had covered earlier in his book *Up from Eden,* published in 1981, which examined the evolutionary journey of humanity, but this time the socio-cultural dimension is far more prominent. He is also more concerned with how bodily processes affect the functioning of human consciousness. Yet, while his model allows for the discoveries in the field of neurology, Wilber certainly does not go so far as to reduce human subjectivity to the mechanics of neurology, as most of those currently concerned with the study of human consciousness are inclined to do. As far as Wilber is concerned, the interior (subjective experience) and the exterior (the human brain) are two separate spheres, and while they might be closely correlated with one another, they can never be reduced to one and the same thing. In addition, Wilber also makes a distinction in terms of the individual and the collective in each of these spheres, thus arriving at four quadrants: (1) the interior-individual (subjective perception), (2) the exterior-individual (cerebral processes), (3) the interior-collective (culture), and (4) the exterior-collective (society). These four quadrants, so he is convinced, need to be recognized as the four essential elements of any integral theory of human consciousness. And this model effectively exposes any attempt to interpret one of these quadrants in terms of the other three as a form of reductionism. Thus in his recent work Wilber counters materialist reductionism (which seeks to explain human consciousness in terms of biochemical processes within the brain), cultural reductionism (which contends that culture is all-determining while the individual counts for nothing), and social reductionism (which regards social structures as being of overriding importance), while being fully aware of the very real influence that these three spheres exert on individual human consciousness.

Wilber's vision of human consciousness has matured in his recent works. Thus it is relevant to ask whether Wilber's system as a whole is able to stand up to criticism. Although over the years Wilber's ideas have been subjected to occasional criticism, it is only in the last few years that his work has been systematically assessed. For instance, in 1997 a conference held in San Francisco was devoted specifically to Wilber's work. At this conference his colleagues in the transpersonal field commented on same aspects of his work. Yet in my opinion a complete assessment of Wilber's work needs to adopt a far wider perspective than that of transpersonal psychology. His vision broadly encompasses four fields of knowledge (not to be confused with the four quadrants mentioned above), and these four fields form the framework of Chapter 7, which attempts to assess Wilber's work from—or at least to situate it within—a broader perspective.

The first field of knowledge reviewed is the materialist philosophy of consciousness, which currently holds a great deal of sway within academic circles and relentlessly reduces human consciousness to neural processes within the brain, or to material processes in general. In this world academics are busy speculating as to the extent to which a computer is a workable metaphor for human consciousness (the weak version), if not the extent to which a computer itself can be said to be conscious (the strong version). Wilber has addressed this dominant viewpoint in only a few places in his work. In my opinion this is an oversight on Wilber's part. If he wishes to attract the attention of the world of academia or to enter into a discussion with the academics, he will need to engage in the discussion in a far more explicit way. It is important to consider the arguments put forward in defense of a totally materialist explanation of human consciousness since there is, in fact, no longer any serious discussion in this field. Many scientists automatically consider a non-materialist explanation of consciousness to be a prescientific aberration—certainly not anything to be taken seriously. Anyone who still believes in a soul— and Wilber happens to be one of those who do—is cast out of the scientific establishment. But has anyone actually succeeded in coming up with an entirely satisfactory materialist explanation of human consciousness, or are we simply witnessing what is essentially religious conviction? And if the materialist establishment has not yet succeeded in coming up with a satisfactory explanation, is it likely to appear at some point in the future (when science is further advanced), or is such an explanation fundamentally impossible? What arguments has Wilber put forward in support of the existence of an independent interior dimension? Do these arguments carry any weight in the current debate regarding individual human consciousness? Surely, if ever there is to be a plausible theory concerning interior subjective experience, this formidable horde of materialists will first have to be taken on.

Secondly, Wilber and his colleagues in the transpersonal field will have to face the criticism that the orthodox psychological community has leveled at transpersonal psychology as a whole. If the phenomena of spirituality and mysticism cannot be accounted for by 'normal' psychological processes such as upbringing, projection, conditioning, learning processes, frames of reference, and the like, what arguments have those who subscribe to the tenets of transpersonal psychology advanced in support of the existence of a transpersonal dimension? The rationale of transpersonal psychology as such hinges on the answer to this question. In view of the fact that, thus far, transpersonal psychology has not really been acknowledged by the academic world (any more than Jungian psychology has seriously been acknowledged), an objective analysis of the situation is hardly an unnecessary indulgence. What is the current status of the thinking regarding human development within the world of academia? The line of thinking which postulates the existence of a series of qualitatively distinct stages that the individual proceeds through step by step during the course of his or her life has been discredited by psychologists in recent decades. This is partly because today's postmodern climate is fiercely opposed to the introduction of qualitative distinctions ('nothing is higher or better than anything else'), and there seems to be precious little empirical evidence of the existence of these stages. Or if evidence does exist, it is not widely accepted. Given that the theme of development is central to Wilber's way of thinking, it is imperative that the arguments for and against should be reexamined. What are Wilber's arguments in support of the existence of qualitatively distinct stages of development during the course of a human life? Anyone who has dared to postulate as many seventeen stages of development, as Wilber does in *The Atman Project* published in 1980, has a lot of explaining to do. While Wilber has certainly touched upon this question in his work since then, in my opinion he needs to consider it further.

The third field of knowledge examined in this last chapter is transpersonal psychology itself. As will be clear by this stage, Wilber is one of the foremost theorists in this field, yet he chooses to adopt a different standpoint from the majority of his colleagues. Whereas most of his colleagues work within the framework presented by depth psychology, the assumption on which Wilber's work is based is very different. Much of the current debate concerning the transpersonal is inevitably obscure because this basic difference of approach has not been explicitly identified. Transpersonal psychology, therefore, finds itself at a crossroads in this respect. Does the framework provided by depth psychology, which is subscribed to by the majority of transpersonal psychologists, allow for further progress? Or would it be better to look for a different context from which to explore the phenomenon of human consciousness, as Wilber has done? I hope to be able to contribute to the debate concerning the basic principles by analyzing the fundamental differences between Wilber's vision and the vision adopted by many of his colleagues in the transpersonal field.

Finally, any assessment of Wilber's vision also needs to consider the metaphysical sources on which his thinking is based. In his very first article published in the *Journal of Transpersonal Psychology* in 1975 under the title of "Psychologia Perennis" (or "Perennial Psychology") Wilber was clear about his objective: he wanted to translate the perennial philosophy into psychological terms. The phrase *perennial philosophy,* popularized by Aldous Huxley, speaks of the understanding of reality which is said—by those who endorse this view—to underlie all of the great religions and philosophical systems. Yet as Wilber himself says at the outset, just as few philosophers are interested in the idea of a perennial philosophy, few psychologists are open to the idea of a perennial psychology. Wilber says this fully convinced that for a vision of humanity to be valid, it must do justice to the whole wealth of human experience, and for this reason it can be said to be scientific (while the so-called scientific materialist vision of man is fundamentally unscientific in that it refuses to acknowledge the undeniable empirical fact of human subjectivity).

Esoteric philosophy, which is also referred to as the perennial philosophy, identifies a number of different planes of existence—usually seven worlds or spheres—extending from the world of matter to the world of Spirit. Between these two extremes are a number of intermediate levels which correspond to human consciousness. Wilber adopted this idea of a layered reality as a guiding principle on which to base his vision of human development. From this point of view development can be conceived of as proceeding step by step through each of these spheres. Individual development begins in the lowest, material field (i.e., in the physical body) and subsequently expands to encompass the psychic or personal levels of existence (which are of an emotional and mental nature). At a later stage it may then move into the spiritual or transpersonal realms. In view of the fact that this profound idea is such a central premise in Wilber's oeuvre, it is important and even essential to reexamine this teaching of the spheres of existence as a teaching in its own right, independent of any correlations with psychology that have since been suggested. Having done so, we are then in a position to question whether, for example, the correlation between the spheres of existence and the stages of development is actually as cogent as Wilber suggests. Do all of the stages of human development postulated by Wilber correspond to the levels of existence described by esoteric philosophy, or is this only true of certain stages? And if this is the case—as we will argue—would it not be more appropriate to make a distinction between primary stages, which have an ontological basis in reality, and secondary stages, which are of a more transitional nature? I hope to be able to contribute to the discussion with regard to this point.

There can also be said to be opposing schools within the field of esoteric philosophy. Many authors in this field, including Réné Guenon, Frithjof Schuon, and Huston Smith, are wary of, if not outspokenly opposed to, modern and postmodern culture. These authors regard the history of Western culture as the decline of a deeply rooted spiritual culture—seen to have existed in the Middle Ages—and the emergence of a culture which is superficial and materialistic. On these grounds they call for spiritual values since lost to be restored. Wilber, who subscribes to the idea of cultural evolution, is diametrically opposed to this way of thinking, however much he might criticize modern materialist culture, which he graphically describes as "flatland." For this reason Wilber has occasionally described his vision as "neo-perennial philosophy," a vision which centers on the notion of evolution.[14] Thus even though he endorses the basic principles of the perennial philosophy which postulates the existence of a layered reality supported by the ground of being, which each person can contact in himself, Wilber chooses to adopt a different standpoint from other authors in the field when it comes to the question of evolution. Thus also in this case it is relevant to ask what arguments have been advanced for and against the actual existence of cultural evolution. Where should the spiritual dimension be situated in this respect—in the past or in the future?

As mentioned earlier, some of Wilber's books were published by a theosophical publishing house.[15] Theosophy can be seen as a nineteenth-century attempt to translate the insights of the perennial philosophy into contemporary Western culture. The principles expounded by Theosophy are also relevant to an assessment of Wilber's vision for two reasons. Firstly, Theosophy also adheres to the idea of evolution and thus readily endorses Wilber's neo-perennialist view. And secondly, Theosophical literature presents a wealth of information regarding the different levels of existence, which sheds light on the basic principle of Wilber's philosophy, that development is essentially a process of expanding from one level of existence to the next and of passing through different closely related stages and spheres. Thus in my opinion the teachings of Theosophy also serve to enrich any discussion about the validity of Wilber's vision.[16]

I

WHO IS KEN WILBER?

"I'm a pandit, not a guru"

Wilber's parents met and married shortly after the Second World War, his father having served as a pilot during the war. Their first and only child was born Kenneth Earl Wilber II on 31 January 1949 in Oklahoma City, the state capital of Oklahoma in the United States.[1] His parents were simply travelling through Oklahoma at the time. Because Ken's father worked for the air force, the family never settled in one place for very long. Every few years they moved from one air force base to another.

As an only child Ken Wilber had a relatively happy childhood. Yet, while his parents allowed him to do largely as he pleased, the frequent moves called for a great deal of adaptability on his part. During his early years the family moved from the island of Bermuda to El Paso, Texas, and from there to Great Falls, Montana. From there they moved to Idaho and then back to Great Falls again, where Ken went to high school. During his last year at high school the family moved again, this time to Lincoln, Nebraska, where Ken completed his schooling (four different schools in four years). The many moves proved to have a formative influence on Ken's character both in a positive sense and in a negative sense: "The good news is that you learn a certain type of non-attachment, because you are moving all the time. So you make friends, but you lose them a year or two later. You make friends, you lose them. So it was rather traumatic. That part was very hard."[2]

In later years whenever things weren't going well, he would blame the fact that he had had a difficult youth. Yet, by the same token, when things were going well, he would feel that in some sense he could thank his youth because it taught him to stand on his own two feet.

His father's side of the family was not particularly close; his mother's side of the family was far closer. His mother had three sisters, two of whom had two sons, and the cousins frequently played together. Because his father's work often took him away from home, Ken was brought up largely by his mother who evoked in him a strong sense of the aesthetic, implicitly encouraging his interest in things like interior design, fashion, and the world of art in general. As a result of her influence, the feminine side of Wilber's character is strongly developed. His father was an outstanding athlete; for years he held the New York State record for sprinting. From his father Ken inherited his athletic build and a disciplined attitude to life—an attitude that would serve him well when it came to the intensive work of writing.

TOP OF THE CLASS

Although both of Wilber's parents were intelligent, neither of them was particularly intellectual. Yet from the start Ken was an exceptionally bright and gifted pupil (a straight A student every year in middle and high school). He had a natural aptitude for intellectual study and was also inclined to invest considerable time and energy in it. At high school he rapidly came to be known as "the brain" because he was at the top of the class year in and year out. This didn't make him particularly popular with his classmates because the pupil who was top of the class effectively set the standard by which the performance of the other pupils was assessed. On leaving high school, as is customary in the United States, as the valedictorian—the pupil with the highest grade average—Ken was invited to give the farewell speech on behalf his classmates.

Because Ken was keen to be popular, he tried to play down his intellectual talent. He certainly didn't relish being known as 'the brain'— through throughout his life it has been virtually impossible for him to throw off this image—and deliberately threw himself into the social side of school life. He became an active member of the student body, twice being elected student body president and once as class president. He also excelled at football, basketball, volleyball, gymnastics, and track and enjoyed not only the sport itself but also the popularity that came with it.

The tension between being engaged in intellectual pursuit and being accepted by his peers would continue to be a significant theme in Wilber's life—despite the fact that his extraordinary powers of reasoning have led him to be recognized the world over. Given his natural gregariousness, it was not easy for Wilber to come to terms with the fact that as a writer he was more or less compelled to lead a relatively lonely existence from a very early age: "People think that I am a born hermit, that I don't want to be with people, that I am anti-social, and that is quite wrong. People that are anti-social show it from about age four or five on. You just can't hide it. But I have exactly the opposite record. I was very sociable and really liked it. The hardest thing about starting writing, when I was twenty-three, was that I had to stop being with people. My two adult interests—writing and meditation—mean that I have basically spent my entire adult life by myself in a corner. Either reading, writing or meditating. That was really a hard transition for me."[3] While still at school Wilber even hosted a television show called "The Indispensibles" in which he interviewed people, a role he was invited to perform on account of his obvious social skills.

During these early years Wilber showed little interest in writing itself; in fact, he disliked it. The compulsory essays he had to write at school held little appeal. Even after he had become a famous author, he rarely looked forward to the actual task of writing. The reason for this is that he sees himself first and foremost as a thinker: "Basically I'm just a thinker. And because I had some new ideas, relatively interesting ideas, I felt I should communicate them. And to communicate them I had to write them down. But I didn't particularly enjoy that part."[4] Once he had decided to write books, in order to develop his fluency as a writer he took Alan Watts—then a popular author—as a model: "I basically taught myself how to write using Alan Watts' books. Alan Watts was one of the clearest writers I had read. He is really a great, clear, elegant writer. I took all thirteen or fourteen of his books and copied every one of them, literally sentence by sentence. I still have the notebooks downstairs. I wrote the books out, so that I could know the style of writing. Just getting a sense of being able to write clearly, and study syntax, seeing how you put paragraphs together."[5] Over the years Wilber has gone on to develop his own clearly recognizable style, which is both abstract and theoretical as well as being extremely direct and personal, and sometimes even lyrical. Yet it is only recently, after having written eighteen books, that he has the feeling that he has finally mastered the art of writing to some extent.[6]

Neither did Ken show any noticeable interest in religious or spiritual matters during his years at high school. On the contrary—in those years he was interested in exact science. In a long autobiographical article on this period written some years later he wrote: "My true passion, my inner daemon, was for science. I fashioned a self that was built on logic, structured by physics, and moved by chemistry. I was precociously successful in that world, obtaining numerous awards and honours, and was at college to corner that success and extrapolate it into a life's destiny. My mental youth was an idyll of precision and accuracy, a fortress of the clear and the evident."[7] And more recently in speaking of this period: "I have always been appreciative of my degrees in science. Take something like the Schrödinger wave equation, or integral calculus. Once you learn that, then you can read Buddha, or you can read Shakespeare. But if you get your college degree in Shakespeare, and try to teach yourself calculus, it is probably not going to happen."[8]

"AN ENTIRELY NEW WORLD"

Wilber's parents thought he would make a good doctor and he enrolled to study medicine at Duke University in Durham, North Carolina. However, that first year of study had a very different outcome from the one that might have been expected, given Wilber's track record to date. From one day to the next, exact science gradually lost its appeal. He suddenly felt that there was absolutely no point in devoting his life to science, for he was aware that what science had to offer was not what he really wanted to know. All of this made him very unhappy. He quit going to class, his grades were barely sufficient—quite a drop by his standards. His parents were unable to understand him. He came home with long hair and talked about some strange Eastern literature they had never heard of. Referring to this turning point in his life at a relatively young age, he himself says: "I went to Duke University and on the day I walked into the campus, I sat down in my dorm, in my room, and knew that I didn't want to have anything to do with it any more. I did not want to study any more of that conventional knowledge. I had already done tons of that, and it wasn't answering my questions. So basically I completely dropped out."[9]

That was in 1968, the era of the hippies and flower power. For a brief period Ken flirted with the trappings of this way of life, but by and large the psychedelic revolution passed him by. Marijuana made him giddy and he avoided the psychedelic scene. In retrospect he is glad things turned out this way: "Basically I did not really do the drug scene. Which actually I think is rather fortunate, for I have seen a lot of people that get into this field through psychedelics who have very strange ideas about spirituality, down the line."[10] Ken set out in search of more reliable methods of entering expanded states of consciousness and began to study the literature of Eastern spirituality. His own experience has shown—and his work reflects the fact—that in the long term the craving for spectacular spiritual experiences effectively runs counter to spiritual development. While spiritual experiences undoubtedly have a place within the process of spiritual development, these experiences are best seen as a side effect rather than a goal.

Early on in his exploration of the literature he came across a passage in the *Tao Te Ching*, a classic volume of Chinese wisdom by the sage Lao Tsu. In terms of the impact it had on his future development, this passage proved to be of huge significance. The *Tao Te Ching* opens with the following lines:

> *The Way that can be told of is not the eternal Way.*
> *The name that can be named is not the eternal Name.*
> *The Nameless is the origin of Heaven and Earth.*
> *The Named is but the mother of ten thousand things.*
>
> *Truly, only he that rids himself forever of desire*
> *can see the Secret Essences;*
> *He that has never rid himself of desire*
> *can only see Outcomes.*
>
> *These two things issue from the same Source,*
> *but nevertheless are different in form.*
> *This Source we can but call the Mystery,*
> *The Doorway whence issue all Secret Essences.*

These words written centuries earlier provoked what was virtually a religious conversion in Wilber. "As I stood reading the first chapter of the *Tao Te Ching*, it was as if I were being exposed, for the very first time, to an entirely new and drastically different world—a world beyond the sensical, a world outside of science, and therefore a world quite beyond myself. The result was that those ancient words of Lao Tzu took me quite by surprise; worse, the surprise refused to wear off, and my entire world outlook began a subtle but drastic shift. Within a period of a few months—months, spent in introductory readings of Taoism and Buddhism—the meaning of my life, as I had known it, simply began to disappear. Oh, it was nothing dramatic; more like waking up one morning, after twenty years of marriage, with the 'sudden' realization that you no longer loved (or even recognized) your spouse. There is really no upset, no bitterness, no tears—just the tacit realization that it is time to separate. Just so, the old sage had touched a cord so deep in me (and so much stronger due to its 20-year-old repression) that I suddenly awoke to the silent but certain realization

that my old life, my old self, my old beliefs could no longer be ener-
gized. It was time for a separation."[11]

At the same time a new sense of direction began to emerge. He told
me: "I did not know what else to do. Back then there were no meditation
centers, there was basically nothing like that. But there was Krishnamurti,
there was Alan Watts, and there was D. T. Suzuki, who was writing about
Zen Buddhism. And I just caught hold of those books. As soon as I read
a few sentences I knew that that was what I was going to do—study these
higher waves of knowing and being. I felt very certain about that. But
then it was very difficult, because there were few ways to actually pursue
this study. You couldn't get a degree in it, and there were few places you
could actually study it."[12]

His first year at college was essentially a lost year. He returned to
Nebraska, where his parents were currently stationed, and got a double
bachelor's degree, one in chemistry and one in biology, and then received
a scholarship in graduate studies in biophysics and biochemistry. But while
ostensibly studying biochemistry, he devoted most of his time to his own
self-devised program of study: "The next two years were spent, almost
literally, in solitary reading and research, eight to ten hours a day. I had
decided to pursue degrees in chemistry and biology, simply because they
came so easily to me that I didn't have to waste time studying them, but
could instead spend every hour out of class pursuing Eastern philosophy
and religion, Western psychology and metaphysics. I recklessly managed
somehow to graduate with enough honors to be offered a scholarship at the
University of Nebraska (Lincoln) in biochemistry/biophysics, and during the
first year of graduate school, continued to do nothing more than read, study,
and take notes—and the names in my notebooks were not Krebs, Miller,
Watson, or Crick. But Gaudapada, Hui Neng, Padmasambhava, and Eckhart."[13]

"LIFE FOR ME WAS SOUR"

This research of the psychological and spiritual and religious literature
was far more than an intellectual quest—for Ken it seemed to be a matter
of life or death. He wasn't doing it with a view to gaining a degree or
because it was likely to enable him to earn a living. He did it because he
had the feeling that that he had no choice—it was a Grail search. And
the search was by no means confined to theory. At the same time he
began to intensify his practice of Zen meditation. At a certain point he
even travelled to Mexico, where Philip Kapleau, the author of the well
known book *The Three Pillars of Zen*, was on holiday. He managed to find

Kapleau and practiced seated meditation with him, a practice he continued seriously under the guidance of Katigiri Roshi.[14] He went on to explore various forms of psychotherapy, including Gestalt therapy and dream analysis, as well as other forms of meditation, including TM and Vedanta. Because he sensed that he derived benefit both from meditation as well as from psychotherapy, the contradictions he detected in the psychological and spiritual literature started to become a source of considerable concern to him.

Ken was clearly going through a crisis which was directly related to his own life: "When I left Duke, with my old belief structures terribly undermined, I was, in the simplest sense of the word, unhappy. Not profoundly depressed, not clinically morose, not even darkly moody—just plain unhappy. This simple unhappiness is really the way Gautama Buddha used the word 'dukkha'; although it is usually translated as 'suffering', it more accurately means 'sour'. The Buddha's first truth: life as normally lived is sour, and awakening to this sourness is the first step on the path to liberation . . . Life for me *was* sour; it was unhappy. And in part I was obsessed with reading all the great psychologists and sages because I was searching for a way out of the sour life; reading was motivated by personal existential therapy, to put it in dry terms. The point is that I had to 'read everything' because I was trying mentally and emotionally to put together in a comprehensive framework that which I felt was necessary for my own salvation. I was particularly drawn to Perls, Jung, Boss, and the existentialists; Norman O. Brown, Krishnamurti, Zen, Vedanta, and Eckhart; the traditionalists, Coomaraswamy, Guénon, and Schuon, but also Freud, Ferenczi, Rank, and Klein—a more motley group you could not imagine."[15]

In order to make extra money Ken offered to coach students. He tutored in law, science, Shakespeare—it made little difference to him. In 1972 a beautiful student, Amy Wagner, turned up on his doorstep and never left. After living together for a year, the two got married. Amy worked long days at a large bookstore, which left Ken free to study undisturbed in the empty apartment. They agreed that they would each pay half of the rent and in order to be able to pay his share of the rent, Ken took on various jobs. For the next nine years he washed dishes, cleared tables in restaurants, worked in a grocery store, as a check-out clerk. He now jokes: "The only real job I've ever had was dishwashing. The only thing I am qualified to do is wash dishes!"[16]

It was actually a lifestyle very much in line with the tenets of the Zen Buddhism he was practicing, which saw value in menial tasks. At that time Ken was meditating for three hours a day and often spent an entire day in seated meditation on the weekend. The unskilled labor he was engaged in also helped to balance his profoundly intellectual work: "I was deeply drawn to the Zen notion of bringing honor to the most menial of tasks, even, or especially, 'lowly' manual labor. If meditation exercised the spirit and writing-thinking exercised the mind, how could I best engage the world in bodily exchange? Because I wanted and valued this gesture of balance, I deliberately sought out and took part-time jobs in manual labor . . . I hardly need tell you that this whole situation was an extraordinary education. It was an education first and foremost in humility. Forget the degrees, forget the books and articles, forget the titles, forget everything really, and wash dishes for two years. It was also an education in *grounding*, in engaging the world in an intimate, concrete, tangible fashion, not through words or concepts or books or courses."[17]

"THE EINSTEIN OF CONSCIOUSNESS RESEARCH"

After he had been living and working in this way for about three years, the first contours of a book that would undertake to bring together spirituality and psychotherapy, East and West, began to emerge in Wilber's mind. Though a number of other books had already been written in a similar vein, Ken was convinced that he was able to offer a fresh and original angle of approach. In the autumn of 1973 he completed a voluminous manuscript entitled *The Spectrum of Consciousness*. He wrote the book over a period of three months and made very few revisions. The basic idea behind *The Spectrum of Consciousness* was that human consciousness could be represented metaphorically as a spectrum of different bands, and that it was possible to reconcile the numerous schools in the fields of psychotherapy and spirituality by relating them to one or more of these bands. Since none of these schools addressed all of the aspects of the human individual, a "spectrum psychology" (which he would later call "integral psychology") was called for. The spectrum model effectively introduces order within the otherwise apparently random fields of psychology and spirituality.

The way in which he produced this first manuscript would prove to be characteristic of his method as a writer: "It just sort of 'shows up' fully written in my head. I just 'see' it. And then it is a matter of writing it down. Typically that was the way I would work during that decade. I would read and study for about ten months. And then at the end of that period, I would wake up one and suddenly 'Book!' I always hated that because I knew that for the next month or two it was going to be horrible. Especially the way I did it then. I would sleep on a sofa, with a typewriter next to me, and I would wake up early in the morning and just start typing. I put a gallon of milk on the table, and I would not move. I would type for maybe fifteen hours, go to sleep, get up, and start typing. I did that non-stop until the book was done. I think it was because I was holding it all together in my mind. Anyway, that's how I would basically work. When that was done, and it was typed up, it was easy, because, I mean, I had the year off! Sitting around and reading was easy. You know, I would lie around the pool, read. . . . And people would see me and say 'That is just the *laziest* guy I have ever seen. Washes dishes, you know, but what does he *do*?' But then ten months later, I would wake up, and 'Book!'"[18]

Nevertheless, even though his first book had been committed to paper, it was another few years before the book was actually published. First, the bulky manuscript, which had been written longhand, had to be typed out. And then there was the process of finding a publisher, and initially things didn't look particularly promising—the manuscript was rejected by approximately thirty publishers. Finally in 1977 the theosophical publishers Quest Books ventured to publish what was to all intents and purposes a difficult book by an unknown author. Yet, as soon as it was published, the book caused an immediate sensation.

The Spectrum of Consciousness was highly praised by many of the leading authors within the field of psychology. For example, Jim Fadiman, who was then the president of the Association for Transpersonal Psychology, wrote: "Wilber has written the most sensible, comprehensive book about consciousness since William James." Jean Houston, past president of the Association for Humanistic Psychology, said: "Wilber might likely do for consciousness what Freud did for psychology." And John White, author and editor of almost a dozen books in the field, described Wilber as the "long sought Einstein of consciousness research."

Virtually overnight Wilber was acknowledged as a leading thinker in the fields of psychology and philosophy, with serious reviews comparing him to Freud, Hegel, even Plato. As a young author it was only natural that he should feel flattered by all of the approval, yet it also left him feeling somewhat embarrassed. Looking back on this period almost ten years later he would say: "I think they [the positive reviews] don't have too much to do with me at all. I think they reflect much more on the wisdom found in the great spiritual traditions. The point is that this spiritual wisdom is so forgotten in modern times, it is so neglected, that when an even vaguely competent person stands up and points to it, and outlines it, and reminds you of its overwhelming importance, then people get a little excited and reviewers appreciate the effort. I think that's what those reviews were all about—I had suggested a way to integrate ancient wisdom with modern knowledge."[19] Still, when the existential psychologist Rollo May described him as the most passionate philosopher he had ever known, Wilber took it as a great compliment: "Rollo May is the brilliant American representative of the great humanistic-existential tradition, and so for him 'passion' is the highest praise. To be honest, that meant much more to me than being compared to a Hegel or a Freud."[20]

Indeed Wilber is best described as a passionate thinker—a man who is deeply moved by what he sees as the truth. The modesty he has retained despite all of the praise that has come his way does him credit and characterizes him as a person. It also reveals that he has always been relatively ambivalent towards the publicity that has inevitably been his lot.

"THE LONELY PURSUIT OF THE WRITER"

Invitations to give lectures and workshops followed one after another and as a young author Wilber was happy to respond to this demand. For a year or so he gave courses at institutions offering adult education and he also gave a large number of lectures on *The Spectrum of Consciousness*. However, he gradually came to realize that lecturing was effectively preventing him from exploring new ground as a creative writer. This typifies Wilber's conception of his task as a writer and also accounts for his relatively reclusive lifestyle.

A few years ago he wrote about the crucial dilemma he found himself faced with: "When I wrote my first book, *The Spectrum of Consciousness*, I was a tender twenty-three, and the attention that book generated catapulted me from obscure biochemistry graduate student to 'New Age teacher'. Offers to lecture and give workshops poured in, and I eagerly took many of them up. It was a heady, wonderful time. And yet, after a year or so of this minor public fame, a stark choice presented itself; it became obvious to me that I could continue this public path and get virtually no new work done, or I could close down the public route and return to a more solitary, and lonely, pursuit of the writer. I kept thinking at the time: 'I can live off what I did yesterday, or continue to create.' That line constantly went through my mind. It was obvious that, at least for me, I would not be able to mix the public and the private very easily; the more I did of one, the less I could do of the other. So, rather abruptly and totally, I stopped any sort of public theatre, and began to concentrate totally on writing. Although I have often chafed under this decision, I have not changed my mind in twenty years."[21]

Even before *The Spectrum of Consciousness* had appeared in print Wilber had already written a popular version of his first book. Published in 1979, *No Boundary* has thus far proved to be one of his most popular works, though the more recent *A Brief History of Everything* (1996) has recently surpassed *No Boundary* in this respect. Not only was *No Boundary* considerably less voluminous than *The Spectrum of Consciousness*, it was also more practical in terms of its approach. Thus at the end of each chapter, in place of a list of references to other works, there were suggestions as to which psychotherapeutic methods or meditative practices were likely to be helpful at different stages. The book clearly conveyed the message that rather than simply thinking about yoga or psychoanalysis, it was essential to actually engage with the chosen method or practice.

In the meantime Wilber was also involved in the work of setting up a scholarly journal. The first of his writing to appear in print, an article also bearing the title "The Spectrum of Consciousness," was published in *Main Currents in Modern Thought* in 1974. *Main Currents* was a journal that had been set up in the forties by a group of theosophists, including Fritz Kunz and Emily Sellon, with a view to signalling new trends in scientific, spiritual, and religious thinking. Shortly after Wilber's article was published, the journal went out of publication. However, Wilber's article had attracted the attention of Jack Crittenden, who contacted Wilber with a plan to set up a new journal. The journal he had in mind was to be similar to *Main Currents* and would center on the ideas presented in Wilber's article. The new journal, *ReVision*, was to fill the gap left by the disappearance of *Main Currents*. Crittenden contacted Emily Sellon, who gave them her blessing, and the first edition of *ReVision* came out in 1978.[22]

Despite the fact that his first two books had met with such a positive response, by now Wilber himself was actually of two minds. While he was writing *No Boundary*, he started to experience the uncomfortable feeling that there was something not quite right with what he had written. Thus not long after he had come through the existential crisis that preceded the writing of *The Spectrum of Consciousness*, he found himself caught up in a major theoretical crisis. The next two chapters cover this period—which effectively laid the basis for Wilber's subsequent intellectual development—in some detail. What was it that concerned Wilber during this period of his life? What he had written in his first two books was not actually wrong, but it was likely to lead to false conclusions. The problems came to light when Wilber attempted to map out the developmental process of the human individual with the aid of the spectrum model he had elaborated in *The Spectrum of Consciousness*. Upon closer examination, the phase of the newborn infant, which many spiritually inclined authors describe as a blissful, almost paradisiacal state lost to the adult, proved to be of an entirely different nature. This early infancy of consciousness was, in fact, far more likely to be a state of physical and emotional bondedness and often one of unlimited narcissism. Having made this sobering discovery, Wilber realized that he needed to revise his model accordingly. And this capacity to constantly subject his own conceptual models to critical examination would continue to be typical of his approach.

Once he had made this fundamental change in his conceptual model, Wilber finally had the feeling that he was now on the right track. He then went on to write a number of new books at a rapid pace. First he wrote *The Atman Project* (1980), a brief study of the complete developmental process of the human individual—from the state of the newly born infant to the state of the enlightened being. Virtually in tandem he also wrote *Up from Eden* (1981), which was published a year later—a relatively detailed study of the phases humanity as a whole has gone through during the course of its evolutionary journey. In writing *Up from Eden* Wilber drew on an article by the Swiss anthropologist and cultural philosopher Jean Gebser, which had also been published in the journal *Main Currents in Modern Thought*. Then, as a contribution to a congress on the sociology of religion, he compiled a small book entitled *A Sociable God* (1982), in which he sketched the outlines of a transcendental—in other words, a non-reductionist—sociology. Given that sociologists are even more inclined to see the human individual in purely materialist terms than materialist psychologists, in *A Sociable God*, which is extremely programmatic in its approach, Wilber attempts to correct this outlook.

Slowly but surely an overall pattern was emerging through the writing of these various books. Working on the basis of the spectrum model, Wilber went on to address various fields of knowledge one after another—developmental psychology, the history of civilization, the sociology of religion, and psychopathology. In doing so Wilber was effectively building bridges between these academic disciplines and the spiritual traditions. And his approach was particularly striking on account of the fact that it was deliberately grounded in the humanities, rather than in exact science, which is far more usually the case (*The Tao of Physics* by Frithjof

Capra, published in 1975, is an obvious example). Chapter 4 examines the issues relating to the philosophy of science that play a part in such comparative studies.

Initially the new journal, *ReVision*, demanded considerable editorial support, which meant that Wilber's presence was urgently needed at the editorial headquarters in Cambridge, Massachusetts. At about the same time Amy was offered a job elsewhere. Over the years the couple had grown apart and in 1981 they finally decided to separate on amicable terms. Wilber moved to Cambridge and devoted himself to the journal. With a view to supporting the journal, which was in dire straits financially, he offered to publish a book of articles that had already appeared in *ReVision*. In less than twenty-four hours he compiled *The Holographic Paradigm* (1982), and the royalties served to provide the journal with much-needed financial support. A collection of Wilber's own essays from various academic journals was published the following year as *Eye to Eye* (1983).

However, Wilber was finding life in Cambridge oppressive, and he gratefully took up the offer of two of his friends, Frances Vaughan and Roger Walsh, both of whom were also colleagues within the integral field, that he should come and live with them in Tiburon, a small town to the north of San Francisco. He found the atmosphere in San Francisco far more conducive. It was here in 1983 that Wilber met Terry Killam, the woman who would come to be his second wife. Only a few days after they first met, the two decided to get married. During the three months leading up to the wedding Wilber worked on *Quantum Questions* (1984), a collection of pieces by famous physicists on the relationship between physics and mysticism, and *Transformations of Consciousness* (1986), a collection of articles relating the spectrum model to recent developments in Western psychoanalytic literature. Then fate struck.

The medical examination that Terry underwent prior to her impending wedding revealed that she had breast cancer. Wilber immediately abandoned the work that engaged him so fully in order to constantly be with his wife. For the next five years the cancer continued to exact its toll and throughout this time Wilber devoted himself to caring for his wife. Having been used to producing a new book virtually on an annual basis, the sudden stemming of this flow of creativity inevitably generated a powerful tension. After Terry, who later changed her name to Treya, died in 1989, Wilber wrote a book about this debilitating period as she had requested. The book was published as *Grace and Grit* in 1991. Wilber then went on to pick up the thread of his earlier work.

THE *KOSMOS* TRILOGY

Initially Wilber was planning to complete a textbook of integral psychology that he had had in mind under the provisional title of *System, Self and
Structure* since the beginning of the eighties.[23] However, it rapidly became
clear to Wilber that there had been a drastic leveling in the psychological
literature since he himself had last published. Holism, the leading philosophy in alternative circles, was now oriented solely towards the exact
sciences, such as physics and biology—largely with a view to acquiring
quasi-scientific status. Wilber was saddened to see how the depth and
detail of the traditional spiritual worldview had been almost entirely ef-
faced in the holistic literature. It was this that prompted him to set aside
the textbook of integral psychology for the time being in order to write
a detailed work expounding the basic tenets of his integral philosophy.
This work evolved into a trilogy, entitled simply *Kosmos*. The first volume
of the trilogy, *Sex, Ecology, Spirituality*, was published in 1995. Wilber uses
the term *Kosmos* to refer to the multidimensional reality described by the
perennial philosophy—a reality that encompasses not only matter, but
also soul, spirit, and ultimately the Divine. Furthermore, as far as Wilber
was concerned, the thinking in alternative circles with regard to spirituality was dominated by an excessively romantic and nostalgic yearning for
the past—an attitude he found misguided. Over the years, some of the
concepts he valued—depth, quality, nested hierarchy, evolution, interiority, even consciousness itself—had come to be rejected as suspect, to such
an extent that, in his opinion, they now needed to be rehabilitated.

Wilber spent more than three years working on the first volume of
the *Kosmos* trilogy, a period he spent in almost total isolation. During
these years of self-imposed isolation he underwent a profound spiritual
transformation. By this stage he had been meditating for twenty years and
had had a number of satori experiences, but this new illumination surpassed anything he had experienced up until then. After he had been
writing continuously for several months without seeing or speaking to
anyone, he entered a mystical state of awareness which persisted for eleven
days. He described this state to me as follows:

> For eleven days and nights, I did not sleep at all. I was awake
> twenty-four hours a day. Towards the end of that time I would
> lie down and my body would go to sleep, and I started dreaming,
> but I was completely aware of the dreaming. Lucid dreaming.
> Then I would go to deep dreamless sleep and I was aware of this

deep dreamless sleep. Then, out of that, I would see the dream arise, and I would be aware of that. And out of that, the gross realm would arise. So it was basically a case of *turiya*, the fourth state [beyond waking, dreaming and dreamless sleep]. . . . Since then, access to that awareness has been present, fairly constantly. There were often glimpses of this before, but now it spontaneously became a type of constant nondual awareness—although there are times that it is more or less apparent, which involves "dropping" identification with this particular body-mind, or rather, recognizing that such a nondual state is always already present. And this "one taste" [Wilber's expression for unity consciousness] is very obvious. It is very straightforward, a very simple, clear, ever-present awareness, described by Ramana Maharshi [a Hindu mystic], it is just *sahaja* [spontaneous enlightenment].[24]

In actual fact Wilber's life shows two parallel lines of development—one venturing into the intellectual realm and the other venturing into the spiritual realm. Behind Wilber the thinker there is always Wilber the mystic, who has experienced in his own awareness what he attempts to convey through his writing. The spiritual intention behind his work is clearly discernible on every page of his oeuvre as he seeks to rehabilitate the spiritual dimension of reality and the individual within Western culture in an academically sound way.

After he had completed the exhausting work of writing *Sex, Ecology, Spirituality* and having already elaborated the second and third volumes of the trilogy in draft form, he felt the need to produce a popular summary of the first volume of the *Kosmos* trilogy. A year later the popular version of *Sex, Ecology, Spirituality* was published as *A Brief History of Everything* (1996). In many respects *A Brief History of Everything* is very similar to *No Boundary*, written shortly after he had completed his first book, *The Spectrum of Consciousness*. The concepts presented in the more complex work are described in a simpler style in *A Brief History*, which helps to further clarify some of the thinking. Nevertheless, *A Brief History* is more than simply a summary of Wilber's largest and most elaborate work to date, for Wilber also introduces a number of new ideas. Furthermore, in *A Brief History* Wilber undertook only to include that which could be asserted without the need for reference works and quotes, as if he were engaged in a personal conversation with the reader. As such, the entire book is written in the form of a long interview, which considerably enhances its readability.

By now Ken Wilber had come to be a relatively controversial figure in certain alternative circles—particularly in the circles in and around San Francisco. This state of affairs was prompted by a number of passages included in the end notes to *Sex, Ecology, Spirituality*, in which Wilber criticizes what he considers to be questionable notions and developments in the countercultural and alternative literature in no uncertain terms. Wilber deliberately included these polemical passages in his book with a view to rousing the stagnation that he felt had the whole field in its grip. However, some of his colleagues found these passages difficult to digest.

In 1996 the journal *ReVision* devoted three consecutive issues to Wilber's recent work. In these three issues of the journal some of his critics commented on Wilber's vision and Wilber was invited to respond to these comments. The resulting discussion continued in January 1997 during a conference held in San Francisco devoted entirely to Wilber's recent work. Several of the authors who had contributed to the *ReVision* series spoke at the conference. True to his principles, Wilber himself did not attend the conference, yet in the meantime he had compiled his contributions to *ReVision* together with several new chapters into a book entitled *The Eye of Spirit* (1997), which was published immediately prior to the conference. And he had also completed yet another manuscript. This was a relatively brief monograph on the relationship between science and religion, which was published the following year by Random House, bearing the title of *The Marriage of Sense and Soul* (1998).

In 1997 Wilber kept a journal of his everyday experiences and less commonplace experiences. He had the impression that as an author who wrote about the inner dimension, he could not honestly evade writing about his own inner life. The manuscript was to be published as *One Taste* (1999) and was a testimony of the nondual state of the mystic, in which there is no distinction between high and low, spirit and matter, sacred and profane. The journal shows Wilber to be a full-fledged mystic, now beginning to reap the fruit of more than twenty-five years of meditation.

Due to the fact that all nineteen of Wilber's books were still in print—an extremely rare feat for an academic author—and given that his various books had been translated into more than thirty foreign languages—making Wilber one of the most highly translated living authors in America—Shambhala Publications and its distributing company Random House decided that it would be appropriate to compile and issue *The Collected Works of Ken Wilber*. This made Wilber the first psychologist-philosopher in history to have his collected works published while he was still alive—and Wilber was only forty-eight! Wilber himself was ambivalent about doing this because it involved so much editorial work. He joked, "Usually they have the decency to wait until you die and stiff somebody else with this dreary editorial job, but nooooo. . . ."

Wilber spent the better part of 1998 editing his seventeen books. Fortunately, there was not much to change, but there was an enormous amount of material to go through, so Wilber worked around the clock. In what has become something of an inside joke, as he was going through his past works, he found a small book he had written and forgotten about. Called *Sociocultural Evolution*, it is published for the first time in volume 4 of the *Collected Works*.

But what made 1998 to 1999 a remarkable year for Wilber—arguably the most productive year of his life—was that, in addition to editing the *Collected Works*, he wrote three new books: *Integral Psychology, A Theory of Everything*, and *Boomeritis. Integral Psychology* is a succinct summary of the two-volume text he had been planning to write (*System, Self, and Structure*) and is undoubtedly his most important psychology book to date. *A Theory of Everything*—deliberately titled to challenge the modern theories in physics that claim to have a theory of everything but actually deal only with the physical realm—is perhaps the most accessible introduction to Wilber's work yet, covering numerous applications in medicine, politics, business, and education—all of which are areas where interest in his work has exploded in the last few years (for example, both the former President Bill Clinton and the former Vice-President of America Al Gore have issued public praise of his work). And *Boomeritis* is his good-natured chastising of his generation—known in America as the "Me generation"—for being too self-absorbed.

Wilber is now in the process of completing his *Kosmos* trilogy—a project that is likely to take several years. In 1999 and 2000 Shambhala has published the first eight volumes of the *Collected Works of Ken Wilber*. And given that Wilber's interest is increasingly turning towards politics, the chances are that he will also produce a monograph on the relationship between politics and religion. The last chapter of *The Marriage of Sense and Soul* gives us a foretaste of this as Wilber seeks to identify a "third way" somewhere between liberalism and conservatism—the two main movements in American politics, and attempts to integrate the Enlightenment of the West—rationalism and individual freedom—with the Enlightenment of the East—spiritual development and realization through meditation. In addition to all of this, for some years Wilber had also been toying with the idea of trying his hand at a very different literary genre. When I interviewed him back in 1995, he said: "Strange as it might sound, I have thought very much about moving into writing novels. First of all, novels don't have footnotes. Every now and then you simply get tired of having to prove every sentence you utter. I think I have earned the right—after a dozen books—to simply suggest a world without having to prove it! But more than that, narrative is an extremely powerful form of communication. Look at what simple works of fiction have actually accomplished. Harriet Beecher Stowe's *Uncle Tom's Cabin* almost single-handedly ended slavery in the States. We have Rousseau's *Emile*, Goethe's *Sorrows of Young Werther*, Thomas Mann's *Buddenbrooks*. The worldwide environmental movement was almost totally started by Rachel Carson's *Silent Spring*—it's not really a novel, but it reads like one, and it does point up the power of narrative. For that matter, Freud himself only received one important award in his life, and that was the Goethe Award for literature. I probably won't be any good at it, so I will end up retiring from philosophy to write really bad novels."[25]

"A FUNDAMENTAL PATTERN"

Before proceeding to cover the books written by Ken Wilber in more detail in the following chapters, it is a good idea to examine whether there is in fact a discernible thread running through the books. When I asked Wilber about this during the 1995 interview, he came to realize that there was a certain logic in the sequence of his books, despite the fact that the books themselves address widely divergent fields of knowledge. He described this logic as follows: "The study of psychology inevitably leads to sociology, which inevitably leads to anthropology, which leads back to philosophy. And then, strangely, bizarrely, that leads to politics."[26] The way Wilber sees it, psychotherapy seeks to identify the reasons why people are unhappy and suggests that maladjusted behavior is one of the most significant contributing factors. But what if the society to which the individual is so ill-adapted is also dysfunctional? Thus psychology inevitably leads to sociology. Yet how can we hope to assess our own society in the absence of any comparative context? Thus in the endeavor to compare our own society with the societies created by other cultures, past and present, sociology leads us to anthropology. And then we are faced with the question as to what criteria we are to adopt with a view to assessing other cultures. Thus anthropology leads us to philosophy. And once we have succeed in identifying the values that need to be created within a culture, as far as Wilber is concerned, we are then more or less bound to develop a political vision in which as many people as possible are enabled to share these values.

Referring to his own books, Wilber went on to say: "My approach has also gone through that basic pattern, from psychology to sociology and anthropology, to philosophy, to political theory. You can see this in the books: *The Spectrum of Consciousness*, *No Boundary*, and *The Atman Project* were my first three books, and they are all recognizable as psychology books, in a broad sense. Then *Up from Eden* and *A Sociable God*, which are anthropology and sociology. Then *Eye to Eye*—a very philosophical work. And then my most recent works, which are, well, hard to describe, because they sort of cover everything."[27]

Wilber anticipates that integral psychology will have a significant effect on the culture as a whole, its impact is certainly likely to extend well beyond the confines of the discipline of psychology proper. In this respect he sees a similarity between integral psychology and psychoanalysis: "Psychoanalysis had much of its greatest impact in fields that were also outside of psychology. It had a major and profound influence in literature, in literary theory, in political theory and discourse (the enormously influential Frankfurt School of Critical Theory—Horkheimer, Adorno, Erich Fromm, Herbert Marcuse, Jürgen Habermas—was a direct attempt to integrate the concerns of Marx and Freud), in art and in theories of art, even in artistic practice (the Surrealists, for example), and in education and educational theories and practices. Because psychoanalysis was in fact plugged into some very important—if limited—truths, it proved itself by completely exploding out of the narrow confines of psychology and having an extraordinary impact on other fields. And I think we are now on the verge of something quite similar happening with integral studies, perhaps not as widespread, but at least quite similar. Its impact is moving rapidly beyond the field of psychology. And many of us have been working in this much more expanded field of integral studies, and this also includes my own recent work."[28]

In Wilber's opinion, if there is any truth in the integral approach, it should ideally serve to integrate all of the various fields of knowledge: "Here's what we are faced with: if the integral orientation has any validity, it ought to apply to every aspect of human endeavor. It ought to have something interesting to say about all of that—from physics to psychology, from philosophy to politics, from cosmology to consciousness. But you cannot do that as an eclecticism, or a smorgasbord of unrelated observations. There has to be something resembling coherence and integrative capacity. The integral orientation must be able to tie together an enormous number of disciplines into a fairly complete, coherent, plausible, believable vision. Obviously, it remains to be seen if this can even be done at all. It might simply be an impossibility, for many reasons— 'fools rush in where angels fear to tread'. But that is what the *Kosmos* trilogy attempts to do—to integrate a comprehensive number of knowledge disciplines. Whether it succeeds or not, well, that definitely remains to be seen. But if nothing else, I think it will help people elevate their own visions to a more comprehensive and inclusive scale."[29]

SO, YET ANOTHER GRAND THEORY?

Ken Wilber can be characterized as a system philosopher—a thinker who seeks to establish the essential coherence of things, to gain an overview of the whole of reality in all of its diverse facets. In this respect Wilber is diametrically opposed to the postmodern spirit of the times, which considers such an approach to be impossible. Nowadays all-encompassing intellectual systems which attempt to explain the whole of reality on the basis of a single underlying theory are treated with huge and widespread scepticism. The era of the grand theories, such as Marxism, psychoanalysis, and evolutionism, definitely appears to have come to an end.

And it is not without reason that such systems are treated as suspect. For, time and time again history has shown that such grandiose systems of thought virtually always result in some form of totalitarianism. Anything that fails to fit within the system in question is rejected or identified as an inimical element, and is thus effectively marginalized—as the jargon would have it. In recent years Wilber's system has also been subject to criticism largely motivated by the same kind of distrust. Some of the critics are of the opinion that Wilber's all-encompassing model is not all-encompassing enough in view of the fact that it fails to appreciate the value of lesser developed cultures or the female perspective on reality. For a philosophy that purports to be an *integral* philosophy, these are criticisms that need to be taken seriously. Thus in the last chapter of this book we will examine whether there is in fact any truth in these criticisms.

However, it would be premature to reject Wilber's vision out of hand as a totalitarian and marginalizing vision. In my opinion the standard criticism leveled by postmodernism—that grand theories are now a thing of the past—does not apply to Wilber's vision in view of the fact that his approach is so radically different. For rather than attempting to pass off a certain *partial truth* as the one and only truth, as many of the major systems of thought evolved in the past have attempted to do, he is far more concerned with *integrating* all of these partial truths as facets of Truth—and he does so in an open-ended way, not in a closed or final way. Thus the strength of Wilber's vision lies in its ability to reconcile different and often apparently contradictory partial truths. In doing so, Wilber relies on a few simple principles. Virtually all of those passionately concerned with the humanities or philosophy labor under the conviction that they are able to make a valuable contribution, and Wilber sees it to be his task to incorporate these individual contributions into a more comprehensive theory. Or, as he himself once put it, with a touch of humor: "Nobody is smart enough to be wrong all the time." If Wilber criticizes a theory, it is rarely if ever because he considers the theory to be completely wrong, but because the theory can be shown to be one-sided or incomplete. His motto might be "Everyone is right—up to a certain point." Another motto might be "The more inclusive the theory the greater the truth." Naturally, it is quite an art to be able to determine the point at which an insight, which in itself contains an element of truth, degenerates in to a one-sided theory. And Wilber appears to have a particular gift in this respect.

However, in addition to this very obvious reconciliatory side, which is expressed in his endeavor to integrate widely divergent visions within a unified system, Wilber also has an uncompromising unconciliatory side, which is fiercely critical of notions that fail to do justice to the truth, at least as he perceives it. In adopting this stance, he is well aware that he is likely to make a few enemies. "All of us in this field are looked upon by conventional theorists as being totally flaky, wacky, off the wall, crazy. We are sort of looked on as the phrenologists of the universe. Well-intentioned but totally nuts. So I have tried to be, in my writing, very critical, very discriminating, very sharp, very intense. . . . It is possible to present a very mystical and integral viewpoint that is not at all flaky. . . Kierkegaard pointed out that truth is revealed if you go at it with an insane intensity and I belong to that tradition. I do regret, however, that some people are upset with this passionate approach and style."[30] On balance, the great majority of readers have found Wilber's occasional acerbic wit to be enlivening and enjoyable; the criticism has come, not surprisingly, almost solely from those who are the brunt of the humor.

Besides evolving systems of thought and assuming the role of the tireless critic, Wilber is also unmistakably a visionary. By his own account, in the process of writing he relies on a form of vision logic, which enables him to assess a number of different points of view simultaneously and to reveal the way in which these different viewpoints relate to one another. The tenacity and passion with which he has sought to communicate and continually further refine his vision over a period of more than twenty years is nothing less than remarkable. Yet as far as he is concerned, he has no choice: "Those who are allowed to see are simultaneously burdened with the obligation to *communicate* that vision in no uncertain terms: that is the bargain. You were allowed to see the truth under the agreement that you would communicate it to others . . . And therefore, if you have seen, you must simply speak out. Speak out with compassion, or speak out with angry wisdom, or speak out with skillful means, but speak out you must. And this is truly a terrible burden, a horrible burden, because in any case there is no room for timidity. The fact that you might be wrong is simply no excuse: You might be right in your communication, and you might be wrong, but that doesn't matter. What does matter, as Kierkegaard so rudely reminded us, is that only by investing and speaking your vision with *passion*, can the truth, one way or another, finally penetrate the reluctance of the world. If you are right, or if you are wrong, it is only your passion that will force either to be discovered. It is your duty to promote that discovery—either way—and therefore it is your duty to speak your truth with whatever passion and courage you can find in your heart. You must shout, in whatever way you can."[31]

"I'M A PANDIT, NOT A GURU"

Wilber makes no apologies for his intellectual approach to spirituality. He likes to compare himself with the figure recognized in India as a *pandit* or a religious scholar.[32] In a relatively recent article he described the role of the pandit as follows: "In India, as I have often pointed out, a distinction is made between a *pandit* and a *guru*. A pandit is a spiritual practitioner, who also has a flair for the academic or scholarly or intellectual, and so becomes a teacher of the Divine, and articulator and defender of the dharma [spiritual truths], an intellectual samurai [warrior]. A guru, on the other hand, is one who engages people directly and publicly, and who gets intimately involved with the ordeal of transforming their karmas. Neither calling is to be taken lightly. I am a pandit, not a guru, and I have made that clear from day one."[33]

Popular conception has it that a guru is familiar with and engaged in the actual practice of spirituality while a pandit has a special capacity for theoretical knowledge. This may well be true, but according to Wilber the generalization does not apply in his case. When I asked him to explain his understanding of the difference between a pandit and a guru, he said:

The real difference between a pandit and a guru is that a guru accepts devotees and a pandit doesn't. Otherwise they can be almost identical. One is not necessarily more enlightened than the other. A guru is like a therapist. A guru takes on devotees, it is a more intense version of a therapist taking on a client. It means you are going to wrestle with their personal karmas [problems]. That's a very deep involvement. And traditionally, the guru actually absorbs, it is said, the karma of the devotee, whatever he does. Even if you look at a therapist, he gets personally involved, wrestling with clients *for years*, in a personal, transformative event. Pandits don't do that. They tend to be scholars, sometimes they are practitioners, sometimes they are very enlightened. They just don't get personally involved. It is an entirely different profession. It is first of all a matter of how you are going to allocate your time. If you are a writer, you spend a year, you do a good book, you can reach a hundred thousand people. If you see clients, you can reach about twenty people a year, if you are a therapist. Or fifty. It is just a different profession. And it is not that one is better. They are both needed. It is just that, for whatever reason, I started as a pandit. I don't think I have any *karmas* [talents] in me to be a therapist. Anybody that has a spiritual understanding and communicates it can be a pandit in that sense. It just means you are knowledgeable about it. Pandits are often scholars. Actually pandits often know more about the tradition then the guru. It is just a different kind of function. And sometimes gurus are not very enlightened . . . And sometimes pandits are *very* enlightened. Milarepa is a good example: a great yogi, but also a great pandit. A lot of them were real scholars. Naropa was a great scholar. Longchempa was a great pandit. Sort of the head of the dzogchen tradition. Plotinus was a perhaps the greatest pandit of all time.[34]

The fact that Wilber's work is sustained by a deeply spiritual motivation will be clear to anyone able to read between the lines of his books. In an interview conducted in the eighties, which subsequently dubbed Wilber "the pundit of transpersonal psychology," Wilber described the spiritual motivation behind his work as follows: "The whole thrust of my work is to make spiritual practice legitimate, to give it an academic grounding so people will think twice before they dismiss meditation as some sort of narcissistic withdrawal or oceanic regression. That's all. I am not doing all this work just to build a nice system, like Hegel, then put my name on it and admire it and go down in history. I'm doing all this so we can just forget it and get down to practice, which is ultimately all that counts."[35]

THE SEVEN FACES OF KEN WILBER

So who is Ken Wilber? As an author, Ken Wilber performs at least seven different roles. These roles are listed below in order of increasing intensity and spirituality. The first four roles are primarily intellectual while the last three are explicitly spiritual.

(1) *Theorist.* First and foremost, Ken Wilber is a highly distinguished thinker who strives to capture the richness of human experience in all of its facets in a theoretical model. He makes no apologies for his theoretical approach; on the contrary, right from the outset he was convinced of the fact that the undertaking was of value. He is not so much a scientist conducting his own research, as a philosopher who seeks to compare the results of scientific research carried out by others and to extrapolate the various implications. In doing so he attaches great importance to the social sciences, particularly developmental psychology. At its core his thinking revolves around a model of the different stages of human development, which has its roots in Western psychology and reaches its fruition in Eastern spirituality.

(2) *Synthesist.* Wilber is equally characterized by the inclusivity he displays as he seek to compare and integrate the results of scientific research conducted by others. His considerations are always geared towards synthesis. Wilber is a system builder, like others before him, but with the distinctive difference that as far as possible he endeavors to incorporate the visions of others within his system. This elevates his model to the stature of a meta model, which serves to situate other models in relation to one another. In doing so his ultimate goal is to formulate a Theory of Everything which is not confined solely to the natural sciences, but also includes all of the other facets of human experience. The criticism leveled by the postmodernists that grand theories are no longer possible does not apply to Wilber's vision in view of the fact that he makes no attempt to inflate partial truths to absolute proportions—as so many great theorists have done in the past—but as far as possible he seeks to integrate partial truths within an overall model. In this way he tries to gain an insight into the 'binding pattern' underlying the various theoretical visions of the individual and reality. Any gaps in the meta model are fleshed out with inevitably speculative theories of his own making.

(3) *Critic.* Wilber tirelessly criticizes notions which in his opinion effectively violate the binding pattern, in that they mistake partial truths for absolute truths. Thus the infinite richness of mysticism is nowadays often reduced to the principles of an exact science such as quantum physics. Wilber regards this as a disastrous development, which rather than underpinning mysticism actually effaces mysticism. His own holistic vision differs from the more popular version of holism in that it has its roots in the humanities and, ultimately, in the spiritual wisdom traditions rather than in the natural sciences. The critical spirit which breathes through all of his work emerges out of the conviction that partial truths need to be seen as partial truths, no more and no less, but never as absolute Truth.

(4) *Polemicist.* Some passages in Wilber's recent work are rather polemical, which has not gone down well with all of his readers. (Some readers were upset by the polemical nature of a number of the end notes in *Sex, Ecology, Spirituality,* while others found the attack refreshing.) This deliberately confrontational approach was prompted by Wilber's sense that current thinking regarding spirituality, both within the field of psychology as well as within Western culture as a whole, is suffering from stagnation. He compares the situation with a river used to transport logs which has since become jammed. Often the only remedy is to explode a few sticks of dynamite so that the logs can once again flow with the current. Wilber is of the opinion that when it comes to erroneous notions that lead a highly persistent existence, sometimes the only solution is to voice severe criticism. In particular, he speaks out against the narcissism of his own generation and against the nihilism of postmodern philosophy, which he sees as being two sides of the same coin.[36]

(5) *Pandit.* Wilber sees himself as a Western pandit or spiritual intellectual, which means that his intellectual gifts are actually entirely in service to a fundamentally spiritual approach to life. His primary motive in writing so many books is to legitimize spiritual practice within secularized Western culture. Essentially this makes Wilber a spiritual thinker. Though Wilber is more open to what science has to offer than many other spiritual philosophers, in the final count his vision does not depend on science. Ultimately the spiritual dimension can only be discovered in the depths of the innermost self, to which neither phenomena nor thoughts have access. Ultimately only the deeper levels of the mind are able to know the Divine.

(6) *Guide.* Despite his reluctance to assume the role of a guru, in certain respects Wilber undoubtedly acts as a spiritual guide for his readers. The passages in his recent work in which he relates to the reader as

a meditation teacher have this quality and are among the most beautiful passages of his oeuvre as a whole[37] (certainly when compared with the approach adopted by some modern gurus in their attempts to communicate the dharma). Particularly when it comes to explaining the so-called pointing out instructions, which are given in some of the mystic traditions with a view to enabling the student to experience the spiritual dimension during the early stages of the practice, Wilber shows his masterful command of the subject. That fact that he is able to reach hundreds of thousands of people through his books to offer such spiritual guidance—something that few true gurus are in a position to do—is an advantage that he feels should not be underestimated.

(7) *Mystic*. Last but by no means least, there is Wilber the mystic, for whom the states described in his works are not simply a matter of theory, but also a matter of intimate personal experience. He first began meditating in 1973 while he was in the process of writing *The Spectrum of Consciousness*. More than twenty-five years later the practice appears to have borne fruit. In *One Taste* he describes numerous mystical experiences, which according to the criteria set down in the spiritual literature point to a more or less continuous state of Enlightenment. Nevertheless, this last aspect takes a back seat in Wilber's work—and rightly so. Rather than basing his testimony on highly personal mystical experiences, he chooses to base it on the broadest possible study of the insights into human consciousness produced by both spiritual and scientific literature. However, we can undoubtedly conclude that Wilber lives what he writes about. As such he is a living example for the many readers of his books who may well ask, "Spiritual development certainly sounds like a wonderful ideal, but can it ever really be a reality in my own life?"

Having made the acquaintance of Ken Wilber as a person, we can now go on to look at the content of his books in some detail. In the next few chapters we will follow Wilber closely, not only in his search of the literature of East and West, but also in his personal life. In doing so we will come to detect a characteristic pattern that has occurred repeatedly in his life. At a number of junctions in his life he has been beset by a fundamental crisis—either intellectual or existential in nature, though it is not always possible to make a clear-cut distinction between the two in Wilber's case—and time and time again he has emerged from these periods of crisis bearing new insights.

2

A FLYING START

"Consciousness is like a spectrum"

WHAT IS TRANSPERSONAL PSYCHOLOGY?

Ken Wilber is considered to be the most important theorist within the field of so-called transpersonal psychology. In order to be able to place his work within the context of psychology as a whole, we first need to examine the meaning of the term *transpersonal psychology*. Among American transpersonal psychologists the discipline of transpersonal psychology is generally regarded as the fourth great school of psychology, following behaviorism, psychoanalysis, and humanistic psychology.[1] Sensing that these first three schools were too limited, psychologists set out in search of a vision of the individual that was deliberately rooted in the spiritual dimension. Transpersonal psychology essentially evolved out of humanistic psychology. Abraham Maslow stood at the cradle of both schools. In 1968 he wrote, "I consider humanistic, Third Force psychology, to be transitional, a preparation for a still 'higher' Fourth psychology, transpersonal, transhuman, centered in the cosmos rather than in human needs and interests, going beyond humanness, identity, self-actualization and the like."[2]

While it makes sense for the four movements in psychology to be ranged in this sequence, as we shall see, it is worth noting that this is a very American way of looking at things. Given that psychoanalysis predates behaviorism historically, it should really be seen as the first school of psychology. It is listed second in this sequence because behaviorism was already well established as a school of psychology in its own right when psychoanalysis was first introduced in the United States. Yet, from a didactic point of view, it is more logical to start with behaviorism on account of the fact that it denies the subjective inner life of the individual (or at least it maintains that it is not scientifically investigable), while the other three schools all accept the existence of and attach increasing importance to the subjective dimension.

A second point to bear in mind is that the American version of the history of psychology disregards the fact that Western scientific psychology started out as an introspective form of inquiry practiced primarily in Germany. Given that transpersonal psychology considers the inner dimension to be central, it is certainly worth examining what this early period in the history of Western psychology has to say about the possibilities and impossibilities of introspection. When Wilhelm Wundt published his *Contributions to the Theory of Sensory Perception* in 1862, it effectively marked the beginning of psychology as an experimental science. Wundt deliberately intended to study the individual from the inside out—and not simply from the outside. In 1874 he published his masterpiece *Physiological Psychology*.[3] (To give some sense of the historical context, Freud's first major publication, *Die Traumdeutung*, was published more than twenty-five years later in 1900 and the American behaviorists first made themselves heard a few decades after that through the work of J. B. Watson.)

Thirdly, the American way of looking at things also fails to take into account a number of other important approaches within the field of psychology, such as that of the Swiss developmental psychologist Jean Piaget (1896–1980).[4] Piaget described the process of human development as consisting of four stages.[5] During the first stage (senso-motor), consciousness is largely confined to the body. Mental capacity develops during the later stages (pre-operational, concrete-operational, and formal-operational, respectively), first in a concrete form, and later in the form of abstract thought. Piaget's early work was published in France in the twenties and thirties, but it was some decades before it was translated into English, which meant that the American public first became acquainted with Piaget's ideas in the fifties. His last works were published in the late seventies, such that his study of the development of the individual effectively spans half a century. Lawrence Kohlberg, who studied the development of moral thought and whose model has since been tested in dozens of countries, also belongs to this tradition. Kohlberg distinguished six stages of moral thought, from the type that is geared toward punishment and reward to the type motivated by a sense of conscience.[6] Wilber continues in the tradition established by Piaget and Kohlberg, as will become clear in the following chapters.

And finally, this particular ranking of the schools of behaviorism, psychoanalysis, and humanistic psychology, which is now thirty years old, also fails to take into account the developments that have taken place within each of these schools in recent decades. For instance, within the world of psychoanalysis an increasing amount of attention has been devoted to the importance of the ego in human development. By the same token, the behavioral schools have gone on to discover the importance of the cognitive element. Having said this, it is possible to gain a relatively clear impression of the place occupied by transpersonal psychology within the field of psychology as a whole by looking at each of the four forces in turn.

The first school within the field of psychology—*behaviorism*—examines the individual purely from the outside. As a school, behaviorism is not interested in the existence of an inner, subjective dimension. Arguing that no one has ever been able to observe a feeling or a thought, let alone come up with scientific evidence of the existence of feelings or thoughts, the behaviorists are solely concerned with explaining externally perceivable behavior, without pausing to speculate on the underlying experiences that might have led to this behavior. Within the field of psychology behaviorism advocates the kind of empiricism that is strictly confined to objectively quantifiable evidence perceived through the external senses. All other human experiences are rejected out of hand as unreliable sources of knowledge. Effectively stripping the individual of what makes him or

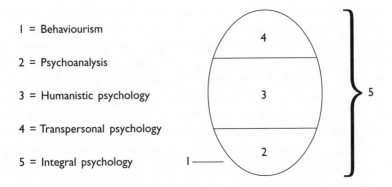

1 = Behaviourism

2 = Psychoanalysis

3 = Humanistic psychology

4 = Transpersonal psychology

5 = Integral psychology

FIGURE 2.1.   The five schools within the field of psychology

her human, the behaviorist will often resort to studying animals with a view to being able to unravel the lawful patterns of human behavior.

So-called cognitive psychology, which currently holds considerable sway within the field of psychology, also falls within this category. Though it speaks of mental processes within the individual, this is simply considered to be a provisional state of affairs. Virtually all cognitive psychologists harbor the notion that these inner processes can ultimately be accounted for by chemical processes within the brain, and that with the right equipment it would or will be possible to objectively quantify these processes. Modern cognitive psychology wishes to have nothing to do with a world of inner subjective experience, dismissing those schools of psychology that do as folklorist psychology. Having adopted this approach, cognitive psychology attempts to answer such questions as, Can computers think? Or even, Is the individual really anything more than a complicated machine? For this reason the approach adopted by cognitive psychology is considered to be a "third-person approach." In other words, rather than studying the individual from the point of view of the first person ("I"), or from the point of view of the second person ("you"), cognitive psychology studies the individual as a third person ("he" or "she"). It is worth noting as an aside that if, for the sake of argument, the individual did possess an inner life, the method applied by the behaviorists is guaranteed to keep it well hidden.

As its name suggests, the second school within the field of psychology—*psychoanalysis*—does recognize the existence of an inner life. Psychoanalysts see the individual as a maelstrom of drives and emotions through which the fragile ego has to wend its way. In this vision, if the human ego is still weak, it can be overwhelmed by the force of these drives and emotions, but once the ego has crystallized to a sufficient extent, it is then able to repress these drives and emotions—which can lead to all kinds of pathology. Psychoanalysis claims that we allow ourselves to be guided by unconscious motives far more often that we are prepared to admit. Believing that the patterns that make for later happiness or unhappiness are effectively established during early childhood, the psychoanalyst focuses heavily on the past. The problems experienced by the neurotic adult can almost always be traced back to events that took place in the past; this being the case, it is thought to be therapeutic for the individual to remember the experiences of the past. The psychoanalyst is particularly interested in the lower, primitive side of the individual—basic impulses and sexuality. However, while psychoanalysis certainly acknowledges the existence of an inner life, it is primarily concerned with what I would call an "interiority-that-was"—an interiority that has to do with the early years of childhood.

In the sixties these two relatively limited visions of the individual met with a certain amount of opposition in the United States. For decades American psychology had been dominated by the two schools of behaviorism and psychoanalysis. A number of psychologists were of the opinion that the view of the individual on which there schools were based—the individual as a mechanism or the individual as a victim of primitive, unconscious impulses—failed by a long way to do justice to the mystery of human experience. Under the inspiring leadership of Abraham Maslow and many others, the school of *humanistic psychology*, which aspired above all to understand individuals in terms of their humanity, emerged on the scene. Humanistic psychologists were less concerned with the past, than with the present. They were less concerned with the animal within the individual than with the human within the individual. Their studies centered on the question of how the individual could function to the best of his or her potential, above all also as a social being. Though this school of psychology has not yet been recognized by the world of academia due to the fact that it is, properly speaking, an ideology geared towards self-realization rather than an academic science, among the general public it met with a far more positive response. Many people breathed a sigh of relief when they first came across the vision of the individual expounded by humanistic psychology. This third school of psychology is primarily concerned with what I would call an "interiority-that-is"—the subjective inner world as it is experienced in the present.

At the end of the sixties some of the humanistic psychologists—but certainly not all—were dogged by the nagging feeling that the vision entertained by humanistic psychology was still not the final word on the individual. Once again it was Abraham Maslow who provided the initial impulse that led to the establishment of a Fourth Force within the field of psychology, which after some deliberation came to be known as *transpersonal psychology*. This school of psychology undertook to subject the divine within the individual to precise scientific investigation. Its exponents were not particularly interested in the past or the present; they were far more interested in the future. What were the further reaches of human potential? Was it possible that human nature was capable of levels of experience and consciousness that the Western individual was still largely unaware of? Where did spiritual and mystical experiences fit into this picture? Were they possibilities that were, in principle, open to any of us? Was it possible that we could learn something from Eastern cultures and religions in this respect? The advocates of transpersonal psychology were primarily concerned with what I would call an "interiority-that-is-yet-to-be" or with an "interiority-that-might-be." According to the vision held by transpersonal psychology, each and every individual is able to apply meditative techniques to raise the level of his or her consciousness with a view to accessing a more expansive or higher state of consciousness.

As was only to be expected, the young science of transpersonal psychology stood even less chance of being endorsed by world of academia than humanistic psychology. As far as many orthodox psychologists were concerned transpersonal psychology was a very long way from being an objective science; worse still, it sought to smuggle the subjective insights of Buddhism or Hinduism in through the back door of psychology. Nevertheless, it is important to emphasize that the express intention of the first transpersonal psychologists was to study the field of spiritual experience in a way that was scientifically sound. *The Journal of Transpersonal Psychology*, a scientific journal devoted to the study of transpersonal psychology set up in 1969, stated its purpose as follows: "The Journal of Transpersonal Psychology is concerned with the publication of theoretical and applied research, original contributions, empirical papers, articles and studies in meta-needs, ultimate values, unitive consciousness, peak experiences, ecstasy, mystical experiences, B values, essence, bliss, awe, wonder, self-actualization, ultimate meaning, transcendence of the self, spirit, sacralization of everyday life, oneness, cosmic awareness, cosmic play, individual and species-wide synergy, the practice of meditation, transcendental phenomena, maximal sensory awareness, responsiveness, compassion and related concepts, experiences and activities. As a statement of purpose, this formulation is to be understood as subject to optional individual or group interpretations, either wholly or in part, with regard to the acceptance of its contents as essentially naturalistic, theistic, supernaturalistic, or any other designated classification."

Some transpersonal psychologists now wish to extend the domain of transpersonal psychology to cover the whole of the field of psychology, based on the reasoning that the transpersonal not only transcends but also encompasses the personal. In my opinion this would simply lead to a hopeless confusion of terminology. In this case it would be better to use the term *integral psychology* to refer to this all-encompassing psychology as Wilber has done consistently in recent years. This integral psychology might well be seen as the "Fifth Force" within the field of psychology in view of the fact that it attempts to describe all of the aspects of human consciousness within a single integral model (see Fig. 2.1).

THE PERENNIAL PHILOSOPHY AS A GUIDING CONCEPT

Though transpersonal psychology was certainly not indiscriminate when it came to smuggling in ideas drawn from the body of religious thought devised by humanity over the centuries, it was virtually inevitable that the first transpersonal psychologists would refer to the mystical traditions of East and West in the attempt to refine their understanding of the spiritual dimension. Countless theories and models have been proposed with a view to charting the more distant realms of human consciousness—Maslow spoke of "the farther reaches of human nature"—but not all of these theories and models were automatically taken on board by the transpersonal community. Given that this was the case, at the beginning of the seventies there was a pressing need for a general theory regarding the realm of the transpersonal—a theory that would not only clearly delineate the experiences that belonged to the world of the transpersonal, but also the way in which the dimensions covered by transpersonal psychology related to the faculties covered by the more conventional schools of psychology.

A few transpersonal psychologists were of the opinion that transpersonal psychology would do best to draw on what was known as the "perennial philosophy," a phrase translated from the Latin *philosophia perennis*, which is popularly attributed to Leibniz.[7] Aldous Huxley introduced the term to a far wider public in his book of the same name, *The Perennial Philosophy* (1944), which was an anthology of mystical texts from East and West. The phrase itself is generally understood to point to a conception of the nature of reality that can be found in most of the great spiritual traditions throughout the world. If indeed there was such a universal conception of the nature of reality, the young science of transpersonal psychology would do well to adopt this as a provisional frame of reference in its endeavor to study human consciousness. After all, had it not declared itself to be in search of a more accurate understanding of the spiritual dimension—an understanding that was generally valid and not encumbered by cultural or religious biases?

The phrase *perennial philosophy* is often used by a group of religious scholars, who are usually mentioned in the same breath—René Guénon, Ananda Coomaraswamy, Fritjof Schuon, Seyyed Nasr, and Huston Smith.

Rather than being a tight-knit group of religious scholars, the five are actually authors who happen to think more or less alike. All of them are convinced that the worldview elaborated and subscribed to by prescientific cultures was far more spiritual and more profound than the secularized worldview that now prevails in the West, dominated as it is by scientific materialism. Guénon presents the striking image of the modern individual yearning under the dominion of quantity while the ancient cultures were primarily concerned with quality. However, this view of things is certainly not endorsed by all religious scholars. Some doubt the existence of a universal doctrine. And the issue is further complicated by the fact that the advocates of the perennial philosophy tend to interpret the essence of this philosophy in different ways.

For example, Aldous Huxley defined the core of the perennial philosophy, somewhat tortuously, as follows: "Philosophia Perennis—the phrase was coined by Leibniz; but the thing—the metaphysic that recognizes a divine Reality substantial to the world of things and lives and minds; the psychology that finds in the soul something similar to, or even identical with, divine Reality; the ethic that places man's final end in the knowledge of the imminent and transcendent Ground of all being—the thing is immemorial and universal. Rudiments of the Perennial Philosophy may be found among the traditionary lore of primitive peoples in every region of the world, and in its fully developed forms it has a place in every one of the higher religions."[8]

Some decades later Ken Wilber reduced the essential message of the perennial philosophy to seven main tenets: "One, Spirit exists, and Two, Spirit is found within. Three, most of us don't realize this Spirit within, however, because we are living in a world of sin, separation and duality—that is, we are living in a fallen or illusory state. Four, there is a way out of this fallen state of sin and illusion, there is a Path to our liberation. Five, if we follow this Path to its conclusion, the result is a Rebirth or Enlightenment, a direct experience of Spirit within, a Supreme Liberation, which—Six—marks the end of sin and suffering, and which—Seven—issues in social action of mercy and compassion on behalf of all sentient beings."[9] I would venture to suggest the following even more concise version: (1) Existence is a whole, (2) which is essentially spiritual in nature and (3) as such contains a number of planes or spheres, ranging from the material to the divine. (4) Each individual is effectively in contact with all of these levels of existence, which means that there is the potential for consciousness to expand from the awareness of matter to an awareness of the Divine. The point is that the perennial philosophy denotes an attitude toward life that appears to be universally valid and that embodies the highest ideals of the spiritual life.

A "PERENNIAL PSYCHOLOGY"

In 1975 Wilber, who was at that stage completely unknown, made his first appearance in the *Journal of Transpersonal Psychology* with an article entitled "Psychologia Perennis"—perennial psychology. In this article he announces, very much in the spirit of the above, what would turn out to be a statement of principle that would infuse the whole of his work:

> In the past few decades the West has witnessed an explosion of interest among psychologists, theologians, scientists, and philosophers alike in what Huxley has called *philosophia perennis*, the 'perennial philosophy', a universal doctrine as to the nature of man and reality lying at the heart of every major metaphysical tradition . . . . What is frequently overlooked, however, is that corresponding to the perennial philosophy there exists what I would like to call a *psychologia perennis*, a 'perennial psychology'—a universal view as to the nature of human consciousness, which expresses the very same insights as the perennial philosophy but in more decidedly psychological language. . . . The purpose of this paper—besides describing the fundamentals of the perennial psychology—is to outline a model of consciousness which remains faithful to the spirit of this universal doctrine yet at the same time gives ample consideration to the insights of such typically Western disciplines as ego-psychology, psychoanalysis, humanistic psychology, Jungian analysis, interpersonal psychology, and the like. At the heart of this model, the 'Spectrum of Consciousness'[10], lies the insight that human personality is a multileveled manifestation or expression of a single Consciousness, just as in physics the electro-magnetic spectrum is viewed as a multi-banded expression of a single, characteristic electro-magnetic wave. More specifically, the Spectrum of Consciousness is a pluridimensional approach to man's identity; that is to say, each level of the Spectrum is marked by a different and easily recognized sense of individual identity, which ranges from the Supreme Identity of cosmic consciousness through several gradations or bands to the drastically narrowed sense of identity associated with egoic consciousness.[11]

We see here that from his very first articles onwards Wilber shows himself to be an *integral* psychologist. He is more than a transpersonal psychologist in that he is concerned to fathom the phenomenon of human consciousness in its totality—both personal and transpersonal. He does not wish to concentrate solely on mysticism or spiritual experience, but above all he is intent on investigating how spiritual experience relates to the more mundane forms of consciousness and identity. Also, right from the outset he is clear about the metaphysical context within which he seeks to pursue psychology—the perennial philosophy constitutes the frame of reference for the whole of his work.

How did Wilber come to this way of thinking? Once again the au-tobiographical article "Odyssey" provides valuable information in this respect, this time regarding the genesis of the spectrum model.[12] During his intensive study of the literature of East and West Wilber rapidly discovered that it was essential to make a distinction between two differ-ent realms within human consciousness—the realm of the personal and the realm of the transpersonal or spiritual. It is this distinction that jus-tifies the existence of transpersonal psychology. In reaching this conclu-sion Wilber was influenced by the distinction that Carl Jung made between the personal and the collective unconscious, and the distinction made by Roberto Assagioli, the founder of psychosynthesis, between personal (psy-chological) psychosynthesis and transpersonal (spiritual) psychosynthesis. Thus in his first attempt to arrive at an integral model, Wilber made the following basic distinction:

personal / transpersonal

The conventional schools of psychology are primarily concerned with how an individual can become an autonomous, rational individual, free of neuroses and other pathological symptoms. Transpersonal psychology addresses itself to a very different matter, namely, how can the autono-mous, rational, and mentally balanced individual align himself or herself with the dimension of the Divine? The personal and the transpersonal schools are not in conflict with one another; they are simply each con-cerned with a different aspect of human consciousness, or, to put it an-other way, they are each concerned with a different band of the spectrum of consciousness. Bearing this in mind, Wilber adopted the following basic principle: only schools that are concerned with the same aspect of consciousness can be considered to be in conflict with one another. Ap-parent differences of opinion between schools that are concerned with different bands of the spectrum of consciousness—such as, for example, psychoanalysis and Buddhism—are, in fact, illusory. This line of thinking immediately serves to create order within the chaotic field of psychology and spirituality, in which the countless schools and different forms of therapy all shout the loudest that they have hold of the truth.

The next subdivision that Wilber introduced within his model related to the humanistic/existential schools in psychology. These schools fall somewhere between the personal and transpersonal schools. On the one hand, they have elaborated a vision of the human being that is far more complete than the vision adopted by the schools of psychology that focus purely on mental awareness, in that in addition to the psyche they also include the body as a factor in the equation. Yet on the other hand, they often (though not always) reject all forms of spirituality and so discount a transpersonal dimension. (And even within this field it is possible to make further distinctions. For instance, atheist existentialists are closer to the personal and theistic existentialists are closer to the transpersonal.)

The situation, which is now somewhat more complex, can be visualized as follows:

personal / existential / transpersonal

Wilber felt that it was possible to refine this still rather basic model even further. For example, within the realm of the personal there are schools that concentrate solely on the conscious ego, as well as schools that study what happens when the ego represses a part of itself, thereby creating what has come to be known as the "shadow." This concept of the shadow, which is borrowed from Jungian psychology, stands for all of the qualities within ourselves that we seek to conceal from the outside world (and often also from ourselves). To the outside world we attempt to present a far more attractive, but often unrealistic image of ourselves, which has come to be termed the "persona" (literally our mask).

This gives us the following picture:

persona / ego / existential / transpersonal

As we have already seen, the existential or humanistic schools are essentially concerned with another facet of human experience. These schools look for ways of integrating the body and the psyche with a view to creating a total organism. Wilber chose the term *centaur* to refer to this approach. The centaur was a creature of Greek mythology with the head, arms, and torso of a human being and the lower body and legs of a horse—a creature that can also be seen as symbolic of mental and physical unity. Therapists working within this field deliberately seek to involve the body in the therapy and believe that the failure to do so is one of the main reasons why forms of therapy based purely on dialogue, such as psychoanalysis, prove unsuccessful. This field includes all of the body-oriented approaches, such as bioenergetics, which was evolved by Alexander Lowen, and all of the schools since derived from bioenergetics.

At this point Wilber felt that it would be helpful to introduce a further distinction within the realm of the transpersonal or spiritual, which is all too often erroneously conceived of as a single homogeneous field. For instance, while some schools concentrate on the various stages of transpersonal or spiritual development that an individual can go though, others choose to concentrate on the final product of this development or the highest stage of consciousness (which, paradoxically enough, according to the mystics is closely related to our everyday consciousness). To put it in Wilber's own words: "The first thing that became obvious to me was that there existed *at least* two different subrealms within the transpersonal sphere, or, if you will, two degrees of transcendence. The lower degree was that of the transcendent witness. In this state, one's awareness transcends mind, body, ego, and centaur, and merely witnesses the fluctuations of those lower realms. . . . But beyond that level of transcendence, there is a radical and ultimate state, where one no longer witnesses reality, one *becomes* reality. The transcendent witness collapses into everything witnessed, high or low, sacred or profane, and disappears as a *separate* entity. In the lesser state, one's deepest self intuits Godhead; in the ultimate state, one's deepest self gives way to Godhead, and *that* is the Supreme Identity."[13] To refer to this ultimate state of consciousness, Wilber used the term *Mind* or *Spirit*.

This gave rise to the following spectrum:

persona / ego / centaur / witness / Spirit

According to Wilber these are the five basic forms of identity, of subjectivity, of "I"-ness, of consciousness, that are possible for the individual. As one moves from the left to the right of the spectrum, there is an increasing *expansion* of consciousness. By the same token, as one moves from the right to the left of the spectrum, there is a progressive *narrowing* of consciousness. The persona is the most restricted form of consciousness and Spirit the most expanded form of consciousness.

Wilber was struck by the fact that there was a remarkable continuity between the personal and transpersonal bands of the spectrum of consciousness. "From that point, it was a very small step to realize how the mystical traditions fit into the overall scheme. Psychoanalysis aimed at uniting persona and shadow to reveal the whole and healthy ego; going deeper, humanistic therapies aimed at uniting the ego and the body, to reveal the total centaur. Just so, the mystic traditions went deeper still and aimed at uniting the centaur and the cosmos to reveal the Supreme Identity, a 'cosmic consciousness.' " [14]

Thus, as far as Wilber could see, the process was actually a remarkably simple process of addition and inclusion:

1. Persona = persona
2. Ego   = persona + shadow
3. Centaur = persona + shadow + body
4. Spirit = persona + shadow + body + cosmos

This covers the four major levels of the spectrum model, which can also be seen to be a hierarchical model. Each time that we move to a deeper level within the spectrum, not only do we transcend the previous stages (because a new element is added), we also encompass the previous stages (because the old elements are retained). From Wilber's point of view the more all-encompassing the perspective, the truer it is. The levels of the spectrum might also be depicted as follows, as a series of concentric circles:

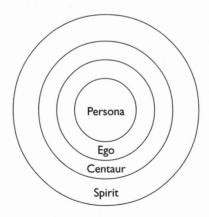

FIGURE 2.2. The spectrum of consciousness (basic version)

If these four levels of the spectrum are taken to represent the primary colors of the spectrum, given that a spectrum is a continuum, which, in principle, can be subjected to an infinite number of divisions, there are also bound to be a number of secondary colors. Between the level of the centaur and the level of the ego Wilber inserted two such secondary bands. Closest to the level of the centaur he identified what he called the "biosocial bands." These represent the influences exerted upon us by the culture within which we live primarily through the medium of language, though we are often unaware of this influence. Our perception of reality is often heavily influenced by the structure of the language we use, for example, by the fact that we rely primarily on verbs in our attempt to describe reality, or alternatively on a large number of nouns. And this differs from one culture to another. Through language our view of the world is subject to the most fundamental distinctions without our even realizing it. These bands give us the feeling that we are separate beings. They also serve as a storehouse of abstract thought in that they provide us with symbols and logic, and are thus partly responsible for the creation of the ego. Between the biosocial bands and the level of the ego Wilber placed what he called the "philosophical bands," which represent a more personal interpretation of the influences exerted by culture. For example, if a particular culture opposes individualism, the way in which we experience this taboo is likely to involve all kinds of personal elements. Thus, as Wilber sees it, the philosophical bands act as a personal filter for reality while the biosocial bands act as a cultural filter for reality.

Finally, between the level of Spirit and the level of the centaur Wilber placed the "transpersonal bands," which represent the "no-man's-land" between the Divine and the individual organism. According to Wilber the transpersonal bands encompass Jung's collective unconscious, extra-sensory perception, the transpersonal Witness, astral projection, out of the body experiences, peak experiences, clairaudience, and other similar experiences. What all of these experiences have in common is that they occur within a domain in which the definite boundary between the individual and the greater whole of the cosmos gradually begins to blur.

The complete spectrum model of consciousness can be visualized as follows in Figure 2.3.

Another way of describing the descent in the spectrum from persona to Spirit might be to say that when we live purely within the confines of the persona, everything that is not part of this persona—

— Persona
— Ego
            — Philosophical bands
            — Bio-social bands
— Centaur
            — Transpersonal bands
— Spirit

FIGURE 2.3.   The spectrum of consciousness (complete version)

the shadow, the physical body, and the universe—is experienced as existing outside of ourselves. However, if we succeed in incorporating the shadow within the persona, thereby creating an integrated ego, we effectively bring the shadow within our inner world. If we then go on to incorporate the body within the ego, we bring an even greater element of reality within our sphere of consciousness. The last stage of this process brings the whole of the cosmos within our field of perception. That is, we no longer experience the cosmos as something outside of ourselves, but as our deepest being. Rather than being purely identified with the individual organism, the self expands to encompass the whole of the cosmos.

THE SPECTRUM OF CONSCIOUSNESS

Once Wilber had worked all of this out for himself, he committed it to paper in a relatively short space of time in his book entitled *The Spectrum of Consciousness*. The book is divided into two parts, "Evolution" and "Involution." Wilber uses the term *evolution* to refer to the process that gives rise to the spectrum of consciousness with all of its bands or colors, and the term *involution* to refer to the process by means of which consciousness returns to its Source—the white Light of the Divine. These two great movements are central to the perennial philosophy and also constitute the framework for all of Wilber's thought.

EVOLUTION—THE MOVEMENT FROM SPIRIT TO EMBODIED INDIVIDUAL

In the preface to *The Spectrum of Consciousness* Wilber is careful to emphasize that the idea of consciousness as a spectrum is simply a helpful metaphor: "Throughout this book, whenever consciousness is referred to as a spectrum, or as being composed of numerous bands or vibratory levels, the meaning remains strictly metaphorical. Consciousness is not, properly speaking, a spectrum—but it is useful, for purposes of communication and investigation, to treat it as one. We are creating, in other words, a *model*, in the scientific sense of the word."[15] In Wilber's eyes, the main value of this spectrum model is that it serves as an integrative conceptual framework for the highly fragmented field of psychology, since all of the existing schools of psychology can be related to one or other of the bands of the spectrum. The spectrum model also delineates a spiritual path that is open to any individual. However, in showing this to be the case, Wilber certainly does not mean to imply that everyone should cram to become a mystic in the shortest possible time; this is only a possibility for the few individuals who are genuinely ready for it. For the majority of people the personal bands of the spectrum will continue to constitute the whole of reality for the time being.

Wilber then goes on to make a distinction between two fundamental forms of knowledge. In line with a large number of authors linked with both Eastern and Western traditions, he makes a distinction between theoretical knowledge and empirical knowledge. Theoretical knowledge is essentially dualistic and completely reliant on the categories of subject and object. This is the kind of knowledge on which science is based. However, as Wilber points out in *The Spectrum of Consciousness*, modern physics has discovered that at the deepest level of matter this polarity can no longer be maintained. Confronted with the collapse of the subject-object paradigm, modern physicists set out in search of a different way of knowing, and it was more or less inevitable that they should end up consulting Eastern philosophy, which speaks of a different way of knowing.[16] This other way of knowing is not symbolic or conceptual, but existential, intimate, and highly subjective. Taoism speaks of conventional knowledge as opposed to natural knowledge, Hinduism speaks of lower knowledge as opposed to higher knowledge, and the same distinction is also to be found in Western mystical literature. Within the field of Western psychology William James speaks of conceptual knowledge as opposed to intuitive knowledge.

According to Wilber, it is this second way of knowing, which is spoken of in all of the traditions, that brings us into contact with Reality. It turns out that Reality itself is actually a form of Consciousness that can be discovered in stages. And, as Wilber rightly points out, the mystical texts refer to this Consciousness in a number of different ways. Some texts say what this Consciousness *is*, some texts say what this Consciousness *is not*, and other texts tell us—by means of instructions rather than descriptions—

how we can *experience* this Consciousness. Although this Consciousness essentially transcends all categories, including the distinction between the inner world and the outer world, for the individual it is likely to be most accessible through inner subjectivity. It is not without reason that the mystical texts speak of a Self that exists within each individual and forms the essence of the universe. This Self is eternal and is not affected by the passage of time, nor by the processes of birth and death. It is present here and now in each activity of consciousness, however humble.

It is within this Self that the whole spectrum of consciousness emerges—not as a progressive development that takes place in time, but simultaneously at each moment. Wilber describes this process as a series of dualisms. At a certain moment the Consciousness that is Spirit begins to contract, giving rise to the polarity between subject and object. Wilber calls this the Primary Dualism, and this first shift creates the conditions that support the concept of space. In terms of individual experience, this contraction marks the transition from identification with the All to identification with the psychophysical organism, which corresponds to the existential level of the centaur. A further contraction—the Secondary Dualism—gives rise to the concept of time. The individual has now "fallen" from the first (intuitive) form of knowledge into the second (conceptual) form of knowledge. The individual now thinks in terms of time and finiteness and no longer in terms of eternity and infinity. A third major shift takes place as consciousness contracts still further into the psyche, such that the organismic bond with the body is broken (the Tertiary Dualism). The fourth and last shift involves the contraction away from and rejection of a part of the psyche (the shadow)—at this stage consciousness is experiencing itself as the persona (the Quaternary Dualism). Though the transitions from one level to another actually occur as a gradual process, this distinction between the four levels of Spirit, organism, ego and persona helps to clarify the situation. Thus we see the emergence of the spectrum of consciousness.

Wilber describes the transition from the level of the centaur—the psychophysical organism—to the level of the ego as follows (this passage is characteristic of the view that Wilber expounds in *The Spectrum of Consciousness*): "We may follow this entire process if we can only understand what I would like to call *organismic awareness*. Organismic awareness is what we—at the Ego Level—ordinarily, but clumsily, refer to as seeing, touching, tasting, smelling, and hearing. But in its very purest form, this 'sensual awareness' is non-symbolic, non-conceptual, momentary consciousness. Organismic awareness is awareness of the Present only—you can't taste the past, smell the past, see the past, or hear the past. Neither can you taste, smell, see, touch, or hear the future. In other words, organismic consciousness is properly timeless, and being timeless, it is necessarily spaceless. Just as organismic awareness knows no past and future, it knows no inside or outside, no self or other. *Thus pure organismic consciousness participates fully in the non-dual awareness called Absolute Subjectivity.* Organismic consciousness and cosmic consciousness are thus one and the same."[17]

Wilber does not actually state in *The Spectrum of Consciousness* whether or not he believes that an individual also goes through this process of the progressive narrowing of consciousness in a literal sense during the first half of his life, though the spectrum model certainly suggests this to be the case and in certain passages Wilber himself appears to subscribe to this view. For instance, he writes in *The Spectrum of Consciousness:* "The process of the Self's involution and evolution is viewed as a universal drama of eternal play . . . but the sole actor in this drama is the one and only Self, playing an infinite number of roles (such as you and me) without ceasing in the least to completely remain itself, spaceless and timeless, whole and undivided. In our limited and temporal state, we divide this drama into two stages—that of involution and that of evolution—while in reality both are phases of one aspect. In highest truth, there is no involution and evolution through time, for whether we realize it or not, the Self remains always above time in the Eternal Moment. The same holds true for the apparent evolution of the spectrum of consciousness . . . For this reason, we have studiously avoided assigning actual chronologies to the four major dualisms. From the standpoint of time, we have only suggested that the four major dualisms do occur in the order that we have outlined, beginning with the primary and ending with the quaternary dualism. This is not to say, however, that these dualisms, as they appear to evolve in history, do not constitute a legitimate field of study. On the contrary, the field is a most important one. The primary dualism, for example, has been approached anthropologically by investigators concerned with that period in man's evolution when he learned to separate himself from his environment.[18] It has also been followed in the individual development of the infant, as the child learns to separate himself from his immediate surroundings.[19] The works of such scholars as Freud, Piaget, Werner, Cassirer, Arieti and others in this area represent a most valuable contribution."[20]

Having said this in *The Spectrum of Consciousness,* Wilber still adopts a "timeless" standpoint: at *every* moment of our lives Consciousness narrows itself to the personal consciousness that we are; but at *any* moment it can also reexpand to encompass the whole cosmos. However, Wilber is not specifically interested in the connection that exists between the course of a human life or the course of evolution and the spectrum of consciousness: "We are not primarily interested in these temporal aspects, however, for man re-enacts his major dualisms in this very moment, and it is only as he views them through the squinting eye of time that he is persuaded to establish a time-table for what actually remains timeless. How, in this very moment, we illusorily separate ourselves from our universe, our bodies, and even our thoughts—that is our primary concern."[21]

Wilber concludes the first part of *The Spectrum of Consciousness* with a tour of the world's great spiritual traditions, such as Platonism, Vedanta, Mahayana Buddhism, Zen Buddhism, Tibetan Buddhism, and the work of a few Western authors in order to show that "the psychological systems of the great metaphysical traditions—from Vedanta to Zen—are in essential, formal agreement with the spectrum of consciousness as we have described it."[22]

INVOLUTION—THE MOVEMENT FROM EMBODIED INDIVIDUAL TO SPIRIT

In the second part of *The Spectrum of Consciousness*, entitled "Involution," Wilber outlines the way back to Spirit, which proceeds through the same phases as the movement from Spirit to embodied individual, but in reverse order. He plots the path that each individual can follow back to God as it were. First he discusses the problem of integrating the shadow to create the ego in some detail. Then in a chapter entitled "The Great Filter," which looks at the veiling effect of language, he describes the traversal of the biosocial and philosophical bands of the spectrum. The integration of the ego and the body to create the centaur is addressed in a chapter on body-oriented therapy (including the school of bioenergetics developed by Alexander Lowen). At this point, according to Wilber, we enter the no-man's-land of paranormal and transpersonal phenomena (referred to by most of the spiritual traditions as "lower mysticism"). As yet relatively little is known about this realm. In the following chapter Wilber goes on to discuss the experience of the unity consciousness of Spirit ("higher" or "true mysticism") in more detail. Having attained unity consciousness, the individual actually lives the nondualist understanding that sees no distinction between high and low or sacred and profane. With this our spiritual voyage of discovery is at an end.

In the last chapter of *The Spectrum of Consciousness* Wilber shows a side of himself that is to persist throughout the whole of his oeuvre—his feeling for the paradoxical nature of Spirit. Despite the fact that the majority of the book is concerned with the stages of development that can be experienced by an individual and the obstacles that he or she is likely to encounter along the way, Wilber now contends that all of this takes place within the sphere of illusion, and that in reality we have never left the level of Spirit. In other words our everyday consciousness is very closely connected with Absolute Consciousness, if we were but able to realize it. Maybe we can attempt to understand this highest mystical insight in the following terms. In all of our attempts to find the Self in the outer world or in the inner world, we have always already been this Self. In other words, we have never really left this Self, and all of our attempts to find it elsewhere actually lead us even further away from it. Thus all of the great spiritual teachings speak of the danger of regarding the method as an absolute. At a certain stage we will have to cease seeking Spirit in order to be able to rest in the Being of Spirit. It is quite remarkable that Wilber should have had such a clear feeling for the more paradoxical aspects of spirituality and that he was also able to articulate this insight so clearly at such a young age. In the last chapter, entitled "Always Already," he outlines how the countless spiritual techniques developed by the various traditions always have the same goal in mind—to make it clear to us that ultimately it is impossible for us to *reach* Spirit, *because we ourselves are already Spirit.* We can never reach Spirit, but—and here is the paradox—neither can we ever lose it. So the search for Spirit finally comes to an end when we realize that the search for something outside of ourselves effectively stands in the way of the realization of the Self.

Nevertheless, many people continue to search for God or Spirit because they experience themselves to be separate from God or Spirit. Many spiritual seekers have the vague feeling that they have somehow lost God somewhere along the way. According to Wilber it is to remove this ultimately illusory impression that the spiritual traditions have developed what are known as "skillful means". We heave no choice but to meditate, to search, to experiment, and to seek the Divine, for it is only in doing so that we can find out for ourselves whether or not Spirit exists. There are certain instructions that apply to this kind of experiment, which has to be carried out within the laboratory of our own consciousness, and these instructions need to be followed very carefully. Wilber goes as far as to say that anyone who refuses to carry out this experiment is not really entitled to voice an opinion on the subject. In *The Spectrum of Consciousness* Wilber emphasizes the fact that these meditative experiments are completely scientific. "These [experiments] are perfectly intelligible, reasonable, and scientific, and any logical positivist or scientist who dismisses them must do so on purely unscientific and emotional grounds."[23] According to Wilber, what all of these experiments have in common is: (1) *active attention*, a relaxed but intense alertness, which is focused on the present; (2) the *stopping* of the formation of thought (the conceptual form of knowledge), as a result of which we are able to be present for what is arising in the moment, and (3) *passive observation* not focused on any particular object, which creates the space for the Subject to reveal itself (and which enables us to make the leap to the second, nonconceptual way of knowing). "And one instant of this pure awareness is itself Mind. Whether we realize it or not, it is always already the case."[24] In discussing these three ingredients, Wilber refers to the work of Hubert Benoit, Krishnamurti, Ramana Maharshi, D. T. Suzuki, and Wei Wu Wei, among others.

CONSCIOUSNESS WITHOUT BOUNDARIES

Because *The Spectrum of Consciousness* was fairly dense and quite abstract for readers coming into contact with these ideas for the first time—the book is infused with all of the characteristics of a young and passionate author who wants to say everything at once in his first book and to substantiate his argument with as many quotes as possible—not long after he had completed the manuscript, and before *The Spectrum of Consciousness* was even published, Wilber wrote a popular version of the book. This came out in 1979 as *No Boundary—Eastern and Western Approaches to Personal Growth*. *No Boundary* explains very clearly how individuals can experience their oneness with the cosmos by continually expanding the boundaries of their identity. *No Boundary* covers the same ground as the second part of *The Spectrum of Consciousness*, but in a somewhat more informal manner.

No Boundary also suggests a number of practical exercises that can help the reader to put what Wilber describes into practice, and it specifies which of the psychotherapeutic approaches or spiritual traditions relate to the different bands of the spectrum, as can be seen in figure 2.4.[25] According to Wilber spirituality is a logical extension of psychotherapy. In the schools of psychotherapy that deliberately make room for spirituality, such as psychosynthesis and Jungian psychology, it is difficult to specify the point at which psychotherapy turns into spirituality. Armed with the information set out above, each individual can choose the most appropriate approach depending on the level at which his or her sense of identity is

— Persona
  — Simple counselling
  — Supportive therapy

— Ego
  — Psychoanalysis
  — Psychodrama
  — Transactional analysis
  — Reality therapy
  — Ego psychology

— Centaur
  — Bioenergetic analysis
  — Rogerian therapy
  — Gestalt therapy
  — Existential analysis
  — Logotherapy
  — Humanistic psychology

— Transpersonal bands
  — Jungian psychology
  — Psychosynthesis

— Spirit
  — Vedanta / Hinduism
  — Mahayana / Vajrayana Buddhism
  — Taoism
  — Esoteric Islam
  — Esoteric Christianity
  — Esoteric Judaism

FIGURE 2.4.   The spectrum of psychotherapy and spirituality

primarily focused. According to Wilber all forms of therapy aim to take us deeper within the spectrum of the consciousness, until we reach the deepest level of Spirit. The figure also shows the importance of psychotherapy for those who wish to pursue a spiritual path. There is little point in trying to become one with Spirit if we still need to undergo some form of psychotherapy in order to deal with problems relating to the personal level. These personal problems prevent us from expanding to deeper levels of consciousness. Thus psychotherapy can often be the first step on the path to Spirit.

No Boundary was Wilber's first attempt at writing a book for the layperson. Adopting a familiar and direct style, he guides the reader through the primary stages on the path to God—persona, ego, centaur, witness, cosmos/Spirit. The basic underlying theme of the book is that we limit our sense of identity unnecessarily by drawing all kinds of dividing lines between the psyche and the body or between the organism and the cosmos. If one by one we were able to remove these dividing lines, we would arrive at a state in which there is no boundary. This highest form of identity is also referred to as "cosmic consciousness." Wilber himself refers to it as "unity consciousness." Speaking of unity consciousness, he says: "So widespread is this experience of the supreme identity that it has, along with the doctrines that purport to explain it, earned the name 'The Perennial Philosophy'. There is much evidence that this type of experience or knowledge is central to every major religion—Hinduism, Buddhism, Taoism, Christianity, Islam and Judaism—so that we can justifiably speak of the 'transcendent unity of religions'[26] and the unanimity of primordial truth. The theme of this book is that this type of awareness, this unity consciousness or supreme identity, is the nature and condition of all sentient beings; but that we progressively limit our world and turn from our true nature in order to embrace boundaries. Our originally pure and unitive consciousness then functions on varied levels, with different identities and different boundaries."[27]

According to Wilber each different level of the spectrum is associated with a characteristic sense of identity and also with certain types of pathology that are likely to occur at that level of the spectrum and which require the forms of therapy or meditation suited to that particular level of the spectrum. In this way the spectrum model serves as an integrative model for the field of psychotherapy, which encompasses an unoverseeable quantity of contradictory approaches. "All these different schools of psychology and religion don't so much represent contradictory approaches to an individual and his problems, but rather they represent complementary approaches to different levels of the individual. With this understanding, the vast field of psychology and religion breaks down into five or six manageable groups, and it becomes obvious that each of these groups is aiming predominantly at one of the major bands of the spectrum."[28]

The centaur level—the level at which the integration of body and psyche takes place—occupies a central position within the spectrum model. The centaur level effectively forms the doorway to the transpersonal and spiritual levels of consciousness. Wilber analyses the reasons why the modern individual has a tendency to dissociate from the body and to identify entirely with the ego. The ego relates to the body as voluntary to instinctive, as deliberate to unconscious. Body-oriented therapists are presently attempting to remove the distinction between the ego and the body by encouraging a total surrender to the body, which gives rise to a feeling of joy. However, as much as Wilber recommends this body-oriented approach, he is careful to comment on the line of thinking that holds that the body is more important than the ego. Insufficient appreciation of the body—which tends to be the case within the schools of psychotherapy that adopt a predominantly mental approach—can easily be replaced by an approach that attaches excessive importance to the body, seeing it as a source of happiness. Somewhat concerned about this development Wilber writes, "Please remember, however, that I am not saying that the body per se—what we call the 'physical body'—is a deeper reality than the mental-ego. In fact, the simple body itself is the lowest of all modes of consciousness, so simple that we have not even included it, by itself, in this book. The body is not a 'deeper reality' than the ego, as many somatologists think, but the integration of the body and the ego is indeed a deeper reality than either alone, and that integration is what we will emphasize in this chapter, even if, for practical purposes, we dwell on the physical body and physical body exercises."[29]

In discussing the levels beyond that of the centaur, Wilber sees value in the ideas expounded by Jungian psychology and the school of psychosynthesis developed by Assagioli. If we learn to drop our identification with the body and with our feelings and thoughts, we can discover a still center within ourselves—the Self. This transpersonal Self, also known as "the Witness," transcends the ups and downs of the personal life and is at home in a world of light, calmness, and peace. Speculating about the nature of this Self, Wilber suspects that this Self is in fact identical in all people because it has no individual attributes. It is immortal and eternal, and though it cannot be perceived objectively or defined, it can be realized: "You needn't try to see your transcendent self, which is not possible anyway. Can your eye see itself? You need only begin by persistently dropping your false identifications with your memories, mind, body, emotions and thoughts. And this dropping entails nothing by way of super-human effort or theoretical comprehension. All that is required, primarily, is but one understanding: whatever you can see cannot be the Seer. Everything you know about yourself is precisely not your Self, the Knower, the inner I-ness that can neither be perceived, defined, or made an object of any sort. Bondage is nothing but the mis-identification of the Seer with all these things which can be seen. And liberation begins with the simple reversal of this mistake."[30]

Once this transcendental Self has been realized, the next and final step is that of unity consciousness. In the last chapter of *No Boundary* Wilber shows that he has also mastered this most paradoxical aspect of mystical literature. There is nothing that we can do to bring about this unity consciousness. We can only create special conditions, as by entering a state of meditation, which facilitate the emergence of this unity consciousness. Gradually spiritual practice evolves from a means to an end—unity consciousness—into the expression of the state itself: "Even if, in our spiritual practice, it appears we are trying to attain enlightenment, we are actually only expressing it. If we take up Zazen, for instance, then deep within we are doing so not to become Buddhas but to behave like the Buddhas we already are."[31]

"AND YET, SOMETHING WAS DEFINITELY WRONG . . ."

At this point let us just stop for a moment and look at what Wilber has achieved in his first two books.

First, Wilber offered the possibility of introducing a sense of order within the field of Western psychology and Eastern spirituality, classifying the leading schools of psychotherapy and the spiritual traditions in light of the four levels of consciousness—persona, ego, centaur, and Spirit. However, while this metaphysical context is certainly intellectually satisfying, it also raises a number of questions. In particular, the way in which Wilber describes the process of the emergence of the spectrum as a phenomenon outside of time makes it difficult to assess his model in scientific terms, given that science is only able to deal with processes that take place within time. And as we shall see in Chapter 3, in the books that he wrote after *The Spectrum of Consciousness* and *No Boundary*, books in which he studies developmental psychology and the cultural history of mankind respectively, Wilber focuses specifically on precisely this aspect of time.

Another important aspect of Wilber's spectrum model—certainly in the form in which it is presented in *The Spectrum of Consciousness* and *No Boundary*—is that the two extremes of the spectrum are represented by personal consciousness (the persona) at the one end and universal consciousness (Spirit) at the other. This calls into question the place occupied by the human body within the model. In view of the fact that the two ends of the spectrum are occupied by the persona and Spirit, the body must be somewhere in between, which does not mesh with Wilber's statement that the physical body is "the lowest of all modes of consciousness." Thus at this stage the spectrum model does not take into account the physical body per se.

Given that the physical body has apparently been left out of the equation, it is odd that Wilber should then outline a path to Spirit which completes its course via the body. It is difficult not to infer from this that in *The Spectrum of Consciousness* Wilber regards the body as being higher than the ego. In his vision the ego is the most contracted form of consciousness, while, when integrated as part of the centaur, the body is part of the organismic or centaur consciousness, which is closer to Spirit because it is closer to the cosmos. Wilber seems to suggest that if we live in the body we are part *of* the cosmos, whereas if we live in the mind, then we only look *at* the cosmos—and in doing so we stand outside of it. This creates a juxtaposition between experience and the intellect in which both spiritual experience and bodily experience end up in the same category. Or, as Wilber himself actually formulates it, organismic consciousness and cosmic consciousness are one and the same thing.

Furthermore, the movement from persona to Spirit as depicted by Wilber is in a certain sense an expansion *outwards*, and not a journey within—which is emphatically the case in many visions of spirituality. In the spectrum model, starting with the inner life of the persona, we move step by step outwards, by encompassing within our consciousness first the shadow, then the body, and then the physical cosmos. In other words, Wilber's spectrum model is an extroverted, outward-oriented model of human development and spirituality. This movement outwards is very much in line with the holistic line of thinking, nowadays so popular, which contends that the physical cosmos forms the basis of reality, and that the physical cosmos and the spiritual dimension can be conceived of as being virtually synonymous. And indeed in *The Spectrum of Consciousness* Wilber frequently refers to the work of physicists such as Einstein, Heisenberg, and Schrödinger. At this stage he is still of the opinion that the revelations of modern physics lend support to a mystical worldview.

Had Wilber left it at these two books, he would undoubtedly have been recognized as one of the leading figures of today's holistic pantheon, and he would certainly have made a valuable contribution to the integration of Eastern and Western thought. But it is a tribute to his intellectual integrity that he did not leave it at that. When he took a close look at what he had written in *The Spectrum of Consciousness* and *No Boundary*, he began to get the nagging feeling that there was something wrong with his spectrum model—something "profoundly wrong." To let him express it in his own words: "The more I thought about this developmental scheme, the more something seemed profoundly wrong. I read and reread what I had written, trying to figure out what was so insistently bothering me. In an unflattering moment, it seemed to me that I had stated the case so carefully that I couldn't crack my own argument; and yet something was definitely wrong."[32] He goes on to say: "This was a very difficult period for me. I physically ached with the effort of trying to straighten things out. Intellectually, it was as if I were racing a motor with the gears disengaged. Had I not the grounding of my manual job, and the steadiness of Zazen, I'm sure I would have busted a rivet here or there."[33]

But precisely what was it that was wrong with the spectrum model? No doubt Wilber had made a flying start with his first two books, but had it also been a false start? The following chapter addresses this important question in more depth.

3

CRISIS AND REORIENTATION

In search of a new footing

When Wilber attempted to apply his spectrum model to the course of a human life, the inherent limitations of the model started to come to light. He suddenly found himself confronted with a problem that was not easy to solve. In *The Spectrum of Consciousness* and *No Boundary* he had made only an occasional reference to the way in which the human individual develops over the course of time. In writing *The Spectrum of Consciousness*, he had adopted a line of thinking that took Spirit, which is essentially timeless, to be the point of departure, and in *No Boundary* he was concerned with the concrete adult individual seeking to enter psychotherapy or wishing to undertake a certain spiritual discipline. Yet how does the individual actually reach the state of adulthood? And how are we to situate the process of development from child to adult in relation to the spectrum model?

The most obvious approach—and one that Wilber himself initially opted for—was to project the cyclic process of evolution and involution he had already described in *The Spectrum of Consciousness* onto the course of a human life. Seen from this point of view, as an infant the individual is unconsciously in union with Spirit or the cosmos. The individual slowly emerges out of this state of union and gradually loses contact with Spirit or the cosmos as it develops through the various bands of the spectrum. First it emerges out of its union with Spirit or the cosmos by learning to regard itself as a separate physical organism. It then severs the organismic psychophysical unity of the centaur by regarding itself purely as a psyche, and finally it fragments the unity of the psyche by regarding itself purely as a persona. At this point the individual has reached the stage of the typical adult who seeks to present himself or herself to the external world in as favorable a light as possible, and who has very little contact with his or her body and none at all with the cosmos as a whole. At this point the individual has reached the furthest outpost of the spectrum of consciousness.

However, at any point the individual is free to go back—an adult can learn to become aware of his shadow by pursuing any one of a number of different kinds of therapy. This will serve to integrate the shadow within the persona, thus restoring the unity of the ego. He can then pursue the process further, becoming aware of his body by engaging in some form of body-oriented therapy. This will lead to the integration of the ego and the body and the restoration of the psychophysical unity of the centaur. He can then go on to become aware of his connection to the cosmos as a whole by following a certain meditative discipline or a spiritual path. This will eventually lead to the integration of the psychophysical organism with the entire cosmos. At this point the individual has expanded to encompass the spectrum of consciousness in the opposite direction.

Regarded from this point of view, the course of a human life can be subdivided into two main phases—the outward journey from infant to adult and the return journey from adult to enlightened individual, though very few people actually reach this final stage. During the first half of life the individual develops an ego, which forms in response to the demands of the external world. During the second half of life the individual retraces his steps, as it were, and regains the sense of identity with Spirit or the cosmos lost during the first half of life. This way of looking at things also offers a particular perspective of the dynamic behind the process of spiritual development. Within this context spiritual development is a process by means of which the individual seeks to regain a sense of oneness that was lost during the process of becoming an adult. Effectively speaking, the individual strives to reenter the paradise lost of childhood.

To adopt the terminology used by depth psychology we might say during the first half of life the individual emerges from the realm of the unconscious or the Self by developing a strong ego, yet during the second half of life the ego seeks to reapproach the unconscious Self. The vision of human development articulated by depth psychology can be visualized in two different ways—as a semicircle or as a complete circle:

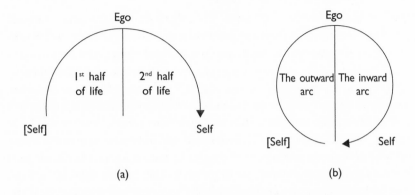

FIGURE 3.1.   The life cycle according to depth psychology (two versions)

The first of these two visions comes from Jungian depth psychology.[1] Carl Jung considered religion to be to be something that typically develops in the second half of life, as the ego seeks to come into contact with the Self, which has been relegated to the background during the first half of life. Similarly, those working in the field of transpersonal psychology use the terms *outward arc* and *inward arc* to refer to these two distinct phases of a human life.[2] The outward arc represents the first half of life, during which the individual develops an ego and comes to occupy a place within the society; the inward arc represents the second half of life, during which the individual becomes more inwardly focused as spirituality starts to play a more important role. Wilber's spectrum model is consistent with both of these visions.

"INSTANTLY THE ENTIRE SCHEME BECAME CLEAR"

Having written *The Spectrum of Consciousness* and *No Boundary*, Wilber now undertook to describe the first half of the life cycle—the outward arc—with the aid of his spectrum model. In doing so, he planned to incorporate a considerable amount of consensus data, drawn in particular from the scientific research studies produced by those working within the field of developmental psychology. In 1978 and 1979 he published the results of his first steps in this direction in *ReVision*, the journal he himself had recently helped to set up. Yet the more he studied the scientific literature covering the first years of life, the more he became convinced of the fact that the state of consciousness of the newborn infant could not possibly be conceived of as the (unconscious) epitome of spirituality that we spend the rest of our lives yearning to return to.

The work of the Swiss developmental psychologist Jean Piaget proved to be of crucial importance in this respect: "This was brought home to me in a very forceful way by one sentence of Piaget. Describing the earliest period of infancy . . . he stated: 'The self is here material so to speak.' Instantly the entire scheme became clear. That early fusion state, which everybody from Freud to Jung to Brown had taken as a state of 'oneness with the whole world in love and pleasure', is nothing but an identity with the very lowest levels of the Great Chain[3], especially the material level (and the biological level via the mother). The infant is not 'one with the whole world'. For starters, the infant is not one with the mental world, the social world, the subtle world, the symbolic world, or the linguistic world because none of those yet exist or have yet emerged. Infants are not one with those levels; they are perfectly ignorant of them. What they are basically one with, or fused with, is just the material environment and the biological mother. No levels higher than that enter this primitive fusion state."[4]

Just as some years earlier Lao Tsu had set him on the right track by pointing him in the direction of Eastern wisdom, this time Jean Piaget provided Wilber with an important key to the nature of the consciousness of the newborn infant. This one sentence led Wilber to realize that all this time he had essentially been on the wrong track. The infant is not more spiritual than the adult. On the contrary, the infant is less spiritual than the adult because the infant is still fully merged with concrete physical reality. Thus, according to Wilber, rather than seeing the transition from baby to adult as a fall out of Paradise, we need to see it as a difficult *emergence* out of a state of unconsciousness—a way forward. And if this is the case, the transition from adult to enlightened individual is not so much a *return* to a spiritual state once lost, as a *continuation* of the process of development already embarked upon. Seen from this point of view, spirituality is essentially a process of continued development.

The weak point of the spectrum model, as Wilber had formulated it thus far, was that it did not account for the prepersonal, in other words the phases preceding the stage of the adult personality. As we saw in the previous chapter, the spectrum model ranged from the personal (the persona) at the one end to the transpersonal (Spirit) at the other. This being the case, so far the spectrum of consciousness had looked like this.

personal / transpersonal

when really it should have looked like this

prepersonal / personal / transpersonal

The first spectrum model, or "Wilber 1" as Wilber himself now terms this first model, recognized only two categories—the personal and the transpersonal. The new spectrum model, "Wilber 2," recognized three categories—the prepersonal, the personal, and the transpersonal. The direction of development changed: in Wilber 1 the individual descends from the personal to the transpersonal; in Wilber 2 the individual ascends from the prepersonal, via the personal, to the transpersonal. Wilber 1 is depth psychology whereas Wilber 2 could be said to be height psychology. Wilber 1 begins with Spirit; Wilber 2 begins with the body. This time, rather than taking the adult individual with a fully developed personality as its starting point, the spectrum model starts with the newborn infant in which the ego or personality has yet to form. Wilber had moved to an entirely new footing, adopting the ground floor of the body, of physical reality, as the starting point of the developmental process. Starting with an awareness of the body, the child *first* develops an ego or personality and only *subsequently* attains a transpersonal Self.

In deliberately creating space within the spectrum model for the realm of the prepersonal, Wilber not only delineated the realm of the transpersonal more precisely, but equally importantly, he also attached far greater value to the middle ground—the personal, the mental, the intellect, and the ego. Rather than being the furthest outpost of the Self, as he had suggested in *The Spectrum of Consciousness*, the ego is now situated halfway between the two extremes of the body and the Self. As such, rather than being diametrically opposed to the spiritual, the ego is now seen to be an important stepping stone along the way. In the process of developing from a child into an adult, we are not so much suppressing the spiritual as completing an important step on the way towards the spiritual. In fact, what we are more likely to suppress as we develop into rational and autonomous individuals is not the spiritual dimension but the physical and often also the emotional dimensions. In this new model the body is shown to be not closer to the Self than the ego, as Wilber had appeared to suggest in *The Spectrum of Consciousness*, but the point furthest away from the Self, as the body and the Self now form the two extremes of the spectrum of consciousness.

Among other things this implies that having reached the personal level there are now *two different directions* that we can go in our development. We can regress towards the body (and the emotions), or we can progress towards the Self. By regressing, we come into contact with our more primitive side; by progressing, we encounter the divine qualities of our nature. By regressing, we delve into our evolutionary past; by progressing, we start to explore our evolutionary future. By regressing, we become aware of the subconscious; by progressing, we expand our consciousness to become aware of the superconscious. [5] The study of the lower dimension is known as "depth psychology"; the study of the higher dimension should ideally be termed "height psychology" and any study which encompasses both dimensions—also including the middle ground of the ego—should be known as "integral psychology." The first version of the spectrum model and the visions of development evolved by depth psychology are really too limited to communicate these nuances. If the personal is taken to be the point of departure, development can only take place in one direction—via the body to the Self. Thus the first spectrum model does not allow for the theoretical distinction between regression to more primitive levels of consciousness and progression to spiritual levels of consciousness. This crucial difference between Wilber's first formulation of the spectrum of consciousness and the revised version of the spectrum model forms the basis of all of his later work. A grasp of this one point is essential to a clear understanding of the vision of Ken Wilber.

If the formulation of the spectrum model in Wilber's first two books is practical and therapeutic, in his later work his approach is more theoretical and metaphysical. Though he also writes about metaphysical subjects in his early work and suggests practical applications for the theories presented in his later work, the way I see it, the basic question he is addressing has changed. In *The Spectrum of Consciousness* and *No Boundary* Wilber is primarily concerned with how the individual can rid himself of his psychological problems and, having done so, how he can come into contact with the spiritual. In his later work Wilber is concerned to show how the individual develops from an infant into adult and from an adult into enlightened individual—a different approach requiring a different footing.

However, Wilber does not completely abandon the thought that development is prompted by the urge to return to a lost state. The fact that we start our individual existence on the physical plane does not mean that that is where we come from. It is more likely to be the case, and here Wilber again adopts the tenets of the perennial philosophy, that we need to seek the source of our existence in the Divine. From this divine Source we descended—by means of the process of involution—until we reached the level of matter, and, having reached the level of matter, the process of evolution takes us back to the Source.[6] However, rather than being a process that takes place during the first half of life, this is a process that is understood to take place over many lifetimes and, as such, can only be understood within the context of the whole of the evolutionary process.

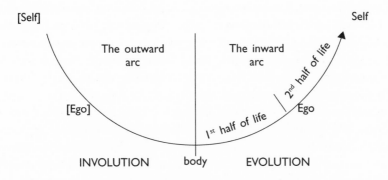

FIGURE 3.2.   The process of involution and evolution according to the perennial philosophy

Both the first half and the second half of our present life are now part of the evolutionary arc, which can also be conceived of as an inward arc, but on a far larger scale. Whereas in Wilber's early work the first half of a human life was perceived as the outward arc and the second half of a human life as the inward arc—with the turning point occurring somewhere in the *middle* of the life cycle—now both the first half of life and the second half of life are seen to be part of the inward arc or the return journey to God. And rather than occurring somewhere in the middle of the life cycle, the turning point now occurs at the *beginning* of the life cycle. In other words each step that we take along the way in terms of our development, from the moment of birth through to the most elevated stages of mystical development, can be seen as a progression towards Spirit. Right from the start, development is seen to be a Spirit-oriented process.

A FORGOTTEN TRUTH

In reformulating his spectrum model Wilber moved closer to the tenets of the perennial philosophy, which speaks of a series of planes extending from the material plane to the Divine. In doing so Wilber was influenced to some extent by a study of the perennial philosophy entitled *Forgotten Truth* written by religious scholar Huston Smith in 1976.[7] In *Forgotten Truth* Smith claims, among other things, that the core of the spiritual traditions (or "primordial" traditions, as he calls them) evolved by prescientific cultures centers on a vision of reality in which both the world and the individual are regarded as a "layered" phenomenon. In this traditional vision reality is conceived of as being made up of a large number of spheres, levels, or realms extending from the material to the Divine.

Smith goes on to show that the worldview adopted by modern science recognizes only one metaphysical dimension, which is that of visible matter. He sees this as the most essential difference between scientific and prescientific cultures. As science emerged on the scene within Western culture, religion was forced to clear the way. This has led many people to believe that religion is unscientific. Yet, as Smith rightly points out, rather than being an inevitable consequence of the fact that the scientific standpoint is true, the loss of the spiritual worldview is due to a *misreading of science*. Strictly speaking, science can only hold forth on matters that fall within its own domain. By definition, it is not qualified to say anything about those things that fall outside of its domain. In other words, the fact that science is unable to prove the existence of the human soul does not mean that the human soul does not exist. It simply means that the human soul does not fall within the realm of visible things. Science cannot prove that the human soul exists, yet it is even less capable of proving that the human soul does not exist. The fact that our inner world of thoughts and feelings cannot be perceived by the senses but only by means of introspection can hardly lead us to conclude that this world of thoughts and feelings does not exist. Yet many psychologists have been seduced into drawing just such a conclusion in the belief that they are being scientific. Perhaps there are other ways of arriving at knowledge of the soul.

Nevertheless, according to Smith there is a remarkable correspondence between the modern worldview and the traditional worldview in the sense that both think in terms of *hierarchy*. But there the correspondence ends. The Western scientific worldview recognizes a hierarchy which moves from the smallest (the subatomic world) to the largest (the cosmos as a whole), whereas the traditional worldview was based on a hierarchy which ascended from the lowest (matter, or sometimes the underworld) to the highest (the Divine). Both visions are hierarchical, but the traditional hierarchy proceeds *from lower to higher* (or from less valuable to more valuable), while the modern hierarchy proceeds *from small to large*. The traditional vision was dominated by the concept of *quality*, whereas the modern vision is dominated by the concept of *quantity*. Smith argues that the material plane of Western science is actually just one of the planes recognized by the traditional worldview, which conceives of many more planes. In making an absolute of the visible plane science effectively denies the existence of these higher dimensions, and this approach, which Smith terms "scientism," is in itself unscientific.

In *Forgotten Truth* Smith depicts the layered worldview of the spiritual traditions as a succession of at least four planes—the earth plane, an intermediate plane, the celestial plane, and the Infinite. In principle, the individual is in contact with all of these planes through the corresponding planes of consciousness of his own being. The individual is connected to the various planes as follows:

— The Infinite	— Spirit
— The celestial plane	— Soul
— The intermediate plane	— Mind
— The earth plane	— Body

FIGURE 3.3.   The world view and the view of the individual depicted by the perennial philosophy

Supported by this vision Wilber proceeded to draw up his spectrum model along these new lines. He now conceived of human development as a consecutive progression through the spheres of existence or the planes of consciousness of the individual. And this applied not only to the development of the individual, but also to the history of mankind as a whole, as Wilber attempts to show in the two books discussed in this chapter—*The Atman Project* and *Up from Eden*. In this vision we begin our development as a primarily physical-emotional being (Body). We then go on to form a predominantly mental personality (Mind). And finally at some stage we are ready to enter the transpersonal (or spiritual) levels (Soul and Spirit). To this day, Wilber's vision continues to be based on this line of reasoning.

THE SEARCH FOR THE SELF

Armed with this new frame of reference, which was more firmly rooted in the perennial philosophy than his earlier model, Wilber now embarked upon an in-depth study of the literature produced by those working within the field of Western developmental psychology. However, the material that he compiled grew to be so voluminous that it was clear that he would have difficulty finding a publisher. It was only when he went on to produce a highly abridged summary of this copious material, incorporating the material he was unable to cover at length in table form, [8] that the book was published relatively rapidly, once again by the theosophical publishers Quest Books, the publishing house that had also published *The Spectrum of Consciousness*.

In *The Atman Project—A Transpersonal View of Human Development* (1980) we find a new Wilber. He now describes human development as a linear process that can be divided up into a large number of stages. [9] In *The Atman Project* Wilber describes as many as seventeen stages of development that mark the territory between a newborn baby and an enlightened Buddha—a considerable number of stages for any developmental model. He also sought to formulate several general mechanisms that underlie the whole of the developmental process and in doing so made a valuable contribution to developmental theory. No other book offers such a broad overview of the process of human development—one that encompasses the prepersonal, the personal, and the transpersonal dimensions of consciousness—in such a concise form. The book has a firm footing in conventional developmental psychology, being based among other things on psychoanalytical (Freud), Jungian (Neumann) and cognitive (Piaget) schools of development—yet it also builds on this foundation in that it postulates a number of transpersonal stages of development drawn primarily from Eastern psychology.

In doing so, Wilber suggests that the insights of Eastern psychology are actually a logical extension of those of Western psychology: "Most of the mystic-sages have left rather detailed records of the stages and steps of their own transformations into the superconscious realms. That is, they tell us not only of the highest level of consciousness and superconsciousness, but also of all the intermediate levels leading up to it. If we take all these higher stages and add them to the lower and middle stages/levels which have been so carefully described and studies by Western psychology, we would then arrive at a fairly well balanced and comprehensive model of the spectrum of consciousness. That, exactly, is the nature and aim of this volume."[10]

DEVELOPMENTAL PSYCHOLOGY AS A STARTING POINT

The subject of spirituality can be approached from the point of view of virtually any school within the field of psychology—the study of the personality (mystics have a certain type of personality), the study of the physiology of the brain (mystical experiences are caused by the presence of certain substances in the brain), perceptual psychology (mystics see the world in a different way), clinical psychology (mystics suffer from a certain kind of schizophrenia), or developmental psychology (mystics go through certain rare stages of development). While the choice of developmental psychology as an angle of approach might seem to be an obvious one given that the literature on mysticism is full of references to "stages on the path," "rungs on the ladder," or "storeys in the fortress of the soul," thus far few authors have attempted it. Regarding the spiritual philosophers of the perennial philosophy as the first developmental psychologists, Wilber justified his choice of the developmental approach as follows:

> Look at any major system of meditation: the Buddha's detailed stages of dhyana/prajna; Patanjali's eight-step Yoga Sutras; Lao Tzu's hierarchic Taoistic contemplation; the encompassing Zen meditation system depicted in the ox-herding stages; the Victorines' multilevel course of *contemplatio*; the specific and detailed stages taught by St. Teresa and St. John of the Cross; the entire tradition of kundalini/tantra-yoga, both Hindu and Vajrajanic. What they all have in common is a view of meditation, not as a relaxation response or a sensory deprivation or a self-regulation strategy, but as a hierarchical unfolding of successively higher structures of consciousness. To be precise, they see it as a developmental process, composed of specifiable stages, such that each stage embodies a distinct structure of consciousness. . . . From the Buddha's stages of dhyana to Kundalini's chakric stages of sublimation, the whole point was that of stages of development. Truly, these traditionalists were not only the first structuralists; they were the first bona fide developmental psychologists.
>
> My point is that in our rush to bridge Eastern and Western psychology, we have looked absolutely everywhere except to developmental/structural psychology. Yet, since the essence of the Eastern traditions is a phenomenological-developmental-structural view of the superconscious realms, and since Western psychology has a rather detailed phenomenological-developmental-structural view of the sub- and self-conscious realms, the most immediate and painless bridge would be simply to add them together, just as they are. Such, anyway, was the approach I took in *Atman Project*.[11]

The Atman Project covers a very extensive theoretical terrain. Wilber starts by discussing the stages of development that a child goes through one after another as the personality matures into the personality of an adult. He then goes on to outline the spiritual stages that may follow. He also presents a differentiated vision of the unconscious and explains how the practice of meditation can help the individual to become aware of these distinct dimensions of consciousness. He then gives a panoramic overview of the three main phases of development—prepersonal, personal, and transpersonal—and comments on the supposed similarities between schizophrenia and mysticism.

In this book we will be concentrating on the developmental process as a whole and the three main phases of this process. The total developmental process that Wilber describes is presented as follows:

Wilber	Smith
17. Ultimate	
16. High-causal	Spirit
15. Low-causal	
14. High-subtle	Soul
13. Low-subtle	
12. Centaur	
11. Biosocial	
10. Mature ego	Mind
9. Late ego	
8. Middle ego	
7. Early ego	
6. Membership	
5. Image body	
4. Pranic body	Body
3. Axial body	
2. Oeroborus	
1. Pleroma	

FIGURE 3.4.   The process of individual development

To gain some idea of the nature of these stages, let's go through them starting from the bottom. Wilber's model identifies far more stages than most other scientific developmental models; nevertheless, the seventeen stages can be subdivided into three main phases—the prepersonal, the personal, and the transpersonal stages of development.

The prepersonal

The first six stages of development are dominated almost entirely by the body and the emotions. According to Wilber, during the first years of life to all intents and purposes consciousness is merged with physical-emotional reality. An infant lives in a world of food, pleasure, displeasure, comfort, discomfort, clutching things, letting go of things—a very concrete world. Obviously, we can only speculate as to the nature of the very earliest consciousness of the newborn infant, or possibly even the state of consciousness of the foetus while it is still in the womb, but, generally speaking, those who have conducted research in this field are inclined to believe that the consciousness of the foetus and the newborn infant is closed in upon itself. To describe this state Wilber adopts the term *pleroma*—a Gnostic term which refers to the chaotic, unordered, primal matter out of which everything emerges. At this stage consciousness is in a deep slumber. As yet, there is no sense of time, space, self, or environment. This state can be described as entirely prepersonal in view of the fact that the personality has yet to develop. And Wilber is now absolutely adamant that this is certainly not a state of transpersonal bliss, as some theorists claim.

However this state of unconsciousness rapidly evolves into the stage of the *uroboros*—named after a mythical serpent that bites its own tail. Consciousness is still largely closed in upon itself, but a vague perception of an outside world is now starting to penetrate the slumber. And at the same time a very vague concept of self is also starting to emerge, though this is still extremely primitive at this stage. The oceanic state of the pleroma, in which there were absolutely no limits, no longer exists; the self is starting to separate from its environment, even if the boundary that separates the two is very indistinct. An infant in this stage experiences fleeting states of pleasure or discomfort, without there being any clear connection between the successive experiences. There is also a vague sense of anxiety in that something else is felt to exist in addition to itself— an outside world that is threatening, an element that disturbs the self-enclosed slumber.[12]

In the following three stages of the prepersonal phase the child comes to associate itself increasingly with its body as the boundary between the self and the outside world becomes ever more sharply defined. The boundary of the self is felt to coincide with the boundaries of the physical body. In the stage of the 'axial body' the child experiences its body as something that clearly belongs to it. If it bites its thumb it feels pain, yet if it bites a teddy bear it feels no pain—this difference rapidly gives the child a sense of its own body. In the stage of the 'pranic body' (from *prana*, vitality) the emotions start to play a part—not subtle feelings, but raw and primitive emotions such as rage, fear, hunger and satisfaction, tension and release. At this stage the child is governed entirely by what Freud termed the pleasure principle—prompted by the whim of its needs from moment to moment, seeking physical pleasure and avoiding discomfort and pain. It experiences pleasure throughout its entire body. In the stage of the 'image body' the child begins to form images of the objects within its environment. The most important image is that of the mother figure. The mother is both the source of the greatest pleasure when she suckles the child and the source of the greatest fear if she withholds the breast. The child's concept of time has now extended beyond fleeting moments, and the child lives in a kind of extended present. The child thinks irrationally with a great emphasis on emotions and images, in what Freud called "primary processes," and is entirely dominated by its desires and emotions. Its capacity to create images, however vague, strongly contributes to the development and enrichment of its emotional body.

Thus the first five stages of development are very much centered on the body. The ego begins its long developmental journey as a 'body-bound' ego—during this phase the self is essentially a 'body-self'. At this point in the developmental process the physical self is the 'true self'. In describing these body-bound stages Wilber uses the image of the typhon, a mythical creature that is half human and half serpent. The child now identifies itself entirely with its own body and no longer with an undifferentiated environment, as was the case during the stages of the pleroma and the uroboros. And because the child now knows itself to be distinct from its environment it can learn to interact with its environment.

Then comes the stage of the so-called 'membership self'—a term that refers to the fact that the child now discovers itself to be part of a social environment in which a certain language is spoken. This is the stage during which the child begins to talk and to communicate with the important persons in its environment. At this point the culture we are born into begins to exert an influence. Through language and other ways a particular view of the world is transmitted to us.[13] The child is not yet able to think logically—it thinks in its own way. It learns to give everything around it a name and begins to attribute more importance to this world of names and forms than to the purely physical world out of which it emerged, which now falls largely into the background. The child also gains a clearer understanding of the concept of time; aided by language it can now refer to past, present, and future. This stage is also character-ized by the emergence of a certain capacity for self-control. Whereas the body-bound stages were almost entirely dominated by the spontaneous expression of physical impulses, the child can now choose whether or not to express a certain impulse or emotion. As the child emerges from the physical spheres and begins to explore the world of language, it starts to become a personality.

THE PERSONAL

Almost imperceptibly the prepersonal stages give way to the personal stages of development. The personal stages are more predominantly men-tal in nature and, once again, Wilber divides these stages into a number of substages. According to Wilber the transition from the prepersonal to the personal is essentially a transition from a method of functioning that is primarily physical to a method of functioning that is more mental. In addition to forming images of itself, the child now starts to think about itself. It begins to develop a sense of conscience based on the values introjected from its parents. This leads to the creation of a three-fold division within the ego, described in Freudian terms as the id, the ego and the superego, and in the terms of transactional analysis as the inner child, the inner adult, and the inner parent. The forming of the ego actually takes place over a good many years. For this reason Wilber divides the process into four phases—an early phase (approximately 4–7 years), a middle phase (approximately 7–12 years), a late phase (approximately 12–21 years) and the point in which the ego is considered to be fully mature (from 21 years).[14]

The child now increasingly identifies with this mental self in the same way that it had previously identified itself with its body. One of the characteristics of the mental self is that besides being able to *transcend* the physical, it is also able to *suppress* the physical, and in Wilber's opinion, this phenomenon is at the core of an important imbalance in the psyche of the modern Western individual, and by extension also within Western culture. The modern individual has lost virtually all contact with his body and functions primarily as a mental self, or, in other words, as an ego. The physical-emotional sphere and the mental sphere, which can also be termed "nature" and "culture," are two of the main spheres of existence. While Wilber makes it absolutely clear that he considers the transition from the first sphere to the second sphere to be a positive development in that it considerably enriches the individual's self-awareness, this does not alter the fact that this transition effectively distorts the individual's relationship with the first sphere, which includes not only the body, but also nature and traditional feminine values.

Towards the end of the late-ego phase (12–21 years) the ego matures, and as it does so, the Self also begins to differentiate itself from the ego. Experiencing itself to be separate from both the body and the ego, for the first time in its existence, the Self is now in a position to integrate the two. This gives rise to what Wilber calls the stage of the centaur, a mythical creature that symbolizes the union of the body and the psyche. During the centaur stage body and ego are integrated with one another to create a higher union, which is described in some detail by those working in the schools of humanistic and existential psychology. Again in this case Wilber sees the emergence of entirely new possibilities—and also new problems. During this stage the individual is concerned with ascribing meaning, self-realization, autonomy, and the realization of potential. At this point intentionality—a key concept in phenomenological thinking—starts to play an important part. Intentionality prompts an individual to ascribe meaning to his life within the context of a personal vision. Life does not necessarily *have* a meaning, but an individual can *give* it meaning by doing in life what he feels compelled to do by his whole being—heart, soul, and body. The centaur's concept of time is once again established in the here-and-now—not in any inept way, as in the case of the of the small child who has no choice but to live in the present, but in an adult way, which is essentially free. The individual now comes to understand that both his memories of the past and his dreams of the future occur in the present. He also learns the nature of true spontaneity—not the body-bound impulsiveness of the small child, but a way of life that is mature and free.

Wilber groups this existential stage with the personal stages, though the centaur is clearly on the threshold of the transpersonal. We could also put it in these terms—the integration of the personality (which also includes the body) does not automatically lead to an awareness of the transpersonal or the spiritual, but it is a important prerequisite for the development of any such awareness. For only once the individual starts to inquire about the meaning of existence, is he open to the answers offered by the various spiritual traditions. In this respect the existential is the gateway to the transpersonal.

THE TRANSPERSONAL

According to the view of the individual subscribed to in the West at this stage there is nothing more—once you have become an autonomous, rational, integrated individual, you have reached the end point of human development. But is this really the end point? Wilber certainly doesn't think so and neither do the world's many mystics. In *The Atman Project* Wilber offers the reader a far more detailed description of his understanding of the various stages of transpersonal development than he had done in his previous works. By now Wilber had completed a thorough study of the various planes of existence described by the perennial philosophy. As we have seen, Huston Smith identified four planes of existence. Traditionally, however, there are said to be seven spheres of existence. After having studied various Eastern texts in some detail, Wilber came up with the following map, which he justified as follows during a transpersonal congress held in September of 1978: "The transpersonal field is immensely complex. . . . The words 'transpersonal' and 'spiritual' seem to be used in a bewildering variety of ways. Since there are no experimental or statistical ways to define these terms, we must arrive at accepted meanings by conventional agreement. I have found a useful 'map' of trans-ordinary states in some Eastern traditions. . . ." [15]

7.	Ultimate	The Absolute
6.	High-causal	The transcendence of all forms
5.	Low-causal	The beginning of transcendence
4.	Subtle	Religious visions, ecstasy
3.	Psychic	Paranormal phenomena
2.	Astral	Out-of-the-body experiences
1.	Gross	Physical body + ego

FIGURE 3.5.   The seven levels of consciousness

According to Wilber the first sphere encompasses not only the physical body but also ego-consciousness, which is closely related to the body. The experiences that belong to the second and third spheres are studied and documented by parapsychology, while the experiences that belong to spheres four, five, six, and seven all fall within the domain of transpersonal psychology. Thus he suggests that within the transpersonal domain there are distinctly different types of spiritual experience corresponding to each of the different spheres. The fourth sphere is typically the realm of religious visions in which the subject is still separate from the object. Experiences that occur in spheres five and six transcend this distinction, bringing about the gradual dissolution of subject-object duality. The experience of the seventh sphere is one in which the individual is fully identified with Spirit, and for this reason Wilber is of the opinion that only the seventh sphere can rightly be described as spiritual.

In *The Atman Project* Wilber uses this model of the seven spheres or states of consciousness, albeit in a slightly revised form, to point to a psychology of the superconscious.[16] However, he now conceives of the second and third spheres—the astral and psychic planes respectively—as both belonging to the low-subtle plane, which gives rise to the following, somewhat simpler model:

6. Ultimate
5. High-causal
4. Low-causal
3. High-subtle
2. Low-subtle (astral/psychic)
1. Gross

FIGURE 3.6.   The six levels of consciousness

In the first stage of the transpersonal phase—the subtle—the Self begins to transcend the personal—language, thought, the ego, and the centaur. The subtle world is divided into a lower realm and a higher realm. To the *low-subtle* Wilber ascribes what are commonly called paranormal phenomena (out-of-the-body experiences, seeing auras, clairvoyance, psychokinesis, and other such experiences and capacities). In *The Atman Project* he also refers to this level as the "astral-psychic" (in other words, a combination of spheres two and three of Fig. 3.5).[17] In this low-subtle or astral-psychic stage the Self continues its developmental journey by transcending the whole of the psycho-physical organism with its rational thought and sensory perception—even if this transcendence does not yet take place in an even and controlled manner.

In the *high-subtle* stage we enter into the realm of religious intuition and inspiration, illuminatory experiences, ecstatic feelings, visions of archetypal gods and goddesses, guides and angels. According to Wilber this particular spiritual realm is characterized more than anything else by visions of archetypal or celestial beings who embody qualities that are part of our deepest being. By meditating on these beings, we evoke these same qualities within our own consciousness.

The second stage of the transpersonal phase, which brings us into contact with the causal level, has to do with experiences of an even more profound nature. Wilber also divides this world into a lower realm and a higher realm, in this case the low-causal and the high-causal level. In the *low-causal* world the individual no longer perceives archetypal divinities but falls back on himself as it were. The many gods of the subtle world are discovered to emanate from the one God, in the same way that the many qualities that have been evoked within consciousness are discovered to emanate from the one Self. The mystic is filled with bliss, wisdom, and compassion and is one with God. Wilber describes this realm in the following terms: "In the low-causal, all of these archetypal Forms simply reduce to their Source in final-God, and thus, by the very same token and in the very same step, one's own Self is here shown to be that final-God, and consciousness itself thus transforms upwards into a higher-order identity with that Radiance. Such, in brief, is the low-causal, the ultimate revelation of final-God in Perfect Radiance and Release."[18]

According to Wilber some mystics then progress to the *high-causal*— entering further into the essence of the Self, the mystic discovers formlessness: "Beyond the low-causal, into the high-causal, all manifest forms are so radically transcended that they no longer need even appear or arise in Consciousness. This is total and utter transcendence and release into Formless Consciousness, Boundless Radiance. There is here no self, no God, no final-God, no subjects, and no thingness, apart from or other than Consciousness as Such."[19]

And even now the inner journey is not yet at an end, for according to some spiritual texts these extremely exalted and rarefied states of consciousness are followed by a great reversal. In all of the stages up to this point the mystic withdraws further and further into himself, as it were, until consciousness attains to the Ground of Being, which is discovered to be the ground of everything. Now consciousness moves outward again, towards the world, for the mystic now knows that everything that exists— gross, subtle, and causal—has never been anything other than this Ground. The Heart Sutra, one of the most well-known mystical texts of Mahayana Buddhism, expresses this realization in the following terms: "Form is no other than Emptiness, Emptiness is no other than Form." This then is the highest state of Enlightenment, also known as *sahaja samadhi* (in other words, spontaneous enlightenment). Wilber writes: "This is also sahaja samadhi, the Turiya state—the ultimate Unity, wherein all things and events, while remaining perfectly separate and discrete, are only One. Therefore, this is not itself a state apart from other states; it is not an altered state; it is not a special state—it is rather the suchness of all states, the water that forms itself in each and every wave of experience, as all experience. . . . This is the radically perfect integration of all prior levels—gross, subtle and causal, which, now of themselves so, continue to arise moment to moment in an iridescent play of mutual interpenetration. This is the final differentiation of Consciousness from all forms in Consciousness, whereupon Consciousness as Such is released in Perfect Transcendence, which is not a transcendence from the world but a final transcendence as the World. Consciousness operates, not on the world, but only as the entire World Process, integrating and interpenetrating all levels, realms, and planes, high or low, sacred or profane."[20]

GENERAL PRINCIPLES OF DEVELOPMENT

In *The Atman Project* Wilber not only identified and described a large number of developmental stages, he also set out to identify the general principles governing the process of development. He called this "the form of development" and describes it in chapter 10, which goes by the same title. Wilber is certainly very good at devising new terms. This can make his books difficult to read in the beginning, but once the reader becomes familiar with Wilber's terms, the great advantage of the new terminology is immediately apparent. No specialist field can do without its own jargon, and though such jargon may initially be incomprehensible to outsiders, it serves to facilitate the discussion within the field for insiders.

The way Wilber sees it, in the most general sense the transition from one stage of development to the next always involves the two processes of differentiation and integration. The process of *differentiation* leads the Self to the awareness that its own identity is distinct from the identity attached to a certain stage of development and at this point the Self is free to proceed to the next stage. The process of *integration* adds the new stage to the previous stage to create a new whole. Thus Wilber sees development as a continual process of transcending and encompassing, transcending and encompassing. Only once the Self has realized that it is distinct from a certain stage of development can it proceed to relate to it, not before. Only once the child knows its awareness to be separate from its body can it learn to relate to and control its body. Thus differentiation is an absolute prerequisite for healthy development, and the same applies to integration.

So the process of development proceeds, borne along on the two wings of differentiation and integration. Yet this is clearly a precarious balance, for the process of differentiation and the process of integration can both go off the rails. Indeed, Wilber bases his vision of psychopathology (the study of psychic disorders) on this very fact. Differentiation without integration leads to *dissociation*. In this case the Self not only knows itself to be distinct from a certain stage, it also becomes totally dissociated from it. For example, thinking can become so detached from the body that it becomes completely separate and gets lost in lifeless abstractions. On the other hand, without differentiation *fixation* is bound to occur, in which case the process of development comes to a halt. For if the individual remains too focused on the body and fails to develop the capacity for abstract thought, the Self will remain bound to concrete reality.

In this respect it is important to note that the integration that has to take place at each stage is a *hierarchical* form of integration, in the sense that the element most recently added to the psyche always governs the psyche. As such, the new element is the defining characteristic of the stage in question and the stage in question is also named after the new element. For example, if the child proceeds from the stage of concrete thought to the stage of abstract thought, the stage now attained is named after the latest additional element—abstract thought. Or, to give another example, the way in which the human individual differs from the animal (in terms of a capacity for self-awareness, language, and abstract thought—faculties that emerged on the evolutionary scene at a relatively late stage) is the most characteristic element of the human individual (even if the human individual also has a great deal in common with the animal world). Wilber—who can also certainly be said to be an evolutionary thinker—differs from evolutionary biologists, who are often inclined to reduce human behavior to the kind of behavior that can also be perceived in animals, in that he sees the constant emergence of something essentially or completely new during the course of evolution—something that cannot be found in any of the previous stages of evolution. In terms of Wilber's view of evolution, the fact that the individual may have come *after* the animal, does not automatically imply that the individual evolved *out of* the animal. Because Wilber is convinced of the existence of involution, he sees qualities appear during the course of evolution that were inlaid during the course of involution.

Each transition from one developmental stage to the next involves what Wilber terms *transformation*. In fact, he sees the whole of the developmental process as nothing more than a series of transformations, during the course of which the Self inhabits a large number of stages or structures of consciousness one after another—first the body, then the mind, then the soul, and finally Spirit. In New Age circles the word *transformation* is often used to refer to the Great Enlightenment that is supposed to await us all, without there being any clear idea as to what we might be able to do to speed up the process. By examining spirituality from the point of view of developmental psychology, Wilber has effectively helped to relieve the concept *transformation* of such excessive expectations. For it is clear that during the process of growing up we have already undergone more than a few radical transformations (at least four according to Piaget)—even if we are no longer able to remember these transformations. According to Wilber spiritual development is simply a continuation of this developmental process—a continuation of the journey we embarked upon as we moved from the prepersonal to the personal.

Repression is another term widely used in psychology, though the term is primarily applied to the prepersonal spheres, to describe how the mental ego represses physical impulses, for example. However, Wilber believes that this repressive mechanism also functions in the same way in the personal and transpersonal spheres. Thus, just as we are able to repress the physical during the transition from the physical to the mental, we are also able to repress the mental during the transition from the mental to the spiritual. We try to force our development, as it were, and to make progress by repressing the stages we have emerged out of, overlooking the fact that these are the rungs we need to stand on as we climb the ladder of development. Thus while repression can occur each time development occurs, it is always to be avoided.

Attachment is another psychological term that Wilber interprets in a wider sense. Just as we can be attached to the physical/emotional realm of existence in a way that gives rise to all kinds of neuroses and symptoms that prevent a healthy transition to the sphere of mental existence—Freud spoke of the famous, if not notorious, 'Oedipus complex' in this respect[21]— according to Wilber, once we expand into the mental sphere of existence we can just as easily become attached to existence at the mental level. He calls this kind of attachment the "Apollo complex"[22]—a reference to the Greek god of clear thinking. Each time we become too attached to a certain level of development, the developmental process comes to a halt. Even if we manage to make the transition from the mental to the spiritual, Wilber believes that we can still fall prey to pathology at these more elevated levels of development. Thus Wilber is certainly not one to depict spirituality as a carefree undertaking. On the contrary, the way he sees it, all kinds of things can go wrong. If we become too attached to the blissful experiences of the subtle stage, according to Wilber we run the risk of developing a "Vishnu complex"[23]—a reference to the Hindu god of bliss. We have to be willing to give up this attachment too if we wish to continue our developmental journey in pursuit of Spirit.

Wilber is clearly of the opinion that typical orthodox psychological concepts (such as repression, fixation, regression, and complexes) or concepts associated with developmental psychology (such as transformation, differentiation, structures of consciousness, and stages), which up until now have been used mainly to describe the transition from the prepersonal to the personal, can also be fruitfully applied to the transition from the personal to the transpersonal—without thereby reducing the transpersonal to the prepersonal sphere or the personal sphere. Wilber has effectively abstracted, or detached, these terms from the physical or mental spheres to which they are generally applied. However, because Wilber posits a larger number of planes of existence than is normally the case, these orthodox psychological concepts suddenly have a far wider field of application.

In this respect Wilber is actually more Freudian in his thinking than Jungian, which is relatively unusual in alternative circles.[24] Freud showed what can happen if a person becomes too attached to the physical level, such that they are unable to complete the transition from the physical to the mental (the Oedipus complex). Yet according to Wilber essentially the same problems can occur in relation to the transition from the mental sphere of existence to the level of the soul (the Apollo complex), and also in relation to the transition from the level of soul to the level of the Spirit (the Vishnu complex). In other words Freud's insights can be abstracted from their application purely to the physical level and generalized to apply to other spheres of existence. It is possible for an individual to become too attached to any sphere of existence—physical, mental, or spiritual, such that their development comes to a halt. Hence Wilber's comment about Freud: "Beyond these lower levels I am no fan of Freud—within them, however, I have searched in vain for a greater genius."[25]

In reading Wilber's description of the human developmental process it is possible to detect a certain concern regarding the concept of spirituality now widely accepted within our culture. Many authors working within the field of modern spirituality deplore the fact that the modern individual has lost virtually all contact with his body and with nature. And many are inclined to attribute the current environmental crisis to the fact that the modern ego is dissociated from the body. This being the case, the intellect is all too readily identified as the villain of the piece and the prescribed remedies often seem to voice a thinly-veiled plea for a return to earlier stages of development—in other words, for regression. Wilber is strongly opposed to this stance and is at pains to point out that the essence of development lies not in *dissociation* but in *differentiation*. He says, let's not forget that the transition from the physical to the mental— and from the mental to the spiritual—is both necessary and desirable, regardless of how unpleasant the side effects may be. In other words, we must continually strive towards differentiation and at the same time avoid dissociation. If we fail to recognize the true value of differentiation, we are likely to come up with the wrong diagnosis and any remedy based on this diagnosis is unlikely to help.

In the last chapter of *The Atman Project*, which discusses the mysterious and intriguing subject of involution, Wilber outlines the metaphysical background to his vision of human development. He thinking is based primarily on the ideas presented in The Tibetan Book of the Dead. In accepting the idea of involution Wilber not only sets himself apart from academic science—which eschews all metaphysical source material opting solely for materialistic metaphysics—but also from the majority of his colleagues within the transpersonal field, who favor an explanation of the underlying mechanism of development that derives from depth psychology. Most transpersonal psychologists tend to see development as being fueled by the processes that repress the Self (during the first half of life) and the release of this repression of the Self (during the second half of life). Wilber, on the other hand, is far more inclined to see development as a natural growth process, which may involve the repression of earlier stages, but this repression is certainly not to be seen as the driving mechanism behind development. In Wilber's vision this growth process towards Spirit (or the *Atman*) is fueled by the urge to regain the awareness of the Self that was lost during the process of involution. This being the case, from start to finish development is essentially conceived of as a voyage in search of the Self—a true "Atman project."

Pause for thought

So how are we to assess this vision of individual development? Can personal development really be seen as a transition from a sense of self that is predominantly attached to the body to a sense of self that is predominantly attached to the mind? And can transpersonal development be conceived of as a continuation of this process of development? Does each individual complete all of the developmental stages Wilber describes or can some of the stages be bypassed? And where do paranormal experiences fit in to all this? Do all mystics experience paranormal experiences, or only a few? At this point I would like to comment on the vision of development that Wilber sets out in *The Atman Project* (we will also return to these questions in Chapter 7). The comments I wish to make have to do with the *existential* and *psychic* stages of development that Wilber inserts between the strictly personal and the transpersonal stages of development. At first glance these existential and psychic stages do not appear to fit within the developmental logic outlined by Wilber, and, to my mind, these stages have a different status from the personal or transpersonal stages.

The existential centaur stage fits perfectly within the logic of the Wilber 1 model described in *The Spectrum of Consciousness* and *No Boundary*. In these first two books development was depicted as a process by means of which the individual becomes conscious of more and more of his whole being—first becoming conscious of the ego, then of the ego plus the body (the centaur), then of the ego plus the body plus the cosmos. However, the Wilber 2 model, described for the first time in *The Atman Project*, is based on a very different logic. In this model development is seen to be a process of transcending and encompassing, of differentiation from and integration, first of the body, then of the ego, and finally of soul and Spirit. By definition, each new process of differentiation must be followed by a new process of integration. Only then is the transition from one stage to the next considered to have been properly completed. This is also the case as the mental self differentiates itself from the body and the body is subsequently incorporated within the new whole during the next phase of integration. Why should the integration of the mental self with the body be identified as a separate stage when, given the logic of the model, the integration of the mental self is already understood to be a necessary component of the completion of the mental stage? It would be more logical for the mental stage to be followed immediately by the transpersonal stages of development, such that differentiation and integration always go hand in hand. Thus, whereas in the Wilber 1 model it proved to be difficult to incorporate the body-self, in the Wilber 2 model the same appears to be the case for the centaur stage.

The second point is that the astral-psychic stage, which follows on from the centaur stage, does not appear to be part of the normal process of development, albeit for different reasons. According to authors who are primarily concerned with the subject, paranormal development is actually more a question of an expansion of the *senses* rather than an expansion of the *Self*. The fact that it is quite possible for spiritual development to occur without the development of paranormal capacities, such that this astral-psychic stage can apparently be bypassed, tends to suggest that the astral-psychic phase is more likely to be a side branch of human development. Within the context of a model that sets out psychological stages of development, a stage can only really be considered to count as valid if each individual is bound to complete this stage. Furthermore, terms such as *extrasensory perception* and *out-of-the-body experience* also point to the fact that it is the physical level rather than the mental level that is being transcended.

The fact that certain conscious forms of clairvoyance can sometimes occur after the mental stage of development has already been completed—and in this they differ from the prepersonal, unconscious forms of clairvoyance—does not mean that they need to be included in a general model of normal personal and transpersonal development. In this case it is as if once we start to outgrow the coat of our personality, which effectively serves to bind us to the physical world, the seams of the coat can sometimes come loose—but this is not strictly necessary. Paranormal capacities are really on a par with extremely good vision or sharp hearing. Properly speaking, they have nothing to do with spirituality or spiritual development. A person can be clairvoyant without being enlightened and enlightened without being clairvoyant.[26]

And a final comment regarding Wilber's assertion that ego consciousness is to be attributed to the physical sphere of existence. Even if it is true that during waking consciousness we are very much bound to the visible world as far as our *senses* are concerned, it is equally true that in terms of our *Self,* or our center of consciousness, during waking consciousness we are actually functioning at a mental level. Only when we turn our attention outward do we find ourselves in the physical sphere of existence, since this is the only world that can be perceived through our physical senses. Once we turn our attention inward, we immediately shift to a level that is ontologically higher—the level of emotions and thoughts. In the model suggested by Huston Smith—which recognizes the four levels of body, mind, soul, and Spirit—mental ego consciousness is placed at a level that is ontologically distinct from the body-bound consciousness of the child. Thus while the ego is attuned to the physical world, it actually belongs to a higher sphere of existence. The astral level is listed as the second of the seven spheres, but (despite the fact that Wilber does just this in Fig. 3.6) it cannot be placed above the ego, which also functions in the mental world that follows the astral world.[27]

Thus in speaking of planes of existence it is important that we specify whether we are referring to spheres of reality or states of consciousness.

Generally speaking, we can say that if we wish to base a model of development on the metaphysical model of the spheres, before we can do so we first need to be clear as to the nature of these spheres. Development can then be depicted as a gradual evolvement through these spheres—the physical stages of the prepersonal being followed by the mental stages of the personal, which are followed in turn by the spiritual or transpersonal stages of development. This developmental logic does not appear to leave room for an existential or astral-psychic stage because one is actually part of another stage, and the other can be skipped.[28]

A FALL FROM PARADISE?

While searching the literature for clues as to the nature of the state of consciousness of the newborn infant, Wilber began to touch on the field of anthropology. Is what we know about the earliest phases of the cultural history of humanity able to tell us anything about this primitive stage of development? he wondered. Has humanity as a whole evolved through more or less the same stages of consciousness that we now see in infants and children? Did our ancestors ever live in a kind of Garden of Eden, only to be driven out, as all of the great myths of tell us? This so-called recapitulation hypothesis has been in and out of favor over the years; nevertheless, Wilber was keen to reexamine the value of the theory. In biology the recapitulation hypothesis is expressed in the idea that ontogenesis is a recapitulation of phylogenesis; in other words, in our individual biological development (as an embryo) we evolve through all of the phases of the life forms of evolution. A more psychologically oriented version of the recapitulation hypothesis holds that in its individual psychic development each child evolves through the phases of thinking that in the past would have characterized humanity as a whole.

Wilber went on to elaborate this theory in a book entitled *Up from Eden: A Transpersonal View of Human Evolution* (1981), which was published the year after *The Atman Project* came out. This voluminous book contains a wealth of material on the cultures of the past, and—because in *Up from Eden* Wilber appears to support the idea of cultural evolution—it is one of his more controversial works. Referring indirectly to the recapitulation hypothesis, in the foreword to the book Wilber notes: "I have chosen to tell the story of mankind's 'painful growth' in terms of several major 'eras'. I have done this mostly as a matter of convenience, and do not hold to the 'rigid era' school of history (although I do hold to a structural/developmental view of individual consciousness)."[29] As the title of the book suggests, Wilber does not subscribe to the idea of a fall from paradise. He is more inclined to see humanity as climbing up out of its past. Indeed, on the basis of his study of the relevant literature Wilber was forced to conclude that far from being the paradise that many believe it to have been, the Eden evoked by so many myths was actually a state of gross unconsciousness—not a state of transpersonal bliss, but a state of prepersonal ignorance.

CULTURAL EVOLUTION

At around this time Wilber discovered the work of cultural philosopher Jean Gebser, through an article by Gebser published in *Main Currents in Modern Thought*.[30] Gebser's two-part main work *Ursprung und Gegenwart* (1949/1953) had not yet been translated into English; nevertheless, Wilber was struck by the extent to which stages of cultural development outlined by Gebser corresponded to the stages of individual development that he himself had described in *The Atman Project*. Indeed, the similarities are remarkable.

Wilber	Gebser
5. Centaur	Integral
4. Ego	Mental
3. Membership	Mythical
2. Typhonic	Magical
1. Pleroma / Uroboros	Archaic

FIGURE 3.7.   Cultural and individual development

As this diagram shows, Gebser does not refer to transpersonal stages of development, though his integral stage sometimes appears to have transpersonal characteristics, in the same way that his archaic stage sometimes seems to have spiritual characteristics (suggestions that Wilber would dispute in both cases). However, when it comes to the prepersonal and personal phases of the cultural historical process, Gebser's stages and Wilber's stages are completely parallel. In Gebser's (and Wilber's) opinion four simple words—archaic, magical, mythical, and mental—enable us to describe the whole of the complex history of the consciousness of humankind. As a tribute to Gebser, and also because Gebser's terms are more readily descriptive than his own terms borrowed from mythology, Wilber used Gebser's terms as a prefix to his own terms. This was how he came to arrive at what appear at first sight to be somewhat affected terms such as *magical-typhonic* or *mental-egoic.* Again let's attempt to gain a brief overall impression of this terrain.

Millions of years ago, in the earliest days of humankind, during the *archaic-uroboric* phase primeval man existed in a state of consciousness that was more animal than human, a state of consciousness that was concerned solely with the struggle to survive and the search for food—as is still true today of animals in the wild. There are very few archaeological remains from this period to give us an idea of the culture of this animal-man.

We know more about the second phase of human culture, the *magical-typhonic* phase, because the primitive people of this era left traces in the form of cave paintings, tools, and settlements. They lived in a state of consciousness that was primarily geared to the physical-emotional level, hunting animals and enlisting support for their hunting from the world of magic, which was closely related to the hunt. Their close ties with the animal world were also reflected in the phenomenon of the totem, which was based on the belief that there was a special bond between an individual and a certain totem animal. The individual suddenly became conscious of his own mortality and magic rituals were devised in an attempt to ward off death. The concept of time encompassed more than the immediate present, but not much more. The people of this era lived in an extended present. In this period religion was the domain of the shaman, who, so Wilber supposes, probably possessed authentic paranormal powers.

In the third phase of human culture, approximately one hundred thousand years ago—the *mythical membership* phase—humanity took another huge step forward. The increasing population called for a certain form of social organization. At this point agriculture began to develop. According to Wilber, the development of agriculture was of great importance in the growth of human consciousness. For agriculture meant that the individual was forced to relate to time in a different way. Now, rather than existing in an extended present, he developed an awareness of the cyclic nature of time, based on the rhythm of the seasons. Agriculture also instilled the need for patience and impulse control, to manage and care for the crops. Calendars were invented and writing was developed (initially purely with a view to noting the quantities of the harvest), language developed, and religion took on a different form. And, most importantly of all, people started to live together in groups (hence the term *membership*), within which stories (hence the term *mythic*) were passed on to the younger generations. With language the individual suddenly had access to the world of symbols, which meant that culture as a whole could flourish. From that point on the individual was less and less a biological being and more and more a cultural being. Tribal communities aggregated into larger communities of up to ten thousand people.

However, according to Wilber, this mentality also had a shadow side, and this point makes *Up from Eden* particularly interesting. For the first time in history groups of individuals began to wage war on a large scale, to foster hatred of other groups—often in a ritualistic manner. Yet at the same time the development of language also led to a growing recognition of the need for communication. The individual began to develop a basic political awareness: as a member of a community he began to concern himself with the well-being of the community as a whole. According to Wilber the development of social awareness was also of great importance for the further development of human consciousness. It was during this period that the institution of kingship was introduced. These kings, who were always considered to have a direct relationship with the ruling gods, were often ritually sacrificed to the gods, until a better replacement was found in the form of priests or ordinary citizens, at which point the kings were free to concentrate on expanding their kingdoms.

In the fourth phase, the *mental-egoic* phase, which Wilber dates around the second millennium B.C., the ego appeared on the scene: "It's incredible when you start to think about it, but sometime during the second and first millennia B.C., the exclusive egoic structure of consciousness began to emerge from the ground unconscious (Ursprung) and crystallize out in awareness. And it is just this incredible crystallization that we must now examine, that last major stage—to date—in the collective historical evolution of the spectrum of consciousness (individuals can carry it further, in their own case, by meditation into the superconsciousness). It was that transformation which set the modern world."[31]

In *Up from Eden* Wilber again emphasized the precarious nature of the development of the human ego, both within the individual and within a culture. Having fully disengaged itself from the preceding stages of development (the environment, the body, the group), the ego can now forcibly *suppress* these stages. Having heroically wrested its existence from the slumber of the unconscious, the ego begins to feel omnipotent, forgetting that it is nothing in comparison with the spiritual reality of the Self. Caught between the vast realm of unconscious nature and the vast realm of the spiritual Self, the ego imagines itself to be the only reality. Nevertheless Wilber is still keen to defend the ego. In his opinion this relative newcomer in human evolution has managed to free itself from the oppressive world of magic and myth, and in doing so has stimulated our mental development to a tremendous extent. The mythology of this period celebrates the conquering of the forces of the unconscious. According to Wilber the dragon-killing or snake-killing hero in these myths represents the ego, which has now succeeded in imposing restraints on the body and the emotions. For the first time these myths convey the theme of resistance to nature, rather than simply glorifying nature, as was the case in the magical-mythical religions. The same resistance was also directed against the cyclic nature of mythical time. The mental individual's concept of time is linear, historical, looking forward into the future and back into the past. This gave rise to feelings of guilt and fear, which the people of the previous cultural phases had not experienced to the same extent. For the first time in history there is now a genuine sense of history. The modern individual has now arrived on the scene.

THE EVOLUTION OF RELIGION

So what place does religion occupy within this cultural historical scheme? When it comes to religion, we tend to think of something that stretches back into a golden past, compared with which our own materialistic culture stands out as distinctly a-religious. Virtually all sociologists are inclined to subscribe to the theory that the modern era is characterized by radical secularization. But Wilber is not unreservedly in agreement with this qualification. There are two points he makes in this respect: (1) If we take a somewhat broader view of the historical time scale, compared with the prehistoric times of the cave dwellers, the relatively recent period of *a few thousand years* ago was clearly the most religious period. Certainly if we look at the emergence of the great world religions and the developments within these religions. Thus there is every reason to speak of religious evolution. (2) The fact that a number of huge spiritual figures— such as Jesus, Buddha, and Lao Tsu—lived in the past does not automatically imply that humanity *as a whole* has reached that same high spiritual level during the same era. These figures were way ahead of their time (and also way ahead of ours!). But the average individual was actually far less developed than is now the case.

Thus in *Up from Eden* Wilber makes an important distinction between the average level of consciousness of a certain period, and the more advanced level of consciousness attained by only a few unique individuals during the same period. In his view both of these levels of consciousness are subject to development, which means that we always have to consider two parallel lines of development: average and advanced, commonplace and rare. And in Wilber's opinion it is possible to detect an increasing deepening of religious experience during the course of history.

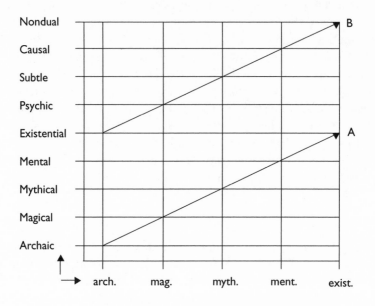

FIGURE 3.8.   The evolution of the average (A) level of consciousness and the advanced (B) level of consciousness

In archaic and magical times the shaman served as an intermediary between heaven and earth. The shaman was the spiritual hero of this cultural phase who provided the primitive magical tribal cultures with a meaningful context. As an individual the shaman had attained the level of consciousness defined in *The Atman Project* as the low-subtle or psychic level.

In mythical times humanity as a whole had outgrown magical thinking and had made the shift to mythical consciousness. Shamanic religion was no longer enough. The people of this era evolved elaborate mythologies full of gods and goddesses engaged in complex relationships with one another. During this period Wilber believes that one mythological figure stood out head and shoulders above the rest—the Great Mother. In its most mystical form—which Wilber refers to as the Great Goddess in order to distinguish it from the more earthly form of the Great Mother—this figure represents what Wilber has defined as the high-subtle or archetypal level.

The mental phase of cultural history saw the development of yet another concept of the divine, this time God the Father. The matriarchal religions with their fertility cultures were fought and suppressed in order to give mental consciousness the space to mature. In its most mystical form the concept of God the Father correlates to the religious insight of the causal level—there is only one God. However, this mystical insight could easily be co-opted by the prevailing religious movements, each of which proclaimed their own favorite God to be the Only True God.

All of the previous magical-mythical cultures had worshipped the Earth Mother, often conducting bloody rituals in an attempt to assure the fertility of the land. During the mental phase of cultural history a whole host of male gods suddenly appeared on the scene. These male gods suppressed the feminine gods, who were generally depicted as devils. Matriarchy gave way to patriarchy on a grand scale. Wilber interprets this as a collective/cultural shift from the body to the ego, from the worship of the physical/emotional sphere (Earth) to an equally intense worship of the mental sphere (Heaven).

In our era, however, God the Father is on the decline. In New Age circles many insist that the return of the Goddess is necessary to redress the balance following centuries of patriarchy. Yet Wilber warns against the attempt to resolve the religious issue by means of regression. Rather than returning to God the Mother, or clinging to God the Father, we need to *progress* to God as Emptiness—a concept of the divine that the mystics also refer to as the 'Godhead'. If the Goddess corresponds to the sphere of the body, and God the Father to the sphere of the mind, the Godhead relates to the sphere of the Spirit, which can only be known in the silence of one's own internal world. As far as Wilber is concerned, God the Mother and God the Father have both served their purpose for the modern individual. They are concepts of the divine that belong to the childhood and adolescence of humanity.

Thus Wilber also sees the evolution of a spectrum of concepts of the divine throughout the course of history:

7.	Emptiness / Godhead	Ultimate
6.	God the Father	Causal
5.	The Great Goddess	Subtle
4.	The Hero	Mental
3.	The Great Mother	Mythical
2.	The Devil	Magical
1.	Uroboros	Archaic

FIGURE 3.9.   The spectrum of concepts of the Divine

In speaking of the future of religion, working on the basis of this same model of development Wilber predicted that both within the individual and within the culture as a whole religious development would follow the spectrum of consciousness:

> This hierarchy of religious experience is not just a historically interesting movement. It has two other related meanings: one is the path of future evolution on the whole, the other is the path of present-day meditation. To take the latter first: a careful survey of reports of present-day meditation shows that advanced meditation discloses, in the same order, the very same higher structures of consciousness first discovered in historical succession by the past *transcendent* heroes of the various epochs. That is, the person today who begins and eventually completes a well-rounded meditation goes first into shamanistic intuition, then subtle oneness, then causal emptiness, then final and complete enlightenment.
>
> Second, because we are now *collectively* at the precise point in history where the exoteric curve [the outward arc] is *starting* to run into the esoteric curve [the inward arc],[32] our analysis suggests that future evolution on the whole will begin to run into the same higher structures first glimpsed, in successive fashion, by the esoteric [mystic] heroes of past ages—and it will do so in the *same order.* If our analysis is generally correct, this fact will necessarily provide a most powerful, *general,* sociological prognosticative tool. And this analysis is supported, not just by the hierarchic ordering of past transcendent heroes, but also by the hierarchic disclosures of present-day meditators.
>
> The point is this: Future evolution on the whole (i.e., the average mode of consciousness) will likely follow the same hierarchic path first glimpsed, stage by stage, by the successive transcendent heroes of the past, *just as* meditation today follows the same hierarchic path, because what all three—past transcendent heroes, present-day meditators, and future evolution on the whole—are following is simply *the higher levels of the Great Chain of Being.*[33]

In other words, in the future we will experience collectively what in the past was only experienced by a select few. The first collective phase, which is yet to be experienced—the phase of the centaur—harks back to the shamanic cultures of the past. The following phases, the subtle and the causal, will draw inspiration from the mystical teachings of the great world religions. Figures such as Christ, Buddha, and Krishna have gone on ahead of us and we will follow in their footsteps.

The spiritual heroes are always a few steps ahead of humanity as a whole, as it were. But just as humanity gradually evolves to higher planes of existence, so do its religious leaders and mystics.

Wilber outlines his vision of the kinds of religious experience and spiritual development that the individual is likely to undergo in the following passage. His ideas here tie in with the 'Trinity' referred to by Mahayana Buddhism:[34]

In *The Atman Project*, I presented evidence (based on Vajrayana, Zen, Bubba Free John, etc.) strongly suggesting that 'religious experience' actually consists of three broad but rather different classes, each with its own techniques, its own path, and its own characteristic visions and experiences.

The lowest class is that of the Nirmanakaya, commonly known as kundalini yoga, which deals with bodily-sexual energies, and their sublimation upward toward the crown-brain center, known as the sahasrara. . . . The next class—that of the Sambhogakaya— goes further, and follows the ascent of consciousness *at* and *beyond* the sahasrara into seven (some say ten) higher realms of extremely subtle consciousness. The third and highest class—the Dharmakaya—follows consciousness to its ultimate root. . . .

In the first class, the emphasis is on the body and on bodily energies. In the second class, the emphasis is on the subtle realm of light and audible illuminations and subtle sounds (nada). In the third class, the emphasis is upon transcending all of the foregoing by uprooting the separate self sense altogether.

The first class talks of trance, of bodily ecstasy, of swooning in release, and is usually accompanied by psychosomatic changes of a dramatic and overt variety (kriyas)—all of which results, at its peak, in certain psychic intuitions and powers. The second class speaks of subtle light and bliss, beyond gross sensations of the physical body, and is usually accompanied by a drastic quieting of the gross psychosomatic body and a release into the subtle realm at and beyond the sahasrara—all of which results, at its peak, in a revelation of the One God, One Light, and One Life, which underlies and gives birth to all lower and manifest realms. The third class speaks of no particular experiences whatsoever, but rather aims for the dissolution of the experiencer itself, the radical undercutting of the subject/object duality in any form—all of which results, at its peak, in the Supreme Identity of the soul and the One God-Light, so that both soul and God are united, and vanish into, the ultimate unity of the Atman.

These three classes are not three different yet equal 'experiences' of the Ultimate Source, but rather successively closer approximations of that Source (the Svabhavikakaya, or Atman-Spirit). They represent successively hierarchic structures of superconsciousness, leading finally to the Origin and Condition of all three realms and classes.[35]

New Age or Dark Age?

Numerous holistic authors would have us believe that we are on the brink of a New Age, but Wilber considers this to be highly unlikely. In the long (perhaps very long) term he sees the emergence of a wisdom culture in which the principles of a transpersonal spirituality or wisdom religion will be commonly accepted. But at this stage humanity still has to complete the task of fully realizing the mental level. If we fail to place sufficient emphasize on the value of rational thought, Wilber warns that we may be in for a Dark Age, in which archaic regression, magical thinking, and mythical religion are mistaken for mystical spirituality. Thus Wilber agrees with many of the critics of the New Age, that, motivated largely by narcissistic self-centeredness, New Age thinking is far more inclined to romanticize the prepersonal than to strive towards the transpersonal on the basis of an authentic mystical spirituality.[36]

Thus Wilber closes *Up from Eden* on a cautiously optimistic note: "While I am encouraged by the glimmerings of a New Age, I conclude with a sober appraisal: we are nowhere near the Millennium. In fact, at this point in history, the most radical, pervasive, and earth-shaking transformation would occur simply if everybody truly evolved to a mature, rational, and responsible ego, capable of freely participating in the open exchange of mutual self-esteem (and even better, to centauric self-actualization). *There* is the 'edge of history.' There would be the *real* New Age. We are nowhere near the stage 'beyond reason,' simply because we are nowhere yet near universal reason itself."[37]

"NO LONGER LOST IN THOUGHTS"

During all of this intensive work of writing Wilber continued to deepen his own spiritual practice. He describes this period in the autobiographical article "Odyssey," which was published a year before *Up from Eden* came out. As his meditation progressed he himself began to gain access to the transpersonal worlds—first the subtle world, and then the causal world. But he found that first he had to overcome what he had called the Apollo complex—the compulsive attachment to the intellect:

> The struggle with my own obsessive/compulsive thinking—not *particular* obsessive thoughts, as per specific neurosis (which is often indicative of an Oedipus-complex holdover), but the very stream of thought itself—was as arduous a task as I would ever handle. It was the most difficult battle I had ever faced; were it 1% more difficult, I would have failed miserably. As it was, I was fortunate to make some progress, to be able eventually to rise above the fluctuations of mental contractions and discover, however initially, a realm incomparably more profound, more real, more saturated with being, more open to clarity. This realm was simply that of the subtle, which is disclosed, so to speak, after the weathering of the Apollo complex. In this realm, it is not that thinking necessarily ceases (although it often does, especially at the beginning); it is that, even when thinking arises, it does not detract from this broader background of clarity and awareness. From the subtle, one no longer 'gets lost in thoughts'; rather, thoughts enter consciousness and depart much as clouds traverse the sky: with smoothness, grace and clarity.[38]

His first real experience of the subtle world had a very profound effect on him: "While in actual meditation, however, the experiences of the subtle realm can be (and usually are) quite extraordinary, awesome, profound. For this is the realm of the archetypes and of archetypal deity—confrontation with which is always numinous, as Jung pointed out. This was a very real and very intense period for me; it was my first direct and unequivocal experience of the actual sacredness of the world, this world which, as Plotinus said, emanates from the One and plays as an expression of It. Oh, I had earlier had brief and initial glimpses into the subtle realm—and even the causal beyond it—but I had not yet really been introduced to, or initiated in, that realm. A Zen master once said that the proper response to the first strong ken-sho (small satori) is not to laugh but to cry, and that is exactly what I did, for hours it seemed. Tears of gratitude, of compassion, of unworthiness, and finally, of infinite wonder. (That is not false humility; I have never met anyone who did not feel unworthy of this realm.) Laughter—great laughter—came later; at this early point, it would have been sacrilegious."[39]

As his meditations deepened, he realized that he also had to give up his attachment to spiritual experiences (the Vishnu complex). Again this was no easy task, for "These were, without doubt, the most profound experiences I had ever encountered."[40] Yet all of these marvellous experiences lost their appeal when he realized that they would never lead to the Self that had these experiences. Having realized this, Wilber began to focus on the transcendent reality of the Self. At this stage of meditation the attachment to rapturous experiences is the greatest obstacle: "The Vishnu complex is precisely the difficulty in moving from subtle soul to causal spirit. The subtle experiences are so blissful, so awesome, so profound, so salutary, that one wants never to leave them, never to let go, but rather to bathe forever in their archetypal glory and immortal release— and *there* is the Vishnu complex. If the Apollo complex is the bane of beginning meditators, the Vishnu complex is the great seducer of advanced practitioners."[41]

These mystical experiences also served to back up his intellectual studies: "This whole period of touring the subtle realms, grappling with the Vishnu complex, and penetrating the Dharmakaya—however partial, initial, and incomplete they all may have been—at least gave me a fairly solid, firsthand introduction to the various higher spheres of consciousness. With that background, I was more easily able and capable of returning to the literature of the transpersonal traditions and doing a rather exhaustive breakdown and classification of the various higher realms, realms too often merely lumped together and called 'transpersonal', 'transcendent' or 'mystic'. This was the point that I subdivided the transpersonal realm into at least four or five major levels based on structural analysis. With these subadditions to the spectrum, and those from *Eden*, I finally felt that I had a more-or-less complete cartography of consciousness, one that, while far from perfect and occasionally somewhat sloppy, had at least the merit of comprehensiveness. Refinements could come over the years."[42]

TO SUM UP...

What Wilber offers us in *The Atman Project* and *Up from Eden* is a fairly complicated theory regarding the development of consciousness, a theory that applies not only to the individual but also to cultures as a whole and a theory that is specifically geared to developments in the field of religion. Basing his argument on the body of thought conveyed by the spiritual traditions, he suggests that there are a number of levels of reality and that development consists in the progression from one level of reality to the next in a certain set sequence. He substantiates this conceptual framework with a huge quantity of scientific data drawn from the literature on developmental psychology and anthropology. Wilber does not believe that progress is simple or that it can be taken for granted; on the contrary, the individual sometimes has to pay a very high price for development. However, according to Wilber the advantages always outweigh the disadvantages. In this context he speaks of the "dialectic of progress."

The theory he presents centers on the concept of structures of consciousness. Each stage of development is characterized by its own distinct structure, which is qualitatively different from each of the other stages of development. A structure can be defined as a certain ordering of elements, though the structure itself does not depend on the nature of these elements. For instance, lead bullets can be arranged in the form of a circle, as can wooden cubes. These same elements could also be arranged as an oval.[43] In the same way the elementary functions that characterize human consciousness, such as perception, desire, emotion, imagination, thinking, and intuition, can also occur in different relationships to one another. In the case of magical thinking, feelings are the dominant factor, in mythical thinking the imagination is the dominant factor, and in rational thinking the intellect is the dominant factor, while the other functions are all present in the background.

According to Wilber's hypothesis each of these structures of consciousness generates its own distinct form of culture or religion. By the same token, all forms of cultural or religious expression can be traced back to the underlying frame of mind that led to the expression, given that the expression itself will show unmistakable signs of this particular frame of mind. And since the principle of development by means of transcendence and inclusion automatically implies that all of the earlier stages of development are still present within our modern Western consciousness, in the same way that the modern individual occasionally shows signs of magical behavior and mythical imagination in addition to rational thought and intuitive consciousness, we can also trace contemporary forms of culture and religion back to more fundamental phases of thinking. For example, in the field of religion we can make a distinction between magical religion (ritualistic religion motivated by primitive impulses), mythical religion (with its focus on nature and a cyclic concept of time), mental religion (with its focus on the individual and a historical concept of time) and mystical religion (which is geared towards interiority with an emphasis on the present).

This same model also makes it possible to draw comparisons between different disciplines, such as developmental psychology, anthropology, clinical psychology, and even animal psychology. In all of these fields there can be said to be *parallel* developments—from a predominantly magical/mythical form of functioning to a predominantly mental form of functioning. Thus, subject to certain limits, a child's thinking can be compared with the kind of thinking that characterizes a schizophrenic or prehistoric man, even if the *content* of these mental worlds is likely to be radically different in each case. In terms of the essential structure of consciousness there are interesting similarities. Clearly, this comparative developmental psychology based on the paradigm of structures of consciousness offers promising possibilities when it comes to interpreting the modern cultural and religious situation.

There is a very striking difference between Wilber's first version of the spectrum of consciousness and this new version of the spectrum model. Whereas the movement prescribed by the first model was *extrovert*, as we saw earlier, the process of development described by the new version of the spectrum model is *introvert* in nature: the individual starts out identifying with the physical body and goes on to discover deeper and deeper layers of interiority—first the personal, then the transpersonal. The process of development shows a progressive deepening (or refinement) of consciousness as the individual gains access to deeper and deeper (or higher and higher) planes of existence. Thus in the second model of the spectrum of consciousness the direction of development is diametrically opposed to the direction of development described by the first model.

Bearing in mind that Wilber wrote both *The Atman Project* and *Up from Eden* before he was thirty, the intellectual competence with which he delved into the various scientific disciplines is bound to command tremendous respect. The fact that, following the initial success of *The Spectrum of Consciousness* and *No Boundary*, he had the strength of character to radically revise his system and to introduce such fundamental changes, certainly testifies to his integrity as a thinker. Whether or not he has reached the right conclusion in all of the details—this is something that specialists in the respective fields of science will have to determine—is at this stage less important than the fact that he has presented us with an inspiring vision, which appears to reconcile the visionary and the scientific.

Wilber would spend the next few years refining his model, and in doing so he began to concern himself with current affairs more so than he had up to this point. The next chapter discusses the six books he published from 1982 to 1987. All of these books were written from the point of view of the vision outlined in this chapter. The intellectual effort that this calls for on the reader's part is more than rewarded in Chapter 5, in which we look at the course of Wilber's life during this same period.

4

FURTHER REFINEMENTS

Scientific and social issues

By this stage Wilber had weathered two crises in his career as a writer. The period that preceded the writing of *The Spectrum of Consciousness* had been as much a personal crisis—his career, his outlook on life, and his happiness were all at stake—as an intellectual crisis. The writing of his first book helped him to overcome this predicament. The crisis he went through prior to writing *The Atman Project* and *Up from Eden* was more of a theoretical crisis—and for that very reason equally devastating for a passionate thinker of Wilber's ilk. However, having come through both of these crises, by the end of the seventies Wilber had the feeling that he had finally laid a solid basis for his later work. He could now turn his attention to further elaborating and consolidating his oeuvre. In doing so he began to focus specifically and increasingly on current affairs.

At this point Wilber became a self-appointed critic of many of the ideas being voiced by the world of transpersonal or alternative psychology. He constantly referred to the perennial philosophy, which he always used as a touchstone in assessing scientific and social issues. His comments initiated a critical movement within the field of transpersonal psychology itself, which made Wilber the "outsider" of transpersonal psychology. In his opinion, many of his colleagues were far too ready to subscribe to the then fashionable holistic thinking that centered on the notion that there was a correlation between Eastern mysticism and Western physics. Wilber insistently rejected the idea that this would lead to the emergence of a 'New Paradigm'. As far as Wilber was concerned, it would take a lot more to bring about a New Paradigm, if indeed such a paradigm were ever to come about.

It was also a time when sects—or new religious movements, to use the somewhat more euphemistic scientific term—were often in the news. In search of a deeper form of spirituality or a form of spirituality more suited to their temperament, many young people joined what were mostly Eastern sects. The excesses perpetrated by these sects (the most tragic example of which was the collective suicide in 1978 of the People's Temple headed by Jim Jones) led many to ask to what extent these groups posed a danger to the mental health of society as a whole. This raised another question, namely how do we make a theoretically justified distinction between a mala fide sect headed by a dubious leader and a bona fide spiritual community concerned with authentic spirituality?

Wilber responded to these trends by publishing a number of books containing collections of articles written by himself and others—and by writing a brief monograph. This chapter discusses each of these books in turn.

TOWARDS A NEW PARADIGM?

Eye to Eye (1983), a bundle of essays that Wilber had published in various journals in previous years, examines the requirements that a possible New Paradigm would need to meet. Wilber argues that for such a paradigm to be able to provide a comprehensive framework for both science and spirituality, it would first need to address a number of philosophical questions, one of which concerns the nature and value of the different kinds of human knowledge. What precisely is the domain of science? Is science qualified to say anything about the different realms of consciousness? What about the social sciences, which aspire to the status of an exact science but really seem to occupy their own domain? And what is the value of the knowledge obtained through activities such as yoga and meditation, for example? Can these activities be considered a valid form of scientific study? Or should they be rejected out of hand as subjective and unscientific?

THE THREE EYES OF KNOWLEDGE

In an attempt to answer these fundamental epistemological questions, Wilber reintroduced a metaphor first suggested by the thirteenth-century Christian mystic St Bonaventura, who claimed that the individual had three "eyes"—the eye of flesh, the eye of reason, and the eye of spirit (which he also called the eye of contemplation). Each of these eyes accesses a particular realm of reality. This metaphor makes it possible to structure the various approaches within the field of science.

First, every individual has an eye of flesh: the capacity for sensory perception which enables the individual to explore the material world. All of the exact sciences—physics, chemistry, biology, cosmology, etc.—are rooted in this faculty. In addition, according to St Bonaventura, there is the eye of reason, the intellect, which enables the individual to perceive meaning in virtually the same direct way that the physical eye perceives objects. The humanities—psychology, philosophy, the study of literature, history, theology, etc.—and also logic and mathematics are based on this faculty. These subjects have their own unique domain, one which cannot be reduced to the visible world of physics. The third eye that St Bonaventura spoke of is the eye of contemplation. This eye is still closed in most people but it can be opened by intensive meditation practice. The opening of this third eye reveals another distinct realm of reality, which is as different from the second as the second is from the first. According to Wilber all spiritual sciences, such as yoga, are based on this capacity for transcendent perception. And, in his opinion, the insights gained as a result of deep meditation, which can only be perceived in deep meditation, transcend both the realm of the senses and the realm of the intellect.

3. The eye of contemplation   — Spiritual insight
2. The eye of reason   — Humanities / Social sciences
1. The eye of flesh   — Natural sciences

FIGURE 4.1.   The three eyes of knowledge and the different types of scientific knowledge they convey

Thus Wilber effectively created an anthropological basis for these three large groups of so-called sciences. The tension between the exact sciences and the humanities could now be traced to the always problematic relationship between the body and the mind that philosophers have called the "mind/body problem." The scientific status of the humanities is as controversial as the ontological status of the inner life of the individual (which in English is generally covered simply by the term *mind*). And while psychologists have traditionally assumed the task of studying this inner dimension, their studies are often confined to the observation of human behaviour in order to ensure that the discipline of psychology is thereby accorded scientific status. As far as Wilber is concerned, however, this is unacceptable in that it effectively reduces the mental to the physical. Wilber calls for the reality of the inner life of the individual to be recognized as a field that can be studied scientifically in its own right. Even if the inner life of the individual cannot be perceived directly by the eye of flesh, the introspective eye of reason is able to study it. Wilber also contends that the inner life of the individual encompasses many levels and that these different levels can only be accessed by means of intensive meditative training.

Wilber then goes on to emphasize that it is extremely important not to confuse these three domains of knowledge—the world perceived by the senses, the dimensions perceived by the intellect, and the realms accessed by transcendent perception. Meaning and value cannot be perceived by the eye of flesh, but the fact that they can be apprehended by the eye of the reason makes them just as real as the objects of the physical world. In the same way, spiritual truths cannot be grasped with the intellect, but only by means of a faculty that transcends the intellect—the eye of contemplation. Thus, in Wilber's opinion, neither the exact sciences (the eye of the flesh) nor philosophy (the eye of the reason) are able to prove spiritual truths—spirituality is a discrete realm of experience with its own forms of research and methods of proof.

The fact that the world of our experience consists of three separate domains can also be argued as follows. First, we are surrounded by a world of physical phenomena that we perceive with our senses. In addition to this each of us has a world of inner experience populated by thoughts and feelings, which can also be perceived, but in this case with an introspective eye. Yet this does not account for the whole of the world of our experience, for the awareness in each of us that perceives the outer world and the inner world—which is generally referred to as the "self"—is clearly distinct from the order of physical phenomena and the realm of thoughts and feelings. It is fundamentally true to say that the self belongs to a different order of reality, which transcends the world of physical phenomena and the realm of thoughts and feelings. One does not have to experience advanced mystical states of consciousness to know this to be true; it is a basic reality that can be ascertained by each individual.[1]

According to Wilber, because of its central position, the faculty of thought is able to engage with all three domains. Thought working in conjunction with the senses gives rise to science—physicists are concerned with the laws and patterns that can be detected in the world revealed by the senses. Thought focusing on its own domain gives rise to the humanities—those who study the humanities attempt to discover the laws of the world revealed by the faculty of thought. And in addressing the transcendent, thought gives rise to spiritual science—or an intellectual interpretation of the spiritual.

Although thought is, by definition, incapable of grasping spiritual reality in its entirety, it is able to form a relatively reliable impression of spiritual reality in the same way that a two-dimensional painting is able to convey the illusion of a three-dimensional reality. This validates the discipline of transpersonal psychology. The study of transpersonal psychology is not the same as actually undergoing transpersonal development—describing the path and traveling the path are two different things. But that does not mean that the processes and stages of transpersonal development cannot be described as rationally as possible, as Wilber endeavors to do in his books.

THREE TYPES OF SCIENCE

Having pursued his argument thus far, Wilber then goes on to draw the rather surprising conclusion that all three of these activities should actually be defined as scientific, in the finer sense of the word, in view of the fact that all three follow the same procedure. In his opinion, rather than being solely concerned with the reality that can be perceived by the senses, an undertaking is scientific to the extent that it tests theories in the light of experience—which is actually the real meaning of the word *empirical*—and human experience clearly encompasses far more than can be perceived with the eye of flesh. (The world of our inner experience is invisible to the senses, yet only an inveterate materialist could argue that, therefore, the world of thoughts and feelings does not exist. Having said this, many who are currently engaged in studying consciousness appear to be of this opinion.)

According to Wilber any scientific inquiry encompasses the following three elements: (1) It follows a specific *procedure*, (2) which gives rise to a certain *perception*, (3) which can then be *compared* with the perceptions yielded by other qualified researchers. Only researchers who have completed the first two steps of the scientific process are qualified to voice an opinion on the matter—in this respect, science is not democratic. In the case of the natural sciences it is easy to identify the three steps of the process. For example, the only way to determine how many moons orbit Saturn is (1) to observe Saturn through a telescope (procedure), (2) to count the number of moons (perception), and (3) to compare this result with results reported by others (comparison). If a sufficient number of qualified observers have come to the same conclusion, the number of moons that orbit Saturn is considered to have been scientifically established. (As far as science is concerned, anyone who refuses to look through the telescope, as the church authorities did at the time of Galileo, forfeits the right to voice an opinion.)

Essentially the same process applies to the humanities despite the fact that in this case the material being studied cannot be perceived in such concrete terms. For example, in order to be able to establish what a certain text—such as *Hamlet*—is about, first one must (1) study the text thoroughly (procedure), as a result of which one will be able to (2) gain a certain understanding of its meaning (perception with the eye of reason), and (3) exchange opinions with others who have also studied *Hamlet* in some depth (comparison). Again in this case, only those who have taken the time to study the text are qualified to voice an opinion. The more profound the text, the more expert the reader needs to be, but for all intents and purposes this is no different from the situation in which an astronomer searches outer space with an advanced telescope. Highly specialist knowledge is required in both cases. And while it is often the case that meaning cannot be definitively established in the intellectual domain, it is clearly possible to reject obviously false interpretations. For example, *Hamlet* is certainly not a book of recipes for exotic dishes—any such suggestion can be rejected out of hand as an erroneous interpretation.

By now we can see where Wilber is heading with this argument. As the step from exact science to the humanities has shown, both can be termed "science," even if each domain is subject to its own rules and its own degree of precision. Having come this far Wilber argues that it is possible to regard the spiritual sciences, such as yoga and meditation, as genuine sciences—again subject to their own rules and with their own degree of precision. Authentic spirituality is not a question of speculative reasoning but the deliberate practice of a meditation technique. A person who meditates (1) follows a certain *procedure,* such as sitting on a meditation cushion and meditating for hours at a stretch, as a result of which he or she is able to gain a (2) *perception* of the nature of spirit, and (3) can compare these experiences with other people who meditate and with his or her meditation teacher, who can assess the authenticity of the experiences. While it is impossible to gain the same degree of precision that prevails in the sensory domain, this does not mean that the results of the practice of meditation are completely random and that anyone can claim whatever they want in this respect. As in this case of other forms of science, individual opinion needs to be assessed in the light of the experiences of qualified researchers.

In this way Wilber justifies the existence of the humanities and the spiritual sciences by pointing out that while they may be less precise than the exact sciences, essentially they follow the same formal procedures. The natural sciences are the most exact of all sciences because the object of their research is so simple, for when compared with the human spirit, the properties of matter are indeed relatively straightforward. As far as Wilber is concerned, the fact that there is so little consensus in the humanities—the apparent contradictions within the field of psychology, which formed the basis for Wilber's first book, are an obvious example—does not mean to say that it is impossible to make general statements that everyone is willing to subscribe to. In the same way, according to Wilber, it is possible to arrive at generally accepted, valid knowledge in the field of spirituality, as he attempted to show with his own spectrum model. Experiences gained during meditation can be compared and related to what the spiritual traditions have to say about such experiences. In his own words:

> If such endeavours as Zen, Yoga, Gnostic Christianity, Vajrayana Buddhism, Vedanta, and others do in fact follow the three strands of valid data accumulation and verification (or rejection), can they legitimately be called 'sciences'?
>
> The answer, of course, depends upon what we mean by 'science'. If by 'science' one means the three strands of knowledge accumulation in any realm, then indeed the purer schools of Zen, Yoga, and so on can be called scientific. They are injunctive, instrumental, experimental, experiential, and consensual. That being so, then we could legitimately speak of 'spiritual sciences' just as we now speak of social sciences, hermeneutical sciences, psychological sciences, and physical sciences (the latter being empirical, the others being phenomenological or transcendental). Many of the meditation masters themselves refer to the science of Yoga, the science of Being, or the science of meditation.[2]

THE PRE/TRANS FALLACY

These three domains of knowledge actually correspond to the three domains of development. As we saw in the previous chapter, development begins in the physical-sensory domain, then expands to include the mental domain, and—by means of meditation—possibly also the spiritual domain. In the process of clearly delineating these three domains of development, Wilber hit upon an insight that can be considered to be one of his most important insights, namely the *pre/trans fallacy*. Wilber defines this theoretical fallacy as follows:

There is an obstacle to the emergence of a comprehensive world view, and by all accounts this obstacle is the most fascinating of all. In its various forms, this obstacle, this fallacy, has infected psychologists from Freud to Jung, philosophers from Bergson to Nietzsche, sociologists from Lévy-Brühl to Auguste Comte; it lurks as equally behind the mythological and romantic world views as behind the rational and scientific; it exists to this day in both the attempts to champion mysticism and the attempts to deny it. Until this obstacle is overcome, until this major fallacy is exposed, a truly comprehensive world view will, I believe, most definitely continue to evade us. This obstacle we call the "pre/trans fallacy."

The essence of the pre/trans fallacy is easy enough to state. We begin by simply *assuming* that human beings do in fact have access to three general realms of being and knowing—the sensory, the mental, the spiritual. Those three realms can be stated in any number of different ways: subconscious, self-conscious, and superconscious, or prerational, rational, and transrational, or prepersonal, personal, and transpersonal. The point is simply that, for example, since *pre*rational and *trans*rational are both, in their own ways, *non*rational, then they appear quite similar or even identical to the untutored eye. Once this confusion occurs—the confusion of "pre" and "trans"—then one of two things inevitably happens: the transrational realms are *reduced* to prepersonal status, or the prerational realms are *elevated* to transrational glory. Either way, a complete and overall world view is broken in half and folded in the middle, with one half of the real world (the "pre" or the "trans") being thus profoundly mistreated and misunderstood.[3]

Wilber illustrated these two variants of the pre/trans fallacy by referring to the work of Freud and Jung, two of the major figures in the field of Western psychology, who are diametrically opposed to one another on this point. As is well known, Freud had little time for religion, considering it to be an illusion, while Jung, on the other hand, was particularly interested in religion. According to Wilber both were laboring under the pre/trans fallacy, albeit in two different directions:

> Freud correctly recognized the prepersonal id and the personal ego, but he reduced all spiritual and transpersonal experiences to the prepersonal level; transtemporal insights are explained as pretemporal id-impulses; transsubject/object samadhi is claimed to be a throwback to presubject/object narcissism; transpersonal union is interpreted as prepersonal fusion. . . . [This view] of course, is not confined to Freud. It is the standard, orthodox, unquestioned Western orthodoxy—Piaget to Sullivan to Adler to Arieti.
>
> In my opinion, Jung errs consistently to the opposite side. He correctly and very explicitly recognizes the transpersonal or numinous dimension, but he often fuses or confuses it with prepersonal structures. For Jung there are only two major realms: the personal and the collective—and as Assagioli himself pointed out, Jung tends to obscure the vast and profound differences between the *lower* collective unconscious and the *higher* collective unconscious; that is, the prepersonal collective and the transpersonal collective realms. Thus, not only does Jung occasionally end up glorifying certain infantile mythic forms of thought, he also frequently gives a regressive treatment of Spirit.[4]

Because these elevationist theories fail to allocate the prepersonal domain its own place within the scheme of things—an error that Wilber himself was also guilty of in his early work—the prepersonal tends to end up in the transpersonal domain. And in Wilber's opinion many transpersonal psychologists still subscribe to the romantic Jungian view, in which the development of the individual proceeds not from the prepersonal via the personal to the transpersonal but from the (unconscious) transpersonal via the personal *back* to the (conscious) transpersonal—a model that fails to recognize the prepersonal for what it is. Thus Wilber is engaged in a polemic not only with Jung, who still holds considerable sway within the world of transpersonal psychology, but also with many of his present colleagues in the transpersonal world. He now deliberately distances himself from the view he presented in his first two books: "In my opinion, besides Jung and his followers, this [elevationist view] and its world view is found, although in different outer forms and to different degrees, in a large (but certainly not total) number of transpersonal psychologists . . . [and also] in my own early works, *Spectrum of Consciousness* and (to a lesser degree) *No Boundary*."[5]

As a result of this confusion of pre and trans, the ego (the rational) is always excessively undervalued and/or the pre-ego (the emotional/physical) is idealized. Because Wilber himself had made this same error in reasoning in his early writing, he is quick to spot spiritual models that fail to sufficiently acknowledge the value of the ego (or the modern world as a whole), or in which the spiritual is sought exclusively in nature, the body, the cosmos, or the subconscious. From this point on, he labels these models as "regressive" or "romantic" in view of the fact that they place the spiritual dimension in the past and show an aversion to modern culture. Clearly, if there is such a thing as a transpersonal dimension, it needs to be set in contrast not only to the personal dimension, but also and even more so to the prepersonal dimension in order to prevent hopeless confusion.

In order to further refine our understanding of this fundamental point, I would also like to add the following. There is always a risk of the pre/trans fallacy whenever a line of reasoning opposes just *two* categories: rational/emotional, theory/experience, man/woman, heaven/earth, West/East, science/religion, spirit/body, conscious/unconscious, etc. These pairs of opposites often tend to lead to facile generalizations: Western culture is predominantly masculine, scientific, and rational in terms of its outlook, whereas Eastern culture is more feminine, religious, and bodily in terms of its orientation. Thus the introduction of spirituality in the Western culture is reduced to reintegrating those things that have been suppressed, such as experience, imagination, feelings, and the body. In reality of course there are *three* categories that need to be taken into account: subconscious, conscious, and superconscious; magic, mental, and mystical; body, soul, and spirit; or body, ego, and Self. Thus in our individual and cultural development we move not from 'good' (body) to 'bad' (ego), but from 'good' (body) to 'better' (ego) to 'best' (Self). In the one model the ego is seen as being the enemy of the spiritual, while in the second model the ego is seen as a stepping stone to the spiritual. In his first two books Wilber subscribed to the first model (Wilber 1), but in his later books he defends the second model (Wilber 2).

Thus transpersonal psychology actually has two enemies: mainstream Western culture, which rejects the existence of the transpersonal dimension out of hand, insisting that the personal dimension is absolute, and the counterculture, which rejects the personal dimension and idealizes the prepersonal dimension (mistakenly regarding it as transpersonal). So Wilber is effectively fighting on two fronts at once as he endeavors, on the one

hand, to convince the intellectual community that transpersonal spirituality is not a relapse into dogmatic religion or infantile religiosity and, on
the other, to convince the New Age community that mystical spirituality
involves more than magical thinking, consulting oracles, or swimming
with dolphins. The fact that both groups are guilty of the pre/trans fallacy,
while each loudly denounces the other, simply makes the situation even
more complicated.

A FURTHER REFINEMENT OF THE DEVELOPMENTAL MODEL

In the meantime Wilber continued to further refine his model of human
development. In *The Atman Project* he still deliberately depicted the process of development as a more or less homogenous progression in which
the self as a whole moves from one stage to the next.[6] However, most
people will be familiar with the example of an intellectual genius who is
emotionally underdeveloped or an emotionally intelligent individual who
has little intellectual capacity. Thus it is clearly more accurate to speak of
different dimensions or lines of development: intellectual development,
social development, moral development, aesthetic development, etc. Psychologists seek to identify the links between these relatively independent
lines of development, and sometimes assume that one line (such as intellectual development, for example) is a prerequisite for another (such as
moral development, for example), though much of this is still unclear.

Thus, in *Eye to Eye* Wilber introduced a number of further refinements in his developmental model in an attempt to clarify these more
complicated issues. He himself has recently defined this phase in his
thinking as "Wilber 3" in order to make a clear distinction between this
new phase and the earlier phases of Wilber 1 and Wilber 2.[7] The difference
between Wilber 2 and Wilber 3 is essentially the difference between
homogenous development and differentiated development, which can be
visualized as follows:

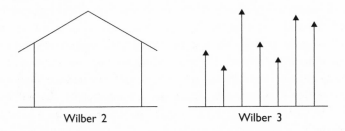

Wilber 2   Wilber 3

FIGURE 4.2.   Homogenous and differentiated development

Wilber now made a new distinction among the self or self-system, the basic structures of consciousness, and the transitional or replacement stages of development.[8] The mechanism of development can be illustrated with the aid of a metaphor that depicts development as the climbing of a ladder—(1) someone climbs (2) the rungs of the ladder and (3) gains a new view from each rung. As the climber climbs the ladder, the view is constantly changing and widening. The climber represents the self or self-system in the individual, the rungs of the ladder represent the basic structures of consciousness, and the different views represent the transitional or replacement stages. The most obvious difference between the basic structures of consciousness (2) and the transitional or replacement stages (3) is that as the process of development progresses, the basic structures of consciousness remain present, while the transitional or replacement stages disappear. To give an example: the body is a basic structure that remains present throughout the whole process of development, but the transitional stage of the typhon (in which consciousness is powerfully identified with the body) is of a transitory nature.

Wilber differs from most psychologists in that he makes out a case for the existence of a self in the individual. He considers the grounds on which the idea of the self is generally rejected to be invalid. It is often argued that because the senses and the faculty of introspection are unable to perceive a self, the self therefore does not exist. Psychologists and Buddhists often find themselves on common ground in their denial of the existence of a self in the individual.[9] Wilber counters this by saying: "The fact that the self cannot see itself doesn't necessarily mean there is no self, just as the fact that the eye does not see itself doesn't mean there is no eye."[10] The fact that the self cannot be perceived does not mean that there is no self. It simply means that the self cannot be made into an *object*. Which is precisely what we might expect given that the self is the *subject*. What is it that looks for a self, if not the self? It is true that the self cannot be perceived. Nevertheless, according to Wilber the existence of a self is indispensable if we are to account for the phenomena of consciousness.[11]

Wilber ascribes different functions to this self.[12] It integrates, coordinates, and organizes the 'stream of consciousness'—the continuously changing process of the inner life. Without such a center the individual would simply be a medley of disparate impressions. Furthermore, the self selects from the stream of consciousness that flows through us by focusing its attention on it. In doing so it also forms the basis for our sense of identity. The self enables us to identify with (or to differentiate ourselves from) something. And finally Wilber also sees the self as the navigator of development—the sense of direction that causes us to become attached or enables us to differentiate ourselves, to continue in our development, or to return to previous stages (or to remain at our current stage). It is the self in us that actually climbs the ladder of development.

As we have said, the rungs of the ladder are the basic structures of consciousness. These basic structures are not conscious in themselves, but are used by consciousness or the self.[13] Wilber identifies some ten basic structures of consciousness and also specifies the ages at which these structures generally begin to emerge:

10.	Causal	experience of Emptiness	approx. 35 years
9.	Subtle	experience of Archetypes	approx. 28 years
8.	Vision-logic	visionary thought	approx. 21 years
7.	Formal-reflexive	abstract thought	11–15 years
6.	Rule/role-thinking	concrete thought	6–8 years
5.	Rep-thinking	thinking in symbols and concepts	15 mnths.–2 years
4.	Phantasmic	thinking in simple images	6–12 mnths.
3.	Emotional-sexual	life force	1–6 mnths.
2.	Sensoriperceptual	sensation and perception	0–3 mnths.
1.	Physical	the physical organism	prenatal

FIGURE 4.3.   The basic structures and the age at which they begin to emerge during development

We recognize some of these stages from *The Atman Project* and *Up from Eden*. However, here Wilber has reduced the seventeen stages described in his earlier books to the more manageable number of ten stages. His formulations have also been brought into line with the literature on psychological development. "Phantasmic" thinking is thinking in images that resemble what it is that they represent; "rep-thinking" is short for "representative" thinking which is based on words and concepts rather than images and does not have the same kind of visual similarity. "Vision-logic" is the form of thought that emerges at the centaur stage.

The basic structures are no longer depicted as occurring in a simple sequence as in the form of a ladder, but more in the form of a tree with branches. This implies that while the various basic structures start to emerge at a certain point in development, it will be some time before they become fully mature. For instance, the basic structure of the body is present from the beginning, but an athlete can spend years perfecting his mastery of the body. Similarly, the faculty of abstract thought first emerges at the age of eleven, but it will only be fully mature at the height of a life of study and reflection.

In addition to this, generally speaking the following temporal dimensions apply. The basic structures are essentially timeless (according to Wilber these structures are part of the unconscious) though they appear in consciousness at a certain moment in the individual's development, at which point the self may or may not be able to identify with the structure in question. This gives rise to a self-stage, which is of a temporary nature in view of the fact that the stage in question will be replaced as the self continues in its development. The basic structures themselves are permanent while the self-stages based on these structures are transitory. The self moves through all of the basic structures one after another, and for each of these basic structures there is also a corresponding self-stage.

According to Wilber this model of the basic structures makes it possible to map the countless stage models within the field of developmental psychology. He demonstrates this using Maslow's model of the hierarchy of needs, Loevinger's model of the sense of self, and Kohlberg's model of moral sense.[14] His point is that "if one takes the hierarchy of basic structures and then subjects each level to the influence of a self-system, one will generate the basic features of the stages of development, presented and described by researchers such as Maslow, Loevinger and Kohlberg. It is almost a process of simple mathematical mapping."[15] A few examples may help to clarify this. If the self is identified with rule/role thinking, the person in question will be able to adopt the opinions of others, but will be unable to subject these opinions to any kind of critical analysis. This is prompted by the need to belong (Maslow) and leads to conformity (Loevinger) and conventional moral thinking (Kohlberg). However, if the self is identified with the next basic structure, formal-reflexive thinking, the person in question will have a sense of conscience and will be individualistic (Loevinger), he or she will experience a need for self-esteem (Maslow), and will be postconventional; in other words, he or she will be capable of thinking for himself or herself (Kohlberg). In this way these developmental models can be *mapped* in relation to the spectrum model of the basic structures.

As such, the model of the basic structures serves a valuable function in that it provides an integrative framework. When the various stage models are held up against the background of the model of the basic structures, we discover (1) that some models are more refined than others in the sense that they identify various substages while another model simply identifies a single stage, and (2) that some models have a greater range than others in the sense that they also include transpersonal stages while other models stick purely to the personal domain.

According to Wilber this process also describes the cultural development of humanity. Again he illustrates his point with the aid of a number of examples:

Since the basic structures are essentially *cognitive* structures, the temporary or phase-limited aspects of the basic structures simply concern the shifts in cognitive maps or worldviews that occur as successively new and higher structures emerge. I'll give several examples, which I'm sure will start to sound familiar:

The world view of the lowest levels—matter, sensation, and perception (treated together)—we have called "archaic," "pleromatic," "uroboric," and so on. This world view (so primitive as to hardly merit the name) is largely undifferentiated, global, fused, and confused—it's the way the world looks when you *only* have physical and sensoriperceptual structures. When the higher structures emerge, the archaic worldview is lost or abandoned, but the capacity for sensation and perception is not. The latter are basic and enduring structures, the former is merely the transitional or phase-temporary cognitive map associated with them.

The world view of the emotional-sexual level we called "typhonic." It is more differentiated than the archaic and more body-stable, but it is still a largely premental world view, bound and confined to the felt present, capable of seeking only immediate release and discharge. When higher structures emerge, the *exclusively* felt-world will disappear; feelings will not.

The world view of the phantasmic and beginning preop we called "magic." Magic is simply the way the world looks when you *only* have images and symbols, not concepts, not rules, not formal operations, not vision. As in the world of the dream, the phantasmic images display magical condensation and displacement, wish-fulfilment, and release. As higher structures emerge, the magical world view per se is abandoned, but images and symbols themselves remain as important basic structures.

The world view of late preop and beginning conop we called "mythic." Myth is the way the world looks when you have concepts and rules, but no formal-operations or rational capacity.

When the higher levels emerge, the mythic world view per se will die down and be replaced, but conop and rule/role will remain as important basic structures. Likewise, as development proceeds into the transrational realms, the exclusively rational world view— the way the world looks when you only have formop—is replaced with psychic and subtle world views, but the capacity to reason remains, and so on.[16]

Thus the model of development that Wilber has elaborated in this way assumes that there is a self within the individual and that the self is surrounded by various structures, ranging from the very dense (such as the body) to the very fine (such as vision-logic, for example). Development is the process by means of which the self returns to itself, starting from the lowest structure and successively differentiating itself from each of the subsequent structures. However, as the self begins to identify with higher and higher structures, it does not lose its capacity to relate to the lower structures, though it does lose the worldview that is characteristic of these structures.

So has Wilber succeeded in identifying the most fundamental line of development—the series of basic structures from which all other lines of development derive? Or does Wilber's model give too much weight to the intellectual line of development? Actually, it is important to bear in mind that the model of the basic structures is not really a model of intellectual development, but rather it indicates the extent to which the self is structured as an autonomous individual. It is certainly not necessary to master any of the basic structures in great detail before it is possible to transcend them. For instance, a person doesn't have to set a new world record for the 100 meters before the self can differentiate itself from the body. Similarly, a person doesn't have to be an intellectual genius before the self can differentiate itself from thought—indeed, it may even be easier for the self to differentiate itself from thought if one is not so caught up in mental sophistication (the way Wilber struggled with the Apollo complex was an example of this, as we saw in the previous chapter).

Wilber explains the fact that the other lines of development appear to lag behind the process of intellectual development by suggesting that the various self-stages emerge as a result of the mediation of the self, which has to act on the structures in the same way that "an enzyme acts on a substrate," which may mean that there is a certain delay in terms of time. In Wilber's opinion it is extremely important to make a clear distinction between the basic structures and the self-stages because "the two do not necessarily—not even usually—follow the same developmental timetable. They emerge in the same order, but not necessarily at the same time. To return one last time to our ladder analogy, the emergence of the basic structures can run far ahead of the self's willingness to 'climb up' them. This, of course, raises many intriguing questions, but they are questions already faced by orthodox developmental psychologists, for it has long been acknowledged that cognitive structures are necessary but not sufficient for moral or self-development. For example, an individual can be at the basic structure of the conop mind but display a moral self-sense anywhere at or below it (but never above it). For just that reason, the actual times of emergence of the basic structures (up to and including formop) are largely *age-dependent* and relatively fixed (as evidenced, for example, by Piaget's cognitive structures), but the emergence of the self-stages is relatively *age-independent* (as Loevinger and Kohlberg have explained for their stage-structures). The hypothesis that the basic structures serve as substrates for the self-stages is compatible with that data."[17]

Wilber returns to the question of the precise relationship between the various lines of development in his later work, as we will see in Chapter 6. However, at this point in his thinking Wilber is already clearly aware that human development is more complicated than the model of Wilber 2 might lead one to suspect.

PHYSICS AND MYSTICISM: AN UNHAPPY MARRIAGE?

Another subject that led Wilber to voice a great deal of criticism during this period was the so-called New Paradigm, which leans quite heavily on exact sciences such as physics, neurology, and cosmology. Having made a clear distinction between the three different domains of reality, Wilber was disturbed by the way in which other authors attempted to relate Eastern wisdom exclusively to the exact sciences. This was particularly true of the literature on the supposed correlation between physics and mysticism. Numerous authors claimed that Western physics had arrived at more or less the same conclusions about the nature of reality—"everything" is "one"—as Eastern philosophy. With the aid of their mathematical equations Western scientists had now (re)discovered what the Eastern sages had intuited. As far as Wilber was concerned, this was an inadmissible simplification of the profound and detailed worldview of the spiritual traditions.

One way of explaining the problem is as follows: East and West, mysticism and physics, or religion and science can be related to one another in two very different ways. The prevailing and most popular way of doing this, which is represented by Fritjof Capra (the author of the trendsetting book *The Tao of Physics*) and his followers, is to assume that physics and mysticism occupy the same domain, which is said to be reality. In this vision everything ultimately consists of matter or energy. From this point of view modern physics is said to have proved the unity of reality. Radically different from the atomism of earlier physics, this holistic New Science, as it is known, depicts the Old Science established by Newton and Descartes as a force that spread individualism and fragmentation. However, all is not lost since the New Science of quantum physics has rediscovered the wholeness of the world, as a result of which it is now possible to heal these cultural ailments. In this version of the history of ideas the line of development proceeds from the Unity of the spiritual traditions via the Diversity of the Old Science to the Unity of the New Science.

However, this scientific holism is regarded as suspect by the more mystical movement within the holism, which counts Wilber and Huston Smith among its followers.[18] They sketch a very different picture of the history of ideas, which is seen as proceeding from Diversity (the teaching of the spheres) via Unity (the materialism that only acknowledges one world) to Diversity (a multidimensional view of reality). In their opinion, rather than focusing on the idea of Unity, we would do better to emphasize the idea of Diversity. They argue that, according to the spiritual traditions, reality consists of several domains, spheres, or layers. The physical world is just one of these layers and, if the truth be known, it is actually the least real and the least interesting. However amazing they may be, the insights that physics has arrived at always pertain exclusively to its chosen domain—that of matter. Physics is unable to tell us anything about the mental world, to say nothing of the spiritual world. The irony is that despite its self-image as an antireductionistic science, physical holism is extremely reductionistic in that it insists that the whole of reality can be perceived with the eye of flesh.

A HOLOGRAPHIC PARADIGM?

With a view to countering the growing influence of the scientific movement within holism, Wilber compiled two collections of essays in a relatively short space of time. The first of these two collections, *The Holographic Paradigm and Other Paradoxes: Exploring the Leading Edge of Science* (1982), included a number of articles written by well-known scientists, such as Fritjof Capra, Stanley Krippner, and Karl Pribram, that had previously appeared in *ReVision*. These articles present the point of view of the New Science—a conglomerate of physics, the study of the brain, and holography. The term *holographic* mentioned in the title of the collection refers to a form of three-dimensional photography based on the mathematical theories of Nobel prize winner Dennis Gabor, which can be used as a metaphor for the working of the human brain. The brain specialist Karl Pribram had suggested some time earlier that the brain might work in accordance with holographic principles. Scientists have yet to discover how the information contained in our memory is stored in the brain. In an analogy with holography, the information may be spread throughout the brain, so that each part of the brain has access to the whole as it were (a holistic idea).[19] When Pribram discovered that the physicist David Bohm was also thinking along the same lines, the holographic paradigm was born.[20]

Remarkably, though Wilber himself had compiled the collection of articles, he was the only author in the whole book who had serious reservations regarding the mystical interpretation of the new scientific developments. In an introductory essay he states his view of the relationship between physics and mysticism and subsequently elaborates on his objections to holographic mysticism in an interview.[21] Among other things, Wilber accuses the physical-holistic authors of reducing the refined worldview of the spiritual traditions to nothing more than the world of matter. In his opinion, rather than discovering the hierarchy of the countless spheres of existence, physics has simply discovered a "holoarchy"—the wholeness of the lowest of the spheres:

> The modern-day physicist, working with the lowest realm—that of material or nonsentient and nonliving processes—has discovered the *one-dimensional* interpenetration of the material plane: he has discovered that all hadrons, leptons, etc. are mutually interpenetrating and interdependent. As Capra explains it: "Quantum theory forces us to see the universe not as a collection of physical objects, but rather as a complicated web of relations between the various parts of a unified whole . . . All [physical] particles are dynamically composed of one another in a self-consistent way, and in that sense can be said to 'contain' one another. In [this theory], the emphasis is on the interaction, or 'interpenetration', of all particles" (*The Tao of Physics*). In short, speaking of these subatomic particles and waves and fields, the physicist says, "They all penetrate one another and exist together."

Now a less than cautious person, seeing that the mystic and the physicist have used precisely the same words to talk about their realities, would thereby conclude that the realities must also be the same. And they are not.

The physicist, with his one-dimensional interpenetration, tells us that all sorts of atomic events are interwoven with one another—which is itself a significant discovery. But he tells us, and can tell us, nothing whatsoever about the interaction of nonliving matter with the biological level, and of that level's interaction with the mental field—what relationship does ionic plasma have with, say, egoic goals and drives? And beyond that, what of the interaction of the mental field with the subtle, and of the subtle with the causal, and the reverse interaction and interpenetration all the way back down through the lower levels? What can the new physics tell us of *that*?

I suggest that the new physics has simply discovered the one-dimensional interpenetration of its own level (nonsentient mass/energy). While this is an important discovery, it cannot be equated with the extraordinary phenomenon of multidimensional interpenetration described by the mystics.[22]

Once again the concept of the different domains is the key as far as Wilber is concerned. In his view, and also according to the perennial philosophy on which his view is based, the domain of physics—the visible world of matter and energy—is only a small part of the whole of reality, which is made up of a series of worlds. Thus in his eyes any representation of the worldview of the mystics which fails to consider this element of hierarchy falls seriously short of the mark.

By way of clarification Wilber says, "Physics and mysticism are not two different approaches to the same reality. They are different approaches to two quite different levels of reality, the latter of which transcends but includes the former. . . . What is new about the new physics is not that it has anything to do with higher levels of reality. . . . Rather, in pushing to the extremes of the material dimensions, it has apparently discovered the basic holoarchy of level-1, and that, indeed, is novel. There, at least, physics and mysticism agree."[23] In other words, Wilber concludes, while the new physics fits within the worldview of mysticism, it does not prove the existence of that worldview.

When asked to do so by *ReVision*, Wilber summed up his objection to holism and the holographic paradigm as follows: "The problem with the popular theories, as well as the general 'new physics and Eastern mysticism' stuff, is that they collapse the hierarchy."[24] In these circles, the rich and multidimensional worldview of the spiritual traditions, which sees a hierarchy of worlds, is flattened to the one-dimensional worldview of physics, in which there is essentially no hierarchy.

When asked what he thought the new physics had actually discovered, Wilber answered: "In my opinion, it is simply the holoarchy of level one, or the fact of material or physical energy interrelation. The biologists discovered the holoarchy of their level—level two—about thirty years ago; it's called ecology. Every living thing influences, however indirectly, every other living thing. The socio-psychologists discovered the holoarchy of the mental level—the fact that the mind is actually an intersubjective process of communicative exchange, and no such thing as a separate or radically isolated mind exists. Modern physics—well, it's what, almost a century old now?—simply discovered the analogous holoarchy on its own level, that of physical-energetic processes. I don't see any other way to read the actual data."[25]

QUANTUM QUESTIONS

Not content to leave it at that, Wilber also turned to the writings of the physicists themselves, in order to include them in the debate regarding the alleged relationship between physics and mysticism, as it were. From these writings he then compiled *Quantum Questions* (1984), a collection of long passages in which prominent physicists discuss their understanding of the scope of physics and its relationship to spirituality.

Wilber wrote a lengthy introduction to the collection, explaining his intention:

This volume is a condensed collection of virtually every major statement made on these topics by the founders and grand theorists of modern (quantum and relativity) physics: Einstein, Schroedinger, Heisenberg, Bohr,[26] Eddington, Pauli, de Broglie, Jeans, and Planck. While it would be asking too much to have all these theorists precisely agree with each other on the nature and relation of science and religion, nevertheless, I was quite surprised to find a very general commonality emerge in the worldviews of these philosopher-scientists. While there are exceptions, certain strong and common conclusions were reached by virtually every one of these theorists. . . . By way of first approximation, we can say this: these theorists are virtually unanimous in declaring that modern physics offers no positive support whatsoever for mysticism or transcendentalism of any variety. . . .

According to their general consensus, modern physics neither proves nor disproves, neither supports nor refutes, a mystical-spiritual worldview. There *are* certain similarities between the worldview of the new physics and that of mysticism, they believe, but these similarities, where they are not purely accidental, are trivial when compared with the vast and profound differences between them. To attempt to bolster a spiritual worldview with data from physics—old or new—is simply to misunderstand entirely the nature and function of each.[27]

Concluding his introduction Wilber says: "After intensively studying all their works for this anthology, I personally believe they would disagree with virtually all of the popular books on 'physics-and-mysticism', but they would wholeheartedly applaud and support those efforts to come to terms with, we might say, the fundamental quantum questions of existence. The individuals in this volume were physicists, but they were also philosophers and mystics, and they could not help but muse on how the findings of physics might fit into a larger or overall worldview. . . . Their aim was to find physics compatible with a larger or mystical worldview—not confirming and not proving, but simply not contradicting. All of them, in their own ways, achieved considerable success."[28]

In a long end note to his introduction Wilber emphasized yet again that the endeavor to prove the claims made by mystics on the basis of the findings of modern physics is not only an error, but it is also detrimental to real mysticism. He also refers to his own early work in this context:

The attempt itself is perfectly understandable—those who have had a direct glimpse of the mystical *know* how real and how profound it is. But it is so hard to convince sceptics of this fact, that it is extremely tempting and appealing to be able to claim that physics—the 'really real' science—actually supports mysticism. I, in my early writings, did exactly that. But it *is* an error, and it *is* detrimental, meaning, in the long run it causes much more harm than good, and for the following reasons: (1) It confuses temporal, relative, finite truth with eternal-absolute truth. . ., (2) It encourages the belief that in order to achieve mystical awareness all one need do is learn a new worldview . . . , (3) In the greatest irony of all, this whole approach is profoundly *reductionistic*. It says, in effect: since all things are ultimately made of subatomic particles, and since subatomic particles are mutually interrelated and holistic, then all things are holistically one, just like mysticism says. But all things are *not* ultimately made of subatomic particles; all things, including subatomic particles, are ultimately made of God. And the material realm, far from being the most fundamental, is the *least* fundamental: it has less Being than life, which has less Being than mind, which has less Being than soul, which has less Being than spirit. Physics is simply the study of the realm of least-Being. Claiming that all things are ultimately made of subatomic particles is thus the most reductionistic stance imaginable! I said this is ironic, because it is exactly the opposite of the obviously good intent of these new age writers, who are trying to help mysticism while in fact they have just sunk it.[29]

TRANSPERSONAL SOCIOLOGY

Another field that Wilber attempted to relate to the transpersonal view during this period was the sociology of religion, which is one of the main concerns of religious studies. In other words, how do social scientists see the phenomenon of religion? It is commonly believed that religion is actually a premodern phenomenon, and that the decline of religion is largely the result of the process of modernization, rationalization, individualization, and secularization heavily influenced by Western culture. Nevertheless, some see religion as fulfilling an important function in that it provides an overall system of meaning, thereby assuring the cohesion of a culture. If this framework were to collapse, people would look for alternative frameworks to provide meaning in an attempt to fill the gap. Sociologists who study the phenomenon of religion make no pronouncement regarding the truth of the various religions.

METHODOLOGICAL CONSIDERATIONS

Western sociology differs from psychology in the sense that so far it has shown little interest in the insights of the perennial philosophy. According to Wilber, this is partly due to the fact that sociology is still a very young science, which emerged in a climate dominated by materialism and reductionism. Wilber sought to rectify this situation by defining the contours of a nonreductionistic, transcendental sociology. To this end, in 1982 he published a brief monograph playfully entitled *A Sociable God: A Brief Introduction to a Transcendental Sociology*. The monograph was also his contribution to a symposium on new religious movements organized by sociologist of religion Dick Anthony and held in 1981. In no more than 135 very concentrated pages, Wilber defined the contours of a completely new specialist field—"transpersonal sociology" or a "nonreductionistic" sociology of religion.

As we saw in the previous chapter, Wilber is largely in agreement with the analysis of religious scholars, that Western culture is increasingly subject to a process of rationalization. Having passed through the archaic, magical, and mythic cultural phases, we now find ourselves, very generally speaking, in a cultural phase that is predominantly mental. But there Wilber leaves the well-trodden sociological path. For, as far as Wilber is concerned, the story doesn't end there:

> I agree with sociologists in general that the course of modern development is marked by increasing rationalization. However, my major point is that the overall trend of rationalization only covers the *first half* of our proposed developmental scheme: archaic to magic to mythic to rational. But the scheme *continues* from rational to psychic to subtle to causal to ultimate, and thus what perhaps distinguishes my viewpoint from other spiritually sympathetic theorists is that I believe the trend of rationalization per se is necessary, desirable, appropriate, phase-specific, and evolutionary. In fact, I believe it is therefore perfectly religious, *in and by itself* (no matter how apparently secular); an expression of increasingly advanced consciousness and articulated awareness that has as its final aim, and itself contributes to, the resurrection of Spirit-Geist.[30]

Secularization as an act of God? Rationality as a step towards spirituality? A highly original and contrary view! As far as Wilber is concerned, mythic forms of religion are progressively losing their credibility due to the effect of Spirit, which wants nothing more than for us to grow up and to trade in infantile forms of religion for real, postrational forms of mysticism. The fact that large groups of people within society are by no means ready for this, and are alarmed by the disappearance of religious frameworks, simply indicates that they are not yet ready to brave the transition from the mythic stage to the rational stage. A pluralistic society, in which different religious points of view are recognized to be equally legitimate, requires an individual-reflexive level of development that few are ready for as yet.

In Wilber's opinion, up until now religious scholars have focused excessively on the prerational forms of religion from the past:

My point is that religious scholars have often seen the trend toward rationalization and concluded that it is an anti-religious trend, whereas for me it is a *pro-authentic-religious* trend by virtue of being trans-mythic or post-mythic and *on its way to* yogic and higher levels of structural adaptation. If indeed rationality is the great divide between subconscient magic and myth and superconscient subtle and causal, then its major purpose in the overall scheme of evolution might be to strip Spirit of its infantile and childish associations, parental fixations, wish fulfillments, dependency yearnings, and symbiotic gratifications. When Spirit is thus de-mythologized, it can be approached *as* Spirit, in its Absolute Suchness, and not as a Cosmic Parent.

When asked to explain the religious world view that rationalization is supposedly "destroying," such scholars almost always point to magic or mythic symbologies, thereby elevating pre-rational structures to a trans-rational status. Since development *does* move from pre-rational myth to rational discourse to trans-rational epiphany, then if one confuses authentic religion with myth, naturally rationalization *appears* anti-religious. If, however, authentic religion is seen to be trans-rational, then the phase-specific moment of rational-individuation is not only a step in the right direction, it is an absolutely necessary prerequisite.[31]

If we accept the transpersonal dimension as a third category in addition to the personal (rational) and the prepersonal (magic/mythic), we come to see the modernization process in an entirely new light. In placing religion in the category of the prepersonal, one can argue that—in view of the fact that the prepersonal has made way for the personal, or the traditional worldview has been replaced by the scientific worldview—the process of rationalization, secularization, and individualization is essentially *antispiritual*. From this point of view those who are in favor of religion will always be inclined to distrust the attainments of modern reasoning. However, this way of thinking fails to take into account the transpersonal, mystical dimension. If after the personal dimension a transpersonal dimension awaits us, we can evaluate modernism in far more positive terms. Maybe primitive forms of religion *do* need to be replaced by modern reasoning, and it is this that brings transpersonal forms of spirituality within our reach. Maybe we need to make a very clear distinction between the prepersonal mind-set, which is predominantly mythic in its approach, and the transpersonal mind-set, which is mystical in its approach.

Strangely enough, those who are in favor of religion and those who are against religion both endorse the same analysis of the process of modernization. The antagonists applaud the fact that modern reasoning has put religion behind it, while the advocates regret the fact. For his part Wilber adopts a third position: when it comes to prepersonal religion, he sides with the antagonists, since in his opinion we have outgrown this form of religion—and rightfully so. Yet at the same time he stresses the fact that the autonomous, rational individual is *not* the end point of human development. There is scope for further development in the direction of the transpersonal domain.

In his early works Wilber attempted to map out this transpersonal terrain—even if only schematically. In *A Sociable God* he tells us how he went about it: "What is specifically needed . . . is some sort of more precise specification of what the higher structure-stages of consciousness might be. For various reasons, I first looked to the psychological systems of Hinduism and Buddhism for possible answers; I later found these answers echoed in Sufism, Kabalah, neo-Confucianism, mystical Christianity, and other esoteric traditions. What struck me about these traditional psychologies is that, although they often lacked the detailed sophistication of modern Western psychologies, they were perfectly aware of the general features of the level-structures so intensively investigated in the West (i.e. physical, sensorimotor, emotional-sexual, lower mental, and logical-rational). Nonetheless, they universally claimed that these levels by no means exhausted the spectrum of consciousness—there were, beyond the physical, emotional and mental levels, higher levels of structural organization and integration."[32]

In *A Sociable God* Wilber also discusses the work of the German sociologist Jürgen Habermas, whose work he greatly admires—he even goes as far as to call him "the greatest living philosopher."[33] Habermas makes a distinction between two different domains—the material economic system and the subjective world of human experience. In our society the first of these two domains has virtually entirely colonized the second domain. Similarly, the world of science is dominated by the exact sciences: in comparison with the exact sciences the social sciences are thought to be of lesser value. Habermas also points to the fact that human knowledge is always motivated by certain interests. In addition to the technical interest of science, which seeks to control the world and aims to compile predictable, repeatable knowledge, there is also the practical interest of the humanities, which seek to understand human existence and to promote mutual understanding. Habermas also identifies a third type of science, which he calls "critical science," and which is characterized by the drive to free people from oppressive social structures. Though Wilber clearly has a great deal of admiration for Habermas' work, he regrets the fact that the spiritual dimension is entirely lacking and attempts to complete Habermas' vision by adding a spiritual dimension. Wilber also divides the field of science into three different types of science: the exact sciences, the humanities, and spiritual science. In this case the third type of science is explicitly spiritual in nature. Within the field of spiritual science Wilber then makes a further distinction between two new interests that motivate the drive to acquire knowledge: an interest in knowledge *about* spirituality (the drive behind Wilber's own work), which he describes as "mandalic" and "soteriological," and an interest in *actual* spiritual development (which can be satisfied by meditation), which he describes as "gnostic" and "liberational."

What Wilber did in fact was to add a vertical dimension to the model that Habermas had elaborated. Just as there is "horizontal emancipation," which endeavors to free people from the entrapment of social structures, according to Wilber there is also "vertical emancipation," which aims to restore the individual's relationship with Spirit by means of the process of transpersonal development. This gives rise to a complete model of the acquisition of human knowledge.

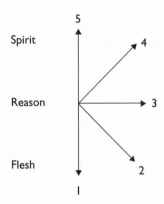

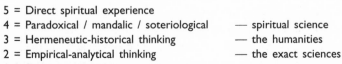

5 = Direct spiritual experience
4 = Paradoxical / mandalic / soteriological   — spiritual science
3 = Hermeneutic-historical thinking   — the humanities
2 = Empirical-analytical thinking   — the exact sciences
1 = Sensory perception

FIGURE 4.4.   The five ways in which human knowledge is acquired

The three types of science are all activities of the intellect—or the eye of reason—which may be focused on any of the three domains of reality.[34] (1) The eye of flesh has access only to the world of sensory perception. This includes the direct, nonsymbolic experience of the body. This information in itself does not lead to science. For this to be possible the eye of reason is needed. (2) Intellectual activity based on information gathered by the senses gives rise to science as the intellect tries to discover the laws of the material reality detected by sensory perception. (3) However, the intellect can also train its analytical powers on its own domain. This gives rise to the humanities, which are concerned with the world of language, meaning, interpretation, hermeneutics, phenomenology, and introspection. Sensory perception does not have access to this domain of reality. As we have seen, Wilber has made a considerable effort to justify the existence of this second type of science. (4) In addition to this, the intellect can also focus on the third domain of reality—the domain of spirituality. This gives rise to spiritual science, which is fueled by an interest in spiritual growth. In this case the intellect endeavors to define spirituality in intellectual terms, which ultimately results in the formulation of paradoxes. (5) The fifth way in which knowledge is acquired is through the individual's experience of the spiritual dimension in a direct and nonsymbolic way.

Wilber is of the opinion that the truth of his model can be demonstrated scientifically because it can be verified. "When we add these various modes and interests of human knowledge to the various levels of structural organization and relational exchange of the human compound individual . . . we have the outlines of a fairly comprehensive (though far from complete) sociological theory: a skeleton, as it were. . . . It is a truly *critical* and *normative* sociological theory, by virtue of the two emancipatory interests that rear their heads wherever structural nonfreedom and nontransparancy arise. This critical (what went wrong) and normative (what should go right) dimension, especially in its vertical form, is not based *on* ideological preference, dogmatic inclination, or theoretical conjecture, but *in* the observable, verifiable, inherently preferred direction of structural development and evolution, a direction that discloses itself in successive hierarchic emancipations that *themselves* pass judgements on their less transcendental predecessors."[35]

In *A Sociable God* Wilber depicts the current status of religion in Western culture in the following way: (1) The established religions are on the wane as a result of the increasing impact of the secularization process. Many are disoriented by this and are currently seeking refuge in *prerational,* dogmatic forms of religion, which include both orthodox Christian groups as well as sect-like Eastern movements. (2) Others, such as the intelligentsia who dominate the media and the universities, will continue to pursue the process of *rational* development and will be satisfied with a humanitarian/secular worldview. (3) A small minority will set out in search of *transrational* forms of spirituality by following a certain spiritual discipline, which can take place within the context of Christian spirituality as well as within the context of Eastern spirituality. As far as Wilber is concerned, at this stage very few people are ready for this. By combining the sociology of religion with a developmental model, Wilber is able to explain why people find the traditional religious message less and less credible. They have essentially outgrown this kind of religiosity and are now looking for forms of religion that match the stage of religious development that they as individuals have reached.

THE NEW RELIGIOUS MOVEMENTS

In the eighties the phenomenon of sects attracted a great deal of attention, not only on the part of the general public but also among sociologists of religion. Does Wilber's sociological theory offer anything by way of a solution? The problems of the new religious movements were discussed in a collection of essays entitled *Spiritual Choices: The Problem of Recognizing Authentic Paths to Inner Transformation* (1987), co-edited by Wilber, Dick Anthony and Bruce Ecker. The book was originally prompted by a seminar on the new religious movements held back in 1980 and 1981 under the auspices of the Center for the Study of New Religious Movements at the Graduate Theological Union in Berkeley, California. Among other things the seminar hoped to bridge the gap between transpersonal psychology and the more academic religious studies.

In *Spiritual Choices* a number of problematic gurus or groups were subject to detailed analysis: the Peoples Temple (the movement headed by Jim Jones which ended in a collective suicide in the Guyanan jungle in 1978), Synanon (a therapeutic community which subsequently degenerated into a totalitarian sect), Scientology (a blend of therapy and religion devised by Ron Hubbard), Psychosynthesis (a kind of spiritual psychotherapy based on the work of Roberto Assagioli: a division in San Francisco rapidly degenerated into a sect), the Unification Church (of Sun Myung Moon), and the movements that grew up around Chögyam Trungpa, Bhagwan Shree Rajneesh, the Maharishi Mahesh Yogi (Transcendental Meditation), Muktananda, Richard Baker, and Da Free John (who is now known as Adi Da Samraj).

The fact that even idealistic and well-meaning spiritual movements can degenerate into tyrannical and totalitarian organizations points to the existence of autonomous psychosocial processes that every group needs to be on its guard against. It is not so much that the teaching itself is culpable, but that people in a religious group readily fall prey to detrimental and regressive group processes. Wherever this kind of degeneration occurs, the members of the group tend to be bound increasingly tightly to the group and adopt a paranoid attitude towards the outside world.

In *Spiritual Choices* Wilber discusses the features that are characteristic of problematic religious movements.[36] Drawing on his spectrum model of human development, he was able to show what a bona fide spiritual movement might look like, as well as all of the things that could go wrong along the way. According to Wilber, the success or failure of the initiative depends on the level of development of the persons involved. This applies not only to the leaders, but also to the members of the movement. The history of many religious movements leads to the inevitable conclusion that any attempt to transcend the personal can easily degenerate into a regression into the prepersonal.

In his analysis of religious movements Wilber referred to a far simpler and more manageable version of his spectrum model:

7.	causal	— emptiness, the spiritual Self
6.	subtle	— archetypes, enlightenment, intuition
5.	psychic	— vision-logic, integration, autonomy
4.	rational	— formal-operational thinking, logic
3.	mythic	— concrete-operational thinking, language
2.	magic	— images, symbols, first concepts
1.	archaic	— body, sense-perception, emotions

FIGURE 4.5.   The spectrum of consciousness (simplified version)

Again in this case rationality is the dividing line, this time between regression (sliding back into the prerational) and progression (ascending to the transrational or spiritual). Wilber goes on to make an important distinction between the *legitimacy* and the *authenticity* of any form of religion.[37] Sociologists generally only talk about legitimacy. Legitimacy relates to the extent to which a certain movement succeeds in creating stability at a certain level of development; authenticity relates to the extent to which a certain movement stimulates development to a subsequent level. According to Wilber, authenticity and legitimacy are both important, though the two are largely independent. In other words, a movement that is not particularly authentic may achieve considerable legitimacy if it is supported by large groups within the society, while a movement that is extremely authentic may have problems in terms of legitimacy if it happens to be opposed by the surrounding culture. The reverse is also conceivable: in a spiritually evolved culture mystical religion has high legitimacy, while mythic or magic religions have low legitimacy. According to Wilber, in the West religion is undergoing a crisis not only in terms of its legitimacy but also in terms of its authenticity, an aspect that not many sociologists have elaborated on to date. Once again Wilber tried to add a vertical dimension to the sociological theory.

The concept of authenticity can be used in two different ways that can easily lead to confusion. In this respect it is similar to the concept of intelligence. Generally speaking, when we say that someone is intelligent, we mean a person of *high* intelligence, but we could also argue that everyone, no matter how limited their mental capacity, has some degree of intelligence. Thus when Wilber talks about "authentic religion," he generally means mystical spirituality, in other words, religion that has a high degree of authenticity. Yet it can also be said that *every* form of religion, no matter how primitive (even voodoo) has a certain degree of authenticity. It is not the case that mythic religions are only legitimate while mystical religions are authentic. Having said this, it is true that mystical religion is more authentic than mythic religion and that—at least in our Western culture—it is harder for mystical religions to justify their existence.

Sect-like religious movements often involve a third factor that can cause all kinds of problems, in that they are often headed by a charismatic leader or founder, in other words a person that wields *authority*. According to Wilber, a "benevolent" form of authority is purely functional in that it serves to promote the development of the disciple or student and is only maintained until the disciple has reached a certain level (as is more or less the case between a teacher and a pupil in a school situation).

In Wilber's opinion a problematic religious movement can be identified as follows:

(1) The approach is predominantly *prerational*. Regression is encouraged. The leaders play on infantile needs (the need to be looked

after, the need to belong, the need to idolize the leader, etc.). Rational thinking is discouraged.

(2) The authority figure is a *permanent* factor. Rather than deliberately seeking to become superfluous, the authority figure seeks to make himself indispensable. The students are encouraged to become dependent and are kept dependent.

(3) The authority lies not in a *tradition*, but is invested in the leader. A tradition can help to ensure that a leader does not deify himself. It also ensures that the student does not idolize the leader any more than is healthy. (That does not mean that there can never be an authentic religious movement that breaks new ground independent of any tradition, but it does mean that this inevitably involves certain risks.)

According to Wilber the tragedy of Jonestown shows how a religious movement can undergo a complete regression, descending as far as it is possible to go. What started out as an idealistic and socially concerned movement later degenerated into a mythic sense of belonging to a group, and subsequently descended further into a magic paranoia which ended in an archaic suicide effected with the aid of sleeping pills. "The dynamic of Jonestown was textbook in the way it followed almost exactly our three 'bad' criteria," he says.[38] The question is not so much which religious movements are misguided or suspect—for, to start with, almost all of them set out with the best of intentions—but how they fall into this regressive spiral and how this can be prevented.

A nonproblematic religious movement is the mirror image of a problematic religious movement. As such it can be characterized as follows:

(1) The approach is predominantly *transrational.* People aspire to spiritual stages of development and practice meditation and live in accordance with ethical guidelines to this end. Rational thinking is incorporated rather than discouraged.

(2) The movement is situated within the context of a spiritual *tradition.* This prevents a situation in which a person considers himself to be all-important and is no longer willing to stand corrected by the wisdom of ages.

(3) The authority figure is *temporary.* In this case the guru assumes a role similar to that of a doctor or a teacher. He represents the

Self of the student which is gradually evoked, at which point the guru becomes superfluous.

And Wilber added two further points:

(4) The leader is not regarded as *perfect*. He or she is also an ordinary individual who will occasionally make mistakes and must be able to admit these mistakes (which seldom happens).

(5) The movement is *not* there to save the world. That only leads to narcissistic fantasies about how important the group is. This actually conceals a dangerous form of arrogance.[39]

THE STAGE MODEL IS COMPLETE

The last collection of essays that Wilber collaborated on during the eighties was the book *Transformations of Consciousness: Conventional and Contemplative Perspectives on Development* (1986), a book that he co-edited with Jack Engler and Daniel Brown. The book contained a number of articles that had previously been published in the *Journal of Transpersonal Psychology*. Wilber's contribution consisted of three chapters in which he discussed the value of the stage model in the diagnosis and treatment of psychopathology.[40] With the exception of Wilber, all of the authors were attached to the prestigious Harvard University. Once again Wilber tried to bridge the gap between transpersonal psychology and a more orthodox branch of science, this time psychiatry.

In the years prior to 1986, Wilber had gone to a great deal of trouble to follow and study the latest developments within the field of Western clinical psychology and psychoanalysis and to relate these developments to his spectrum model. At this point these schools were increasingly placing the emphasis on the ego and the value of its functions, and less on the more primitive drives, as had been the case in traditional psychoanalysis. The authors of this new collection of essays all subscribed to the idea that virtually all forms of psychopathology can be seen as thwarted development. Indeed, it is one of the basic principles of Wilber's work that wherever there is development, there is also the possibility of pathological development, not only in the personal domain but also in the transpersonal domain.

In *Transformations of Consciousness* Wilber acknowledged the importance of Western insights regarding mental health and mental illness:

"One of the aims of this volume is to begin to flesh out this skeleton [of the spectrum model] by bringing together, for the first time, both of these major schools of development—conventional and contemplative. For if it is true that the conventional schools have much to learn from the contemplative schools (especially about possibly higher development), it is equally true—and, we believe, as urgent—that the contemplative schools surrender their isolation and apparent self-sufficiency and open themselves to the vital and important lessons of contemporary psychology and psychiatry."[41]

Wilber outlined in great detail the many different forms of psychopathology that can occur at every stage of development. He presented yet another version of his spectrum model, which now encompassed nine stages: three prepersonal stages, three personal stages, and three transpersonal stages (plus a last stage, which can no longer really be said to be a stage). It was this version of the spectrum model that Wilber went on to use in all of his subsequent books. He then linked a certain form of psychopathology to each of the nine stages. And finally he did the same thing with different kinds of therapy or meditation. In this way the whole field of psychiatry and clinical psychology was clearly mapped out, as can be seen in the following figure which presents a summary of Wilber's ideas:

Stage	pathology	therapy
10. ultimate	ultimate pathology	nondual mysticism
9. causal	causal pathology	formless mysticism
8. subtle	subtle pathology	theist mysticism
7. psychic	psychic pathology	nature mysticism
6. vision-logic	existential crisis	existential therapy
5. formal-reflexive	identity crisis	introspection
4. rule/role thinking	script-pathology	script-analysis
3. rep-thinking	neuroses	insight therapy
2. phantasmic	narcissism/borderline	structuring therapy
1. sensory	psychosis	relaxing therapy

FIGURE 4.6.   The spectrum of stages, pathologies, and methods of treatment

This model is the apotheosis of Wilber's attempts to create models during the seventies and eighties. Thus it is worth taking the time to run through the different stages one by one:

Prepersonal pathologies and the appropriate therapies:

(1) *Sensory.* Impairment during the first, predominantly physical, stage can lead to psychosis in later life; sedative medication is likely to be most effective in this case.

(2) *Phantasmic.* Impairment during the second, predominantly emotional, stage is likely to make the person emotionally unstable and highly susceptible to powerful emotions, both positive and negative. This kind of pathology is referred to as narcissistic or borderline pathology. In this case it is necessary to introduce an element of structure within the highly unstable inner life; hence structuring therapy is recommended.

(3) *Rep-thinking.* If impairment occurs in the third, more mental, stage the person will have a tendency to repress emotions and feelings, which is typical in the case of neurotic pathology. The solution is to encourage the expression of the emotions and to stop the repression; therapy that offers an insight in this respect is likely to be most effective.

Personal pathologies and the appropriate therapies:

(4) *Rule/role thinking.* Pathology at this level is expressed as a sense of insecurity regarding the roles that one is supposed to play within society. The person in question does not know how to behave in different social situations. In this case the most suitable form of therapy is script analysis, in other words, the analysis and objective criticism of the erroneous ideas that the person has about himself.

(5) *Formal-reflexive.* At this stage one experiences an identity crisis because one is unable to shape one's own life. All kinds of hypothetical possibilities present themselves, but the person finds it difficult to make a pragmatic choice. Introspection will help in this case since the person needs to learn to identify what he or she really wants in life.

(6) *Vision-logic.* At this stage personal pathology reaches a peak. The person asks "Does what I'm doing have any meaning? What difference does it make?" At this point it is important to learn

that ultimately one is thrown back upon oneself in life, and that we ourselves can give our lives meaning by devoting ourselves to something unreservedly.

Transpersonal pathologies and the appropriate therapies:

(7) *Psychic.* This is the first stage of spiritual practice, also known as the Path of the Yogis.[42] The first spiritual experiences, which are the result of meditation or which can occur spontaneously, can lead to the inflation of the ego, because the person is unable to deal with the spiritual power and believes himself to be enormously important. At this point a person can also become unbalanced because the body and the soul are not sufficiently integrated. One can also believe that it is impossible to combine spirituality and everyday life. The recommended treatment is to learn to bring the inner life and the outer life into alignment, to incorporate meditation as a part of everyday life, and to promote good physical and psychic health.

(8) *Subtle.* This is the middle stage of spiritual practice, also known as the Path of the Saints. The person experiences the Self as something above or outside himself and subsequently learns to identify with it. One can shrink away from this Light and cling to the personality, or one can become excessively absorbed in the Light and remain stuck at this level (this is the so-called Vishnu complex). Both of these imbalances need to be avoided. Remedy: continue to practice meditation until stability has been established.

(9) *Causal.* This is the advanced level of spiritual practice, also known as the Path of the Sages. Pathology or imbalance at this level expresses itself in two different ways: one continues to cling to the idea of a separate Self (failure to differentiate), or one disappears into Emptiness and does not come back (failure to integrate). Remedy: realize that one does not have to turn away from Form in order to be able to experience Emptiness. Having done so, one then sees Form as the expression of Emptiness.

Wilber's message to conventional psychiatry was that the three basic forms of pathology in Western psychiatry—namely psychosis, narcissistic or borderline pathology, and neuroses—actually relate to three very different *levels* of consciousness: the physical level, the emotional level, and the mental level. Thus, broadly speaking, psychosis is a disturbance that occurs at a physical (and emotional) level, in which the person in question experiences a distorted relationship to the world of space and time. Narcissistic or borderline problems occur at an emotional level. In this case the person in question is not sufficiently able to set emotional boundaries: he will either feel overwhelmed by the world (borderline) or he will try to control the world (narcissism). And neurosis is a disturbance that occurs at a mental (and emotional) level in which the person represses his feelings and is too mental. Whereas the narcissist needs to learn to suppress his feelings, the neurotic person needs to learn to express his feelings. Thus the recommended forms of therapy are precisely the opposite in both cases.

Using somewhat simpler language, Wilber describes the process as follows.[43] All children start by developing a sense of a *physical or bodily self* as they discover the boundaries of their own body. This serves to establish the basis of a stable sense of self. During this phase the child acquires the faculty known as "object permanence"; in other words, the child understands that objects have their own independent existence outside of himself, even if he is not looking at them or if they disappear from his field of vision. The child then goes on to develop an *emotional self* as he learns to set emotional boundaries and is therefore able to make a clear distinction between his own feelings and those of others (in precisely the same way that during the preceding stage he learned to make a distinction between his own body and the bodies of others). At this point the child has acquired what Wilber refers to as "emotional object constancy." The child learns to deal with emotions, which is extremely important in that it enables the child to enter into relationships. Hence borderline pathology is always characterized by patterns of instability in relationship. And finally the child develops a *mental self* that is able to make a clear distinction between its own thoughts and the thoughts of others. At this point the child is now independent at a mental level. The self climbs the physical, emotional, and mental rungs of the ladder of development one after another, gaining a very different view of itself and the world around it each time it steps from one rung to the next.

This view of personal development is diametrically opposed to the popular thinking regarding psychological growth and spirituality, in which pathology at a certain level is used as an excuse to return to the previous level where these disturbances do not occur. Yet there is a high price to pay for stopping the process of development.

In this way one can contrast the pathology that occurs at an emotional level, such as narcissism, with the condition of the body which poses fewer problems. In Alexander Lowen's system of Bioenergetics the individual is identified with his body and all pathology is explained by the fact that he has betrayed the body.[44] The individual's real needs are equated with the needs of the body (such as the need for food, sleep, sex, and relaxation). The physical self is considered to be the true self, whereas the emotional self is regarded as a false self more concerned with its image and its narcissistic needs than with its real needs.[45] However, this view turns the relationship between the two levels upside down and presents a totally inaccurate picture of the normal process of development. The disturbances that occur at an emotional level are not (permanently) resolved by returning to the physical level, but rather by establishing a healthy emotional self. This emotional self has its *own* needs, which are entirely legitimate and produce a deeper sense of satisfaction than the needs of the body alone.

We can clarify this as follows. It is true that the body forms the basis of a healthy personality, but the personality does not end there. The pyramid of a healthy personality can only be built on the basis of a firmly anchored sense of the body, but if the pyramid is never erected, we are not any closer to home. The tragic thing about views of this kind is that they start out as a fully justified plea for a reappraisal of the true value of the body in an endeavor to treat psychological disorders. But unfortunately, this reappraisal turns into an excessive focus on the body, as a result of which the body is glorified at the expense of the inner life of the individual.

In the same way disturbances at a mental level can be seized upon as an excuse to call for a return to a way of life based more on the emotions. In a number of very successful books, such as *Care of the Soul*, Thomas Moore has advocated an approach to life that centers largely on the imagination.[46] In this view the true self is not the physical self, but the emotional self (the self that is treated with such misgivings by the therapists who focus primarily on the body). In this case the emotional self, which relies on magical thinking, is elevated at the expense of the mental self, which is depicted as impassive and detached. This gives people carte blanche to wallow in personal feelings and encourages a wholesale return to magical times.[47] Regrettably, it is a fact that thought can suppress the emotions; thus a call for true recognition of the emotions is justified. But again in this case it is important to guard against an equally detrimental excessive appreciation of emotionality at the expense of the intellect and spirituality. It is not fair to compare the derailments of the spirit with the harmonious soul. Certainly those who seek to scale the heights have a long way to fall. But does that risk mean that we should no longer attempt to climb? Isn't the attempt in itself the glory of the individual? A balanced view of the individual will give the body, soul, and spirit their rightful place within the scheme of things, acknowledging their proper relationship to one another and viewing that hierarchy from the overall perspective of development.[48]

Above all, the aforementioned authors—and their legions of followers—fail to make a clear distinction between differentiation and dissociation. Rather than seeing symptoms they identify as undesirable as *distur-bances* (dissociation) in what is essentially a desirable development (from a physical self, to an emotional self, to a mental self), they see them as *typical* of the stage of development in question. Thus while they are right to call attention to the different kinds of dissociation that plague the modern Western individual, they underestimate the importance of the need to differentiate as part of the healthy development of the self. As a result, the remedy that they propose for the spiritual ailments of the Western individual is not only inevitably regressive, but in many cases it is worse than the complaint it proposes to heal.

In Wilber's vision the true self of the individual is not bound to the body, or to the emotions—or any other level of existence, no matter how elevated. During the first phases of its development the self identifies with and then differentiates itself from the body and the emotions on the way to a stable mental self. As part of this process physical needs give way to emotional needs, which in turn give way to mental needs and spiritual needs. Wilber's model is able to explain both narcissistic pathologies (excessive emotionality) and neurotic pathologies (the suppression of the emotions), yet at the same time it retains an overall perspective of healthy personal development. It recognizes the possibly harmful side effects of this process of development, and the therapeutic value of the insights offered by authors such as Lowen and Moore, but it holds fast to the belief that healthy human development can only take place within the context of a process of progressive differentiation.

Wilber moves beyond the domain of conventional psychiatry by discussing the pathologies that are associated with the personal and transpersonal domains. He puts forward a convincing argument that, in addition to the pathological disturbances that are generally recognized, a large number of other kinds of pathology are also related the higher stages of development: "These first three [stages] and their associated pathologies (psychotic, borderline, and neurotic) correspond with the first three basic structures or rungs in the ladder of overall development. . . . The remaining basic structures or rungs (levels 4 through 9) each involve another and crucial [stage] of self-development, and lesions at those [stages] also generate specific and definable pathologies (which in turn respond to different treatment modalities or therapeutic interventions)."[49]

Wilber also claims that many therapists are still caught up in the pre/trans fallacy because they either (1) deny the existence of the spiritual, seeing it as something infantile that needs to be overcome (which is more or less the Freudian point of view), or (2) mistake the primitive in the individual for the spiritual, as a result of which there is an endless fascination with myths, magic symbols, and dreams, among other things (which is more or less the Jungian point of view). Wilber concludes his discussion of modern psychiatry with the following words:

> Currently, models less comprehensive than the one proposed here are being used to diagnose and treat clients, with an apparent collapse of what seem to be very different diagnostic and treatment categories. . . . A major confusion among various theorists stems from what I have called the 'pre/trans fallacy'. . . . In my opinion, such theoretical (and therapeutic) confusions will continue to abound until the phenomenological validity of the full spectrum of human growth and development receives more recognition and study.[50]

However, in saying this, Wilber certainly does not mean to imply that the last word on consciousness has been said. He ends with a modest note that clarifies his standpoint: "I would like to be very clear about what this presentation has attempted to do. It has not offered a fixed, conclusive, unalterable model. Although I have at every point attempted to ground it in the theoretical and phenomenological reports of reputable researchers and practitioners, the overall project is metatheoretical and suggestive, and is offered in that spirit. . . . My point is, that given the state of knowledge *already* available to us, it seems ungenerous to the human condition to present any models *less* comprehensive—by which I mean, models that do not take into account both conventional and contemplative realms of human growth and development."[51]

Transformations of Consciousness brought to a close a period in which, with remarkable persistence and consistency, Wilber thought of new ways in which to apply the idea that had first presented itself to him ten years earlier as a young biochemistry student: the possibility of mapping the entire field of Western psychology and Eastern spirituality by seeing human consciousness as a spectrum. As a collection the articles in *Eye to Eye* summarize this period very effectively. Some of these articles led to separate books on topics such as physics and mysticism; the New Paradigm; new religious movements, the process of human development; and the treatment of pathologies that thwart development.

However, Wilber's prodigious output was followed by a noticeable silence. In the years that followed it seemed doubtful that he would ever write again. Life itself had knocked on his door—and none too gently, as we shall see in the following chapter.

5

LOVE, DEATH, AND REBIRTH

Years of test and trial

By the beginning of the eighties Wilber had produced an impressive oeuvre in a relatively short time. Over a period of a few years he had written *The Spectrum of Consciousness, No Boundary, The Atman Project, Up from Eden, A Sociable God, The Holographic Paradigm,* and *Eye to Eye.* He had also set up the journal *ReVision* with Jack Crittenden. After he and his first wife Amy Wagner parted on friendly terms, he lived in Boston for a short time while he was helping to start up the journal, but didn't really feel at home there. So when Roger Walsh and Frances Vaughan invited him to come and live with them in San Francisco in 1983, he gratefully accepted. Walsh and Vaughan more or less took pity on Wilber, who was somewhat at loose ends. They both wanted to help him find a partner and tried to pair him off with various single women from their circle of acquaintances. After five or six attempts, none of which proved to be very successful—Walsh and Vaughan were never able to agree on who was the most suitable woman—they came up with a new candidate in the form of Terry Killam. As far as Ken was concerned, they needn't have gone to the trouble of arranging the various meetings—he was quite happy to get by on his own. But this time it was different. And the remarkable thing was that this time Roger Walsh and Frances Vaughan both felt that Terry would prove to be the right partner for Ken.[1]

"LOVE AT FIRST TOUCH"

During their first brief meeting at a party held by their mutual acquaintances, Ken and Terry had little opportunity to talk. But when Ken put his arm around Terry in the early hours of the morning, they both experienced an immediate sense of recognition. "It was love at first touch. We hadn't said five words to each other. And I could tell by the way she looked at my shaved head that it definitely was not going to be love at first sight. I, like almost everybody, found Terry quite beautiful, but I really didn't even know her. But when I put my arm around her, I felt all separation and distance dissolve; there was some sort of merging, it seemed. It was as if Terry and I had been together for lifetimes."[2]

A week later they were able to arrange a proper date, and from that moment on, Ken and Terry were virtually inseparable. Although they had both recently resigned themselves to the fact that they might always be single, they were now convinced that they were made for each other. Ken introduced Terry to Samuel Bercholz, his publisher in Boulder, and less than two weeks after they had first met, he asked her to marry him. Before the wedding could take place a few months later, they first had to attend to the necessary preparations. Or as Wilber put it laconically: "The wedding was set for November 26 [1983], a few months away. In the meantime we busied ourselves with all the necessary preparations. That is to say, Terry busied herself with all the necessary preparations. I wrote a book."[3] The book was *Quantum Questions*, a collection of passages taken from the writings of famous physicists which showed that, contrary to the claims being made by most of the holistic authors of the day, physics actually offered very little support if any for a mystical worldview.

Referring to this misconception Wilber said: "I disagreed entirely with books such as *The Tao of Physics* and *The Dancing Wu-Li Masters*, which had claimed that modern physics supported or even proved Eastern mysticism. This is a colossal error. Physics is a limited, finite, relative, and partial endeavor, dealing with a very limited aspect of reality. It does *not*, for example, deal with biological, psychological, economic, literary, or historical truths; whereas mysticism deals with all of that, with the Whole. To say physics proves mysticism is like saying the tail proves the dog."[4]

In the meantime their friends and acquaintances had been informed of the forthcoming wedding. A month before their wedding day Terry underwent a routine medical examination simply as a matter of precaution. The doctor found a lump in her right breast but didn't think that it was anything serious. Terry, however, suddenly felt a sense of dread. She didn't want to postpone the wedding, even if it might have been more convenient given that December was such a busy month. On the contrary, she suddenly felt that there was no time to waste. Now that she had finally found the right man, she didn't want to take any chances so the wedding went ahead as planned. They were intending to spend their honeymoon in Hawaii, but just before they left, Terry was examined for a second time. The doctor who examined her was of the opinion that the lump was probably a benign growth, but that it needed to be removed, though the operation could wait until after the honeymoon. Terry's mother, who had had cancer and recovered, wasn't satisfied with this opinion and insisted that Terry consult a specialist. The specialist felt that the operation couldn't wait even a few weeks, and ideally the growth should be removed the same day. The tumor turned out to be malignant.

Suddenly the rosy world that they had been living in for the last few months fell apart. *Cancer.* The stark reality of the word began to make itself felt. Ken and Terry initially looked to the information they had been given by the medical establishment in an attempt to find their bearings. They had a huge need for reliable information about the how and the why of the illness. As they read up about it, they discovered that cancer was not only a physical *illness*, it was also a *sickness* surrounded by all kinds of cultural values. Anyone who suffers from an illness must not only seek the right medical treatment, he or she must also learn to deal with the sickness. Was it possible that there were also psychological factors that caused a person to develop cancer? Many theories contend that this is the case, particularly in New Age circles. And, so they discovered, the less that is known about an illness, the more the culture is inclined to provide us with information about the sickness—information that is not always correct.

Thus besides taking in all of the strictly medical information, Ken and Terry also had to find a way to deal with the sickness of cancer. They discovered that, so far, medical science had made little progress with most forms of cancer. Their doctor gave them the hard facts: none of the forms of treatment currently available substantially prolonged the patient's life. The treatments could only make the time that was left more enjoyable— if such a word was appropriate given the invasive impact of many of the conventional forms of treatment (surgery, chemotherapy, radiation). Despite the fact that the doctors themselves were aware that these treatments were often of little use, they tended to cling to them because they were consistent with their medical convictions. Ken and Terry then turned to the medical and alternative literature on cancer. Whereas the conventional literature was often negative, the tone of the alternative literature was positive. But the evidence was often based on poorly researched, anecdotal cases of miraculous cures. When they drew up a list of the different views of cancer they came across in the literature, they ended up with as many as eleven different interpretations, varying from scientific explanations to religious convictions.

Christian	— Illness is God's punishment for sin
New Age	— Illness is a lesson from which we can learn something
Medical	— Illness is simply a physical disorder
Karma	— Illness is the result of past action
Psychological	— Illness is due to suppressed emotions
Gnostic	— Illness is an illusion, only Spirit exists
Existential	— Illness is part of our finite, mortal existence
Holistic	— Illness is the result of a combination of many different factors
Magical	— Illness is retribution for evil thoughts
Buddhist	— Illness is an inseparable part of life
Scientific	— Illness has causes but no meaning

FIGURE 5.1.   Different interpretations of the phenomenon of illness

They were particularly interested in the extent to which we ourselves are responsible for the illnesses we develop. Wilber suspected that when it came to cancer psychological factors played a relatively small part:

I think cancer is caused by a dozen different things. . . . People have physical, emotional, mental, existential and spiritual dimensions, and I would guess that problems on any and all of those levels can contribute to illness. Physical causes: diet, environmental toxins, radiation, smoking, genetic predisposition, and so on. Emotional causes: depression, rigid self-control and hyper-independence. Mental: constant self-criticism, constant pessimistic outlook, especially depression, which seems to affect the immune system. Existential: exaggerated fear of death causing exaggerated fear of life. Spiritual: failure to listen to one's inner voice.

Maybe all of those contribute to a physical illness. My problem is, I don't know how much weight to give to each level. Is the mental or psychological cause of cancer worth 60% or 2%? But that's the whole point, you see? That's the whole issue. Right now, from all the evidence I've seen, I'd say that with cancer it's about 30% genetic, 55% environmental (drinking, smoking, dietary fat, fiber, toxins, sunlight, electromagnetic radiation, etc.), and 15% everything else—emotional, mental, existential, spiritual. But that means that at least 85% of the causes are physical, seems to me.[5]

In order to be able to cope with the sickness and to use the years that might be left to her in a way that was as meaningful as possible, Terry decided to change the things in her life that the alternative theories about cancer identified as causative factors—even if this was not actually the case. Faced with the prospect of death, she felt that it was a good idea for her to set her house in order and to make changes that she should have made anyway. She focused in particular on what might have been the spiritual causes of her illness. For example, had she listened to her own inner voice enough over the years? Had she followed her calling in life? Or had she allowed herself to be guided by illegitimate motives, such as ambition, competition, and comparisons with other people up until now? As she looked at these issues, the theme that constantly emerged was the essential nature of the feminine and the masculine, particularly with regard to spirituality. She began to define this as the difference between "being" and "doing," and was especially interested in seeking to find the right balance between these two fundamental human principles in her own life. As far as she was concerned, doing was synonymous with producing, achieving, changing, competition, aggression, and hierarchy, whereas being was synonymous with acceptance, inclusion, compassion, care, and equality. In our predominantly masculine society we attach a great deal of importance to what someone *does*, and far less importance to how someone is *being*. She herself had been very attached to all of the things she had done, both at college and at work, but now she was keen to discover who she really was. What did she really want to do in life? What kind of activity would allow her to express her deepest being most effectively? What was her true calling in life? Where did her task lie? Had she honored her own femininity sufficiently in her life up until now?

Writing about this process later, Wilber said: "We came to refer to her search for her 'work' as a search for her 'daemon'—the Greek word that in classical mythology refers to 'a god within,' one's inner deity or guiding spirit, also known as a genii or jinn, the tutelary deity or guiding spirit; one's daemon or genii is also said to be synonymous with one's fate or fortune. Terry had not yet found her fate, her genius, her destiny, her daemon, not in its final form, anyway. I was to be a part of that fate, but not quite the main focus that Terry thought; I was more of a catalyst. Her daemon, really, was her own higher Self, and it would soon be expressed, not in work, but in art."[6]

Recalling the way in which he had discovered his own calling as a writer in the period when he first began writing, he said:

I, on the other hand, had found my fate, my daemon, and it was my writing. I knew exactly what I wanted to do, why I wanted to do it; I knew why I was put here, and what I was supposed to accomplish. When I was writing I was expressing my own higher Self; I had no doubt or hesitation about that at all. Two paragraphs into the writing of my first book, when I was twenty-three years old, I knew I had come home, found myself, found my purpose, found my god. I have since never doubted it once.

But there is a strange and horrible thing about one's daemon: When honored and acted upon, it is indeed one's guiding spirit; those who bear a god within bring genius to their work. When however, one's daemon is heard but unheeded, it is said that the daemon becomes a demon, or evil spirit—divine energy and talent degenerates into self-destructive activity.[7]

In Wilber's case, it would rapidly become apparent just how true this was.

In determining the right treatment for the physical aspect of the illness, Terry finally decided on a combination of a partial mastectomy and radiation, supplemented with all of the alternative forms of therapy that were available—meditation, visualization, and diet. She also decided to keep a journal of her experience and was keen to do something for other cancer patients. Finding the right balance between being and doing, between fighting against her illness on the one hand and accepting it on the other, would prove to be the most important theme during the last phase of her life.

In the summer of 1984 Wilber was working on his next book. "I, of course, was writing a book, *Transformations of Consciousness: Conventional and Contemplative Perspectives on Development*, which I coauthored with Jack Engler and Daniel P. Brown, two Harvard professors who specialized in East/West psychology. The essence of the book was that if we take the various *psychological* models offered by the West (Freudian, cognitive, linguistic, object relational, etc.) and combine them with the *spiritual* models of the East (and Western mystics), then we arrive at a full-spectrum model of human growth and development, a model that traces human growth from body to mind to soul to spirit. What's more, using this overall map of human development, we can rather easily pinpoint the various types of 'neuroses' that men and women may develop, and consequently choose more accurately the type of treatment or therapy that would be most appropriate and effective for each problem. The *New York*

Times called it 'the most important and sophisticated synthesis of psychologies East and West to emerge yet.'"[8]

"I WENT INTO A PROFOUND DEPRESSION"

Terry then suddenly discovered that she was pregnant, which, given her physical condition, was inadvisable from a medical point of view, since it would only make the cancer worse. However, though neither of them had felt that they wanted children initially, this led them to decide that they would start a family once Terry was well again. With this in mind they started to look for a more suitable setting for a home. Eventually they settled on Incline Village in the state of Nevada—a village on the banks of Lake Tahoe, the largest mountain lake in the United States, which is situated northeast of California at an altitude of 2,000 meters, a four-hour drive from San Francisco.

During the months before they could move to Lake Tahoe, Terry deepened her spiritual practice by going to a Buddhist retreat, where she developed a greater sense of equanimity in the face of her physical condition and the ever-present threat of a recurrence. And indeed, although the doctors had felt that it was extremely unlikely, it rapidly became apparent that the cancer had returned. Strengthened by her meditations, Terry initially accepted the news simply as a piece of factual information. Now that she was more rooted in the Self, she was less alarmed by the deterioration in her physical condition. But not long after that, she suffered a setback. Ken and Terry discussed the various options and decided that as a precaution the wisest course of action was for Terry to have a mastectomy. Once again they spent Christmas in the hospital as they had done the previous year. The doctors were now of the opinion that any risk had been eliminated, since they believed that the return of the cancer had only been a local recurrence and all of the tissue that had been affected had now been removed. The future looked hopeful, especially since they were finally able to move into their new home.

But unfortunately the ordeal wasn't over yet. A number of specialists they spoke to now appeared to believe that the cancer had in fact spread to the surrounding tissue. Thus at this point there was little choice but to step up the conventional treatment and Terry had her first dose of chemotherapy. The fact that this meant that she would probably never be able to have children affected her very profoundly. By way of support, while she lay in the hospital bed, Ken read her passages from *No Boundary*, the book in which he had explained how a person can find the Self or the "Witness" within themselves. He too drew some solace from it, for he too was beginning to feel the strain of the last few months:

> Physically then, Terry managed the chemotherapy treatments fairly well, all things considered. What we overlooked, what caught us from behind, what very nearly destroyed us both, was the emotional, psychological and spiritual devastation that the whole ordeal was having on each of us. As the months wore on, and the ordeal intensified, Terry's shadow elements surfaced and intensified, and I went into a profound depression.[9]

As a result of the chemotherapy Terry began to lose her hair. Given that Ken also had a bald head, they were able to joke about it. They had themselves photographed by a friend of Terry's to capture the moment on film for posterity. In fact, during their many visits to the different hospitals Ken was sometimes thought to be the cancer patient! The real patients drew some comfort from the fact that he could still be so vital and good humored despite his illness. Nevertheless, despite these lighter moments, their relationship was now starting to crack under the strain. Wilber later described the situation in which they found themselves:

> Here was the situation. In the past year and a half: Terry had one operation followed by six weeks of radiation, a recurrence, a mastectomy, and was now in the middle of chemotherapy, all the while confronted with the unrelenting possibility of an early death. In order to be with Terry twenty-four hours a day, I chose to stop writing, dropped three editorial jobs, and generally turned my life over to her fight against cancer. I had recently—big mistake— stopped meditating, because I was too exhausted. We had moved out of the Muir Beach house, but the Tahoe house still wasn't ready. We were in effect building a house while trying to do Terry's chemotherapy on the run, as if building a house or doing chemo weren't madness-enough-inducing endeavors on their own.
> And *that*, we would both realize, was the easy part. When we finally moved into the Tahoe house, the really gruesome ordeal began.'[10]

Once they had settled in their new home, Ken began to drink increasingly heavily, though fortunately it seemed to have little effect on his presence of mind. This went on for a number of months. The trials of the last few years began to take their toll. That year, in 1985, Incline Village, the village they had moved to, was hit by a strange viral disease, one of the symptoms of which was a feeling of total exhaustion.* Ken was one of the victims of the disease and suffered from it for more than two years. But for a long time he was not aware that he had the illness, so he assumed that his malaise was due to other causes. This situation was exacerbated still further by yet another factor:

> But my central problem, the overriding problem, was simply that, in my desire to do anything to help Terry, I had for a year completely submerged my own interests, my own work, my own needs, my own life. I voluntarily chose to do this, and I would do it again unhesitatingly under the same circumstances. But I would do it differently, with more of a support system for myself in place, and with a clearer understanding of the devastating toll that being a full-time support person can take.[11]

Like Terry, Ken felt his own health slipping away:

> I had not been able to do any sustained writing for over a year and a half. Up to that period, writing was my life blood. It was my daemon, my fate, my fortune. I had written a book a year for ten years; and, as men often do, I *defined* myself by doing, by my writing, and when that suddenly stopped I was suspended in midair without a net. The landing hurt.
>   And most egregious of all, I had stopped meditation. The strong taste I had of the Witness slowly evaporated. I no longer had easy access to the "center of the cyclone." I had only the

---

*Only very recently it has become clear that this "virus" Wilber caught is actually a condition now diagnosed as RNase Enzyme Deficiency Disease (REDD). According to Wilber, it is held responsible for illnesses such as multiple sclerosis, myalgic encephalomyelitis, ALS, inflammatory rheumatoid arthritis, Gulf War Syndrome, and fibromyalgia. Typically, the disease can become latent for a decade, until it manifests itself as a condition of chronic fever, caused by "hypoxia" or lack of oxygen in the cells. As Wilber wrote in a recent e-mail communication to his friends and colleagues: "You feel like you are suffocating most of the time, and you're often bedridden around the clock (literally). Also fortunately for me, this means mega meditation. It also means depression, sadness, and pain, not so much for the pain in this body, but the pain of what this body can't do." Reflecting on the time with Treya when he caught the disease, he writes: "I sometimes think of this thing as a war wound I got when taking care of Treya, and sometimes that makes it easier to bear."

cyclone. And it was that, more than anything else in my case, that made difficult times so hard to bear. When I lost access to pure open awareness—to the Witness, to my soul—I was left only with my self-contraction, with Narcissus, hopelessly absorbed in his own image.[12] I had lost my soul, it seemed, as well as my daemon, and so I was left only with my ego, a frightening thought under any circumstances.

But I suppose the simplest and most crushing mistake I made was this: I blamed Terry for my woes. I had freely and voluntarily chosen to set aside my own interests in order to help her, and then when I missed those interests—missed my writing, missed my editorial jobs, missed meditation—I just blamed Terry. Blamed her for getting cancer, blamed her for wrecking my life, blamed her for the loss of my daemon. This is what the existentialists call "bad faith"—bad in that you are not assuming responsibility for your own choices.[13]

Only when Ken discovered that his wretched condition was partly due to the virus was he able to see things in a more balanced light. While this was a huge relief, it also meant that he was less and less available for Terry. Now that his own problems were demanding attention, he simply could not summon up the energy to be there for her, come what may. Their relationship was under serious pressure at this stage, to the point that they almost separated. It took months of relational therapy before their relationship began to flourish again. From then on Terry tried not to claim so much of Ken for herself, while he made more of an effort to express his own needs. This whole process led him to be keenly aware of the fact that meditation alone cannot resolve psychological problems such as neuroses, which need to be tackled with the appropriate psychotherapeutic tools. As they worked through this antagonism, the deep love that they had felt for one another returned.

"MY PATH HAS BEEN BUDDHIST"

They decided to move back to San Francisco and rented a house there. Now both found time to devote themselves to their spiritual practice. Speaking of his own spiritual path, Wilber said:

Although I had not yet started meditating again, both Terry and I had begun the search for a teacher we could both embrace.

Terry's essential path was vipassana, the basic and core path of all forms of Buddhism, although she was also very fond of Christian mysticism and practiced the *Course in Miracles* daily for about two years. Although I was sympathetic to virtually any school of mysticism, East or West, I found the most powerful and profound form of mysticism to be Buddhist, and so my own practice had been, for fifteen years, Zen, the quintessential Buddhist path. But I was always attracted to Vajrayana Buddhism, the Tibetan form of tantric Buddhism, which is by far the most complete and well-rounded spiritual system to be found anywhere in the world. I was also drawn to several individual teachers who, although schooled in a particular tradition, transcended any categorization: Krishnamurti, Sri Ramana Maharshi, and Da Free John.

But Terry and I could never quite agree on a teacher, not one we could both follow wholeheartedly. I liked Goenka very much, but found vipassana to be much too narrow and limited for an overall approach. Terry liked Trungpa and Free John, but found their paths a bit too wild and crazy. We would finally find "our" teacher in Kalu Rinpoche, a Tibetan master of the highest accomplishment.[14] In fact, it would be at an empowerment given by Kalu that Terry would have a stunning dream that made it clear to her that she had to change her name [to Treya]. In the meantime we continued the search, visiting, seeing, hanging out with, practicing with, the wildest assortment of teachers one could imagine: Father Bede Griffiths, Kobun Chino Roshi, Tai Situpa, Jamgon Kontrul, Trungpa Rinpoche, Da Free John, Katagiri Roshi, Pir Vilayat Khan, Father Thomas Keating. . . .[15]

In the meantime Terry's health continued to deteriorate. She had developed diabetes largely as a result of the chemotherapy and was soon dependent on insulin injections. Her vision also started to deteriorate, as is sometimes the case with diabetes. Fortunately, the violent mood swings she had been suffering disappeared once her blood sugar level returned to normal. Throughout this period she continued to open up to the possibilities inherent in true femininity. She rapidly discovered that very little is known about the nature of women's spirituality. Feminine spirituality appears to be far less goal-oriented than the masculine variety, it is not divided up into such distinct stages, it is more diffuse and is geared more towards the body and the earth rather than the mind. Terry began to appreciate the importance of typically feminine values such as care, nurture, and support:

Suddenly it seems OK to be what I am. To have an amorphous
professional life. To get involved in various projects that move me
and inspire me. To learn more about creating environments in
which things can happen. To bring people together, to network. To
communicate, to make ideas known. To let it unfold and not try
to force myself into a form, a structure, a profession with titles.

What a sense of relief and freedom! Just living is OK! Being
is OK, doing isn't necessarily necessary. It's a kind of allowing. Of
letting go of this society's overly masculine and hyper-doing values. To work on the whole issue of women's spirituality, the feminine faces of God. To settle down, to till the soil in one place and
see what will grow there.[16]

One of the first things to emerge from this new way of being was
Terry's involvement in setting up the Cancer Support Community, an
organization that provided free assistance for cancer patients and the people
who supported them. The Cancer Support Community was initially
modeled on a similar organization known as the Wellness Community,
but they came to feel that an approach that saw cancer as an illness, and
ultimately sought to win the battle against the illness, was too masculine.
The more feminine approach they had in mind focused more specifically
on creating optimal quality of life throughout the time that was left. At
the same time, Terry also felt a strong need to express herself artistically
and in doing so she rediscovered a side of her nature that she had lost
touch with years ago. Making things, rather than doing things or thinking
about things, proved to be a source of delight. Maybe that was where her
calling lay? At first she scarcely dared to believe it. Firing pots, producing
fused glass designs, writing, working with people—she suddenly seemed
to have found her niche in life:

All these things! The love of which has always come to me spontaneously, never planned. Where did all this go? How did it get
lost? I'm not sure. But whatever happened, it seems to all have
come back again. The simple pleasure of being and making, not
knowing and doing. It feels like coming home! Is this what Ken
talks about when he said he discovered his daemon? Mine is not
flashy, not of the mind, not of the incredible feats he seems to
accomplish. But that's the point, I now see—mine is quieter,
more amorphous, more gentle, I think. More background, more
feminine, more invisible. More of the body. More of the Earth.
And more real for me![17]

However, while her inner development flourished, when it came to her physical condition the prospects were bleak. Despite her positive inner experiences, Terry was again found to be suffering from cancer. She appeared to take in the news impassively simply as a piece of factual information. Inwardly something valuable seemed to have happened. She seemed to have completely accepted her illness, while at the same time she was doing everything she could to get well. She experienced what had happened to her as a rebirth, and as a symbol of this transformation she changed her name from "Terry," which is really a man's name, to "Treya," a derivative of *estrella*, the Spanish word for star. In this respect she also came to be a teacher for Ken when it came to the typically feminine forms of spirituality.

Because conventional medicine had little more to offer at this point, Terry and Ken now turned to the alternative circuit and went to see a paranormal healer, a woman named Chris Habib. Although Ken especially was very sceptical about her ideas, they both agreed that she gave them the most restorative medicine there was—humor. From then on they tried to face the bleak future with a certain amount of lightness.

At the suggestion of Ken's publisher Sam Bercholz, Ken and Terry attended a meeting in Boulder, Colorado, at which Kalu Rinpoche was to lead a rare Buddhist ceremony. The ceremony was held over a period of four days and was attended by sixteen hundred Buddhists. During the ceremony Terry dreamt that her name was now definitively "Treya." Wilber also had a meaningful dream, that Kalu Rinpoche gave him a book that somehow contained all of the secrets of the universe. Following on from that they went to a ten-day retreat led by Kalu Rinpoche not far from Los Angeles.

When it came to adopting a spiritual practice, Wilber still felt most drawn to Buddhism:

I do not think that Buddhism is the best way or the only way. And I would not especially call myself a Buddhist; I have too many affinities with Vedanta Hinduism and Christian mysticism, among many others. But one has to choose a particular path if one is to actually *practice*, and my path has been Buddhist. . . .

Where I do think Buddhism excels is in its completeness. It has specific practices that address all of the higher stages of development—psychic, subtle, causal, and ultimate. And it has a graded system of practice that leads you, step by developmental step, through each of these stages, limited only by your own capacity for growth and transcendence.[18]

In *Grace and Grit* Wilber elaborates briefly on the three main schools of Buddhism—Hinayana, Mahayana, and Vajrayana—which are generally conceived of as corresponding to different stages of spiritual development.[19] Hinayana Buddhism lays the foundation with the aid of meditation techniques (such as *vipassana*) that serve to cultivate an awareness of internal states. Mahayana Buddhism then adds another dimension by placing the emphasis not on one's own enlightenment but on the well-being of all living beings. Within the Mahayana tradition there are specific practices (such as *tonglen*) that deliberately address the suffering of others—practices that were very relevant to the situation in which Ken and Treya found themselves. These practices help to overcome the inborn aversion to suffering and transform it into a deep sense of compassion.

The third school, Vajrayana or Tibetan Buddhism, goes even deeper in that it is based on a single uncompromising principle: there is only Spirit. In this tradition the search *for* Spirit gives way to resting and abiding *in* Spirit which is always omnipresent. However, the process itself is divided up into three stages: the "external tantras" teach you to receive the divine energies by means of visualization; the "lower inner tantras" teach you to see yourself as one with the Divine, and the "higher inner tantras," which are also known as *mahamudra* or *maha-ati*, teach you to relinquish all sense of separation between the Self and Godhead and to be completely absorbed in Emptiness. According to Wilber, these three stages correspond to what he has referred to as the psychic, subtle, and causal stages of development.

Causal	Vajrayana	Higher inner tantras
Subtle	('the diamond vehicle')	Lower inner tantras
Psychic		External tantras
	Mahayana ('the great vehicle')	Tonglen
	Hinayana ('the small vehicle')	Vipassana
Developmental stage	*Buddhist doctrine*	*Meditative practices*

FIGURE 5.2.   The three main schools of Buddhist philosophy

It was above all the practice of *tonglen* that helped to deepen Treya's sense of compassion for all living beings. It also helped her to accept her own suffering and to come to terms with the prospect of an early death. It cured her once and for all of any desire she may have had to embrace cheap theories about the causes of cancer and how cancer could be cured. On the basis of these new insights she wrote an article entitled "Attitudes and Cancer: What kind of help really helps?" which was published in the *Journal of Transpersonal Psychology* in 1988 and later picked up by the *New Age Journal*. In the article she called for a different and more feminine approach to illnesses such as cancer and rejected the idea popularly subscribed to in New Age circles that people themselves cause their own illnesses.[20]

"I DO NOT CONDEMN THE *ENTIRE* NEW AGE MOVEMENT"

Boulder, Colorado, the home of the Naropa Institute—a Buddhist University set up by Chogyam Trungpa—among other things, appealed to Treya and Ken so much that in 1987 they decided to go and live there. Once they had moved in, Treya devoted herself to making fused glass art work, and Wilber's own creativity also started to reemerge. Over a period of just one and a half months he wrote an eight hundred-page manuscript entitled *The Great Chain of Being*.[21] After years of trial the spell was finally broken and his inspiration began to flow again.

One of the chapters of *The Great Chain of Being* addresses the issue of whether people make themselves ill, as is so often claimed in the New Age literature on the subject. Relating the phenomenon of illness to the perennial philosophy on which all of his work was based, Wilber came to the conclusion that illness can originate at any level of reality. Thus in seeking to treat the illness, it is important to treat it at the right level:

(1) The basic argument of the perennial philosophy is that men and women exist within the Great Chain of Being. In other words, we are made up of matter, body, thought, soul and spirit.

(2) In seeking to treat an illness it is extremely important to try to establish the level or levels at which the illness originally developed—physical, emotional, mental or spiritual.

(3) The main treatment (but not necessarily the only treatment) should be introduced at the same level—physical intervention for physical illnesses, emotional therapy for emotional disorders, spiritual methods for spiritual crises, etc. If there are a number of causes,

a combination of different forms of treatment that address the levels in question is likely to be most effective.

(4) The correct identification of the level at which the illness originally developed is very important, for if the origin of illness is incorrectly diagnosed, in the sense that the illness is said to stem from a higher level than is actually the case, the diagnosis is likely to generate feelings of *guilt* in the patient, while if the illness is thought to have developed at a lower level than is actually the case, the diagnosis is likely to create a sense of *despair*. In both cases the treatment is likely to be ineffective and there is also the added disadvantage that the patient is burdened with feelings of guilt or despair that are prompted purely by a faulty diagnosis.[22]

Wilber added:

The general approach to any disease, in my opinion, is to start at the bottom and work up. First, look for physical causes. Exhaust those to the best of your ability. Then move up to any possible emotional causes, and exhaust those. Then mental, then spiritual.

This is particularly important, because so many diseases that were once thought to have a purely spiritual or psychological origin, we now know have major physical or genetic components. . . .

Now this is not to say that treatments from other levels can't be very important in a supporting or adjuvant fashion. They most definitely can. In the simple example of the broken leg, relaxation techniques, visualization, affirmations, meditation, psychotherapy, if you need it—all of those can contribute to a more balanced atmosphere in which physical healing can more easily and perhaps readily occur.

What is not helpful is taking the fact that these psychological and spiritual aspects can be very useful, and then saying that the reason you broke your leg is that you lacked those psychological and spiritual factors in the first place. A person suffering any major illness may make significant and profound changes in the face of that illness; it does not follow that they got that illness because they lacked those changes. That would be like saying, if you have a fever and you take aspirin the fever goes down; therefore having a fever is due to an aspirin deficiency.

Now most diseases, of course, don't originate from a single and isolated level. Whatever happens on one level or dimension of being affects all the other levels to a greater or lesser degree. One's emotional, mental, and spiritual makeup can most definitely influence physical illness and physical healing, just as a physical illness can have strong repercussions on the higher levels. Break your leg, and it will probably have emotional and psychological effects. In systems theory this is called "upward causation"—a lower level is causing certain events in a higher level. And the reverse, "downward causation", is when a higher level has a causal effect or influence on the lower.

The question, then, is just how much "downward causation" does the mind—do our thoughts and emotions—have on physical illness? And the answer seems to be: much more than was once thought, not nearly as much as new agers believe.[23]

Wilber mentions in passing that the metaphor of the Great Chain of Being also helps to explain why visualization or the *imagination* appears to be an effective tool in healing disease: metaphysically speaking, images are closest to the body because they carry an emotional charge. By the same token, abstract words and concepts are further removed from the body:

All things considered, then, psychological mood plays some part in every illness. *And that component should be exercised to the maximum*, I agree entirely. In a close election, that component may be enough to tip the scales in favor of health or illness, but it does not single-handedly stuff ballot boxes.[24]

Turning to the New Age public as a whole, Wilber explained his objections to many of the ideas that were popular in those circles:

This is not a blanket condemnation of the *entire* new age movement. There are aspects of that movement—it's a large and varied beast, after all—that are indeed based on some genuinely mystical and transpersonal principles (such as the importance of intuition and the existence of universal consciousness). It's just that any genuinely *trans*personal movement always attracts a very large number of *pre*personal elements, simply because both are *non*personal, and it is exactly this confusion between "pre" and "trans" that is one of the major problems with the new age movement, in my opinion. . . .

In the new age movement, I believe, a small percentage of genuinely mystical or transpersonal or transrational elements and principles (levels seven through nine [see figure 4.6 on page 144]) have attracted a huge number of prepersonal, magical, and prerational elements (levels one through four), simply because both are nonrational, noncon-ventional, nonorthodox (levels five and six). And these prepersonal and prerational elements then claim ... that they have the authority and the backing of a "higher" state, when all they are doing, I'm afraid I have to conclude, is rationalizing their own self-involved stance. As Jack Engler pointed out, they are drawn to transpersonal mysticism as a way to rationalize prepersonal inclinations. It's a classic "pre/trans fallacy."

I would also conclude, with William Irwin Thompson, that about 20% of the new age movement is transpersonal (transcendental and genuinely mystical); about 80%, prepersonal (magical and narcissistic). You can usually find the transpersonal elements because they don't like to be called "new age." There's nothing "new" about them; they are perennial.[25]

As Wilber goes on to explain, we are actually dealing with three different kinds of thinking, three different groups within society, not two:

In the field of transpersonal psychology, we are constantly having to deal as delicately and as gently as we can with the prepersonal trends, because they give the entire field a "flaky" or "goofy" reputation. We are not against prepersonal beliefs; we just have trouble when we ourselves are asked to embrace these beliefs as if they were transpersonal.

Our "flakier" friends get rather mad at us, because they tend to think that there are only two camps in the world: rational and nonrational, and so we would join with them *against* the rationalist camp. But there are in fact *three* camps: prerational, rational, and transrational. We're actually closer to the rationalists than to the prerationalists. The higher levels transcend but include the lower. Spirit is translogic, not antilogic; it embraces logic and then goes beyond, it doesn't simply reject logic, and then, but only then, move beyond it with its added insights. Buddhism is an extremely rational system that then supplements rationality with intuitive awareness. Some of the "flaky" trends, I'm afraid, are not beyond logic but beneath it.

So what we are trying to do is tease apart the genuine, uni-versal, "laboratory-tested" elements of mystical development from the more idiosyncratic, magical, and narcissistic tendencies. This is a difficult and tricky task, and we don't always get it right.[26]

"AND THAT IS WHAT TREYA HAD DONE FOR ME"

For the first time in three years Ken and Treya appeared to be leading a more or less normal life: he resumed his writing and his meditation practice while she devoted herself to working in the garden or making fused glass pictures. But in the autumn of 1987 Treya noticed that her vision was beginning to deteriorate, and when she was examined, she was found to be suffering from cancer again: this time not only was there a tumor in the brain, there were also tumors in both lungs. It was clear that the cancer had mestastasized.

After having found out everything they could about the possible forms of treatment, they decided to go to the Janker Clinic in Bonn, which prescribed a very aggressive therapy against advanced stages of cancer. They installed themselves in the hospital there and prepared for a stay of several months during which the last major battle against Treya's illness would be fought. At this point they began to seriously consider the fact that Treya was possibly embarking upon the last phase of her life. The doctors in America had given her just six months to live.

The treatment appeared to be successful and, together with Treya's parents, they also found time to travel through Germany, Switzerland, and France. A visit to Notre Dame in Paris left them both suitably im-pressed: "What moved Treya and me to tears, literally, was Notre Dame. One foot inside and you knew immediately you were in sacred space; the profane world of cancer, illness, poverty, hunger, and woes, all checked at the magnificent doors. The lost art of sacred geometry was everywhere apparent, inviting your awareness to assume the same divine contours."[27] They also visited the Musée de L'Orsay, which was then hosting a Van Gogh exhibition. Agreeing with Schopenhauer's conception of art, Wilber later remarked, "Great art is mystical, no matter what its actual content. I never believed art had that power until I saw Van Gogh. It was simply stunning. Take your breath away, take your self away, all at once."[28]

Forced to spend a few days alone outside the hospital when Treya was not allowed to receive visitors because she had a lung infection, Ken thought about what meeting her had meant to him. From one of the towers of an old fort on the Drachenfels mountain he looked out over the Rhine landscape, the sky above him and the earth below:

I looked up: Heaven; I looked down: Earth. Heaven, Earth; Heaven, Earth. And that's what started me thinking of Treya. In the past few years she had returned to her roots in the Earth, to her love of nature, to the body, to making, to her femininity, to her grounded openness and trust and caring. While I had remained where I wanted to be, where I myself am at home—in Heaven, which, in mythology, does not mean the world of Spirit but the Apollonian world of ideas, of logic, of concepts and symbols. Heaven is of the mind, Earth is of the body. I took feelings and related them to ideas; Treya took ideas and related them to feelings. I moved from the particular to the universal, constantly; Treya moved from the universal to the concrete, always. I loved thinking, she loved making. I loved culture, she loved nature. I shut the window so I could hear Bach; she turned off Bach so she could hear the birds.

In the traditions, Spirit is found neither in Heaven nor in Earth, but in the Heart. The Heart has always been seen as the integration or the union point of Heaven and Earth, the point that Earth grounded Heaven and Heaven exalted the Earth. Neither Heaven nor Earth alone could capture Spirit; only the balance of the two found in the Heart could lead to the secret door beyond death and mortality and pain.

And that is what Treya had done for me; that is what we had done for each other: pointed the way to the Heart. . . . When we were first together, we were sometimes irritated by these differences, me the absent-minded professor . . . ; Treya always hugging the ground. . . .

But we soon came to see that that was the entire point, that we were different, that maybe this applied to many men and women, and that, far from being whole and self-contained people, we were each half-people, one of Heaven, one of Earth, and that was exactly as we should be. We came to appreciate those differences—not just honor them, but be thankful for them. I will always be at home in ideas, Treya will always be at home in nature, but together, joined in the Heart, we were whole; we could find that primal unity which neither alone could manage. Our favorite Plato quote became: "Men and women were once whole but were torn in two, and the pursuit and desire of that whole is called love."

The union of Heaven and Earth, I kept thinking, as my eyes looked up, looked down. With Treya, I thought, I am beginning, just beginning, to find my Heart.[29]

It was then that Ken suddenly realized that the woman he loved was dying. Naturally he had known that it was a possibility for some time, but only now did the stark reality of it actually hit him. He began to drown in self-pity and ended up in a local pub in a neighboring village, where a group of old men were dancing. They invited him to join them and after initially declining the invitation, Ken allowed himself to be persuaded and joined in. Despite the fact that he didn't understand a word of German there was a sense of contact between him and the old men; they wouldn't allow him to leave and went on dancing for two hours.

Looking back on this incident, he admits with disarming honesty: "I would like to claim that my big satori about accepting Treya's condition, that my coming to terms with her likely death, that my becoming finally responsible for my own choices about setting aside my interests and doing anything to support her—I would like to claim that all of that came from some powerful meditation session with blazing white light and spontaneous insights pouring over me, that I grabbed a handful of Zen courage and plunged back into the fight, that I reached high for some transcendental epiphany that set me straight at once. But it happened in a little pub with a bunch of kindly old men whose names I do not know and whose language I did not speak."[30]

The treatment failed to have the desired effect and the cancer now appeared to have spread to Treya's liver. She tried both to fight for her life and to accept her fate—the uniting of these two principles had now become the guiding theme of her life. Between two sets of treatment they returned to Boulder briefly to catch their breath. Both lived from moment to moment and discovered a deep joy in it. At the same time they kept doing everything they could to stem the advance of the illness. To this end Treya tried a form of enzyme therapy developed by Kelley and Gonzales. At this point Treya's was no longer exclusively concerned with overcoming her illness. She was far more inclined to focus on the good that she still had, or had had. She wrote in her journal that the pressure of the illness had dissolved certain inner limitations and released a new flow of creativity in her.

Back in Bonn it was clear to them that the doctors had given up on Treya. The enzyme cure was now their last hope. On their return journey they visited Cologne Cathedral where Treya came to the following insight: "At this moment in church, kneeling before the masses of candles flickering in the soft gloom, the only thing I could think of that gives life meaning is helping other people. Service, in a word. Things like spiritual growth or enlightenment seemed like nothing more than concepts. Full development of one's potential also seemed trite and egocentric unless it leads (as it often does) to ideas or creations that help relieve suffering. What about beauty, my art work, creativity? Well, for today at least, it didn't seem very important, except perhaps for the art that adorns sacred places like this cathedral. Human relationships, human connections, indeed gentle loving relationship with all forms of life and all of creation, only seemed important. Keeping my heart open, always my biggest challenge, letting down defenses, being open to pain so joy can also enter."[31]

When the enzyme cure also failed to have any effect, they both knew that Treya's last hour had come. Yet despite the fact that the doctors had given her only a few months to live, she felt wonderfully light. Even during this critical phase she wrote in her journal: "Each breath is so incredible, so joyful, so dear. What am I missing? What could be wrong?"[32] In the summer of 1988, ill as she was, she gave a glowing speech during a symposium organized by the Windstar Foundation, in which she looked back over the five years of her illness. Among other things she said:

> Learning to make friends with cancer, learning to make friends with the possibility of an early and perhaps painful death, has taught me a great deal about making friends with myself, as I am, and a great deal about making friends with life, as it is.
>
> I know that there are a lot of things I can't change. I can't force life to make sense, or to be fair. This growing acceptance of life as it is, with all the sorrow, the pain, the suffering, and the tragedy, has brought me a kind of peace. I find that I feel ever more connected with all beings who suffer, in a really genuine way. I find a more open sense of compassion. And I find an ever steadier desire to help, in whatever way I can. . . .
>
> Because I can no longer ignore death, I pay more attention to life.'[33]

Ken also tried to sum up what he had learnt during his years as a support person—always being there for someone who is seriously ill. He wrote an open letter to all of their friends and acquaintances, which was later published in the *Journal of Transpersonal Psychology* under the title "On being a support person."[34] Those who undertake to support a person suffering from an incurable illness find themselves in a paradoxical situation—they spend all of their time caring for the person they are supporting but can never call attention to their own problems. Over time this is bound to tear them apart. So a support person also needs to be supported either by friends or by a therapist. In this situation Ken discovered that he was of most use to Treya when he was able to act as an emotional sponge, feeling what she went through without immediately coming up with practical solutions—if indeed there were any in the face of an incurable illness. But above all he learned to see the situation as an opportunity for spiritual growth—a form of meditation in action.

"And all in all," he concluded in his letter, "I'd rather be writing."[35]

DEATH AND REBIRTH IN THE TIBETAN BUDDHIST TRADITION

During this period Ken was meditating in accordance with the guidelines of the dzogchen tradition conveyed to him by Pema Norbu Rinpoche—a tradition primarily concerned with the experience of Spirit in daily life. He also went to see their spiritual teacher Kalu Rinpoche and drew strength from the Tibetan view of death and life after death. In *Grace and Grit* he explains the Tibetan view as follows:

All of the great wisdom traditions maintain that the actual moment of death is an extremely important and precious opportunity, and for this reason: At the moment of death, the person has dropped the gross physical body, and therefore the higher dimensions—the subtle and the causal—immediately flash in the deceased awareness. If the person can recognize these higher and spiritual dimensions, then the person can acknowledge immediate enlightenment, and do so much more easily than when in the dense and obstructing physical body.

I'll be very specific here, because this is exactly the type of training that Treya had been practicing in preparation for her possible death. This explanation is based on the Tibetan system, which seems to be the most complete, but it is in essential agreement with the mystical traditions the world over.

The human being has three major levels or dimensions: gross (the body), subtle (the mind), and causal (spirit). During the dying process, the lower levels of the Great Chain dissolve first, starting with the body, starting with sensation and perception. When the body dissolves (ceases functioning), the subtler dimensions of mind and soul come to the fore, and then, at the actual moment of death, when all levels dissolve, pure causal Spirit flashes forth in the person's awareness. If the person can recognize this Spirit as his or her own true nature, then enlightenment is realized on the spot, and the person returns permanently to Godhead, as Godhead.

If recognition does not take place, then the person (the soul) enters the intermediate state, the "bardo," which is said to last up to a few months. The subtle level emerges, and then eventually the gross level emerges, and the person is then reborn in a physical body to begin a new life, taking with them, in their soul, whatever wisdom and virtue (but not specific memories) they may have accumulated in the previous life.

Whatever we might think about the notion of reincarnation or the bardo or afterlife states, this much seems certain: If you at all believe that some part of you partakes of the divine, if you at all believe that you have some sort of Spirit that transcends your mortal body in any sense, then the moment of death is crucial, because at that point the mortal body is gone, and if there is *anything* that remains, that is the time to find out, yes?

Of course, near-death experiences and near-death research seems to support this claim. But all I would like to emphasize is that there are specific meditation exercises that precisely rehearse this entire process of death and dissolution, and these meditative exercises were exactly what Treya was practicing when she described "dissolving into all space."[36]

Around this time Wilber wrote an essay on the subject of reincarnation for a book entitled *What Survives?*[37] In the essay he was able to explore the subject in more depth. Wilber differs from most of the authors who write about the subject in that he sees the doctrine of reincarnation first and foremost as a *spiritual* hypothesis. As we have already seen several times, in addition to science and the humanities Wilber also identifies a third type of science—the spiritual sciences, which are specifically concerned with meditation. According to Wilber the truth of the theory of reincarnation can only be experienced within one's own consciousness. In his opinion, the so-called proof of reincarnation compiled by parapsychologists carries little weight since "in most cases these can be shown to be only a revival of subconscious memory trace from *this* life."[38] Wilber argues that the spiritual traditions teach us that it is not so much the personality that reincarnates, but the transpersonal soul, which does not contain any specific memories but can be characterized by the qualities of virtuousness and wisdom. The individual soul continues to reincarnate until it attains Enlightenment (becomes one with Spirit) and is then released from the need to reincarnate.

According to Wilber the various stages of the dying process as described in Tibetan Buddhism can be rehearsed during meditation while a person is still alive. Having already gone through this process several times during his life, the person will then be able to experience his own dying process consciously, which is considered to be of the greatest importance in this tradition. The Tibetans believe that at the moment of death a person moves through eight stages that make up the Great Chain of Being, as can be seen in the following figure. The different stages are given very descriptive names.

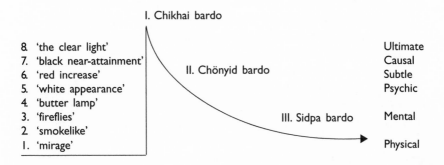

I. Chikhai bardo

8. 'the clear light'		Ultimate
7. 'black near-attainment'		Causal
6. 'red increase'	II. Chönyid bardo	Subtle
5. 'white appearance'		Psychic
4. 'butter lamp'		
3. 'fireflies'	III. Sidpa bardo	Mental
2. 'smokelike'		
1. 'mirage'		Physical

FIGURE 5.3.   The process of reincarnation in the Tibetan Buddhist tradition

Once the person has passed through these eight stages, death has occurred and for a short time the person is able to experience the Clear Light (the Tibetan expression for Spirit). However, if this level is beyond the person's attainment, there follow three *bardo* states (which relate to the nature of existence between two lives). According to Wilber these three bardo states correspond to the causal, the subtle, and the gross levels of existence. In the first or *chikhai bardo* (1) the deceased is still at the level of the Clear Light. If he is unable to remain in this rarefied state of consciousness, he will descend through the spheres to the *chönyid bardo* (2), where he will see countless visions of peaceful and wrathful deities. If he also passes through this realm the moment of rebirth is approaching and he will enter the *sidpa bardo* (3) before returning to the physical world. According to Wilber, proof of the existence of all of these stages of consciousness can be discovered in meditation while we are still alive:

The contemplative evidence strongly suggests that the data, the actual experiences that accompany the dying process—for example, the "white appearance," the "red increase," the "black near-attainment," or whatever terms we want to use—exist and are very real. Further evidence of their reality is found in the fact that they have actual ontological referents in the higher dimensions of the Great Chain of Being. The three experiences just mentioned, for instance, refer respectively to what I have called the psychic, the subtle and the causal structures of consciousness. Indeed, they refer very precisely to those levels, despite the various different and legitimate explanations that might also be given for them. In my opinion, then, the levels are real, they have actual and definite ontological status, and thus the experiences of those levels are themselves real.[39]

People who have gone through a near-death experience often report seeing a bright light or meeting a being of light and traveling through a tunnel. Wilber suggests that these experiences may relate to the subtle level of consciousness, which is said to be characterized by light, wisdom, and bliss. However, since this is only a near-death experience and not actual death, they have not yet reached the eighth stage of the Clear Light. Nor according to the Tibetan system do they have any access to the bardo states. Compared with the relatively pleasant dying process—the ascent to the Clear Light—the bardo experiences—the descent to the physical world—are often far more disturbing and they are certainly not always positive. Some are distinctly nightmarish. But even if those who have had a near-death experience have not completed the postmortem journey, according to Wilber they have in any event experienced the first phases of the journey, which in Wilber's opinion offers further support for the Tibetan model:

One does not hear about this "downside" to the death process from the NDE people. They are just tasting the early stages of the overall process. Nevertheless, their testimony is powerful evidence that this process does in fact occur. It all fits with a remarkable and unmistakable precision. Moreover, it is not possible to explain away their testimony by claiming that all of them have studied Tibetan Buddhism; in fact, most of them have not even heard of it. But they have essentially similar experiences as the Tibetans because these experiences reflect the universal and cross-cultural reality of the Great Chain of Being. It now appears that there is simply nō other way to read the really extensive data gathered on this subject.[40]

This is not the place to examine this view of reincarnation in detail, for it would take us too far away from the line of our narrative. Nevertheless a few observations are called for. For it is doubtful that the Tibetan view of reincarnation is indeed as generally valid as Wilber suggests.[41]

Treya died in January 1989 in their home in Boulder with Ken and their family and their friends around her. The moving description of Treya's last days and hours is too personal to be summarized here. What is relevant in this context is how Wilber looks back on this period. His years of service in looking after Treya had provided him with insights that no amount of intellectual study could have yielded. When, some time after her death, he tried to formulate what he had learnt from Treya, he wrote:

> I had a dream. But it wasn't a dream, it was more of a simple image: a raindrop fell into the ocean, thus becoming one with the all. At first I thought that this meant Treya had become enlightened, that Treya was the drop that had become one with the ocean of enlightenment. And that made sense.
>
> But then I realized it was more profound than that: I was the drop, and Treya the ocean. She had not been released—she was already so. Rather, it was I who had been released, by the simple virtue of serving her.
>
> And so, there it was: that was exactly why she had so insistently asked me to promise that I would find her. It wasn't that she needed me to find her; it was that, through my promise to her, she would therefore find me, and help me, yet again, and again and again. I had it all backwards: I thought my promise was how I would help her, whereas it was actually how she would reach and help me, again, and again, and forever again, as long as it took for me to awaken, as long as it took for me to acknowledge, as long as it took for me to realize the Spirit that she had come so clearly to announce. And by no means just me: Treya came for all her friends, for her family, and especially for those stricken with terrible illness. For all of this, Treya was present.[42]

Personally, he is sceptical about the possibility of meeting Treya again after death:

I don't think any of us will ever actually meet Treya again. I don't think it works that way. [43] That's much too concrete and literal. Rather, it is my own deepest feeling that every time you and I— and any who knew her—that every time we act from a position of integrity, and honesty, and strength, and compassion: every time we do that, now and forever, we unmistakenly meet again the mind and soul of Treya.

So my promise to Treya—the only promise that she made me repeat over and over—my promise that I would find her again really meant that I had promised to find my own enlightened Heart.

And I know, in those last six months, that I did so. [44]

After Treya's death Wilber fulfilled his promise to her to incorporate the entries she had made in her journal in a book. The book, which came to be entitled *Grace and Grit: Spirituality and Healing in the Life and Death of Treya Killam Wilber* (1991), expresses the theme that became the motto of the last years of her life: a person must be able to fight for her life as well as being able to accept death if death proves to be unavoidable. In contrast to Wilber's previous works, *Grace and Grit* is a very personal book. Given the subject matter it was the only appropriate style. After this Wilber rapidly went on to pick up the thread of his earlier work and began to write theoretical books again—and once again he began to churn them out at the amazingly rapid pace his readers had become accustomed to.

And, certainly in terms of his writing, the best was yet to come.

6

AN EVEN BROADER HORIZON

A multidimensional view of Spirit

It seemed that the time had finally come for Wilber to write the textbook on transpersonal psychology that he had had in mind since the beginning of the eighties. He made several references to this work in *Transformations of Consciousness*, the chapters of which were in fact a summary of the material that Wilber had compiled to date. But once again his focus was diverted.[1] It had been some time since Wilber had last published and virtually all of the concepts that he had used in his works—depth, hierarchy, quality, development, higher and lower—were now regarded as highly suspect and had been declared taboo, even in transpersonal circles. The all-effacing holism that reduced all things to the same level, and that often went hand in hand with marked anti-intellectualism and veiled materialism, was at odds with Wilber's endeavor to examine in detail how the kosmos fits together. As far as Wilber could see, an increasing number of people were now under the sway of a romantic and regressive ideology, which regarded spirituality as a return to a state once known that had since been lost—to the carefree world of the child, or the paradisiacal state of primitive man. As a result, the present culture was invariably depicted as antispiritual. Thus Wilber was completely at variance with the prevailing spirit of the times in repeating his plea for the marriage of rationality and spirituality, in the hope that he might be able to salvage something of the depth of the worldview of the spiritual traditions.

This prevailing romantic-regressive view, which was still gaining ground, was diametrically opposed to what Wilber had tried to show in the books he had written in the past: in growing up to become adults we do not move further away from Spirit, but rather *we get closer to it*. The issue hinged on the precise relationship between rationality and spirituality. Surely God could not object to the fact that we grow into adult individuals capable of rational thought? In Wilber's view, the process of becoming an adult was a profoundly spiritual process because in his opinion it enabled Spirit itself to flourish.

So once again Wilber set the work on his textbook of transpersonal psychology aside[2] and undertook to assimilate the entire modern and above all, postmodern spirit of the times in order to confront it with the extensive field of spirituality. Where did the contemporary individual have to look in order to find Spirit? To the past, when the world's religions still wielded a significant influence? Or is Spirit still at work in our time, albeit in a less obvious way? Might Spirit actually be responsible for the decline of the traditional forms of religion? In Wilber's view, many of those who advocate a spiritual way of life have completely misinterpreted the real spiritual significance of modern culture and its achievements. Instead they focus purely on the past in the belief that in the past people were more spiritual. In Wilber's opinion this misconception needs to be eliminated if we are ever to gain an accurate insight into authentic spirituality.

THE *KOSMOS* TRILOGY

Thus Wilber set himself the task of writing a comprehensive study of the place that Spirit might occupy in our Western, secularized culture. It rapidly became apparent that he had compiled far more material than could be incorporated within even a very thick book. It was as if the past few years had acted as a dam that now broke under the force of the water gathered behind it, producing a huge waterfall of insights and creativity. Wilber decided to divide the material up into three volumes, which left him with a plan for a trilogy that he entitled simply *Kosmos*. In choosing to use the word *Kosmos* (spelled with a capital K), he was referring explicitly to the traditional understanding of the world which encompassed not only the physical reality perceived by the senses—the domain of science—but also the realms of life, soul, and spirit. As he had already argued in *Eye to Eye*, for a New Paradigm to be valid, it would have to recognize at least three dimensions: the physical, the mental, and the spiritual. Now Wilber delineated four different domains of reality: the physiosphere or material world, the biosphere or the world of living things, the noosphere or the realm of thought, and the theosphere or divine domain.[3]

Modern science recognizes only one dimension: the world perceived by the eye of flesh. Within these parameters the only form of knowledge

that passes for true knowledge is knowledge that relies on sensory perception. In light of this analysis Wilber might also have been expected to
resort to a romantic-regressive view—after all, hadn't science prevailed
over the traditional religious worldviews on all fronts and given rise to an
extremely superficial, materialistic outlook? But in fact the opposite is
true. For Wilber maintains that:

(1) The contemporary scientific view of reality is undeniably poorer
    and more one-dimensional than the traditional view of reality,
    but that

(2) nevertheless the modern-day individual is richer, more differen-
    tiated, and more evolved that his primitive predecessors.

This paradox can be explained with the aid of the traditional worldview. In
his individual and collective development the individual passes through the
stages outlined in the traditional understanding of reality, but at a critical
moment he decided only to rely on what his senses were able to tell him
about reality. This resulted in the materialistic-scientific view that now
dominates Western culture. Above all, the rise of technology probably encouraged people to place their trust in scientific knowledge, even if it related
purely to the material domain (a fact that is all too often overlooked).

The first volume of the *Kosmos* trilogy was published in 1995 under
the arresting title *Sex, Ecology, Spirituality*. The book was the product of
more than three years of intensive labor during which time Wilber had
lived virtually as a recluse. *SES*, as it rapidly came to be known, is a
remarkable book in many respects. The sheer size of it—the book runs to
800 pages, and the 270 pages of notes would fill a good sized paperback
on their own—gives the reader the impression of having entered a world
in which it is difficult to maintain one's footing. Moving at a vertiginous
pace, the reader is inundated with views on the works of contemporary
and traditional authors, which are supplemented and clarified with Wilber's
own observations and analyses. The notes to the book came as a surprise
to a number of Wilber's readers in that some of them were written in a
sharp, polemical, and sometimes humorous style, since Wilber had decided not to hold back in criticizing what were in his opinion extremely
dubious trends in the transpersonal and alternative worlds.

As far as Wilber was concerned, at this point honest criticism was the
only possible approach left open to him. Even highly respected
transpersonal institutes had since succumbed to the antimodern, regressive thinking about spirituality and his own work was increasingly being

associated with these circles. This being the case, he wanted to make it clear once and for all that his view of spirituality was diametrically opposed to *any* form of retro-romanticism. The truth had to be stated in plain terms—regardless of the consequences. And in any event one of the consequences was positive: the themes that Wilber had explored at length in his previous books over the years, albeit in a more collected tone, were suddenly being openly discussed and criticized. Yet, while this clearly raised the pitch of the debate regarding the basic tenets of transpersonal philosophy, from that point on, at least in some transpersonal circles, Wilber became a controversial figure.

POPULAR HOLISM FALLS SHORT

It is virtually impossible to do justice to the rich content of *Sex, Ecology, Spirituality* in a few paragraphs; nevertheless it is possible to depict the broad outlines. The book is made up of two parts, Book One and Book Two. In Book One Wilber recapitulates the stage model of development that he had described earlier, now adding a number of new elements. Wilber took the current state of affairs in sciences such as physics and biology—the sciences on which popular holism was also based—as his starting point. At the same time he developed his own system of metaphysics, which centered on the "holon," a concept he borrowed from Arthur Koestler.

According to Wilber everything that occurs in reality—an object, a thought, an experience—is both a part and a whole, hence the combination of whole and part to create the word *holon*. We see this very clearly in the physiosphere: an atom is part of a molecule, but it is also an independent whole in its own right. The same phenomenon also occurs in the noosphere: a word is part of a sentence, but it is also an independent unit in its own right. According to Wilber holons differ in terms of their degree of depth or consciousness. The more levels a holon encompasses, the deeper or more conscious it is. For example, a human being has more depth than an animal. By the same token, an animal has more depth than a plant. Seen from this point of view, the process of evolution can be understood as a process of deepening or of growth in consciousness.[4]

The popular form of holism refers to reality—in other words, the reality that can be perceived by the senses—as one great Whole, as one great System, or as a Web of Life that encompasses a hierarchical series of units ranging from minuscule to vast—from the world of subatomic particles to the cosmos (with a small c!) as a whole. Some authors see the biosphere, of which the individual is a part, as the largest unit of description. At this point the small step to an ecological view of life is rapidly accomplished: the extent to which the individual separates himself from the biosphere as a whole will be the extent of his undoing, and to the extent that he conforms to the greater Order of the biosphere, he will discover his true destiny.

At first sight this might appear to be a plausible analysis, but Wilber challenges it in no uncertain terms. First he points out that a holistic series that progresses from small to large—in other words, a series that relies on what is essentially a *quantitative* criterion—will always keep us bound to the visible reality of the physical cosmos. The traditional hierarchy, on the other hand, is one that proceeds from low to high—which is a *qualitative* criterion—and as a result it is of an entirely different order. In moving from the physiosphere to the biosphere, and from the biosphere to the noosphere, rather than moving in space, we are moving in depth or height, and it is precisely this dimension of depth that Wilber wishes to focus on. Each new stage of evolution introduces new elements that cannot be explained on the basis of the previous stages. This is also known as "emergent evolution."[5]

According to Wilber the individual is not simply part of the biosphere as a whole; the human individual transcends the biosphere on account of the fact that he encounters within his being dimensions that do not occur in the biological realm. In other words, we discover the spiritual dimension not by looking at what we have in common with all of the other realms of nature (the biological dimension is the greatest common denominator of all living beings), but by looking at what distinguishes us from the lower realms of nature, that is, our capacity for rational thought. This faculty represents a further dimension of depth of reality that *first manifests in the human being*. And so, Wilber argues, the spiritual dimension must exist further along the same route—also within the human individual, not in a presupposed unity of all biological beings. In this sense Wilber has no hesitation in seeing the human individual as the pinnacle of visible creation.

Yet Wilber also insists that it is essential for us to live in harmony with the principles of ecology. He points out that though the lower can exist without the higher, the reverse is not the case. Even if all life on the planet were to be exterminated, the matter that provides the basis for it would continue to exist. (Or, to pursue the argument still further, if all molecules were to disintegrate, the atoms of which they are made up would continue to exist). In view of the fact that the noosphere cannot exist without the biosphere, it is essential that we treat the biosphere with respect. However, this does not justify the wholesale reduction of the noosphere *to* the biosphere, despite the fact that many contemporary eco-philosophers appear to be heading in this direction. Wilber suggests that we make a distinction between the concepts of "nature" and "Nature." Thus, nature (with a small n) refers to the biological and ecological realm, which we as individuals have transcended, but which nevertheless we also have to integrate. Nature (with a capital N) encompasses *all* levels of existence—not only the biological level, but also the mental and spiritual levels. In a certain sense it was inevitable that we would separate ourselves from nature and our biological roots. But, by definition, it is impossible for us to separate ourselves from Nature in view of the fact that it is the whole of reality, which means that we can never step outside of it. According to Wilber, not only do we have to live in harmony with biological nature, as the ecologists have rightly impressed upon us, we also have to live in harmony with Nature. This means living in harmony not only with the body, but also with the soul and spirit, not only with the cosmos, but also with the Kosmos.

Thus we are not so much part of *nature* but part of *Nature*, while biological nature is actually part of us, since only a part of our being is biological in its make-up. A larger part of our being—the mental and spiritual parts of our make-up—transcends the biological. This does not alter the fact that within the broader context of Nature we have to take good care of biological nature. A healthy ecology is the basis for mental and spiritual life on earth. The biological body is an indispensable cornerstone of our being, but our being cannot be limited to the body. Because contemporary ecologists fail to make a distinction between nature and Nature, they are turning what is in itself a justified concern for nature into an ecological nature religion, which is no longer appropriate for the modern individual.

In so-called deep ecology, which styles itself as a spiritual movement, the idea that the human individual is the pinnacle of creation is considered to be outdated. Instead, the advocates of deep ecology call for a view of reality that sees the individual as inextricably bound up with nature, claiming that the hierarchical thinking that places the individual above nature is old-fashioned. Wilber warns against the extremely reductionistic implications of this view, which fails to emphasize the most essential aspect of the human individual—the mental and spiritual aspects that transcend the biological level. In failing to recognize this inner dimension, deep ecology is actually extremely superficial! In a deep ecology worthy of its name the full depth of existence would be whole-heartedly acknowledged.

At this point Wilber introduces another enlightening distinction as he points out the difference between the terms *fundamental* and *significant*. In his view physics is the most *fundamental* science in view of the fact that it is concerned with the building blocks of creation, but for this very reason it is also the least *significant* because in focusing purely on the physical dimension, it has to disregard so many other valuable dimensions. In Wilber's opinion it would be a serious error to attempt to squeeze human activities such as philosophy, literature, or mysticism within the limited confines of physics, or even within the somewhat broader but still very limited confines of ecological biology. The humanities, and even more so the spiritual sciences, are concerned with deeper dimensions of reality, and must therefore be included in any all-encompassing and truly holistic paradigm.

The idea that the human individual transcends nature does not give him the right to tyrannize nature. On the contrary, because the individual spans so many more levels of being than animals and plants, he is charged with the far more difficult task of integrating all of these levels. Animals are not faced with this problem and indeed might appear to be in an enviable position. We can see deep peace in the eyes of a cow, but would we really want to trade in our psychological turmoil for this kind of peace? Animals are unable to enter the realm of thought—the level that distinguishes us from animals and makes us *human*. This is a theme that Wilber returns to repeatedly: because there are so many more levels of being at play within the individual—the physiosphere, the biosphere, the noosphere, and sometimes even the theosphere—there is far more that can go wrong. But the rewards of human existence are also that much greater: compared with the lower stages of evolution, human existence offers a far richer inner world that should never be denied. Development always comes at a price, but it is always a price worth paying.

Wilber's view can also be explained in another way. People working in alternative psychological circles often emphasize the importance of being "grounded," in other words the importance of being in contact with the body, given that the body forms the basis of our existence. Yet again in this case we can say that while the body is the most *fundamental* aspect of our being, since without a body we would cease to exist,[6] at the same time it is also the least *significant* aspect of our being, because the body is simply a material reality that we have in common with all other biological forms of life. And while we need a healthy basis in order to be able to develop harmoniously, if we insist on focusing exclusively on the basis, there is little possibility of further development. Or, to put it another way, it is important that we take care of our roots in the biological realm, but at the same time we must not forget that ultimately development is concerned with the flowering of our mental and spiritual abilities.

Wilber's greatest objection to the popular holistic models is their blunt denial of the inner dimension: "If we look at all these [holistic models], we notice a startling fact. All of these [models] claim to be holistic, to cover all of reality in an encompassing fashion. That is . . . the systems theorists would claim that the resultant 'big picture' covers the whole of reality, from atoms to cells to animals, from stars to planets to Gaia, from villages to towns to planetary federations. . . . And yet, and yet. Something is terribly wrong. Or rather, terribly partial. All of these [models] represent things that can be seen with the physical senses or their extensions (microscopes, telescopes). They are all, all of them, how the universe looks from the *outside*. They are all the outward forms of evolution, and not one of them represents how evolution looks from the inside, how the individual holons feel and perceive and cognize the world at various stages. . . . So [these models] themselves are not wrong (once we have revised a few errors), but terribly partial. They leave out the insides of the universe."[7]

In other words, they fail to acknowledge the existence of the Kosmos. In other words, it is absolutely essential that the current version of holism, which is based on the natural sciences, should be supplemented with knowledge of the inner dimension, and thus according to Wilber we need to refer first to psychology and second to the spiritual traditions. For it is in this interior realm, and not in the world of quantum physics or evolutionary biology, that we will find the spiritual dimension.

INDIVIDUAL AND CULTURAL PROGRESS

Wilber had already described the evolutionary stages of consciousness at some length in *The Atman Project*, which discussed development from the point of view of individual psychology, and in *Up from Eden*, which examined development from the point of view of the collective culture. In *Sex, Ecology, Spirituality* Wilber describes these parallel processes of development again. This time Jean Piaget serves as a guide to individual development and Jürgen Habermas acts as a guide to socio-cultural development.

Wilber explains why he chooses to draw on Piaget's system:

> Nowhere have the vicissitudes of the mind's developmental emergence been chartered in greater detail than in the works of Jean Piaget; and although nobody imagines that Piaget's system is without its own inadequacies, nonetheless the wealth of research and data that he and his colleagues generated over a four-decade

period stands as one of a handful of the truly great contributions to psychology (and philosophy and religion).

Without, therefore, endorsing all of the Piagetian system, I would like to draw on his data (and some of his conclusions) to point out very carefully the nature of the mind's development from archaic to magic to mythic to mental, as it appears in today's ontogeny [individual development].[8]

As far as Habermas is concerned, like Wilber he too is a social philosopher who has studied the problem of cultural evolution in considerable depth by comparing the forms that society took in the past with the forms that society takes today. In doing so Habermas deliberately incorporates Piaget's ideas regarding cognitive development and Kohlberg's ideas regarding moral development. In his opinion there is clearly a parallel—albeit in a formal sense, and not in terms of every last detail—between the development of the individual and the evolution of humanity as a whole. Although few philosophers now endorse the theory that individual development recapitulates cultural development, Habermas believes that a modified version of this theory is still valid and useful.

According to Habermas (and Wilber), broadly speaking, cultural history can be divided up into three main periods.

	nature of the culture	level of identity	types of thinking	stages of the Self
3	rational	ego	formop	world centric
2	mythic	group	conop	socio/ethnocentric
1	magic	body	preop	bio/egocentric
	Gebser	Habermas	Piaget	Wilber

FIGURE 6.1.   The three stages of individual and cultural development

During the first phase the culture is magical, the individual identifies himself primarily as his body (and is therefore also heavily identified with his biological relatives), his thinking is pre-operational (thinking based on images), and his basic orientation is biocentric or egocentric. In the second phase the culture is more mythical, the individual is primarily identified with the role that he plays within society (and therefore with the group to which he belongs), his thinking is concrete-operational (thinking based on concrete concepts), and his basic orientation is sociocentric or ethnocentric. During the third phase, the phase in which we now find ourselves, the culture is rational, the individual has become an autonomous individual (with an ego), his thinking is formal-operational (thinking based on abstract concepts), and his basic orientation is what Wilber would describe as worldcentric.

Thus in Wilber's view the development of the ego goes hand in hand with the broadening of the mental horizon from identification with one's own body and kin, to the social group to which one belongs, to humanity as a whole, and by extension to all living beings. As part of this process egocentrism gradually recedes in light of the growing capacity to empathize with others. According to Wilber egoism is, paradoxically enough, the result of a *lack* of ego rather than too much ego, a fragile sense of self rather than a strong sense of self. Again in this context Wilber defends the ego that in alternative circles is seen as the root of all evil (which leads people to call for a regression to states that are prior to the ego). As far as Wilber is concerned the ego is not opposed to the spiritual but is a necessary step on the way towards the spiritual.

In the literature produced by the social sciences these three phases— magical, mythical, and rational, or egocentric, ethnocentric, and worldcentric— are known as preconventional, conventional, and postconventional respectively. The conventional level is regarded as the benchmark. Seen from this point of view, the preconventional toddler still lives entirely in his own closed world, the conventional child is geared to the group of which he is a part, while the postconventional adolescent deliberately distances himself from the group in order to be able to form his own opinions. How do these three concepts relate to the concepts of prepersonal, personal, and transpersonal outlined in this book? At first glance one might think that the three levels are synonymous, but as can be seen in the following figure, this is not the case.

4. 'post-postconventional'	transpersonal
3. post-conventional	**personal**
2. **conventional**	prepersonal
1. preconventional	prepersonal

FIGURE 6.2.   Core concepts in the social sciences and transpersonal psychology

As is indicated by the terms printed in bold, the norm is one step higher in the transpersonal literature: in this case the personal level is regarded as the benchmark, which corresponds to the postconventional rather than the conventional. The social scientific literature does not have a term that corresponds to the transpersonal level in view of the fact that so far social scientists have shown little interest in the field of spirituality (a state of affairs that Wilber endeavored to rectify with his book *A Sociable God*). This being the case he is forced to use the construction "post-postconventional," in other words, a state of consciousness that transcends the rational individual autonomous level of the ego, and for this reason can be said to be "transpersonal." Wilber is convinced that there is a vast amount of empirical and phenomenological evidence that testifies to the existence of these four stages in the cultural and individual development of the individual.

There is not yet much scientific evidence of transpersonal or post-postconventional stages, but this is hardly surprising given the relative rarity of these stages in our culture. Nevertheless, we are not entirely without guidelines, for according to Wilber in this respect the mystics of the past are our guides. The great mystics may have lived in the past but, as Wilber has observed, not only were they way ahead of their own times, they were also way ahead of *our* time. In this sense they actually represent our future.[9] Thus as far as Wilber is concerned, mystic spirituality is not a nostalgic look back to the past, but rather essentially looks forward. Wilber then goes on to describe the four stages of mysticism that he had already outlined in his earlier work. This time he describes these stages in greater detail by referring to individuals who represent these four stages: Emerson, Teresa of Avila, Meister Eckhart, and Ramana Maharshi.

In Wilber's opinion the work of the American mystic Ralph Waldo Emerson is a good example of the experience of a *nature mystic*, who apprehends a deeper reality within the visible aspect of nature (and who has developed faculties that are typical of the psychic stage). He sees the Spanish mystic Teresa of Avila as a typical example of a *theistic mystic*, in her emphasis on the relationship of the soul to God (which is characteristic of the subtle stage). *Monistic mysticism*, in which the distinction between the soul and God is abandoned in favor of a sense of identity with the divine (which is characteristic of the causal stage), is described in the work of the German mystic Meister Eckhart (who used the term *Godhead* to refer to this sense of identity). And finally, *nondualist mysticism*, which sees no distinction between God/Godhead and the world (and is characteristic of the ultimate stage), is also evident in Eckhart's work and is even more apparent in Eastern traditions such as Hinduism (Ramana Maharshi) or Zen Buddhism.

Wilber considers the type of thinking that becomes possible at the existential centaur level to be crucial in this respect because it prepares the way for the transpersonal stages of development. He calls this type of thinking "vision-logic" or "network-logic," referring to the capacity to recognize that different and apparently contradictory views can be true at the same time if they are perceived as partial truths within the greater whole of the Truth. In his opinion this is an absolute prerequisite for the kind of global open-mindedness that does not degenerate into indiscriminate tolerance: "It is the integrative power of vision-logic, I believe, and not the indissociation of tribal magic or the imperialism of mythic involvement that is desperately needed on a global scale. For it is vision-logic with its centauric/planetary worldview that, in my opinion, holds the only hope for the integration of the biosphere and noosphere, the supranational organization of planetary consciousness, the genuine recognition of ecological balance, the unrestrained and unforced forms of global discourse, the nondominating and noncoercive forms of federal states, the unrestrained flow of worldwide communicative exchange, the production of genuine world citizens, and the enculturation of female agency (i.e., the integration of male and female in both the noosphere and the biosphere)—all of which, in my opinion, is nevertheless simply the platform for the truly interesting forms of higher and transpersonal states of consciousness lying yet in our collective future—if there is one."[10]

THE FOUR QUADRANTS

In *Sex, Ecology, Spirituality* Wilber added a radical new idea to his model by explicitly introducing three different dimensions in addition to the individual-psychological dimension that had been central in his work up until this point: the material dimension, the social dimension, and the cultural dimension. He arrived at these four quarters after having compared the numerous models of development presented in the scientific and philosophical literature, which led him to discover that this complex mass of material could be ordered on the basis of a simple classification criterion. Some models were concerned with individual development, while others were concerned with collective development; some studied the individual from the outside while others studied the individual from the inside. This gave rise to four quadrants defined by two axes: the interior/exterior axis and the individual/collective axis.

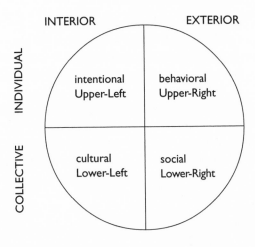

FIGURE 6.3   The four quadrants of consciousness

For the same reason there are also four distinct disciplines in the social sciences—separate fields of study that often find it difficult to relate to one another. The behaviorism of modern cognitive science focuses exclusively on the "exterior-individual" or the behavioral aspect of the individual and considers the other aspects to be irrelevant, incapable of investigation, or even nonexistent. On the other hand, introspective psychology (and also psychotherapy for example) is specifically interested in the "interior-individual" or intentional aspect of consciousness and seeks to make the inner experience of the individual the object of serious study. The cultural sciences study the "interior-collective" or cultural aspect of consciousness by looking at the mentality of different groups of people, while sociology studies the "exterior-collective" or social aspect of consciousness, focusing exclusively on group processes that can be perceived objectively. Each of these disciplines tends to see itself as the only one that is right, which has inevitably led to disastrous fragmentation within the social sciences. We are now faced with the task of studying all of these phenomena in relation to one another.[11]

Up until now Wilber had focused mainly on the Upper-Left quadrant in his works. The core of his early work was essentially a stage model of individual personal and transpersonal development (the Wilber 3 stage of his thinking, see Chapter 4). However, Wilber was now convinced that this quadrant needed to be supplemented with the other three quadrants. Although he had already outlined the socio-cultural correlations of the individual stages of development in *Up from Eden*, in *Sex, Ecology, Spirituality* he proceeds to do so in a more systematic manner. In light of this new phase in his thinking, Wilber refers to his recent view of development, as depicted by the four quadrants, as "Wilber 4."[12] Wilber 4 not only describes the nine stages of development identified in Wilber 3, but it also sets out these nine stages within the context of the other three quadrants, which gives rise to a complex rose-like figure containing 36 cells.

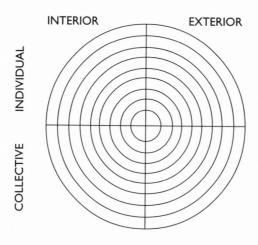

FIGURE 6.4.   The four quadrants with their nine levels

One of the main advantages of this four-quadrant model is that it makes it possible to identify all kinds of precise correlations between domains that might not appear to be at all related to one another at first sight. It also enables us to transcend meaningless platitudes, such as the obvious fact that there is an interaction between the individual and the culture and between consciousness and the brain. With the aid of this model we can be more precise about the nature of the interaction. This is best illustrated if we look at one of the levels in detail, such as the level of abstract thought.

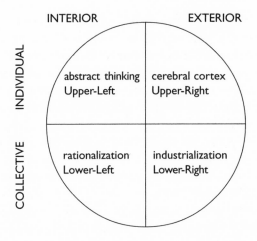

INTERIOR   EXTERIOR

INDIVIDUAL

abstract thinking   cerebral cortex
Upper-Left   Upper-Right

COLLECTIVE

rationalization   industrialization
Lower-Left   Lower-Right

FIGURE 6.5.   The four quadrants of consciousness: an example.

The individual is capable of abstract thought (Upper-Left quadrant) on account of the fact that the neocortex has developed in the brain (Upper-Right quadrant). This does not mean that the neocortex generates thought, but that it is a necessary prerequisite for it. Individuals who are capable of abstract thought will create a culture (Lower-Left quadrant) that is rational (as opposed to the older magic and mythic cultures), while the social order (Lower-Right quadrant) will be dominated by industrialization—the production of goods in a rational technical way. By the same token the human individual will also be influenced by the culture and the society in which he finds himself. According to Wilber, all four quadrants are necessary for an integral theory of consciousness. None of the four quadrants may be reduced to any of the others. We cannot resort to the simplistic view that cerebral processes determine everything, or that we are entirely formed by the culture in which we live, or that our social position has an overriding impact on our thinking, or that our thinking develops completely independently of any other environmental factors.

An early version of this way of thinking can be found in the work of the economist E. F. Schumacher, who is known for his plea for a small-scale approach ("small is beautiful"). In a lesser known work, *A Guide for the Perplexed* (1977), like Wilber he too calls for a hierarchical view of reality which recognizes the various levels of existence—matter, life, consciousness, and self-awareness—that find their expression in minerals, plants, animals, and people respectively.[13] In the same book Schumacher also makes a distinction between four fields of knowledge: (1) one's own invisible inner experiences, (2) the invisible inner experiences of others, (3) one's own visible outer appearance, and (4) the visible outer appearance of others.[14] Clearly there is a striking similarity between these four fields of knowledge and Wilber's four quadrants.[15] Schumacher says that there are two things that we can be sure of: our own inner experiences and the visible outer appearance of others. And there are two other things that we are far less sure of: how we are perceived from the outside and what goes on in the invisible inner world of others.[16] Wilber formulates these four domains as follows: (1) the intentional, (2) the cultural, (3) the behavioral, and (4) the social. Wilber differs from Schumacher in that he presents these four domains in a circle, which reveals all kinds of interactions. He also relates them to the different levels of existence and establishes explicit links with the various fields of science. Nevertheless in my opinion Schumacher clearly deserves a certain amount of credit for the original idea.

According to Wilber these four quadrants can now be reduced to three segments: the whole of the exterior domain (individual and collective, behavioral and social) can only be described in objective or 'it' language; the interior-individual or intentional can only be described in 'I' language; and the interior-collective or cultural domain can only be described in 'we' language.

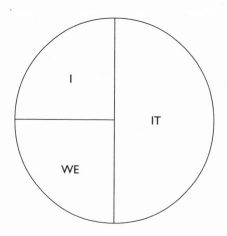

FIGURE 6.6.   The three segments: 'I,' 'we,' and 'it'.

Like the four quadrants, none of the three languages can be reduced to any of the others. A scientist examining the brain will always describe the brain in terms of 'it' language (neurological processes), while we can only ever describe our own experiences in 'I' language. A purely neurological theory of consciousness will always fall short because it cannot account for the element of subjective experience. Wilber goes on to associate these three segments—the 'I,' the 'we,' and the 'it'—with the traditional disciplines of aesthetics, ethics, and science, each of which is searching for the Beautiful, the Good, and the True.

THE COLLAPSE INTO FLATLAND

In Book Two of *Sex, Ecology, Spirituality* Wilber looks at why Western culture has chosen to reject this multidimensional view of reality. Why are these traditional concepts not generally accepted? According to Wilber the reason for this is that over the centuries the modern individual has become an inhabitant of "flatland," where in order to be valid knowledge must be based on the physical reality perceived by the senses, while the inner world of the human individual is treated as suspect and often dismissed out of hand as subjective. Wilber then goes on to present an in-depth analysis of the process of modernization that has dominated Western culture since the age of the Enlightenment.

Some believe that the process of modernization has brought nothing but good, while others contend that it has killed off all religiosity. But according to Wilber modernism has both a positive side and a negative side. The good news of the modern era is—and here Wilber joins ranks with social scientists such as Max Weber and Jürgen Habermas—that art, ethics, and science are now clearly differentiated from one another and have been able to develop without the imposition of constraints. In the past both art and science were heavily restricted by the prevailing religion, but following the division of Church and State and the emancipation of science, this is fortunately no longer the case.

However, the downside of this development is that science, which due to the nature of its investigation is solely concerned with the domain perceived by the senses, has since come to dominate or "colonize" (to use Habermas's term) both art and ethics, which are dismissed as unscientific despite the fact that they represent domains that are just as relevant or possibly even more relevant than the world perceived by the senses. Particularly as a result of the rise of technology and the industrialization based on technology, Western culture has become increasingly one-dimensional—a world that Wilber refers to as "flatland."

According to Wilber the best way to deal with this situation is not to seek to return to the time before art, ethics, and science were differentiated—an era that was definitely not as rose-colored as the romantics would have us believe—but to make a progressive effort to integrate art, ethics, and science. However, this does not mean that art and ethics are to be given a scientific foundation, even if such a thing were possible, but that science should heed the requirements of ethics, and that art should be recognized as a valuable and fully legitimate human activity. As individuals it is up to us to learn to function in all three spheres—'I,' 'we,' and 'it'—or in all four quadrants of life.

ASCENDING AND DESCENDING SPIRITUALITY

A second new framework that Wilber introduces in *Sex, Ecology, Spirituality* in addition to the four quadrants is the notion of ascending and descending spirituality. According to the traditional view, which Wilber feels is best expressed in the West by Plato, Plotinus, and the Neoplatonist schools of thought, there are two fundamental movements in the Kosmos: an upward movement that ascends from matter to Spirit and a downward movement that descends from Spirit to matter. In other words, the Kosmos is a multidimensional whole of ascending and descending streams of divine Love. Or to express it in Eastern terms: by ascending towards Spirit, the individual acquires wisdom; by descending towards matter, the individual expresses compassion. Ascending spirituality is masculine, celestial, and transcendent; descending spirituality is feminine, earthly, and immanent.[17]

For a long time the West has been held in the grip of a spiritual ideal that focuses purely on the ascent from matter to Spirit. The individual was advised to reject the so-called lower reality of the body and sexuality and to aspire towards the Divine. However, when science removed religion from its pedestal, the aspiration changed: we ourselves would turn the world into a paradise. Although this in itself is a respectable endeavor, it degenerated into a lifestyle of maximal consumption that focuses purely on the visible world. All sense of proportion has been lost. All forms of ascent—spiritual growth, thinking in terms of stages, qualitative distinctions—are treated with suspicion; while the various forms of descent—Marxism, humanism, liberalism, consumerism—often result in an extremely one-dimensional view of the human being.

Within the context of flatland—where things that are not visible are not real and physical needs are the only real needs—the ideal of descending spirituality has degenerated into an attempt to create heaven on earth by simply denying the existence of heaven. However, it is one thing to endeavor to satisfy the physical needs of humanity, but it is another thing entirely to claim that physical needs are the *only* real needs. Wilber often refers to this last notion as a "completely descended" view of things. Again in this case the distinction between the terms *fundamental* and *significant* helps to clarify the matter. The need for food is the most fundamental human need; thus working to solve the food crisis in the world a highly ethical form of action. But if this is taken too far, and intellectuals are murdered for attempting to satisfy "higher needs" that are in fact more significant, as has happened in Marxist countries, all sense of proportion has been lost.

According to Wilber there is only one way of resolving this situation: we have to reinstate the traditional notion of the multidimensional Kosmos. In doing so, we do not need to return to the Middle Ages, nor do we have to set aside the achievements of science. On the contrary: if anything, the scientific search for knowledge gains even more of an emphasis when set against the background of the traditional worldview, certainly if we see it as a multidimensional approach that encompasses many different forms of knowledge—natural science, social science, and spiritual science. According to Wilber we also need to preserve the ideal of ascending spirituality if we want to continue to be able to see the process of human development in the right perspective. Only then will the ideal of descending spirituality that seeks to create a better world retain sufficient depth. In the ideal society *all* of the individual's needs are met—physical needs, psychological needs, *and* spiritual needs. Above all the inner needs tend to be overlooked in the materialist Western society, and this is true not only in capitalist countries but also in socialist countries.

In presenting this multidimensional view of things Wilber was able to show how popular holism is in fact a distortion of the traditional spiritual worldview. Holism often sees itself as the great adversary of materialism, the reductionistic approach of the atomism that currently reigns supreme in the world of science, which attempts to reduce everything to subatomic particles. However, as far as Wilber is concerned the conflict between holism and atomism—the world is a whole versus the world is made up of particles—is actually rearguard action that masks the real issue: do people in our culture still have access to depth and interiority?

Though it styles itself as spiritual, in its excessive emphasis on natural sciences such as quantum physics and biology, holism is in fact extremely reductionistic. Wilber describes this as "subtle reductionism" in contrast to the "gross reductionism" that tries to reduce reality to subatomic particles. Subtle reductionism is more treacherous: it rejects atomism but attempts to conceive of reality as a Whole that contains nothing more than the physical reality that can be perceived by the senses. According to Wilber only the traditional worldview of the multidimensional Kosmos does away with both gross reductionism and subtle reductionism in that it sees every-thing in its right relationship to everything else and, in particular, it also includes the dimension of interiority.

AN INTERVIEW . . . WITH HIMSELF

Because Wilber was well aware that the first part of his *Kosmos* trilogy would be too much for many readers to digest, shortly after he had com-pleted *Sex, Ecology, Spirituality*, he wrote a popular summary of the trilogy which also covered themes from the second and third volumes of *Kosmos* (feminism and postmodernism respectively). This summary was published a year later under the playful title of *A Brief History of Everything* (1996).[18] Wilber wrote the book in the form of a fictitious interview in which he was both the interviewer and the interviewee—a device that helped to make the book very accessible. While writing the book, he decided that he would rely solely on his own ready knowledge, and apart from a handful exceptions he would dispense with quotes and references so as not to encumber the book any more than was necessary.[19] *A Brief History of Everything* will undoubt-edly replace *No Boundary* as Wilber's most popular book.

A Brief History of Everything is made up of three parts. In Part One Wilber discusses the emergence of matter and life; in Part Two he dis-cusses the unfolding of consciousness through the various stages of devel-opment—prepersonal, personal, and transpersonal—and in Part Three he discusses the problems of flatland, the modern denial of the existence of the Kosmos, and the superficial world of our contemporary culture. This last theme is elaborated even more clearly in *A Brief History of Everything* than in *Sex, Ecology, Spirituality*.

THE FOUR QUADRANTS REVISITED

In *A Brief History of Everything* Wilber explains the relationship between the four quadrants with the aid of a simple example. The thought "I'll go to the grocers" is not a single isolated event. Naturally it starts out with the thought that occurs to the person concerned, which evokes images, concepts, and memories (Upper-Left quadrant). At the same time there are all kinds of chemical processes going on in the brain—brain waves, neurotransmitters, perceptible behavior (Upper-Right quadrant). But the individual thought is expressed via the cultural phenomenon of language and only has any meaning in relation to a specific cultural background (Lower-Left quadrant); and then there are also socioeconomic factors such as the existence of shops (Lower-Right quadrant). Thus even something as simple as a single thought will always involve four aspects: intentional, behavioral, cultural, and social.

According to Wilber this kind of analysis also needs to be applied to the possibility of a future spiritual culture. Many holistic authors are expecting to see some kind of transformation in the near future, or they claim that our culture has reached a turning point, but Wilber is far more restrained in his expectations. He asks: what would a spiritual culture that takes all four quadrants into account look like?

> So what we will want to talk about, I suppose, is how this coming transformation—and the higher spiritual stages—will appear and manifest in all four quadrants. What is a higher Self? What is a higher brain functioning? What is the transformation of the body as well as of the mind? What is a higher or deeper culture? How is it embedded in wider social systems? What is more profoundly developed consciousness? How is it anchored in new social institutions? Where is the sublime?
>
> What would all of this look like? How can we help it along in all of these quadrants, and not just focus on Self, or just Gaia, or just the World Federation? For all of these will emerge together, or they will emerge not at all.[20]

Thus according to Wilber spiritual development in individuals will have an impact on the culture and the social order as a whole. Spiritual development is not an isolated, subjective phenomenon that has no effect on the outer world. According to Wilber spirituality also has an inescapable political dimension.

The model of the four quadrants can also be simplified in another way.[21] The four quadrants can be divided up into a Left half and a Right half. These two opposing halves appear to be responsible for a great many philosophical and scientific controversies:

From virtually the inception of every major knowledge quest, East and West alike, the various approaches have fallen into one or another of these two great camps, interior versus exterior, Left versus Right. We find this in psychology (Freud vs. Watson), in sociology (Weber vs. Comte), in philosophy (Heidegger vs. Locke), in anthropology (Taylor vs. Lenski), in linguistics (hermeneutics vs. structuralism)—and even in theology (Augustine vs. Aquinas)!

Occasionally you find an approach that emphasizes both the Left and Right Hand dimensions, which of course would be my recommendation, but mostly you find a bitter war between these two equally important, but rarely integrated, approaches. So I think it's crucial to understand the contributions that both of these paths have made to our understanding of the human condition, because both of them are absolutely indispensable.

And, as we'll soon see, it's virtually impossible to understand higher and spiritual developments without taking both of these paths into account.[22]

According to Wilber each of the four quadrants has its own form of valid knowledge. In the Upper-Right quadrant (behavioral) valid knowledge is objective *truth* sought through the empirical establishment of perceivable facts. In the Upper-Left quadrant (intentional), however, the valid knowledge is subjective *truthfulness*, the accurate perception of one's own inner state. What matters in this case is honesty, not only in relation to other people but also in relation to oneself. In the Lower-Left quadrant (cultural) it is more a question of the reaching of mutual understanding between different individuals, what Wilber calls *justness* or "the common good." And the Lower-Right quadrant (social) is concerned with the way in which the individual fits within larger systems or wholes. Wilber refers to this as *functional fit*. This is the domain of systems theory.

In this part of the book Wilber also discusses postmodernism, a philosophical movement that has a great many supporters in the academic world of the humanities. The main proposition of postmodernism is that the typically modern value of progress can no longer be upheld in a century that has witnessed two world wars. The postmodernists argue that it is not possible to express valid value judgements of any cultural or religious forms of expression. What we are left with is an interminable cultural diversity in which nothing is more valuable than anything else. Wilber points to the contradiction inherent in this standpoint—if it is impossible to make valid value judgements, postmodernism itself cannot claim to be true!—and he attempts to incorporate the useful insights of postmodernism in his model. He agrees that with the idea that everything needs to be seen in its cultural context, as the postmodernists claim, but he adds that these contexts are ranged in a series, as he has shown in many of his books. The very existence of this series makes it possible to express value judgements since the higher stages of development are, by definition, more valuable than the lower stages.

GLOBAL CONSCIOUSNESS AS A PLATFORM

In Part Two of *A Brief History of Everything* Wilber again explains the nine-stage model that he had described in *Transformations of Consciousness*, this time in a somewhat more informal manner. In his view human development is a process that is moving towards global consciousness. During the first stages of development the ego is bound to the body, or biocentric; it then learns to adapt to the surrounding culture, becoming socio- or ethnocentric; and subsequently it attains a certain level of independence, developing a rational ego that can think universally or globally, and becomes worldcentric. Thus this global consciousness is the result of a long and difficult process of development. During this process the horizon of the self expands from its own organism, to the group to which it belongs, to humanity as a whole.

Wilber then says that all subsequent spiritual or transpersonal stages of development will have this global consciousness as a platform. This involves an attitude of tolerance and the recognition of the validity of different points of view. This does not mean that there should be unquestioning acceptance of phenomena such as ethnocentrism or racism, on the pretext that everyone is entitled to their own opinion. In other words, any view that is less all-encompassing than the worldcentric point of view is likely to be subject to criticism. The modern individual who sees himself as a world citizen will simply not countenance views in which certain people or a certain religion are seen as privileged.

Once again Wilber describes the four stages of spiritual development, which in his opinion follow on from the stage of the rational ego:

Some traditions are so sophisticated they have literally hundreds of minute divisions of the various stages and components of consciousness development. But, based on the state of present research, it is fairly safe to say that there are *at least four major stages* of transpersonal development or evolution.

These four stages I call the *psychic*, the *subtle*, the *causal* and the *nondual*. These are *basic structures*, and so of course each of them has a different *worldview*, which I call, respectively, *nature mysticism, deity mysticism, formless mysticism, and nondual mysticism.*[23]

According to Wilber these future stages of individual development can be characterized as follows. The *psychic* individual perceives a deeper reality within the visible aspect of nature. Wilber speaks of the World Soul or the Eco-Noetic Self in order to indicate that this is not simply a piece of systems theory solely concerned with objectively perceivable elements. The *subtle* individual leaves the visible world and achieves a blissful unity with his own higher Self, which is sometimes experienced as a deity outside of himself. The *causal* individual goes a step further and discovers the Emptiness, which forms the basis of all reality, out of which this Self has emerged. Thus the Self, which can ultimately never be perceived as an interior or exterior object, is experienced as Emptiness.

At this point in a certain sense the spiritual journey has come to an end. Yet according to Wilber in some spiritual traditions there is an even deeper stage—that of *nondual mysticism*. In this case the world is no longer experienced as something that can be perceived, the nondual mystic becomes one with the world, or, to be more precise, the nondual mystic *becomes* the world. All distinction between inner and outer, subject and object, disappears. In the passages in which Wilber describes this stage he shows his command of these subtle mystic nuances. It is as if he wants to give the reader a foretaste, even it is only through reading his book, of the nondual world of "One Taste" in which Spirit is omnipresent. This is Wilber at his best:

This is definitely not a state that is hard to get into, but rather one that is impossible to avoid. It has always been so. There has never been a moment when you did not experience One Taste— it is the only constant in the entire Kosmos, it is the only reality in all of reality. In a million billion years, there has never been single second that you weren't aware of this Taste; there has never been a single second where it wasn't directly in your Original Face like a blast of arctic air.

Of course, we have often lied to ourselves about this, we have often been untruthful about this, the universe of One Taste, the primordial sound of one hand clapping, our own Original Face. And the nondual traditions aim, not to bring about this state, because that is impossible, but simply to *point it out* to you so that you can no longer ignore it, no longer lie to yourself about who you really are.[24]

Wilber concludes his description of the nondual view with the words: "So the call of the Nondual traditions is: Abide as Emptiness, embrace all Form. The liberation is in the Emptiness, never in the Form, but Emptiness embraces all forms as a mirror all its objects. So the Forms continue to arise, and, as the sound of one hand clapping, you are all those Forms. You are the display. You and the universe are One Taste. Your Original Face is the purest Emptiness, and therefore every time you look in the mirror, you see only the entire Kosmos."[25]

In the Grip of Flatland

This exalted view is certainly not commonplace in our Western culture. In Part Three of *A Brief History of Everything* Wilber goes on to analyze the reasons why this should be so, basing his analysis on a number of cultural-historic considerations. In his eyes it is extremely ironic that the most advanced culture in history should harbor the most superficial worldview. In his opinion this is due to the fact that the multidimensional Kosmos has collapsed into the cosmos of matter, giving rise to the prevailing ideology of "flatland." Given that this is the case, we are now faced with the task of surfacing from this derailment—which in a certain sense was unavoidable—by once again spelling out the many dimensions of the Kosmos one by one. The subjective domain of art and religion needs to be reinstated, without us having to return to the prescientific eras of the past. According to Wilber we need to seek out ways that will lead us to a contemporary and progressive form of spirituality. In this respect Wilber joins ranks with the German idealist philosophers of the eighteenth century, who in his opinion made a certain amount of progress in this respect before the West resorted to a materialistic worldview.

Wilber then divides contemporary culture into two camps—the Ego camp and the Eco camp. While the rationalists in the Ego camp tend to emphasize the progress of Western history and are occasionally guilty of *repressing* biological reality in the process, the romantics in the Eco camp often tend to reject the achievements of Western culture, calling for a *regression* to states that existed in the past, which are considered to be more spiritual. As far as Wilber is concerned, both of these approaches are dead ends. Instead he calls for a future-oriented, *progressive* spirituality that includes both the biosphere and the noosphere within the greater whole of the theosphere or mysticism.

According to Wilber a culture based on these spiritual insights is not safeguarded against problems. On the contrary, in comparison with a relatively undeveloped culture, in a more developed culture there is far more that can go wrong. The 'culture gap' between the lowest stages of development and the highest stages of development within a more developed culture is constantly increasing as it were, since even in a highly enlightened society each individual always has to start from scratch. In other words, in a more developed culture the developmental process gets longer and longer, which means that there is more opportunity for things to go wrong along the way. But, as Wilber points out, in order to be able even to acknowledge the existence of the culture gap, we will first have to say farewell to the ideology of flatland.

THE EYE OF SPIRIT

In 1996, the year in which *A Brief History of Everything* was published, three issues of *ReVision*—the journal that Wilber had helped to set up at the end of the seventies but with which he had had no ties since the beginning of the eighties—were entirely dedicated to Wilber's view. This was the first time that his colleagues within the transpersonal field gathered together to voice their criticism and appreciation of his work. The series was prompted by the polemical nature of some of the endnotes in *Sex, Ecology, Spirituality*, which had alarmed a number of the transpersonal theorists. But, even more importantly, Wilber's main opponents within the transpersonal field—people such as Stanislav Grof and Michael Washburn—were forced to clarify their standpoint in relation to Ken Wilber's view. In the last of the three issues Wilber was then given an opportunity to respond to the various points of criticism in some depth.

Following the publication of this series of articles in *ReVision*, in January 1997 a conference aimed at a wider audience was organized to discuss Wilber's views. With the exception of Stanislav Grof and Michael Washburn, the authors of the articles in the *ReVision* series appeared as speakers at the conference. True to his principles Wilber himself did not appear at the conference. However, immediately prior to the conference a new book was released, entitled *The Eye of Spirit: An Integral Vision for a World Gone Slightly Mad* (1997), which contained the reflections that had been published in *ReVision* together with a number of new essays.

In *The Eye of Spirit* Wilber presented an analysis of his own intellectual development—it is this analysis that we have been following in this book. Naturally his views had evolved over the twenty years that had elapsed since he wrote *The Spectrum of Consciousness*. Some of those who were criticizing his work were basing their criticism on ideas that he himself had already rejected or further elaborated. It was this that led Wilber to plot the line of his own intellectual development.

THE INTEGRAL APPROACH

The foreword to *The Eye of Spirit* gives the impression that Wilber is increasingly interested in the relationship between spirituality and politics. He will undoubtedly write a monograph on the subject at some point. He says that he is in search of a "liberal God," in other words, a view of religion that is compatible with science or with the spirit of free investigation—that gave rise to science. The political landscape in the United States is divided up into two camps. In the one corner is the liberal camp which stands for individual economic and political freedom but is often averse to religion. In the other corner is the conservative camp, which wishes to center on religion (in other words, Christianity which is predominantly mythical) and to honor community values, but often proceeds to sacrifice the intellectual freedom of the individual in the process by prescribing how the individual is supposed to attain salvation. In this instance economic tyranny is opposed to cultural tyranny.[26] Wilber is one of a number of more progressive thinkers who are currently investigating the option of a "third way."

Again in this case Wilber endeavors to unite the best of both traditions—seeking to integrate conflicting views has by this point become second nature to him. Is there not an overall view which regards the spiritual as central in all dimensions of life but still allows scope for intellectual freedom? Don't we need a view of Spirit that goes beyond mythical, dogmatic religion?

> In short, can we not find a spiritual liberalism? a spiritual humanism? an orientation that sets the rights of the individual in deeper spiritual contexts that do not deny those rights but ground them? Can a new conception of God, of Spirit, find resonance with the noblest aims of liberalism? Can these two modern enemies—God and liberalism—in any way find a common ground?
>
> I believe that there is no more pressing question, of any variety, now facing the modern and postmodern world.[27]

Wilber goes on to add: "Almost all of my books (especially *The Atman Project*; *Up from Eden*; *Eye to Eye*; *A Sociable God*; *Sex, Ecology, Spirituality*;

and *A Brief History of Everything*) are prolegomena to exactly that topic: the search for a liberal God, a liberal Spirit, a spiritual humanism or humanistic spiritualism, or whatever word we finally decide will capture the essence of this orientation."[28]

He himself uses the word *integral*:

I have chosen the word integral to represent this overall approach. Integral means integrative, inclusive, comprehensive, balanced; the idea is to apply this integral orientation to the various fields of human knowledge and endeavours, including the integration of science and spirituality. This integral approach is important not simply for politics alone; it deeply alters our conception of psychology and the human mind; of anthropology and human history; of literature and human meaning; of philosophy and the quest for truth—all of those, I believe, are profoundly altered by an integral approach that seeks to bring together the best of each of these fields in a mutually enriching dialogue. This book is an introduction to just that integral vision.[29]

Although the inner world of consciousness has been mapped out by a number of contemporary explorers, it has been charted above all by countless generations of spiritual seekers from cultures other than the West. The comparative study of all of these systems led Wilber to the idea that consciousness forms a kind of spectrum that stretches from the material to the spiritual, with numerous intermediate levels. The field of transpersonal psychology was particularly interested in this spectrum of consciousness. Nevertheless, Wilber is not suggesting that transpersonal psychology should automatically adopt all of the ideas that have come from the East.[30] According to Wilber recent research has also revealed a number of the shortcomings of the wisdom traditions. First, Eastern thinkers have failed to pay sufficient attention to the prepersonal stages of development. It was Western psychologists—those who followed in Freud's footsteps—who discovered all of the things that can go wrong in early youth. All forms of psychopathology can be classified as disturbances in the development of a mature personality. Second, according to Wilber, Eastern traditions have ignored the fact that spiritual development is not simply a subjective matter, but a process that also has social, cultural, and even biochemical correlates (See Fig. 6.7).

In the integral view that Wilber advocates, the worlds of East and West come together in an ingenious way. He himself likes to refer to it as an approach that encompasses "all levels" and "all quadrants." But what does this mean? According to Wilber the East has contributed to this approach in that it has managed not to lose sight of the fact that reality is layered, rather than being limited to the physical reality that can be perceived by the senses. Besides the level of matter, there are also other levels of existence that relate to life, soul, and spirit—and ultimately to God. These higher levels have a lot to do with our own interior. The West has contributed to this approach in that it has discovered that the human individual does not exist in isolation but is embedded in material and socio-cultural contexts. By combining these two schemes Wilber has arrived at an integral approach that encompasses "all levels" and "all quadrants," or "AQAL", in short.

Nine levels intersected by four quadrants give rise to 36 cells, each of which represents an aspect of consciousness. Some of these cells, particularly those that relate to the spiritual stages of development, have not yet been filled in. Nevertheless this scheme makes it possible to speculate on what a spiritual culture and society might look like. In this view the inner world of the individual is not the only aspect to be plotted in relation to the levels of existence through which consciousness evolves; the other

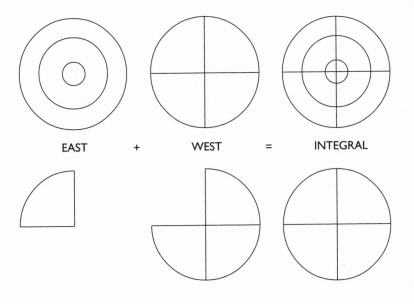

EAST   +   WEST   =   INTEGRAL

FIGURE 6.7.   The integral approach unites East and West (two versions)

three quadrants also do the same thing. Thus socio-cultural developments keep pace with individual development, and vice versa. And, according to Wilber, the material component, that is, the brain, also evolves in line with individual development.

This is one of the ways in which Wilber's scheme differs quite strikingly from the traditional depiction of the levels of existence. He no longer regards matter as the lowest level of reality, as he previously did, but as an aspect of reality that exists as a true parallel to all of the different levels. States of higher consciousness leave traces in the brain, as EEG measurements have shown. Even the highest state of mystical consciousness can be monitored with physical instruments. Secondly, Wilber regards the four quadrants as being of equal value. Rather than treating the Upper-Left quadrant as primary and regarding the other quadrants simply as contexts that influence the inner life of the individual, as far as Wilber is concerned, all four quadrants are constantly interacting with one another. It is as if Spirit expresses itself in four different ways.

IS HUMANITY EVOLVING?

Looking back on *Up from Eden* Wilber returned to the subject of cultural evolution, which many consider to be the most controversial aspect of his view. Can we really still believe in the idea of progress given the amount of human suffering in our century alone? The evidence tends to suggest that modern-day individuals are becoming more and more superficial, materialistic, and violent. Given that this is the case, isn't it terribly naive to claim that history is a process of progress and spiritual development?

Wilber takes this criticism very seriously: "Obviously, if consciousness evolution is to be used as any sort of explanatory principle, it faces several stern difficulties. What is therefore required is a set of tenets that can explain *both* advance and regression, good news and bad news, the ups and downs of an evolutionary thrust that is nonetheless as active in humans as it is in the rest of the Kosmos. Otherwise, we face the extremely bizarre situation of driving a virulent wedge right through the middle of the Kosmos: everything nonhuman operates by evolution; everything human does not."[31]

Wilber asked what principles might serve to rehabilitate the idea of cultural evolution, and in doing so reunite humanity with the rest of the Kosmos, while still being able to account for the ups and downs in the process of the development of consciousness. He came to the following conclusions.

The normal process of development proceeds by means of differentiation of the new stage and hierarchical integration of this new stage with all of the preceding stages. But there are all kinds of things that can go wrong along the way. For example, each new stage brings with it new problems not encountered at the previous stage. These problems can be extremely disturbing for the person concerned. Development can also occur too rapidly, which can lead to dissociation (a loss of contact with the preceding stages) or even repression (the previous stages are unconsciously repressed). A higher stage can even be held in the grip of preceding lower stages, which prevents it from functioning as it should.

This was what happened during the Second World War. According to Wilber atrocities such as Auschwitz, which are commonly cited as a counterargument to the idea of cultural evolution, were not the result of sound rationality—as the romantics have always claimed—but of a rationality that had fallen under the spell of a primitive *Blut und Boden* mythology. According to Wilber true rationality is capable of seeing through the narrow-mindedness of this group-bound mythology. In his opinion it is rationality that lays the foundation for a global culture based on tolerance.

It is easy to compare the problems of the modern era with the imagined advantages of the past, but if we take everything into the equation and weigh things up honestly, the present is seen to be an improvement on the past—even if it the picture is not quite as rosy as the naive faith in progress might have led us to believe. As far as Wilber is concerned, history is the development of Spirit, even if it occurs in fits and starts and occasionally falters.

THE EVER-PRESENT SPIRIT

The Eye of Spirit closes with a number of singularly beautiful passages in which Wilber induces in the reader an experience of transpersonal stages of consciousness, to the extent that this can be done via the written word. Once again he attempts to convey to the reader the insight of nondual mysticism, that ultimately everything is Spirit. This insight puts a definitive end to the search for Spirit, which was always based on the mistaken impression that Spirit was somehow absent. But throughout the search, both in the inner world and in the outer world, Spirit is always already present as the witnessing awareness itself. To understand this is the highest insight:

In other words, the ultimate reality is not something seen, but rather the ever-present Seer. Things that are seen come and go, are happy or sad, pleasant or painful—but the Seer is none of those things, and it does not come and go. The Witness does not waiver, does not wobble, does not enter the stream of time. The Witness is not an object, not a thing seen, but the ever-present Seer of all things, the simple Witness that is the I of Spirit, the center of the cyclone, the opening that is God, the clearing that is pure Emptiness.

There is never a time that you do not have access to this Witnessing awareness. At every single moment, there is a spontaneous awareness of whatever happens to be present—and that simple, spontaneous, effortless awareness is ever-present Spirit itself. Even if you think you don't see it, that very awareness is it. And thus, the ultimate state of consciousness—intrinsic Spirit itself—*is not hard to reach but impossible to avoid.*

And just that is the great and guarded secret of the Nondual schools.[32]

The reader might remember that Wilber also concluded his first book, *The Spectrum of Consciousness*, with this great insight. As vague as his understanding may have been at that stage, even at such a young age he already had a clear understanding of this truth. Twenty years on this understanding, which has since been deepened by years of meditation, has matured, and is now a more or less constant component of his daily existence.

According to Wilber, those who are able to rest in Spirit experience a sense of liberation, openness, and release from the woes of the objective world. Because Spirit can never be seen, at a certain point we give up all attempt to perceive it, and it is then that we find ourselves resting in Spirit. We discover that we could have done so all along without problems, without effort. Like a mirror we allow the experiences of life to file past without leaving a trace. Nevertheless we are fully present and fully conscious in every experience, but without any attachment.

Thus, as I right now rest in this simple, ever-present Witness, I am face to face with Spirit. I am with God today, and always, in this simple, ever-present, witnessing state. Eckhart said that "God is closer to me than I am to myself," because both God and I are one in the ever-present Witness, which is the nature of intrinsic Spirit itself, which is exactly what I am in the state of my I Amness. When I am not an object, I am God. (And every I in the entire Kosmos can say that truthfully.)[33]

According to Wilber, a person who experiences this enlightened state of consciousness will inevitably be moved to help others attain the same level of understanding. This is the classic bodhisattva ideal of Mahayana Buddhism. All of the talents and qualities that a person possesses—intelligence, compassion, artistic abilities, athletic abilities, discernment, combativeness, healing powers—are now expressed in their purest form as they are uplifted by Spirit and by the deep conviction that Spirit will ultimately overcome all obstacles.

THE INTEGRATION OF SCIENCE AND RELIGION

After having written *The Eye of Spirit* Wilber again felt the need to write a relatively simple book that would not suffer from the fact that it swamped the reader with quotes, footnotes, academic discussions, and other such asides. The book should only have one theme, and it was a theme that occurred to him spontaneously: the relationship between religion and science.[34] For many years he had considered this to be the most pressing issue of the modern world. Science and religion are still at odds with one another. Large parts of the world population espouse one religion or another; in the West many are drawn to science. Science gives us truth; religion gives us meaning. How can these two worlds be reconciled with one another?

In fact this is just another way of formulating the more fundamental question as to how our inner world and our outer world hang together. In philosophy this question is referred to as the mind/body problem. It is still a mystery how consciousness and the brain interact with one another. What seems to be so straightforward in our own experience—the fact that we gain impressions through our senses and express our feelings through gestures—is an intractable problem for those who are preoccupied with the precise relationship between the two. While Wilber does not claim to have hit upon the answer to a question that has confounded philosophers for centuries,[35] he does emphasize that, to start with, we need to see the two domains as equal partners. The Left Half is just as valid as the Right Half. A huge quantity of scientific evidence at least confirms the existence of such a thing as an inner dimension (Wilber is referring to the humanities in particular). Thus in *The Marriage of Sense and Soul*, published in 1998, he was not so much concerned with religion per se, but with the total inner world of the individual and with opposing the tenets of flatland ideology:

Flatland accepts no interior domain whatsoever, and reintroducing Spirit is the least of our worries.

Thus our task is not specifically to reintroduce spirituality and somehow attempt to show that modern science is becoming compatible with God. That approach, which is taken by most of the integrative attempts, does not go nearly deep enough in diagnosing the disease, and thus, in my opinion, never really addresses the crucial issues.

Rather, it is the rehabilitation of the *interior in general* that opens the possibility of reconciling science and religion.[36]

A CLOSER LOOK AT SCIENCE AND RELIGION

Wilber starts out by saying that in order for it to be possible to bridge the gap between science and religion, both will need to make an effort meet one another halfway. This does not mean that they will have to renounce their ideals, but that they will need to review their own essence and methods. Wilber asks both science and the religion to subject their aims and methods to close scrutiny.

What is science when it comes down to it? Can natural science, which is inevitably materialistic given the nature of its methods, serve as an example for other forms of science? What does it mean to say that knowledge must be based on empiricism? This is often interpreted to mean that knowledge must be based on information obtained by means of sensory perception. But as Wilber has endeavored to show in numerous places throughout his oeuvre, this results in an inadequate description of our world of experience. The doctrine of the three eyes recognizes the fact that in addition to physical experience there is also such a thing as mental experience and spiritual experience. These three types of experience form the basis for the three types of science: natural science, the humanities, and spiritual science. Thus according to Wilber all three forms of science should be regarded as empirical.

What these three types of science have in common is their scientific method. According to Wilber this involves three steps: (1) injunction, (2) apprehension, and (3) affirmation or rejection. In *The Marriage of Sense and Soul* he substantiates this statement by setting out his own philosophy of science.[37] Once again he shows his ability to integrate different philosophical movements with one another. The school of empiricism has always insisted on the fact that scientific knowledge must be based on experience—this relates to step 2, apprehension. Philosopher of science Thomas Kuhn has argued that scientific knowledge is not simply there for the taking, but the result of a certain research program or paradigm—this relates to step 1, injunction. And the philosopher Karl Popper believed that knowledge can only really be said to be scientific if it is refutable (or "falsifiable" as he called it)—this relates to step 3, affirmation or rejection. Thus Wilber arrived at an integral philosophy of science that incorporates all of the valuable contributions of the most influential schools of thought.

Science has nothing to lose by relinquishing its narrow-minded idea of what constitutes the "empirical." On the contrary, its field of research will simply increase in size. In the same vein, Wilber also suggested that religion should take a good look at itself. In his opinion this is essential if there is ever to be any rapprochement between science and religion:

> Just as science can, by its own admission, expand its scope from narrow empiricism to a broad empiricism, so religion can, as it were, restrict its scope from dogmatic proclamations to direct spiritual experience. In this move, with both parties surrendering an aspect of their traditional baggage that in fact serves neither of them well, science and religion would fast be approaching a common grounding in experiential data that finds the existence of rocks, mathematics and Spirit equally demonstrable.[38]

Religion will only have something of value to offer the modern world if it returns to its roots in direct spiritual experience:

> It is only when religion emhasizes its heart and soul and es-sence—namely, direct mystical experience and transcendental consciousness, which is disclosed not by the eye of flesh (give that to science) nor by the eye of mind (give that to philosophy) but rather by the eye of contemplation—that religion can both stand up to modernity and offer something for which modernity has a desperate need: a genuine, verifiable, repeatable injunction to bring forth the spiritual domain.
>
> Religion in the modern and postmodern world will rest on its unique strength—namely contemplation—or it will serve merely to support a premodern, predifferentiated level of development in its own adherents: not an engine for growth and transformation, but a regressive, antiliberal, reactionary force of lesser engagements.[39]

EARLIER ATTEMPTS AT INTEGRATION

In order to make his own view of science and religion that much more distinct, Wilber discusses earlier attempts at integration in some detail.

He examines the approaches proposed by romanticism, idealism, and postmodernism one after another. In his opinion each of these proposals falls short in relation to a number of essential points.

In Wilber's terminology romanticism stands for the attempt to return to a presupposed unity with the world that has been destroyed by the process of rationalization and modernization. In this context religion is situated entirely at the level of premodern thought. Nature is often deified and the direct experience of the body and the emotions is considered to be more essential than the intellect. In this respect all antirational approaches to spirituality— including in Wilber's opinion much of the New Age movement—can be termed "romantic." Joining forces with the criticism voiced by several German idealist philosophers, Wilber points out that nature is indeed divine but that this is even more so the case for the much maligned intellect. For as the old adage says, God slumbers in nature, begins to awaken in the human being, and is fully awake in the enlightened individual. The limitations of the intellect cannot be transcended by returning to the prerational, but by continuing to the transrational level of mysticism. As far as Wilber is concerned, German idealism was the last great philosophical movement that was still searching for openings for spirituality before the West was struck by the ideology of flatland. Yet in Wilber's opinion the stance of the idealists was considerably weakened by the fact that they did not have a methodical approach to spirituality, such as meditation, and in the absence of any such method could only rely on (essentially accurate) philosophical reflections.

Thus in *The Marriage of Sense and Soul* Wilber arrived at a more precise formulation of the paradox that our culture is both the most developed and the most superficial in the whole of human history:

The modern West is actually an intense combination of good news, bad news. The self or *subject* of rationality was *deeper* than the subject or self of mythology. . . . However—solely because of the collapse of the Kosmos—the *object* of rationality (which was confined to sensorimotor flatland) was much less deep than the object of mythology (which was the Divine order, however crudely or anthropomorphically depicted). Thus, a *much deeper subject confined its attention to a much shallower object.* And there, in a nutshell, the combination of dignity and disaster that is the paradox of modernity: a deeper subject in a shallower world.[40]

The postmodernists have elevated this superficiality to the status of a religion. So Wilber also examines the postmodernist philosophy that is currently setting the tone in the humanities. He makes a distinction between an extreme version of postmodernism, which he rejects, and a more moderate version, which he wishes to incorporate in his integral view. Extreme postmodernism denies the possibility of objective truth, qualitative distinction, or all-encompassing theory. Yet despite its passion to put everything into perspective, it does not go so far as to apply the same principle to its own standpoint—this is the essential contradiction in postmodernism that Wilber repeatedly points to. Nevertheless, in his opinion the more moderate version of postmodernism has made a very valuable contribution to a better understanding of reality. Wilber is entirely in agreement that our knowledge of reality is always relative and always has a subjective component. But this subjectivity of all knowledge should not lead us to conclude that therefore everything is true—and thus nothing is true. In Wilber's system this subjectivity is presented as the fact that our experience of reality is always colored by the stage of development at which we find ourselves. In this sense there is indeed no such thing as objective truth. But Wilber is firmly convinced that as we move from stage to stage we get closer and closer to this truth.

THE INTEGRAL AGENDA

At the end of *The Marriage of Sense and Soul* Wilber outlines the implications of this integral view of reality. And these implications affect both science and politics.

Wilber sees a new role for science. Its domain will increase enormously if in addition to examining the world revealed by sensory perception, it is also able to explore the mental and spiritual domains. Without knowing it, psychology has already charted much of this territory, particularly in the field of developmental psychology. Wilber has shown that many of the findings of orthodox psychology were consistent with the traditional notion of the Great Chain of Being. Transpersonal psychology then attempted to penetrate this inner domain still further. And it was not a coincidence that the worldview of the spiritual traditions served as a useful guide in this respect. But, according to Wilber, the really new contribution made by science is the discovery that the individual-psychological dimension is embedded in a number of socio-cultural contexts. And this insight also needs to be incorporated in an integral worldview. Wilber even sees a new role for strictly empirical science, in that all of the higher levels of consciousness leave their mark on cerebral processes. Even the highest stages of meditation can be examined with the aid of physical instruments. The physical world is not simply the lowest world in the series of spheres, argues Wilber, but a true parallel of these spheres on all levels.

According to Wilber, the existing research on higher states of consciousness now needs to be related to the findings of the more orthodox scientific approaches:

> What remains to be done is to begin correlating this data with the simultaneous and corresponding changes in the other quadrants, thus generating an "all level, all-quadrant" integral view. For example, what happens to brain physiology, neurotransmitter levels, and the organic body itself when individuals move through these higher developmental stages? How might these higher worldviews affect our political, social, and cultural institutions? If these higher stages are in fact stages of our own greater potentials, what types of integral techniques could facilitate this evolutionary growth? How will the higher stages of growth affect our democratic institutions, our educational policies, and our economics? How will higher development alter the practice of medicine? law? government? politics?
>
> In short, how will these stages of our own higher evolution manifest in all four quadrants? What higher art and science and morals await us? And what should we do about it now?[41]

Wilber outlines the political consequences of this integral view by pointing to the two kinds of Enlightenment that the world has known to date. Western Enlightenment brought us individual freedom and rights, an accomplishment that needs to be retained in any contemporary spiritual view. Eastern Enlightenment went further in that it offers us an insight into the spiritual stages of development that are open to all of us. According to Wilber, this progressive spirituality, which does not look back to the past but forward to the future, is very much in tune with the spirit of the times:

> The result, we might say, is a liberal Spirit, a liberal God, a liberal Goddess. In common with traditional liberalism, this stance agrees that the state shall not legislate the Good life. But with traditional conservatism, this stance places Spirit—and all its manifestations—at the very heart of the Good life, a Good life that therefore includes the relationships in all domains, from family to community to nation to globe to Kosmos to the Heart of the Kosmos itself, by any other name, God.[42]

THE TASTE OF ONENESS

Having placed such a strong emphasis on the importance of spirituality, eventually Wilber was more or less bound to write about his own experiences in this respect. So in 1997 he kept a journal in which he noted both his ordinary day-to-day concerns and his extraordinary mystical experiences. It also gave him an opportunity to try out a different literary genre on the way towards what might become a more personal style of writing. The journal was published in 1999 as *One Taste: The Journals of Ken Wilber*. Wilber uses the words *One Taste* to refer to the nondual experience of oneness of everything that exists—both in the inner world and in the outer world. This understanding, which can be regarded as the most profound mystical experience, has been his constant companion in recent years.

A DAY IN THE LIFE

The journal gives us an insight into Wilber's day-to-day existence. He leads a very disciplined life, spending the majority of his time meditating, reading, thinking, writing, and . . . weightlifting.[43] On a typical day he gets up between three and five o'clock in the morning, meditates for an hour or two, and then works until one or two in the afternoon. Then he spends an hour or so weightlifting, a practice that he has stuck to faithfully in recent years because it helps him to keep both feet on the ground. In the afternoon he does chores and then eats a meal at about five o'clock before going to a movie or staying in to watch a video. He has a huge collection of videos that have been screened on television. Or he might visit acquaintances, do some correspondence, read something light, and make some telephone calls. He goes to bed at about ten o'clock.[44] By his own admission, he is able to get by with relatively little sleep because meditating induces such a state of deep relaxation.

When he is compiling material for a new book, he reads a few books a day:

> If I'm researching, it's plain old-fashioned homework—you just read and read and read. I usually try to go through two to four books a day, which means I skim through them very quickly, making a few notes where necessary. If I find a really important book, then I'll slow down and spend a week or more with it, taking extensive notes. Really good books, I'll read three or four times.

When I'm writing, it's a little different. I work at a very intense pace, in some sort of altered state, where I seem to process information at a frightening rate. I'll sometimes put in fifteen-hour days. In any event it's truly exhausting, physically exhausting, which is the main reason I took up weightlifting.[45]

Over the years he has become increasingly aware of the importance of physical exercise: "For almost twenty years, I've done hatha yoga as my main physical exercise. Five years ago, I also began weightlifting, which has been an extraordinary help in writing, meditation, and immune system health—a true testament to integral practice. I'm 48 [in 1997], and I don't ever remember being this comfortable in the body."[46]

The conscious effort to maintain good physical and mental health is an important part of an integral spiritual lifestyle. Profound spiritual experiences can lead people to disregard the lower dimensions. But, according to Wilber, being Enlightened does not automatically mean that you know everything and are capable of anything. For example, you will still need to learn how to drive a car or how to maintain a relationship: "You can be in One Taste consciousness, and still get cancer, still fail at a marriage, still lose a job, still be a jerk. Reaching a higher stage in development does *not* mean the lower levels go away (Buddhas still have to eat), nor do you automatically master the lower levels (enlightenment will not automatically let you run a four-minute mile). In fact, it often means the opposite, because you might start to neglect or even ignore the lower levels, imagining that they are now no longer necessary for your well-being, whereas in fact they are the means of expression of your well-being and the vehicles of Spirit that you now are. Neglecting these vehicles is 'spiritocide'—you are neglecting to death your own sacred manifestation."[47]

PITFALLS ON THE PATH

The journal also offers an insight into Wilber's meditation practice and the mystical experiences to which it has given rise. His years of meditation have borne fruit: Wilber has personally experienced each of the stages of spiritual development he describes in his model. In *One Taste* he discusses at some length the problems that new and advanced meditators are likely to encounter. According to Wilber, to begin with, meditation is a matter of finding the inner Self, the awareness that witnesses everything that passes through consciousness. Then the meditator has to make the step from this individual Self to the universal dimension of "One Taste," which in contrast to the often spectacular mystical experiences that precede it, is extraordinarily simple.

According to Wilber there are two crucial errors that meditators can make. They can attempt to perceive the Self as an *object* and are fated never to find it because the Self is not an object but the *subject* of all experience. The second error that they can make is to imagine that the step from the Self to the One requires an *effort* on their part. Again they will never succeed in making the transition because the highest state of consciousness can never be achieved by means of effort, but, paradoxically enough, is always already the case. The step from the individual to the universal can never be made *from* the individual level, but happens spontaneously once the insight begins to dawn that the individual is an expression of the universal.

He puts this insight into words quite sublimely as follows:

So here are the steps.

Rest as Witness, feel the self-contraction. As you do so, notice that the Witness is *not* the self-contraction—it is aware of it. The Witness is *free* of the self-contraction—*and you are the Witness.*

As the Witness, you are free of the self-contraction. *Rest in that Freedom,* Openness, Emptiness, Release. Feel the self-contraction, *and let it be,* just as you let all other sensations be. You don't try to get rid of the clouds, the trees, or the ego—just let them all be, and relax in the space of Freedom that you are.

From that space of Freedom—and at some unbidden point—you may notice that the *feeling* of Freedom has no inside and no outside, no center and no surround. Thoughts are floating in this Freedom, the sky is floating in this Freedom, the world is arising in this Freedom, and you are That. The sky is your head, the air is your breath, the earth is your skin—it is all that close, and closer. You are the world, as long as you rest in this Freedom, which is infinite Fullness.

This is the world of One Taste, with no inside and no outside, no subject and no object, no in here versus out there—without beginning and without end, without ways and without means, without path and without goal. And this, as Ramana [Maharshi] said, is the final truth.[48]

Though he may not have taken on his readers as personal students, in these passages Wilber acts as an authentic spiritual teacher as he endeavors to use the written word to point out the way on the path towards Spirit. He goes on to explain that the Feeling of Being is not quite like any other feeling:

> It's not quite right to describe One Taste as a "consciousness" or an "awareness," because that's a little too heady, too cognitive. It's more like the simple Feeling of Being. You *already* feel this simple Feeling of Being; it is the simple, present feeling of existence.
>
> But it's quite different from all other feelings or experiences, because this simple Feeling of Being does not come and go. It is not in time at all, though time flows through it, as one of many textures of its own sensation. The simple Feeling of Being is not an experience—it is a vast Openness in which all experiences come and go, an infinite Spaciousness in which all perceptions move, a great Spirit in which the forms of its own play arise, remain a bit, and pass. It is your own I-I as your little-I uncoils in the vast expanse of All Space. The simple Feeling of Being, which is the simple feeling of existence, is the simple Feeling of One Taste.
>
> Is this not obvious? Aren't you already aware of existing? Don't you already feel the simple Feeling of Being? Don't you already possess this immediate gateway to ultimate Spirit, which is nothing other than the simple Feeling of Being? You have this simple Feeling of Being now, don't you? And you have it now, don't you? And now, yes?
>
> And don't you already realize that this Feeling is Spirit itself? Godhead itself? Emptiness itself? Spirit does not pop up into existence: it is the only thing that is constant in your experience—and that is the simple Feeling of Being itself, a subtle, constant, background awareness that, if you look very closely, very carefully, you will realize you have had ever since the Big Bang and before—not because you existed way back when, but because you truly exist prior to time, in this timeless moment, whose feeling is the simple Feeling of Being: now, and now, and always and forever now.
>
> You feel the simple Feeling of Being? Who is not already Enlightened?[49]

CONTINUITY OF CONSCIOUSNESS

As Wilber's meditation deepened, he noticed that he was retaining a certain degree of consciousness even while he was sleeping. Our waking consciousness is normally interrupted by periods of sleep, but he found that in his experience this was less and less the case. As he fell asleep, he would witness the world around him disappearing and being replaced by the dream world. As his dreams became more and more "lucid," he consciously observed the content of the dream.[50] And the thread of consciousness also persisted when the dream came to an end. For Wilber, dreamless sleep, which is normally a period of unconsciousness, became a conscious experience. When he wakes up out of this state, the world appears before his mind's eye, but waking, dreaming, and dreamless sleep are all conscious experiences.

Wilber points out that this cycle can also be experienced in deep meditation. In meditation the world disappears from view and the meditator concentrates on his inner world. In doing so, he can experience all kinds of phenomena that are not dissimilar to the experiences of the dream world. Formless and imageless meditation can induce a state of objectless consciousness that can be compared with dreamless sleep, even if, in this case, the meditator does not lose consciousness. Thus it is understandable that intensive meditation practice is likely to make it easier to remain conscious during sleep.

This cycle is also similar to the cycle of reincarnation, as described in the Tibetan Book of the Dead, for example.[51] When a person dies, the outer world fades from his senses and his consciousness concentrates on the inner world of images. In the Tibetan view of reincarnation, during the process of death the individual ascends to the level of the Absolute, which is known as the Clear Light. Only those who have spent a great deal of time meditating during their lives will be able to make this transition consciously; others will lose consciousness for a short time and will only regain consciousness when the soul is already embarking on its next incarnation. The experience of the Clear Light can be compared with the state of dreamless sleep; the Tibetans compare the phenomena experienced during the process of incarnation with dream experiences. Also in this case, the practice of meditation during one's life can influence the process of reincarnation.

Thus the self conquers not only sleep but also death; likewise, our memory not only unites the days of our life, but also the many lives in the existence of the reincarnating soul.

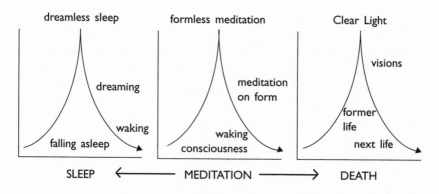

FIGURE 6.8.   The relationship between sleep, meditation, and death

A person who has attained constant consciousness or continuity of consciousness during his or her life has in a certain sense also mastered the cycle of life and death:

> To *consciously* master the waking-dreaming-sleeping cycle is therefore said to be the same as being able to *consciously* choose one's rebirth: to master one is to master the other, for they are identical cycles through the Great Nest of Being, gross to subtle to causal and back again. Even so, that cycle, however exalted, is nothing but the cycle of samsara, or the endless rounds of torturous birth and death. Mastering that cycle is, at best, an aid to the ultimate goal: the recognition of One Taste. For only in One Taste does one step off that brutal cycle altogether, there to rest as the All. Neither gross nor subtle nor causal are the ultimate state, which is the simple Feeling of Being, the simple Feeling of One Taste.[52]

For Wilber these spiritual states are a daily experience, even if they are not yet constantly sustained.[53]

THE COLLECTED WORKS

In 1997, the year in which Wilber kept the journal that was subsequently published as *One Taste*, he also began the mammoth operation of editing all of the works that he had published to date for the edition of the *Collected Works of Ken Wilber*, which was planned for the year 2000. Few authors are involved in such an undertaking while they themselves are still writing. Volumes of collected works are generally published after the author in question has died—as in Jung's case—and are compiled by the author's followers. In any event, with the publication of his collected works Wilber was more likely to gain admittance to the world of libraries and universities, which are not particularly inclined to include his paperbacks in their collection. Only time will tell whether the publisher of the *Collected Works* has succeeded in this respect. But in any event the project gave Wilber an opportunity to reflect on his oeuvre as a whole and to determine his current standpoint in relation to his earlier work.

The forewords that Wilber wrote for the various volumes of the *Collected Works*, some of which are quite comprehensive, are a rich source of information because they describe the mood in which the books contained in the volume were written. Some of the volumes also contain material that was published years ago, which varies from forewords to books written by other authors to lengthy articles. Volume IV of the *Collected Works* even contains an entire book *(Integral Psychology)* that had not been published previously and another manuscript *(Sociocultural Evolution)* that Wilber initially forgot that he had written (the text was written in around 1983). Wilber also answers some of the criticism leveled at his books, particularly the criticism invoked by *Sex, Ecology, Spirituality*. All in all these forewords serve to highlight the individual books, but in order not to interrupt our narrative too much, here we will leave it at that. For those who are interested, the contents of *The Collected Works of Ken Wilber* are as follows (only book titles are listed here):

Vol. I	*The Spectrum of Consciousness, No Boundary*
Vol. II	*The Atman Project, Up from Eden*
Vol. III	*A Sociable God, Eye to Eye*
Vol. IV	*The Holographic Paradigm, Quantum Questions, Transformations of Consciousness, Sociocultural Evolution, Integral Psychology*
Vol. V	*Grace and Grit*
Vol. VII	*Sex, Ecology, Spirituality*
Vol. VIII	*A Brief History of Everything, The Eye of Spirit*
Vol. VIII	*The Marriage of Sense and Soul, One Taste*

Wilber has occasionally been accused of being excessively critical of others. At the end of the foreword to part VIII of the *Collected Works*, he responds to this accusation as follows:

The real intent of my writing is not to say, you must think this way. The real intent is: here are some of the many important facets of this extraordinary Kosmos; have you thought about including them in your own worldview? My work is an attempt to make room in the Kosmos for all of the dimensions, levels, domains, waves, memes, modes, individuals, cultures, and so on, ad infinitum. I have one major rule: *Everybody* is right. More specifically, everybody—including me—has some important pieces of truth, and all of those pieces need to be honored, cherished, and included in a more gracious, spacious, and compassionate embrace. To Freudians I say, Have you looked at Buddhism? To Buddhists I say, Have you studied Freud? To liberals I say, Have you thought how important some conservative ideas are? To conservatives I say, Can you perhaps include a more liberal perspective? And so on, and so on, and so on. . . . At no point I have ever said: Freud is wrong, Buddha is wrong, liberals are wrong, conservatives are wrong. I have only suggested that they are true but partial. My critical writings have never attacked the central beliefs of any discipline, only the claims that the particular discipline has the only truth—and on those grounds I have often been harsh. But every approach, I honestly believe, is essentially true but partial, true but partial, true but partial. . . .

And on my own tombstone, I dearly hope that someday they will write: He was true but partial. . . .[54]

INTEGRAL PSYCHOLOGY

When the first four volumes of *the Collected Works of Ken Wilber* came out at the end of 1999 (the other four volumes were published during the course of 2000), Volume IV contained a surprise for the reader in the form of a brand new book entitled *Integral Psychology*.[55] Not only was it a manuscript that had not yet been published, it was also a highly condensed summary of the textbook on transpersonal psychology that Wilber had been planning to write since 1982, which had been given the working title *System, Self, and Structure*. Wilber had probably come to the conclusion that in view of his busy writing schedule, the book might never be

1250 per mo rent.

per mo is needed
as.

per mo is needed

(40K @ 7% Loan
140,000)

Do I have to
for the PLACE
y its self.

,000.

Cancel ma

written and thus decided to publish the basic ideas in this form. He also wanted to shake off once and for all the critics that persisted in basing their criticism primarily on his earlier works.

In Volume IV Wilber issues the following statement, which can be read as a kind of warning in advance: "Contained herein is the book *Integral Psychology*, which was written specifically for this volume and is published here for the first time. *Integral Psychology* is a condensed version of an as-yet unpublished two-volume text of psychology, spirituality, and consciousness studies. As such, *Integral Psychology* is at this time the definitive statement of my general psychological model, and my other writings in the field should be coordinated with its views."[56] The book is dedicated to the nineteenth-century German psychologist Gustav Fechner, who advocated a nonmaterialist view of human consciousness yet was very much involved in launching psychology as a scientific discipline in the West. It is clear that Wilber sees him as a kindred spirit.

Integral Psychology presents a very complex picture of the individual. As he did previously in *The Atman Project*, at the back of the book Wilber has included numerous charts showing how his model relates to the work of a hundred or so different authors from East and West.[57] This method of comparison shows that thinking in terms of stages is far more common than one might suspect given the current cultural climate in the field of psychology. It also makes it clear that developmental psychologists differ in terms of how much of the spectrum they cover (does the psychologist simply describe the personal, or does he or she also describe the transpersonal?) and the degree of detail (how many subdivisions are there within the personal or the transpersonal?). A brief glimpse at these charts also shows that very few Western authors have so far attempted to map out the transpersonal world.

With the aid of the now familiar four quadrants Wilber shows how an integral psychology combines the best of premodern, modern, and postmodern knowledge:

(1) First, an integral psychology recognizes the existence of an inner dimension in the individual. In other words it is once again a psychology with a soul. This inner dimension is also conceived of as being layered such that development can take place. And third, in the depths (or heights) of this inner dimension there are levels that transcend the limits of the personal. This is, broadly speaking, the Eastern contribution to the integral model of human consciousness.

(2) In addition to this, an integral psychology also recognizes that this inner dimension is embedded in several contexts, including

those of the body, culture, and society. Though it strongly opposes the reduction of the inner dimension to these contexts, an
integral psychology definitely acknowledges the influence exerted
by them. These three contexts (body, culture, society) also undergo development. This is, broadly speaking, the Western contribution to the integral model of human consciousness.

Thinking in terms of stages of development has come in for heavy criticism
within the academic world in recent decades. Nevertheless, as the following
simple example shows, there is no escaping it. In line with a number of other
authors Wilber distinguishes three stages of moral growth: (1) *egocentrism*, in
which one is solely concerned with one's own well-being; (2) *socio-* or *ethnocentrism*, in which one is primarily concerned with the well-being of the group to
which one belongs; and (3) *worldcentrism*, in which humanity is seen as a whole.
In all of these cases we can say that the individual finds his identity by determining which group he belongs to. In the first case he himself is the only
member of the group, in the second case the group might be his family or his
country, and in the third case the group is humanity as a whole. We cannot help
but express a value judgement of these three stages: ethnocentrism is more
valuable than egocentrism, but is more limited than an ethic that encompasses
the whole of humanity. And, thus far in our argument, we are still within the
confines of conventional science. Wilber then suggests that we should continue
this trend of broadening the spiritual horizon by formulating a transpersonal
ethic in which we not only wish the best for all people, but for all living beings.
And having gone this far it is possible to conceive of a stage in which we wish
the best for all beings in all worlds of existence, as in the case of the Bodhisattva
vow in the Mahayana Buddhist tradition. And finally our compassion expands
to include all manifest and unmanifest reality.[58]

    This example also shows how well the ladder metaphor of human devel-
opment communicates a sense of what actually happens. On each rung of the
ladder one sees more of the environment and one expands one's spiritual
horizon. This graphic insight is lost in the alternative metaphor that Wilber
uses in *Integral Psychology*, in which development is depicted as a stream with
different waves. However, the advantage of this second metaphor is that it
allows more scope for fluid transitions between the different stages. Another
advantage of the ladder metaphor is that it puts an end to the kind of
relativism that regards all standpoints as being equally valid. Though all standpoints are indeed relative (while we are still on the different rungs of the
ladder), we can specify precisely what position they occupy on the ladder as
a whole. In other words relativism itself can also be put into perspective.

In *A Theory of Everything*, which we have yet to discuss, Wilber lists the building blocks that he considers to be essential components of any integral psychology:

—multiple levels or *waves* of existence, a grand holarchy spanning the entire spectrum of consciousness, matter to body to mind to soul to spirit (or beige to purple to red to blue to orange [See Fig. 6.9 on page 229] to . . . subtle, causal, nondual). Moving through those levels of development, there are

—numerous different *streams*, modules, or lines of development, including cognitive, moral, spiritual, aesthetic, somatic, imaginative, interpersonal and so on (e.g. one can be cognitive orange, emotional purple, moral blue, and so forth). Moreover, at virtually any stage of development, one is open to

—multiple *states* of consciousness, including waking, dreaming, sleeping, altered, nonordinary, and meditative (many of these altered states can occur in any line at any level; thus, for example, one can have a variety of religious experiences at virtually any stage of development).

—numerous different *types* of consciousness, including gender types, personality types (enneagram, Myers-Briggs, Jungian), and so on. These types can occur in levels, lines and states.

—multiple *organic* factors and brain states (this Upper-Right quadrant today receives most of the attention from psychiatry, cognitive science, and neurobiology; but as significant as it is, it is still only "one-fourth" of the story).

—the extraordinarily important impact of numerous *cultural* factors, including the rich textures of diverse cultural realities, background contexts, pluralistic perceptions, linguistic semantics, and so on, none of which should be unwarrantedly marginalized, all of which should be included and integrated in a broad web of integral-aperspectival tapestries. (And, just as important, a truly "integral transformative practice" would give considerable weight to the importance of relationships, community, culture, and intersubjective factors in general, not merely as a realm of *application* of spiritual insight, but as a *mode* of spiritual transformation).

—the massively influential forces of the *social* system, at all levels (from nature to human structures, including especially the techno-economic base, as well as the profoundly important relationship with nonhuman social systems, from Gaia to ecosystems).

—although I have not mentioned it in this simple overview, the importance of the *self* as the navigator of the great River of Life should not be overlooked. It appears that the self is not a mono-lithic entity but rather a society of selves with a center of gravity, which act to bind the multiple waves, states, streams, and realms into something of a unified organization; the disruption of this organization, at any of its general stages, can result in pathology.[59]

We can expect quite a lot of a book that has had such a long incubation period, particularly if the author of the book is Ken Wilber. *Integral Psychology* might have been even more valuable had Wilber made a point of answering the criticism that has been leveled at the concept of development over the years, particularly in view of the fact that development plays such a crucial role in Wilber's system. Has such criticism always been prompted by ideological (in other words postmodernist) motives, or are there in fact other alternatives to development that are more respectable? Those who object to the idea of development have consistently maintained that development is a learning process. If all developmental models have at least three phases, as Wilber claims—(1) preconventional, (2) conventional, and (3) postconventional—can we not see this process as a learning process? In the second phase one acquires knowledge that one did not have in the first phase, and in the third phase one learns to be creative with the knowledge that one acquired in the second phase. This would also explain why people are able to develop in so many different directions (intellectual, moral, ethical, and so on). They have simply acquired more knowledge and gained more expertise in certain areas.

Wilber might also have examined why Western psychology has reso-lutely avoided having anything to do with the idea of the soul. It is not simply because—by definition—flatland materialism does not recognize such a concept, but it is also because one way or another we are saddled with circular reasoning. A psychology *without* a soul is not psychology, but a psychology *with* a soul is no longer a science. If we attempt to explain the fact that people are able to think by attributing the capacity for thought to the existence of the "power of thought," we have in fact explained nothing, but simply accepted in advance something that needs to be explained. This would also mean a materialistic explanation of consciousness is the only explanation considered to be valid, which is also unsatisfactory (we will have a chance to look at this in more depth in the next chapter). Having said all this, it is to Wilber's lasting credit that in *Integral Psychology* he had the courage to discuss the concept of the self (or the soul) at all, given that for so long this was considered to be taboo in Western psychology.

BOOMERITIS

In the forewords to parts VII and VIII of the *Collected Works* Wilber was clearly on to something that would keep him busy for a while to come. For some time he had hinted that ultimately his ideas would have to result in a socially relevant political theory. He first mentions "Spiral Dynamics" in *Integral Psychology*. Don Beck, one of the authors of *Spiral Dynamics*, was called in to advise on the racial problems in South Africa. In the book he and Chris Cowan outline a developmental model that can usefully be applied to groups in society.[60] In the view presented by Beck and Cowan, which draws on the work of Clare Graves (a contemporary of Abraham Maslow), there are eight stages of thought, which are, purely for the sake of convenience, denoted with a certain color.[61] These eight stages are divided up into the first six stages, which are referred to as "subsistence" levels or stages, and which are said to form the "first tier"; and the top two stages, which are referred to as "being" levels or stages, and which are said to form the "second tier" of the model.

8	synthesis-oriented, holistic	turquoise	late centaur
7	process-oriented, systematic	yellow	middle centaur
6	pluralistic, network-oriented	green	early centaur
5	scientific, success-oriented	orange	rational
4	conformist, absolute-religious	blue	membership
3	power-gods, egocentrism	red	egocentric
2	magical-animistic, ancestor worship	purple	magical
1	archaic-instinctive, geared to survival	beige	archaic

GRAVES / BECK / COWAN   WILBER

FIGURE 6.9.   The stages of consciousness according to Graves, Beck, Cowan, and Wilber

Contrary to the suggestion evoked by the two tiers of the model, according to Wilber the two tiers do not represent the division between the personal and the transpersonal. In his opinion the three highest stages of thought all relate to the vision-logic of the centaur stage. Like Wilber, Beck and Cowan also believe that these stages of thought are present in every individual. Tensions between different groups within a society can be identified and where possible resolved with the aid of this model.

As far as Wilber was concerned, the model devised by Beck and Cowan had a great deal of appeal, not only because it attributed strong social relevance to the stages of thought, but also because it gave him an opportunity to situate his often fraught relationship with his colleagues in the transpersonal field and with the alternative world as a whole within a broader context. For many years Wilber had had the feeling that the post-war generation to which he belonged—a generation also known as the *baby boomers*—was peculiarly afflicted by a mind-set that critics often refer to as narcissism. The often outspoken nihilism of the academic postmodern world had also been a thorn in his side. In his opinion the narcissism and nihilism that hid behind much contemporary philosophy and social science was one of the greatest obstacles to the flowering of mature spirituality in Western society. His exasperation and concern regarding this situation led him to write the book *Boomeritis*, the title of which is meant to indicate that he considers this mentality to be a diseased manifestation of what is potentially a healthy and even a very refined state of mind.[62]

However, not content with *Boomeritis* in its essay form, Wilber decided to rewrite the entire manuscript as a novel and postpone its publication by a year. Since its main subject was the pathology of extreme postmodernism, the novel was to embody most of its characteristics, by being heavily autobiographical, self-absorbed, provocative, and even shocking, philosophical in a literary fashion, and as discontinuous as an MTV television program. Interestingly, the book spilled over into the writings Wilber posted on the Internet even before the novel was published, making it a truly multimedia affair. In some of these postings the main characters of the novel commented on real life events, most notably the attack on the World Trade Center on September 11, 2001. Wilber's response to that disastrous event, aptly titled "The Deconstruction of the World Trade Center," demonstrated that integral political principles could be applied even to these atrocities.

What is at stake here? The "green" front has wrested itself away from the rationalist and dogmatic religious movements that preceded it and believes itself to be the bearer of a new paradigm or a new spiritual consciousness. It rejects all forms of universalist thought because it believes that in the past this has inevitably led to the oppression of dissidents. The postmodern argument—that there is no longer any generally valid truth, that everyone's way of looking at things is determined by the group and the culture to which they belong, and that any attempt to assess this way of looking at things in relation to external standards is illegitimate—simply plays into the hands of the latent narcissism in the modern individual. (Their own universalist pretensions cause the postmodernists to overlook the fact that postmodernism is also a time-and-place-bound truth—an inherent contradiction that Wilber never fails to point out.) Wilber is not against postmodernism as such, but he is against the extreme expression of it that has taken root in the American universities. As we have seen, he is fully aware that an integral psychology must acknowledge the huge influence that culture and society have on the individual, but he refuses to give up the search for generally valid truths, or to deny the existence of the individual self as the extremist postmodernists have done.[63]

Swimming against the postmodernist tide, which argues away the existence of the subject and thus any possibility of speaking about depth, quality, responsibility, and the adoption of an intrinsic stance, Wilber continues to call for the rehabilitation of the subject. Not the subject conceived of by modernism, which was naively thought to be a fully autonomous being—an illusion that has rightly been shattered by postmodernism—but a more qualified subject: a rehabilitation that fully acknowledges the fact that the individual is bound by context, but does not deny the individual's ultimate relative autonomy and responsibility. This call for objective truth and respect for the facts, which might come across as somewhat old-fashioned, is likely to fall on deaf ears among those who adopt a narcissistic approach to life, but it will undoubtedly fall on fertile soil among those who genuinely long to become mature.

The pervasive influence of the green front, which rejects all forms of development and hierarchical thinking, is also evident within the transpersonal community. These circles now depict Western civilization as an ethnocentric, eurocentric, racist, and rationalist culture that is hostile to nature, the body, and women, and embrace the counterparts to any of these stances as a form of spirituality. Compared with Western society, multicultural societies in which all peoples can have their say, and alternative societies that are concerned with nature, the body, and the expression of the emotions—societies in which all forms of suppression are banned—have now acquired the mystique of a true paradise. Yet this overlooks the fact that other cultures can and have been just as racist as Western culture—ethnocentrism is a stage of development that all human beings go through, not the privilege of a certain culture—and also that it is possible to speak out against the devastation of nature without having to revert to a nature religion. The people in these circles are also inclined to reject universalist ideas, which also include the perennial philosophy on which Wilber's early reflections were based.

Wilber endeavors to turn this discussion to his advantage by seeing to it that his model does justice to both general human factors *and* culture-bound factors. He also expresses the hope that some of those who subscribe to the ideas of the green culture of the day will be sensitive to his plea for a new view of traditional spiritual values. At the same time he is well aware that this will only apply to a handful of people, given that the majority of the human race is currently preoccupied with very different issues: "In other words, most of the work that needs to be done involves ways to make the lower (and foundational) waves more healthy in their own terms. The major reforms do not involve how to get a handful of Boomers into second tier, but how to feed the starving millions at the most basic waves; how to house the homeless millions at the simplest of levels; how to bring healthcare to the millions who do not possess it. An integral vision is one of the least pressing issues on the face of the planet."[64]

Surprising words for a philosopher who has spent so many years exploring subtle issues of psychology and spirituality. This passage heralds a phase in Wilber's thinking in which he is more and more explicitly concerned with politics.

A THEORY OF EVERYTHING

In order not to leave it simply at criticism and to demonstrate that ultimately he is more interested in constructing views, models, and theories than in deconstructing them—which seems to be a popular pastime of the postmodernist philosophers—at the same time as he was writing *Boomeritis* Wilber also wrote a book entitled *A Theory of Everything*.[65] As he had done in *Boomeritis*, in *A Theory of Everything* he elaborates the ideas that he had outlined in the forewords to parts VII and VIII of the *Collected Works* in book form. When it comes to diagnosing the evils of our time, *A Theory of Everything* relies on *Boomeritis* but it then proposes a remedy based on the integral view that Wilber has developed over the years.

Wilber also discusses the many fields in which this integral view might usefully be applied, varying from healthcare to politics and from management to education.

So what would an integral view of politics entail? It would certainly attempt to do justice to as many different standpoints as possible. Thus, as we might expect, Wilber does not express a preference for the politics of the left or the right. Following in the footsteps of many other contemporary political philosophers, he is far more interested in identifying a "third way."[66] His four-quadrant model proves to be extremely useful in the field of politics in this respect.

Wilber distinguishes three dimensions in his political theory:

1) The different political movements identify different factors as the *cause* of human suffering. As far as the liberals are concerned, the cause lies outside of the individual; as far as the conservatives are concerned, the cause lies within the individual. The liberals always point to the influence of social structures while the conservatives insist that any problems are due to shortcomings on the part of the individual. According to the liberals if you have been unfortunate in life, it will often be through no fault of your own (you were born into a certain class, or you were not given certain opportunities). Yet the conservatives believe that you yourself are to blame (you may not have done your best, or you may have failed to develop your talents). Liberal politics calls for the restructuring of society to create equal opportunities for everyone; conservative politics calls for the reinstatement of values and standards, often within the closed circle of the family. In terms of the four quadrants the liberals seek causation on the right-hand side while the conservatives are more inclined to look to the left-hand side.[67] Any integral political theory will attempt to honor both standpoints.

2) According to Wilber, it needs to be generally acknowledged that considerable *development* takes place within the subjective domain. Babies are not born as fully mature individuals; they have to go through a long process of development before they arrive at that level. While the conservatives embrace the idea of development, they stop at the stage of conventional mythic belief, which is essentially sociocentric and considers religious salvation to be synonymous with the membership of a certain religion, or even a subdivision of a certain religion. According to Wilber the

modern world has outgrown this stage of thinking; thus in this respect the liberals have gone further in their development. Liberalism originally emerged as a result of the rejection of dogmatic religious thinking and, as such, it corresponds to the level of postconventional rational thought. Unfortunately, however, according to Wilber, the liberal stance often goes hand in hand with a materialistic worldview and denies of all forms of development—including the development that enabled the liberals to arrive at the rational level! Hence Wilber says: "So here is the truly odd political choice we are given today: a sick version of a higher level versus a healthy version of a lower level—liberalism versus conservatism."[68]

3) Political movements differ in terms of the degree of emphasis they place on the *individual* as opposed to the *collective*, in other words, the degree of emphasis they place on individual freedom as opposed to the influence exerted by the collective. At this point in the discussion the four quadrant model becomes relevant: the upper two quadrants stand for individual freedom while the lower two quadrants stand for influence exerted by the state or the community. Both variants can be found on the left-hand and right-hand sides of the political spectrum.

Wilber's reflections also take him into the field of world politics as he discusses recent publications by leading political analysts. Many base their systems either exclusively on the Lower-Right quadrant, by focusing on the trend towards globalization and "americanization," for example, or exclusively on the Lower-Left quadrant by mapping out the cultural power blocks across the different continents. These analyses tie in perfectly with the model of the four quadrants, but Wilber also calls for the inclusion of a "vertical analysis." As we mentioned earlier, his developmental model distinguishes three main phases: if things go according to plan, each individual develops from an egocentric baby into a sociocentric child and from a sociocentric child into a worldcentric adult. In terms of world politics most if not all conflicts are caused by the seemingly ineradicable ethnocentrism of different peoples who deny one another the right to exist. If there is ever to be a peaceful world culture, this pervasive ethnocentrism will need to be overcome. The problem is that this cannot be achieved by imposing Western cultural values on the whole world (something that other cultures are fiercely opposed to, particularly if they are religious cultures). Nor does an indiscriminate pluralism, in which all cultures are allowed to go their own way without having to take any notice of external standards, appear to be the answer. Wilber's model offers, in theory at least, the possibility of finding an external standard that can help us to identify the nature of cultural and political issues. Given the extent to which his thoughts are based on insights from both East and West, Wilber certainly cannot be accused of Western ethnocentrism. The framework of the integral philosophy that he has elaborated on the basis of these insights is able to accommodate the idiosyncrasies of cultures and peoples, but it does so within the context of an overall view of human consciousness in general and the way in which it develops.

We could draw a three-dimensional world map by indicating the progress that each continent has made in the vertical dimension of spiritual growth. Regions where tribes are at each other's throats would be the lowlands; regions in which there are more elaborate cultural contexts, such as states and religious groups, would be depicted as somewhat more hilly; and the few regions in the world where a truly worldcentric view is evolving would form rare mountain peaks. If we then looked at the political mindscape as a whole, we would see that the vast majority of the landscape is hilly and that it is of the utmost importance for us to discover how divergent cultures can live in peace with one another. In his books Wilber has often been critical of multicultural philosophies—most of which are American—that claim to be based on the noble ideal of tolerance of different cultures but inadvertently pave the way for fragmentation and disintegration and all of the ensuing consequences through their lack of critical perspective. In other words, in Wilber's opinion tolerance should be limited when it comes to intolerant, ethnocentric groups.

Wilber has also expressed a certain amount of scepticism regarding the notion that the process of globalization itself is enough to bring about a peaceful world culture. He makes his point by taking the Internet as an example—at the moment a worldwide network that facilitates communication between peoples and cultures is being used for the most part to exchange pornographic material. Again in this case a vertical analysis that focuses on the development of consciousness is urgently required. If the Internet is a reflection of the content of the consciousness of humanity, there is little prospect of the rapid dawning of a worldwide culture of peaceful and discriminate tolerance. And even if we do see the dawning of such an enlightened society, in Wilber's opinion every human child will always have to start from the first stage of development—that of the egoistic and narcissistic babe in arms. For this reason developed cultures do not have fewer problems than cultures that are not as developed; they actually have more problems because the individual members of the culture have more ground to cover to reach the collective level of consciousness. And the longer the process of development, the more likely it is that something will go wrong along the way.

But just as our Western society, which is currently making the transition from a ethnocentric society to a worldcentric society, albeit hesitantly, has been able to function relatively efficiently under a written constitution that embodies worldcentric ideals (all men are equal before the law), it might also be possible to draw up an "integral Constitution," which not only ensures that all people are treated equally, but also acknowledges possibility of the growth of consciousness: "The question remains: exactly how will this be conceived, understood, embraced, and practiced? What precise details, what actual specifics, where and how and when? This is the great and exhilarating call of global politics at the millennium. We are awaiting the new founding Fathers and Mothers who will frame an integral Constitution, a Constitution that will call us to our more encompassing future, that will act as a gentle pacer of transformation for the entire spiral of human development, honoring each and every wave as it unfolds, yet kindly inviting each and all to even greater depth."[69]

THE INTEGRAL INSTITUTE

Naturally it is possible to find leads for the practical application of this integral philosophy in all kinds of different fields: healthcare, management, nature conservation, politics, art, research on consciousness, spirituality, minorities policy, feminism, administration of justice, international relations, child-rearing, and education. Many of these fields are discussed in *Kindred Visions*, a book-in-progress that contains essays by dozens of well-known authors working in all kinds of disciplines.[70] The book can be seen as a true *Festschrift* in honor of Wilber. After having spent more than two decades working in isolation as a philosopher and writer, Wilber has apparently entered a phase in which he can serve as a source of inspiration for new studies and research carried out by others.

With a view to supporting this initiative, Wilber recently began to set up an Integral Institute that will coordinate the various activities and will also be able to finance much of the new research. The provisional statement of intent reads as follows:

Integral Institute is a nonprofit organization dedicated to the integration of body, mind, soul, and spirit in self, culture and nature. This integral vision attempts to honor and integrate the largest amount of research from the greatest number of disciplines—including the natural sciences (physics, chemistry, biology, neurology, ecology), art, ethics, religion, psychology, politics, business, sociology and spirituality. Integral Institute is dedicated to the proposition that piecemeal approaches to the world's problems—war, hunger, disease, famine, over-population, housing, technology, education—not only no longer help but often compound the problem, and they need to be replaced by approaches that are more comprehensive, holistic, systematic, encompassing—and integral.

Integral Institute functions as a network of many of the most influential integral theorists, and information clearing house, a source of substantial funding for integral research, and a coordinating center for hundreds of integral researchers from around the world.[71]

The institute has already set up departments of integral psychology, integral business, integral politics, and integral healthcare. Among other things the institute intends to carry out longitudinal research on transformation, to award scholarships, to finance advertising campaigns for important transpersonal texts, to establish chairs at universities, to provide support for lecturers and students engaged in various integral studies, and also (on a limited scale) to finance projects in the Third World that are an example of integral development aid. The institute will also endeavor to make integral philosophy more prominent on the Internet by maintaining an integral website: www.integralinstitute.org.[72]

The rapid realization of these high-minded plans suffered a considerable setback in the summer of 2000 when there was panic on the stock exchange. Because most of Wilber's financial backers came from the volatile world of the new economy, the plans had to be revised when many of them suddenly needed the funding they had promised in order to be able to survive the stock market crash. For the first year after the institute was set up, numerous representatives working in the fields of psychology, business, politics, and healthcare attended the meetings of the various departments of the institute which were held at Wilber's home in Boulder, where there were animated encounters and discussions. One of the first initiatives designed to ensure that these contacts were productive was the decision to set up core teams—smaller groups that would work on compiling integral textbooks relating to the different fields. For example, the textbook on Integral Psychology would inform future students of the added value of the integral point of view. Similarly, in the textbook on Integral Politics future students should be able to find an explanation of the principal standpoints within the political spectrum and the way in which these views, which are by their very nature one-sided, can be incorporated within an integral framework. And a textbook on Integral Management should portray the many schools and movements in the literature on management in relation to the integral point of view. Obviously, projects such as these will require years of preparation and, not only that, in this initial stage they are catering exclusively to those in academic circles. As yet, an Integral Institute that serves as a visible beacon that lights the way for everyone within the culture is still a thing of the future. The fact that the textbook projects are focusing on academic circles also indicates that academic acceptance is still high on Wilber's agenda. Nevertheless, as a gesture to a wider audience, a number of the Integral Seminars on the program will also be released on video.

"BY FAR THE MOST PRODUCTIVE YEARS OF MY ENTIRE LIFE"

In *One Taste* Wilber describes his meeting with Marci Walters, a student at the Naropa Institute who was then in her late twenties.[73] The two began dating and Marci gradually became the woman in Wilber's life. I had a chance to meet Marci when I visited Wilber in the autumn of 1997 to discuss my plans for this book—she has the most winning smile that I have ever seen. However, on a trip to Denver Wilber confided in me that he thought that the issue of children would prove to be a time bomb under the relationship. "Women in their forties have children; women in their thirties want children. . . ."[74] Nevertheless, it looked as if Wilber might have found a future life partner in Marci.

Wilber and Marci got married on 21 June 2001 and spent their honeymoon in Hawaii. The happiness that Wilber had found in his personal life was paralleled by unprecedented literary productivity on his part. During these years he completed the manuscripts of many of the volumes of the *Collected Works, Integral Psychology*, the essay version of *Boomeritis*, and *The Integral Vision* (which later became *A Theory of Everything*). And at the same time his plans for an Integral Institute also began to take shape. These years were essentially characterized by the theme of Wilber's increasing engagement with the world through his plans for an institute and through is more intensive interaction with colleagues in the various fields. However, only a year after they got married, rumor had it that he and Marci had separated. Wilber himself explained the situation in an online interview: "This is something Marci and I have discussed at least every week since we have been together. After the first month we were dating, I said: 'This is going to be a tragic relationship. We are going to be together for five years, and then we will have to separate so you can have babies.' "[75] It proved to be a prophetic statement. While onlookers might be surprised to learn that the two have separated so soon after getting married, Wilber is very clear about why they got married. "We had a legal ceremony last year, yes. We lived together as husband and wife for five years—to my mind we were married for five years, and it really does not matter to me whether the legal ceremony occurred at the beginning, the middle or the end of that period. I wanted to have the ceremony to celebrate the time we had together, a type of exclamation mark to the whole thing. Marci wanted me to marry her from the start, and I really should have. . . . Those five years were by far the most productive years of my entire life."[76]

TOWARDS A POST-METAPHYSICAL SPIRITUALITY

So how is Wilber's thinking likely to develop over the next few years? In the spring of 2001, Edith Zundel and I conducted an interview with Wilber for the German magazine *Transpersonale Psychologie und Psychotherapie* which offers a number of insights in this respect.[77] The interview was prompted by a critical essay by the German psychologist Hans-Willi Weis published earlier in the same magazine.[78] In his critique of Wilber's work Weis refers among other things to the work of the German philosopher Jürgen Habermas. In his book *Nachmetaphysisches Denken [Postmetaphysical Thought]* published in 1988, Habermas was extremely critical of what he called "closed worldviews," such as the worldviews subscribed to by those in New Age circles, which could only ever exist in small subcultures in the modern era. As far as I was concerned, as well as being a superb opportunity to get Wilber and Habermas—who is known to be very much admired by Wilber—to enter into a debate, at least on paper if nothing else, this interview was also an opportunity to cross-examine Wilber regarding his precise relationship with the perennial philosophy, which Wilber outlines as a background philosophy in many of his books, without going as far as to espouse concrete esoteric doctrines.[79]

In the interview Wilber makes it clear that he is completely in agreement with Habermas in his rejection of retro-romantic approaches to spirituality such as those that are popular in New Age circles. This is one of the reasons why he recently distanced himself from the transpersonal world in America, why in Wilber's eyes has acquired all of the characteristics of a closed subculture. But he then goes on to voice fierce criticism of the advocates of the perennial philosophy: "I do not identify myself with the perennial philosophy, and I have not done so for over fifteen years. As I have stated on many occasions, I categorically reject most of the work of the major perennialists, including Schuon, Coomaraswamy, Pallis, Guenon, etc. . . . My major criticisms of the perennial philosophy are numerous and too detailed to summarize here. But perhaps my strongest criticism is that we can no longer conceive of 'levels of reality' in a separative ontological sense. I reject entirely the notions of levels of reality as separate ontological. . . . Rather, any levels of reality must be conceived in a post-Kantian, post-metaphysical sense, as being inseparable from the consciousness that perceives them. This consciousness is investigated, not by metaphysical speculation, but by empirical and phenomenological research."[80]

Partly as a result of this interview Wilber decided to publish the third volume of his *Kosmos* trilogy earlier than planned.[81] And he is even considering the possibility of referring to a new phase in his thinking: Wilber 5.[82] Although it is still too early to draw any definitive conclusions at this stage, a number of general observations are called for.[83] It goes without saying that it would be inappropriate to attempt to introduce the idea of higher spheres, complete with their own invisible inhabitants, within the discipline of academic psychology, and Wilber is wise to adopt the tactic of setting this point aside for the time being, but this approach clearly falls short of an integral philosophical view of reality. In my opinion it is impossible to argue passionately in favor of the irreducibility of the inner dimension and to speak out very fiercely against the prevailing flatland philosophy without elaborating the ontological consequences that this entails. If we postulate the existence of an inner reality, the status of this inner reality needs to be philosophically described.

Whereas the premodern philosophers were uncritical and naive in their willingness to believe in the existence of realities other than the world that could be perceived by the senses, under the influence of the pervasive flatland ideology the modernists have since dispensed with this way of thinking in no uncertain terms. But does this mean that the modernist view should prevail? Huston Smith, the author of *Forgotten Truth*—a book that Wilber has praised on numerous occasions—does not think so. As far as Huston Smith is concerned, the traditional view of reality was fundamentally ontological. In his opinion the fact that the emergent scientific stance subsequently rejected this multidimensional view is based on flawed reasoning: "Searching for the way things are, we found that the modern reduction of reality to a single ontological level was the result of science. But its psychological, not its logical result; this was our further finding. *Nothing in what science has discovered controverts the existence of realms other than the one with which it deals.* Meanwhile our growing understanding of the scientific method shows us that there are things science bypasses. Whether these neglected items belong to a distinct ontological scale, science, of course, does not say; it says nothing whatever about them. . . . *Since reality exceeds what science registers,* we must look for other antennae to catch the wavebands it misses" (italics mine).[84]

As is clear from the above, the search for an integral view of reality that is as complete as possible is far from over. Yet Wilber has given us all kinds of ideas about how such an integral view might look. Hopefully the subjects he has touched on will inspire many people not only to apply these ideas in a practical way in their own lives, but also to reflect on these ideas to some extent. If the Wilber debate were to become simply "the world according to Ken Wilber," however fascinating and edifying that might be, it might well mean that Wilber would ultimately be interred in the gallery of the great, undoubtedly surrounded by a multitude of followers. Yet someone of Wilber's stature deserves more than that. The ideas that he has presented deserve to be examined in any academic and social discussions of culture, politics, religion, and mental health.

7

KEN WILBER IN PERSPECTIVE

The backbone of Wilber's model

Hopefully the preceding chapters will have served to convey an overall impression of the vision of Ken Wilber and the way in which this vision has developed over the years. This last chapter attempts to evaluate his vision. The fact that this is no easy task will be clear to anyone who has followed the argument at all closely thus far. Wilber has turned his attention to various specialist fields and only the specialists in these fields are suitably qualified to assess whether or not Wilber has the right end of the stick. In view of the fact that, in Wilber's terminology, there is a spectrum of consciousness, we can also expect there to be a broad spectrum of criticism.[1]

Although individual thinkers have criticized isolated parts of Wilber's vision from various angles over the years—and Wilber himself has responded to these points—countless aspects of his work have still not been subject to discussion, despite the fact that, in my opinion, Wilber's vision certainly calls for such discussion. With a view to structuring future discussion of the work of Ken Wilber, this chapter suggests a framework that allows for as broad an evaluation of his work as possible. To this end, rather than seeking to elaborate on the criticism that Wilber's work has elicited over the years, I feel it would be more fruitful to establish an agenda that will facilitate a systematic treatment of his work.

The backbone of Wilber's model is formed by the basic idea that reality is *layered*—the Great Chain of Being—and that, as such, reality can be conceived of as a series of spheres ranging from matter to God. And given that this is the case, according to Wilber, human development can essentially be seen as a gradual progression through the various planes of existence both individually (psychologically) and collectively (culturally). Drawing on this metaphor Wilber has succeeded in creating order within the complex and seemingly obscure world of psychology and spirituality. In this chapter we will be concentrating on this basic thread running through Wilber's vision. If this basic idea is able to withstand the test of criticism, we can then proceed to focus on the criticism of more detailed aspects of his work. If, however, the basic idea fails to hold water, there is little point in losing ourselves in the many abstruse details.

In its simplest form the Great Chain of Being is said to be made up of four great links, that Wilber has termed *body, mind, soul,* and *spirit,* using the same terminology as Huston Smith. According to Smith all of the religious traditions of the world subscribe at least to this fourfold division.[2] The division applies not only to levels of consciousness but also to levels of reality, and the anthropological terms are used simply because they are best suited to the purpose. Within the prevailing cultural climate these four terms actually represent a series of increasing *improbability.* Materialist science only recognizes the body and rejects the idea of an independent inner dimension that is usually vaguely referred to as "mind" or "soul" without any further distinction. This doctrine, known as dualism, is dismissed out of hand by established scientists who consider it to be inferior to materialism, which was once known as monism. Indeed, those working within conventional science attempt to describe the whole of reality—thus also the reality of human consciousness—in terms of physics.

As we have seen, Wilber's writing is largely motivated by the desire to rehabilitate the inner dimension as such within science and metaphysics. To what extent is Wilber right about this inner dimension? And why does the idea of an inner dimension prompt such scepticism on the part of physicists and materialist psychologists? This is the first hurdle that needs to be scaled in the endeavor to assess Wilber's vision. If the existence of an inner dimension cannot be made sufficiently plausible, there is little point in discussing the possible subdivisions within this dimension. Thus we will start by setting Wilber's vision against the visions offered by contemporary cognitive science, which seeks to explain human consciousness in materialist terms. Has any substantial progress been made in this respect—progress that would justify a materialist vision of consciousness? Or are we simply witnessing an almost fundamentalist belief in materialism?

If the existence of an inner dimension can be shown to be in any way plausible, the next task is to formulate an accurate picture of this inner dimension. In seeking to do so we enter the terrain of orthodox psychology, which aspires to be a science of consciousness (or *mind,* to use Smith's terminology). While it is true that many psychologists confine themselves to studying human behavior, the original intention of psychology has always been to penetrate the inner world of consciousness or subjective experience. There are numerous schools within orthodox psychology, but since Wilber's model is predominantly a stage model presented in terms of developmental psychology, we will focus specifically on the field of developmental psychology. Is Wilber right to describe development as a universal phenomenon that applies not only to the realms of nature but also to cultures and individuals? In elaborating on the personal half of the developmental process, was it wise for Wilber to draw from the work of Jean Piaget, the founder of developmental psychology, to the extent that he did? Wilber's vision of development can be described as "Piaget plus"[3] in view of the fact that he initially erected a transpersonal superstructure on a Piagetian foundation. Is the foundation firm enough? Or has Wilber since refined his vision of development to such an extent that the often voiced criticism of the idea of stages no longer applies to the system he now sets forth?

If we get as far as providing sufficient evidence of the existence of human development, we then come to the third hurdle: that of the transpersonal *soul* (in this context the term *soul* is used in the way that Huston Smith used it to refer to the individual spiritual element in the human individual). Is transpersonal psychology right when it postulates the existence of this spiritual dimension in the individual? And what are the fundamental options within the field of transpersonal psychology? In considering this question we are bound to examine Carl Jung's vision of human development and spirituality. Wilber and Jung are essentially the mouthpieces of the two main alternative visions within this field: most of Wilber's transpersonally oriented opponents adopt a typically neo-Jungian stance in the sense that they advocate a vision of human development and spirituality that is rooted in depth psychology, while Wilber's vision is rooted in what might be described as height psychology. Wilber has voiced fierce criticism of Jung's vision in a number of his books. What precisely is his main objection to Jung (and, by extension, the contemporary neo-Jungians)? And how do those who are inclined to support Jung's vision answer this criticism? And which side is right, if it is possible to determine who is right?

The fourth and last hurdle has to do with *spirit*—the fourth and final level in Smith's series. This leads us into the sphere of metaphysics, in other words to as broad a consideration as possible of philosophical questions that are concerned with the nature of reality. These questions include: is the individual really one with God is his deepest being? Do the various spheres that are said to make up the Great Chain of Being really exist? Is there a philosophy that accommodates this kind of multidimensional worldview? From his first publications onwards Wilber has deliberately made it clear that all of his reflections are made within a certain metaphysical context as is provided by the so-called perennial philosophy. Is it appropriate for Wilber to confront the mental world of academia with this metaphysical body of thought? Does this strengthen or weaken his position from a scientific point of view? Is the content of the perennial philosophy un-equivocal, or are there different versions of the perennial philosophy? And how are we to evaluate Wilber's statements regarding the more esoteric teachings such as reincarnation, the process of involution and evolution and the inner makeup of the human individual? And last but not least, how does Wilber's recent "post-metaphysical" phase fit in this picture?

MATERIALIST SCIENCE: THE DOMAIN OF MATTER

In contemporary philosophy human consciousness is often considered to be simply one of the by-products of the body or the brain. The body is visible and tangible; compared with the body consciousness seems elusive and insubstantial. However, this conclusion is actually a direct result of an *initial stance* that is essentially extrovert in its approach. Anyone who wishes to argue purely on the basis of what can be perceived by the senses will only come across material phenomena. This is also known as the "third-person approach." The whole of Western culture places its faith in the reality of the external world, and does not trust the reality of the inner world. In the East things are very different. There the world is seen as *maya* or illusion while consciousness is considered to be a deeper reality or even the only reality. However, this conclusion is also a direct result of the initial approach. Generally speaking, Easterners are inclined to be more introverted and therefore attach more value to what is going on within their own consciousness. This basic fact should make us aware that our vision of human consciousness is influenced by our culture. It should also instill a certain degree of humility since it may well be the case that Western science has only got hold of half of reality.

The materialist science that prevails in the West sees the individual as being entirely synonymous with the body. Most of the scientists cur-rently studying human behavior are of the opinion that consciousness can be completely reduced to processes that take place within the brain. The idea of an inner dimension is categorically rejected as unscientific. For has anyone ever been able to perceive a soul? But where does the burden of proof lie if the existence of the soul is at issue? Does it rest with those who believe in the existence of the soul, as the scientists claim that it does? It might initially appear to, given that nothing in the reality that can be perceived by the senses points to the existence of a soul. Yet upon closer investigation it turns out to be precisely the other way around.

IS THERE AN INNER DIMENSION?

Everyone has access to two worlds: the external world around them and their own inner world. This is the only valid point of departure for all contemplation of consciousness. The inner world and the external world are both real, and any philosophy that purports to be an integral philosophy needs to take both worlds into account. The insubstantial inner world appears to be of an order that is entirely different from the tangible external world. This was what originally gave rise to the obvious concept of a soul that lives in the body. Those who maintain that human consciousness is nothing more than a by-product of cerebral processes must undertake to prove this to be the case since they are essentially attempting to reduce what are experienced to be two very different realities to a single reality: that of visible matter.

That fact that at the beginning of this century psychology abandoned introspectionism in favor of behaviorism, which meant that rather than studying consciousness, psychology began to study behavior, can be excused to some extent.[4] For it is far easier to study human behavior than the inner life of the individual, which is played out in hidden depths. Yet when there is also a requirement—though it may not have been explicitly expressed— that it must also be possible for the *causes* of the observed behavior to be perceived by the senses (in other words, it must be possible to find the causes in the brain), psychology as the science of the soul is dealt a finishing blow. Anyone who is only willing to recognize cerebral processes as scientifically acceptable causes of human behavior is committed to materialism at the outset. But this is hardly a scientific attitude; it is an ideological choice. The fact that cerebral processes are of an order that is entirely different from that of subjective experience has still not been addressed.

In recent decades it has been common for cognitive scientists, who are often committed to a materialist view of human consciousness, to compare the individual with a computer, since both show signs of intelligent behavior. The question being examined is generally formulated as follows: do computers, or machines in general, show evidence of consciousness (or, to use a philosophical term, "intentionality")?[5] According to the philosopher Franz Brentano (1838–1917), one of the founders of phenomenology, mind differs from matter in that it shows intentionality or the capacity to refer to an object, while matter does not. The existence of advanced chess computers that are able to compete with the best chess players in the world appears to suggest that the question can be answered in the affirmative. But are these chess computers *aware* that they are playing chess? This is far more difficult to answer. As yet, there is no evidence to suggest that these computers possess this kind of self-awareness.

The more extreme representatives of this movement in philosophical psychology sometimes formulate the question even more radically. They actually go as far as to question whether human beings really show signs of consciousness?[6] Working on the basis of the assumption that people are in fact simply extremely complicated machines, rather than asking whether computers possess consciousness, they ask whether human beings possess consciousness! The way they see it, we are nothing more than straightforward material systems, which for reasons that we haven't yet explained, somehow manage to generate consciousness as a by-product.[7] Daniel Dennett, the most important representative of this materialist way of thinking, proposes the following strategy. Initially we can assume that not only human beings but also computers and other pieces of equipment that show signs of intelligent behavior possess consciousness (in other words, we adopt an 'intentional stance' towards them), but ultimately none of them do, since they are all simply material systems. (The opposite view might be equally valid: it is sometimes useful in science to take a "mechanical stance" towards human beings, knowing fully well that they are conscious.) According to Dennett, therefore, our only option is to explain consciousness in terms of material processes that are not self-aware, for if we attempt to explain consciousness as a phenomenon that is generated by conscious processes, we simply beg the question, and in his eyes that would mean the end of psychology as a science. "Accepting dualism is giving up," he says succinctly in his book *Consciousness Explained.*[8]

Is the belief in the existence of an inner dimension, which cannot be explained purely by cerebral processes, really unscientific? The philosopher Huston Smith for one certainly doesn't think so. Responding to Dennett's accusation that those who believe in a soul are begging the question, he points out that it is important that we should not commit ourselves to a materialist solution at the outset, since in doing so we fail to address the essential question as to *whether or not consciousness can be reduced to matter.* If a materialist answer is the only answer considered to be acceptable, the question can hardly be said to have been examined impartially.[9] Indeed, if only a materialist answer is acceptable, materialism is begging the question, since it claims that the individual is a material being because materialism is the only acceptable point of view.

In my opinion the physicist's scepticism regarding the existence of an inner dimension would be justified if as human beings we did not have the capacity for introspection. But each one of us has direct and immediate access to our own inner world—a world that asserts its existence at every moment as an undeniable fact. In choosing to regard sensory perception as the primary source of scientific knowledge science has automatically confined itself to materialist territory. As far as physics is concerned this is not such a bad thing, in view of the fact that its assigned task is to study visible matter, but for psychology such a choice is disastrous, given that its mandate is to study subjective experience. And contrary to what many philosophers of consciousness would have us believe, there is as yet not one materialist theory of consciousness that does justice to subjective human experience.

"THE HARD PROBLEM"

In December of 1995 the authoritative journal *Scientific American*, a bastion of scientific materialism, published an article entitled "The Puzzle of Conscious Experience" by American philosopher of mind David Chalmers.[10] In this article Chalmers argues that not one of the materialist theories of consciousness elaborated to date has been able to come up with a plausible argument to explain how physical processes are able to give rise to subjective experience. If we are to believe these materialist theories, the implication is that cerebral processes could actually occur just as effectively *without* consciousness. Certainly a salient point. Chalmers makes a distinction between what he calls the "easy" problem which is concerned with the question as to how our senses initially process incoming signals, and the "hard" problem which is concerned with the question as to how the resulting cerebral processes are able to give rise to subjective consciousness. So far, none of the cognitive scientists has been able to come up with a convincing answer to this question.[11] So, according to Chalmers, it is high time that we recognized the fact that consciousness is irreducible. He goes on to suggest that human consciousness is still an unknown *physical* quantity.[12]

In *The Eye of Spirit* Wilber quotes Chalmers much discussed article with approval. Yet Wilber is of the opinion that Chalmers' suggestion that consciousness should be conceived of as a separate category does not go far enough. First, referring to his own model of the four quadrants, he shows that in addition to making a distinction between the exterior (Upper Right) and interior (Upper Left) dimensions of the individual, as Chalmers proposes, if we wish to arrive at an integral theory of the consciousness, it is also essential to make room for a social (Lower Right) and a cultural (Lower Left) dimension.[13] In Wilber's opinion the scientific debate regarding consciousness is limited by being too confined to the question as to whether consciousness can only be studied objectively—by means of the so-called third-person approach—or whether, in addition to this, we also need to draw on our own introspective experience—the first-person approach. According to Wilber there is also another option in the form of a second-person approach, which relates to the intersubjective world of culture and dialogue and not only to the monologic world of I and it. Summing up, Wilber now calls this "the 1-2-3 of consciousness."[14] Secondly, as we have seen, according to Wilber the interior dimension is made up of at least nine layers, all of which recur in all four quadrants. Compared with the comprehensiveness of Wilber's all-level and all-quadrant approach, the contemporary philosophical treatment of the question of consciousness comes across as extremely meager.

BACK TO INTROSPECTION

Given that, as yet, materialist science is unable to account for the existence of the thinking subject, maybe we would be well advised to reconsider the path of introspection with renewed interest and a little more openness. In doing so, it is important to take to heart Huston Smith's statement that none of the discoveries made by physics contradicts the existence of an interior dimension since the interior dimension falls entirely outside of the domain of physics: reality encompasses far more than physics is able to register.[15] Simply by means of introspection every individual has direct and immediate access to their own inner world—this is something that no materialist theory of consciousness can prevent. We may not be able to penetrate the inner world of another individual from the outside, but we can certainly explore our own inner world from the inside. As was mentioned in earlier chapters, Western psychology chose to abandon introspection as a valid method of research relatively early on. Yet the fact that psychology has seen fit to reject introspection should not lead us to forget that introspection is the primary means of access to information regarding the interior dimension. How else would we know that there are such things as thoughts and feelings? It is a pity that Western psychologists did not think to look to Eastern cultures—which have centuries of experience of introspection and have developed what are often highly systematic methodologies, such as yoga, with a view to exploring consciousness—before they abandoned introspection as a method of research.

Wilber is firmly convinced that psychology should actually be a science of introspection.[16] For this to be possible, however, the purely scientific approach currently adopted by psychology would need to be supplemented by an approach more typical of the humanities, which would center on the *interpretation* of one's own inner world. At a later stage this initial approach would need to be completed by a 'spiritual-scientific' form of research, in which the researcher regards his *own* consciousness as the primary field of research, since it is only in this way that the deepest regions of the human psyche can be explored. By proceeding in this way Eastern cultures have discovered a great deal about the interior world of the individual—an undeniable achievement that a purely objectivist psychology can never hope to match. Only extreme prejudice on the part of Western psychology could reject this world of empirical knowledge in advance. Transpersonal psychology is virtually the only school of psychology that has been willing to consider Eastern models of human consciousness.

Over the years Wilber has deliberately made more and more space within his model for the physical dimension. In *The Spectrum of Consciousness* there is hardly any mention of the body. In *The Atman Project* the body is seen as the lowest rung of the ladder of development. In *Eye to Eye* the body is seen as the vehicle that houses the eye of flesh—the most basic perceptual mechanism for acquiring knowledge, specifically geared to the world that can be perceived by the senses. And this continues to be the case until in *Sex, Ecology, Spirituality* the body is no longer seen as the lowest rung of the ladder, but as a reality which as it were runs parallel to the whole of the interior dimension. The interior dimension can never be reduced to the body or cerebral processes, but it leaves its mark on both and, in Wilber's opinion, this is something that Eastern cultures have not yet sufficiently grasped. According to Wilber each phenomenon of consciousness—also the most elevated mystical states of consciousness—creates a recognizable pattern in the brain that can be studied by exact science. Thus in his recent work Wilber accepts all of the discoveries of contemporary neurology without subscribing to the reductionism in which the research results are virtually automatically couched.

ORTHODOX PSYCHOLOGY:
THE DOMAIN OF THE PERSONALITY

Although many psychologists claim to adhere to a materialist vision of the human individual, in practice they actually engage in a certain form of dualism in that they believe the world of the psyche to be real. This is true not only of clinical psychology, which deals with psychological disorders, but also of a discipline such as developmental psychology which thinks in terms of background inner structures that influence the thought patterns of the individual. While the process of development can also be interpreted from a materialist point of view, in which case the higher stages of development are thought to be nothing more than the result of more complex connections in the brain, in Wilber's vision development hinges on an *interior* component, and these inner structures are seen to be an inherent aspect of consciousness itself rather than being physical in nature.

THE REALMS OF NATURE

So how should we imagine this interior dimension? In Wilber's model the interior dimension is layered like everything else that is produced by and subject to evolution. One way of illustrating this is to consider the different realms of nature that have emerged during the course of evolution. The mineral kingdom, the plant kingdom, the animal kingdom, *Homo sapiens*—all have a physical component, so evolution can be conceived of as a process that introduces increasing complexity. According to science the only thing that differentiates people from animals is the number of neuronal connections; in other words, the difference is purely in the complexity of the brain. But this argument lapses back into materialism and, as we have already seen, materialism is unreliable as a basis for the philosophy of consciousness. Are there other ways in which the various realms of nature can be related to one another, ways that also take the interior dimension into account?

Once again the work of E. F. Schumacher contains a model that helps to throw light on the question. In *A Guide for the Perplexed* Schumacher notes that an unprejudiced analysis of nature shows that nature is hierarchically organized.[17] Historically philosophers saw the various realms of nature—minerals, plants, animals, and human beings—as the visible links of a single Great Chain of Being. Between human beings and God there were thought to be a hierarchy of angelic realms, such that the chain continued without any break from matter to spirit. Each link in the Chain introduces a new element, an element that does not exist in the previous link and most typifies the new link. Schumacher depicted the relationships between the various realms of nature as follows:[18]

man	=	m+x+y+z		z	=	self-awareness
animal	=	m+x+y		y	=	consciousness
plant	=	m+x		x	=	life force
mineral	=	m		m	=	matter

FIGURE 7.1.   The realms of nature seen from the point of view of matter

Minerals consist purely of matter (m), while plants consist of matter plus life (x). This involves an evolutionary leap—there is an element of discontinuity. The biological life exhibited by plants cannot be reduced to matter. Animals have a material body and are also subject to the cycle of birth and death, yet in addition to this they are also conscious (y). This involves a second evolutionary leap: the emotions exhibited by animals cannot be explained by biological or material reality. The next evolutionary leap introduces the phenomenon of self-awareness (z) in man. In the traditional view human beings differ from animals because they are self-aware. Thus while science is only able to detect increasing *complexity* in the physical organism, traditional philosophy also sees an increasing *quality* of interiority. Schumacher also points out that the factors m, x, y, and z show a progression of increasing rarity and vulnerability.[19] Within the material universe life is a rare phenomenon, but conscious life is far rarer. And life that is self-aware is even rarer still. This rarity goes hand in hand with increasing vulnerability. Matter cannot be destroyed, but living organisms can die and human beings can lose their self-awareness.

Schumacher concludes his fascinating analysis by saying: "Matter (m), life (x), consciousness (y), self-awareness (z)—these four elements are ontologically—that is, in their fundamental nature—different, incomparable, incommensurable, and discontinuous. Only one of them is directly accessible to objective, scientific observation by means of our five senses. The other three are nonetheless known to us because we ourselves, every

one of us, can verify their existence from our own inner experience."[20]
According to Schumacher the degree of reality of experience increases
with each evolutionary leap, as does the depth of subjectivity and inner
freedom. In this respect it is true to say that "the most real world we live
in is that of our fellow human beings."[21] According to Schumacher the
later links in the chain can accurately be described as 'higher' as long as
we remember that "higher always means: greater interiority, greater depth
and a greater capacity for intimacy; while lower means: greater exteriority,
less depth and a lesser capacity for intimacy."[22]

We can also add that a particular life form is primarily characterized by
the factor that distinguishes it from the preceding link in the chain. For
instance, minerals are purely matter, but plants are first and foremost *living*
beings (though they too have a material component). Animals are first and
foremost *sentient* beings (though they are also subject to the cycle of birth
and death and they too have a material body), and human beings are first
and foremost *thinking* beings (though they also have feelings, are subject to
the cycle of birth and death, and have a material body). Having come this
far we could say that mystics are first and foremost *visionary* beings in
whom the eye of contemplation has opened (they are also able to think and
feel, are subject to the cycle of birth and death, and have a material body).

So what do we actually know about the interior dimension of the
various realms of nature? In fact, we can only speculate about the inner
life of plants and animals given that we can only observe them from the
outside. We cannot even know the inner world of another human being
firsthand; the only inner world we can know directly is our own. However,
on the basis of analogy it is certainly reasonable to conclude that other
people also experience an inner world in the same way that we do. Otherwise it would be impossible for us to lead a normal social life. Proceeding on this basis, is it possible to say something about the interior dimension
of the lower realms of nature? Schumacher suggests that it is.[23]

man	= M	M	= man
animal	= M–z	z	= self-awareness
plant	= M–z–y	y	= consciousness
mineral	= M–z–y–x	x	= life force

FIGURE 7.2.   The realms of nature, seen from the point of view of
the individual

If we refer to the human individual with all of his faculties as "M," the inner life of an animal could be conceived of as occurring within the context of a reduced form of human consciousness—equivalent to human consciousness minus mental self-awareness. In the same way, the inner life of a plant could be conceived of as a reduced form of animal consciousness—equivalent to animal consciousness without sentience. Similarly, a mineral can be conceived of as biological life minus the life force.

The fact that development is always a question of "transcendence" and "inclusion," as Wilber has repeatedly claimed, is also aptly illustrated by the realms of nature. Plants not only transcend minerals because they are alive; they also incorporate the mineral kingdom in the sense that they too have a physical component. Animals not only transcend plants because they are sentient; they also incorporate the essential elements of plant life because they breathe and have a body. And human beings not only transcend animals because they are able to think; they also incorporate the essential elements of animal life because they too feel emotions, breathe and have a physical body. And, in the same way, the mystic not only transcends the average human being because in the mystic the faculty of intuition is awakened, but the mystic also incorporates all of the aspects of human life in that he too thinks, feels, breathes, and has a body. Nothing human, animal-like, plant-like, or mineral-like is alien to the mystic.

This makes it easier to understand why the nondualist experience of "One Taste," which Wilber considers to be one of the most profound mystical experiences, can only occur once all of the preceding stages of development have been completed. In other words, *we can only integrate that which we have already transcended.* We can only encompass the world as a whole if we have already transcended the world as a whole. However, this should not be taken to mean that the individual turns further and further aside from the world during the process of development, only to return to the world after having reached the highest stage. For each time a new element is introduced, it is immediately integrated with the essential aspects of the preceding stage. In other words, the individual returns to the world as it were at each step along the way.

Furthermore, it should also be noted that this process of evolution or development involves far more than a simple stacking of levels, as some of Wilber's critics have claimed, since each new element influences all previous and more primitive levels. For instance, human emotions are profoundly affected by thought and cannot simply be conceived of as animal emotions, though the individual is also likely to experience more primitive emotions that are also characteristic of the animal world, such as rage, fear, and joy. Yet, by the same token, the addition of new faculties can also undermine the more positive aspects of the preceding stages. For instance, the mind is quite capable of repressing the vitality of animal, emotional, and biological life to a very considerable extent. Very few human beings show the kind of vitality that can be seen in animals; few human beings move as gracefully as a deer. Developmental disorders can be conceived of as abortive differentiation, in which case higher stages fail to appear, or unsuccessful integration, in which case lower stages are repressed. There is scope in this traditional model for all kinds of developmental disorders, but, broadly speaking, the process of development is seen to consist of the twin processes of differentiation and hierarchical integration.

The objection to the idea of hierarchy from the point of view of ecological, feminist, and indigenous ideology (and many of Wilber's critics voice their objection on these grounds) often focuses on this aspect of repression. However, those who object tend to overlook the fact that repression is an undesirable complication within what is essentially a desirable developmental process. The fact that the human being transcends the animal certainly does not mean that human beings are thereby entitled to mistreat animals. On the contrary, the human being's higher state of consciousness also makes him more responsible for all less evolved beings. Besides, the endeavor to protect animals is a typically human undertaking! The only alternative to this hierarchical vision of reality is flatland, in which nothing is higher than anything else and nothing is lower than anything else and in which there is absolutely no possibility for growth and development. In rejecting all reference to a higher or deeper dimension because in the past this doctrine has been used to repress other populations or life forms, our postmodern culture tragically condemns itself to a world that will only deal with the lowest sensory dimension— material reality and bodily needs. In such a world there is no longer any place for the inner life of the individual.

This model can also be used to illustrate the fact that development or evolution occurs not only in a vertical direction but also in a horizontal direction. Rocks can be larger than human beings, plants can be older than human beings, animals can be faster than human beings or may have keener vision than human beings—*but none of the preceding life forms is able to think like a human being.* The faculty that distinguishes us from the other realms of nature is what makes us human beings. Human beings themselves can also differ from one another in the same way: some may be taller, some may be older, some may be able to run faster—but none of these properties is specific to the human being. Wilber's plea for the value of thought as a specifically human faculty that is, as such, a step closer to the spiritual needs to be seen in this light. In his opinion we access the spiritual via the doorway of the mind, and not by reverting to physicality, vitality, or emotionality, which are levels of consciousness that are specifically characteristic of the lower realms of nature.

I have dwelt on the traditional view of nature at some length because Wilber's work is firmly rooted in this tradition and his vision of human development cannot be understood outside of this context. Because he has such a profound command of this age-old concept, he is able to address the results of scientific research without falling into the reductionist pitfall as so many scientists have done. Scientific researchers of consciousness have always had a considerable problem with the subjective and qualitative aspect of consciousness, and have often chosen to concentrate purely on the objective and quantitative aspects of consciousness. Wilber has simply suggested that we need to honor both aspects if we are ever to arrive at an integral vision of consciousness.

THE STAGE PARADIGM

Developmental psychology proceeds on the basis of the assumption that the individual develops the ability to think over a number of years, and this is particularly true of the capacity for abstract thought. The field of developmental psychology is currently dominated by two conflicting visions: Piaget's stage approach and an approach based on the theory of learning which sees the individual (and the child) as systems that have the ability to process information.[24] The first of these visions derives from biology, the second from cognitive science. Those who favor this second theory believe that rather than developing through a series of stages children simply acquire an increasing amount of knowledge in different fields during the course of their development. But the mere acquisition of knowledge does not actually constitute development. From this point of view the differences between children and adults are seen to be quantitative rather than qualitative. This controversy has not yet been resolved and many developmental psychologists work on the basis of a combination of the two paradigms.

J. H. Flavell describes the situation as follows: "The conservative term trends seems to be a more realistic descriptor than the more radical term stages, at least until some future Piaget [Wilber?] can convince us that the postinfancy developmental changes in the cognitive system are as truly fundamental and deep-lying as those that take place between early infancy and early childhood."[25] In the past developmental psychologists made a sharp distinction between children and adults, yet, according to Flavell, contemporary researchers are now focusing increasingly on the unexpected cognitive skills of young children, the equally unexpected cognitive deficiencies of adults and the cognitive inconsistency of both groups. As a result, the distinction between the child and the adult is less and less clear.

Having said this, Flavell is still of the opinion that it is possible to identify a number of trends that can be detected during the transition from childhood to adulthood.[26] There is an increase (1) in the ability to process information; (2) in domain-specific knowledge; (3) in the capacity for abstract thought (thought that is not tethered to concrete reality and can explore hypothetical possibilities); (4) in the capacity for quantitative thought (thought that is more precise than the typically qualitative thought patterns of the child); (5) in the sense that the element of play is inherent in thinking; (6) in the capacity for meta-cognition (the ability to observe and direct one's own thoughts and feelings); and (7) in the command of abilities that already exist in children in a rudimentary form.

To give an example of this last trend, some authors point to the fact that very young children are apparently able to philosophize—an ability that is generally associated with a far later age. The American philosopher Gareth Matthews, who believes that thinking in terms of stages can result in a patronizing attitude towards children, has written several books on the subject.[27] He goes as far as to say that philosophy is largely a child's activity in view of the fact that it is prompted by a sense of wonder about reality which is still very much alive in children and often lost in adults. In his book *The Philosophy of Childhood* (1994) he quotes the example of a five-year-old girl who said to her father: "I'm glad that there are letters." When asked to explain, she went on to say: "If there weren't any letters there wouldn't be any sounds. And if there weren't any sounds, there wouldn't be any words . . . And if there weren't any words, we wouldn't be able to think . . . and if we weren't able to think, there wouldn't be a world."[28] He sees a certain similarity between this reasoning and the doctrine expounded by the Greek philosopher Parmenides, who emphasized the unity of thought and being. Yet to show that it is precarious to interpret statements made by children in this way, let me give a similar example. Wilber quotes a similar incident as an example of the kind of word magic that, according to the stage model, is typical of the magic-mythical thinking of the five-year-old. According to Piaget, at this stage of development the child believes that the name of something is actually part of the object to which it refers or that the name actually exists within the object. A child of five can say, "If there weren't any words it would be very bad. You couldn't make anything. How could things have been made?"[29]

Wilber's stage model shows that while mental faculties initially emerge very early on in development, these faculties mature over the course of time. A child may be able to use concepts before he or she is seven years old, but a seven-year-old is highly unlikely to show the kind of philosophical finesse that draws on a fully mature capacity for abstract thought. Nevertheless, regardless of the age at which it is first thought to appear, in terms of developmental psychology, the ability to use concepts is clearly of a higher order than the ability to deal only with two-dimensional images or words. For whereas two-dimensional images refer to a concrete object and also look like the object to which they refer, a word refers to the same object without looking like the object, which makes dealing with words a more complex task from a cognitive point of view, and dealing with concepts, which refer to a whole class of objects, is more difficult still.

Wilber does not pursue the finer details of Piaget's body of thought, particularly when it comes to the explanation of the various stages identified by Piaget. In the more literary version of Piaget's thought, development is said to occur in at least three stages: the stage of reflecting reality (perceiving things), the stage of processing reality (thinking about things), and the stage of processing thought (thinking about thoughts). Wilber sees this to be an immutable series of stages, which is bound to occur in this order because each stage builds on the previous stage. Yet when it comes to explaining as opposed to simply describing these stages, Wilber leaves aside Piaget's mathematical-logical approach and opts instead for a metaphysical approach, in which he relates the stages of development to the planes of existence described in the perennial philosophy.[30]

Furthermore, over the years Wilber has increasingly distanced himself from the stance that development is first and foremost a question of cognitive development—which would imply that only intellectually gifted people have access to spiritual realms. He now sees the development of the intellect as one of many possible lines of development, as we saw in Chapter 4. Development that occurs primarily along emotional lines can also take the individual into spiritual dimensions, as has long been recognized in India where such development is pursued as bhakti yoga, or the path of love. Nevertheless, Wilber still holds to the idea that the personality must be formed to some extent before spiritual or transpersonal development is possible. Also in the case of emotional development it is possible to distinguish prepersonal, personal, and transpersonal stages of development.

PHILOSOPHY OF DEVELOPMENT

In the phase of his thinking that he now refers to as Wilber 3, Wilber focused intently on theoretical issues related to the idea of development. A discipline known as philosophy of development, which is concerned with the principles of developmental psychology, can be helpful in such an undertaking.[31] Under what conditions can development actually be said to have occurred? What dimensions of development can we identify as being distinct from one another? Is it legitimate to draw a comparison between individual and cultural development? The discipline of the philosophy of development deliberately avoids subscribing to a particular belief in progress; its aim is to subject the assumptions linked to the idea of human development to critical examination.

Those working in this field recognize three models of development: (1) the *mechanistic* model, which attempts to explain and predict development exactly, (2) the *organismic* model, which sees development as a purposive process, and (3) the *narrative* model, which interprets development as a life story that is meaningful to the person concerned. The first model derives from the world of physics (the approach that conceives of development as the processing of information also belongs in this category), the second model has a biological background, and the third model falls within the sphere of the humanities. The third model does most justice to the specifically human dimension of meaning. Yet, given that all three models reflect a certain aspect of the truth, those concerned with the philosophy of development attempt to integrate these three approaches. In doing so they suggest that there is a hierarchical relationship between the three models: the narrative interpretation is to be preferred, but where this is not possible, we need to fall back on organismic interpretation, and if the organismic interpretation does not apply, we then have to resort to a mechanistic interpretation.[32]

The authors of *Philosophy of Development* define development as "a process of more or less gradual change, resulting in (what can be reconstructed as) one or more qualitatively different stages for which the prior stages are necessary conditions."[33] In their eyes a model of development is always a *reconstruction* in retrospect of events that have already taken place. In reconstructing the various elements, it is important to make a distinction between describing the developmental process and evaluating the developmental process. Not all developments are desirable despite the fact that the term itself often has positive connotations. A sound theory of development will include arguments to account for both negative and positive aspects. The authors of *Philosophy of Development* also answer the fierce criticism that the idea of development has had to contend with from the postmodernist movement, which sees development as a typically modern notion that can no longer be upheld in a century that has witnessed the raging of two world wars. "All we can do," according to the leading postmodernist philosopher J. F. Lyotard, "is gaze in wonderment at the diversity of discursive species, just as we do at the diversity of plant and animal species."[34] Under the influence of postmodernist philosophy, thinking in terms of *stages* has largely given way to thinking in terms of *styles*, and it is now considered to be inconceivable to attach value judgements to these styles.

This last point remains to be seen. In my opinion it is possible to draw a parallel between human development and the realms of nature outlined above. Biology is faced with an overwhelming diversity of plant and animal species, but rather than simply observing that there are different biological styles that do not seem to be related to one another, and leaving it at that, by developing the theory of evolution biologists have managed to introduce order within a hugely complex situation, showing that the various species emerged one after another and from one another. This description of the process of evolution has lead some philosophers—including the likes of Wilber and Schumacher—to conclude that intrinsically human beings are worth more than animals because a greater depth of consciousness finds expression in human beings. We could also say that human beings span more of the planes of existence, or that they are closer to the goal of development, namely union with Spirit. Having acknowledged this to be the case, Wilber sees scope within the humanities for discussing, describing, and evaluating development. In other words, it is not necessary for us to confine ourselves to "gaz[ing] in wonderment at the diversity of discursive species" and Wilber uses two arguments to explain why this is so. First, he sees an inner contradiction in the assertion that no one stage is worth more than any other in view of the fact that the statement itself claims to have a clearer insight. Secondly he points out that a later stage always has access to an earlier stage, but that the earlier stages do not have access to the later stages. For this reason too the later stages can be said to be higher.[35]

The philosophy of development draws from Habermas in emphasizing the distinction between the logic of a model and the dynamic of a model. The *logic* of a model describes the various stages as a strictly linear sequence. The *dynamic* of a model examines how development actually occurs in reality. Since no one develops precisely according to the book, the dynamic aspect of the developmental process is also worthy of study. Wilber's approach is repeatedly criticized on account of the linear nature of his model, but those voicing such criticism have failed to grasp that the linear aspect simply depicts the logic of the model. Anyone who has studied Wilber's work in any depth will know that he also makes it abundantly clear that in reality developmental processes can be subject to all kinds of complications, such as fixation, regression, and dissociation. If we conceive of development as the climbing of a ladder, as Wilber likes to do, the logic of a model of development describes the ladder itself while the dynamic of a model of development explains the way in which people climb the ladder. And people can climb the ladder in all kinds of different ways, occasionally descending to the bottom of the ladder before climbing higher. They can also fall from the ladder at any rung. But far from denying the existence of the ladder, these differences simply confirm the fact that the ladder exists. This is why the metaphor has proved to be so useful when it comes to understanding the process of human development.

The philosophy of development also makes a distinction between horizontal and vertical reconstruction. *Horizontal reconstruction* involves identifying the specific dimension that shows signs of development within a certain domain (such as increasing refinement in terms of aesthetic sensitivity within the domain of art, for example). *Vertical reconstruction* involves identifying the stages through which this development occurs, and possibly the final stage or goal of the process. In his Wilber 3 model Wilber elaborates on these theoretical nuances of thinking in terms of stages in considerable detail. In his more recent work he identifies countless dimensions (or "streams") of development and continues to maintain that within a certain dimension development always occurs in stages (or "waves").

And finally, those working within the discipline of the philosophy of development also make a distinction between the *structure* of a developmental process and the *content* of a developmental process. In this particular context *content* refers to the concrete content of a cultural expression, while *structure* refers to the stage of development typically exemplified by the statement in question. In this way Wilber makes a distinction between the underlying or basic features of consciousness without which the surface features of consciousness could not exist. The terms *structure* and *content* are also associated with major philosophical traditions, and while a detailed discussion of these traditions is beyond the scope of this chapter, it is worth noting that the structuralism that has been developed in French circles (by de Saussure, Lévi-Strauss, Barthes, Lacan, and later by Derrida, Foucault, and Deleuze, who are generally said to be neostructuralists) is primarily concerned with the general structures on which individual cultural expressions are based, while the discipline of hermeneutics, which is predominantly a German affair (associated with such figures as Schleiermacher, Dilthey, Heidegger, Gadamer, Apel, and Habermas, who is admired by Wilber) is interested in the historically determined interpretations of these cultural expressions. Both movements clearly represent an aspect of the truth and only an integral approach can hope to combine the valid insights of both.

Both of these philosophical camps are very much concerned with language and thus fall within the category of the narrative model of development, but each focuses on a different aspect of language. A linguistic statement conveys the specific, time-bound content, in which hermeneutics is interested, through the vehicle of an abstract, timeless structure, which is the domain of structuralism. Those pursuing the philosophy of development seek to integrate both of these fields of interest to create what they call depth hermeneutics, in which concrete individual or cultural forms of expression are taken as a basis for penetrating to universal structures of consciousness. In this respect Piaget's work can be seen as a successful form of depth hermeneutics in view of the fact that he took the concrete statements of children as a point of departure in seeking to identify general structures of human consciousness (such as concrete operational thought, for example). The depth-hermeneutic approach is also characterized by its primary focus on how these structures of consciousness are generated, and for this reason the approach is also known as "genetic structuralism." Wilber's work fits with this genetic-structuralist tradition and indeed Wilber has made countless substantial theoretical contributions to the thinking in this field.

The authors of *Philosophy of Development* present a convincing case in support of the fact that under certain conditions it makes sense to talk about stages of development. From their point of view every model of development is always a rational reconstruction of events that need to be substantiated by the arguments of all of the parties concerned (also including the individual who happens to have undergone the process of development). And there must always be scope for revision. They differ from Wilber in the sense that they deliberately disregard visions of development that seek to comment on the history of the world à la Hegel or that seek a basis for the process of development in metaphysical categories: "With regard to the alleged universal claims of developmental theories we admit that this notion in classical developmental theories—above all in Hegel's *Odyssey of the Mind*—has an undeniably strong metaphysical dimension."[36] Yet Wilber has deliberately sought to expand developmental theory with a view to incorporating this metaphysical dimension. Only time will tell if this really leads to a deeper insight into the nature of development. In his recent writings, however, Wilber distances himself more and more from this metaphysical undertaking.

TRANSPERSONAL PSYCHOLOGY:
THE DOMAIN OF THE SOUL

If the existence of an interior dimension is accepted as being sufficiently plausible and if, in addition to this, we can also provide reasonable evidence to support the idea that during the course of his life the individual accesses deeper and deeper realms of this interior dimension—such that it is valid to speak of development—the next question is, where does the process of development end? Is the autonomous, rational individual the end point of the process, as theorists in the West have always claimed? Or is the spiritually aware, enlightened individual the end product of the process, as people in the East have been saying for centuries? If human enlightenment is indeed the ultimate goal of the process, abstract thought is not the pinnacle of development, but simply an interim stage that leads on to spiritual stages of consciousness. At this point we enter the realm of transpersonal psychology, which is predominantly concerned with the process of spiritual development.

In the *Textbook of Transpersonal Psychiatry and Psychology* (1996) the editors point to two paradigms in transpersonal psychology that are respectively defined as being "additive" or "dialectic."[37] *Additive* models conceive of the spiritual dimension as something that is added to the personal dimension, in which case spiritual development is considered to be a logical extension of personal development. Wilber, who sees personal development as giving way to transpersonal development, belongs to this camp. *Dialectic* models differ from additive models in that they situate the spiritual dimension in the past, in which case spiritual development is conceived of as a return to something that has been lost somewhere along the way, regardless of the form that this may take. Jung and all of the latter-day neo-Jungians, such as Washburn, belong to this camp, as do those working within the broader context of depth psychology, such as A. H. Almaas and Stanislav Grof. Michael Washburn has suggested the terms "ladder model" and "spiral model" to describe the two approaches. Unfortunately, those who compiled the *Textbook* do not address the question as to why these two paradigms currently hold sway within the world of transpersonal psychology. I would venture to suggest that this is because the majority of those working within the field are still approaching the question of spiritual development from the point of view of depth psychology (the spiral model), while pioneers such as Wilber have abandoned this way of thinking and set out in search of a height psychology of spirituality (the ladder model). Eventually a choice will need to be made between these two mutually exclusive options.[38]

WILBER VERSUS JUNG

Wilber has made a number of strong statements about Carl Gustav Jung at various points in his work. From these statements we can attempt to distill Wilber's opinion of Jung. Wilber's main objection to Jung is that Jung only refers to the two categories of the ego and the Self or, in other words, the personal and the collective (or transpersonal).[39] In Wilber's opinion this is far too broad a definition of the transpersonal given that it also encompasses the prepersonal and thus encourages the pre/trans fallacy. With only two categories it is easy to confuse the prepersonal with the transpersonal, or primitivism with spirituality, or the mythic with the mystical, or archaic images from our evolutionary past with the spiritual archetypes of our spiritual future.

Given that few of Jung's followers make these distinctions these days, Wilber is of the opinion that Jung has prompted an extremely regressive movement in psychology: "Consciousness is simply divided into two great domains: personal and collective. And the tendency is then to take anything collective and call it spiritual, mystical, transpersonal, whereas most of it is simply prepersonal, prerational, preconventional, regressive."[40] Obvious examples of this kind of thinking can be seen in the literature produced by writers inspired by Jung who interpret the wild or primitive aspect of our nature as spirituality.[41] These writers point to the differences between this state of natural wildness and the unnaturalness of the cultivated Western individual, equating the naturalness with spirituality. However, according to the spiritual traditions the individual is not a primitive being with a thin cultural veneer but a spiritual being charged with the task of emerging from nature (the body) and culture (the personality) in order to discover his deepest spiritual identity. From this point of view, rather than being seen as something that prevents us from accessing our true nature, culture is regarded as a factor that makes an essential contribution to the process of our humanization.

Wilber is well aware of the fact that this is a complicated and delicate subject: "For almost half a century, the Jungian paradigm has been the major—and only—viable theory of transpersonal psychology in the West. I personally believe that the Jungian model has many strong points—but even more weak points—and that this debate will in fact be the most heated area of discussion in the coming decade, simply because so many people are involved in its outcome. But in any event the dialogue between the Jungian model and the general transpersonal field will continue to be a source of rich mutual stimulation and challenge."[42]

In Jung's vision the individual begins the process of development in a state of unconscious union with the Self (mind in its totality), from which the ego (the conscious part of the Self) slowly extricates itself. Because the gravitational power of the Self is so strongly present during the initial phases, this is a process of emerging and falling back again. In mythology this is symbolized by the archetypes of the Hero (the ego) and the Great Mother (the unconscious). Only once the ego has gained sufficient strength is it able to engage in a new relationship with the Self, only this time the relationship is conscious. Jung called this process, which may occur during the second half of life, "individuation." His vision suggests the image of a spiral, in which the ego first extricates itself from the Self in order to reunify with the Self—but at a higher level. During the first half of life the ego represses the Self; during the second half of life this repression will have to be released if the Self is to be able to return to consciousness.

Wilber juxtaposes this spiral model of human development with his ladder model. In this second vision, rather than beginning the process of development from a state of fusion with the Self, the individual starts out completely merged with the physical body. As the ego and the corresponding mental faculties begin to develop, the body is increasingly relegated and both the body and the emotions are often repressed as part of this process. In this vision it is not necessary for the individual to retrace his steps in order to be able to reach the Self. On the contrary, the individual has to continue his development, so that body and the ego can both be transcended in the spiritual stages of development, which have nothing to do with the prepersonal stages of development that occur during early infancy. This is a crucial point in Wilber's thought. In short, according to Wilber we are not dealing with just two principles—the ego and the Self—but with at least three: the body, the ego, and the Self (or, to use the traditional terms, body, soul, and spirit). In this respect Wilber and Jung (and with him all neo-Jungians) are diametrically opposed.

Nevertheless, the value of the ego is heavily emphasized both in Jungian psychology and in Wilber's work, albeit with a subtle difference. In Jungian psychology it is considered to be important to develop a strong ego because a strong ego is indispensable when it comes to engaging in a conscious confrontation with the power of the collective unconscious. In Wilber's psychology a strong ego is important because it is seen to be a step closer to the spiritual dimension, which in this case is further ahead along the road of development traversed thus far. As far as Wilber is concerned, the step from the body to the ego brings us closer to spirit, whereas in depth psychology the step from the body to the ego is considered to be a move away from spirit or the Self.

Wilber's vision of spiritual development is not a form of depth psychology and would in fact be better described as height psychology. In this respect Wilber is following in the footsteps of the Italian psychiatrist Roberto Assagioli, the founder of the psychosynthesis movement.[43] Assagioli was speaking and writing about the superconscious—as a realm of the unconscious that exists in addition to the subconscious discovered by depth psychology—back in the thirties. Freud spoke about the personal unconscious, which is primarily made up of primitive impulses, and, as is widely known, would have nothing to do with religion. Jung, on the other hand, had a strong interest in religion—this difference was partly responsible for the rift between Freud and Jung—and believed that beneath the personal unconscious there ran an even deeper layer that he called the "collective unconscious," the realm of the so-called archetypes. In other words, Jung consistently worked within the context of depth psychology. Assagioli broke radically with this way of thinking, claiming that the unconscious contained both a lower dimension and a higher dimension, which he referred to as the "superconscious." As far as he was concerned, this superconscious realm (in which he situated the Self) was the realm of spirituality. Towards the end of his life Assagioli undertook to write about the realm of the superconscious, but unfortunately he died before doing so. Wilber has since studied the superconscious in considerable detail and has discovered and identified a number of layers that he has described as the psychic, the subtle, the causal, and the ultimate. Very few psychologists have chosen to follow the path marked out by Assagioli, but Wilber is one of them.

WILBER'S MAIN OPPONENTS

A number of theoretical points of view have more or less crystalized since transpersonal psychology first emerged as an academic discipline at the end of the sixties. Though he has also turned his attention to cultural and philosophical issues that extend way beyond transpersonal psychology, Wilber counts as the leading theorist in the field. Nevertheless, there are a number of alternative visions within the world of transpersonal psychology, two of which are worth examining here.

One of Wilber's most important contemporary opponents is the psychiatrist Stanislav Grof, the author of *Realms of the Human Unconscious* (1975), *Beyond the Brain* (1985), and *The Adventure of Self-Discovery* (1988) among other works. Grof has the honor of having introduced the term *transpersonal*. He has also done a great deal to establish the transpersonal community, setting up organizations and organizing congresses all over the world. Grof's model of consciousness is based on the framework suggested by Jung, in which there is a personal layer and collective layer. However, Grof's contribution has been to suggest that there is third layer between these two, which he has called "the perinatal," because it has to do with the circumstances surrounding birth. While the personal unconscious was primarily Freud's territory and the collective unconscious was Jung's territory, the psychoanalyst Otto Rank was a pioneer in the field of perinatal psychology. In his well-known book *The Trauma of Birth* (1929) Rank wrote that the transition from the peaceful environment of the womb to the cold and threatening external world is so radical for each infant that traces of this traumatic experience can still be detected in later life. Grof, who has pursued this line of reasoning, is of the opinion that the abrupt transition from the womb to the world also has certain positive effects in view of the fact that the battle that the baby fights to be born can also generate a euphoric feeling of triumph, or even rebirth.

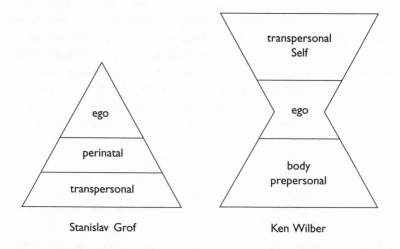

FIGURE 7.3.   Grof versus Wilber

Leading his patients back into their past with the aid of LSD, Grof discovered that not only were they able to reexperience the events of their earliest childhood, but they were also able to reexperience the events surrounding their birth. Some were able to delve even further back into the past and reexperience the peaceful state of being in the womb, which Grof related to the mystical state of unity. Grof claims that in failing to pay sufficient attention to this realm of perinatal experience, Wilber underestimates the importance of an event as radical as birth. He goes as far as to refer to Wilber's "surprising conceptual blind spot" and "astonishing omission."[44] Grof evidently considers the reexperience of one's own birth to be of decisive importance in the process of coming into contact with the spiritual dimension. Grof is also of opinion that the rebirth experience is an essential element of the ritual and spiritual life of many non-Western cultures,[45] adding that in his opinion spiritual development does not occur in a straight line but that it is a process in which progression alternates with regression.[46]

Wilber answered this criticism by saying that spiritual development is not so much dependent on the reexperience of biological birth, but on the experience of an existential crisis in which one is inescapably faced with the issue of one's own finiteness. These two crises are inextricably interwoven in Grof's work, which according to Wilber is in conflict with the teachings of the spiritual traditions: "You do not find the necessity to relive clinical birth in any of the major spiritual manuals and techniques. It is rarely if ever mentioned in any of the ascetic practices, shamanic techniques, or contemplative yogas. You do not find it in the great classics of the perennial philosophy or in any of the major wisdom tradition texts. Nor do you find it in the vast majority of the Western depth psychologists, including James and Jung and the general Jungian tradition."[47] He concludes his response to Grof's criticism by saying "Grof is assuming exactly that which he is supposed to demonstrate—namely, not that there exists an existential level lying between all personal and transpersonal development (all parties agree that is so), but that the essential core of that existential level is a stencil of clinical childbirth (which virtually nobody but Grof maintains, and for which he has presented no generalized evidence)."[48]

Wilber also refutes Grof's often voiced criticism that Wilber's model is not sufficiently empirically grounded, pointing to the fact that, on the contrary, the model is based on extensive empirical research: "Stan [Grof] has a disturbing tendency to describe his research as being THE clinical data. He repeatedly says that it is necessary 'to test theoretical adequacy against the clinical data.' I agree totally. But by 'the clinical data' Grof means basically *his* data (hallucinogens and hyperventilation), whereas the vast majority of researchers I have relied on are exactly those who pioneered direct clinical and experimental evidence, from Jean Piaget's groundbreaking *méthode clinique* to Margaret Mahler's exhaustive videotaped observations, from Loevinger's tests of self development to Kohlberg's and Gilligan's pioneering moral investigations based on empirical evidence—not to mention the vast phenomenological evidence presented by the contemplative wisdom traditions themselves. *The Atman Project*, for example, was directly based on the empirical and phenomenological and clinical evidence, clearly cited, of over sixty researchers from numerous approaches (and hundreds of others in an informal way)—the bulk of which cannot be adequately handled in Grof's model. And yet Grof keeps saying that my approach cannot handle THE clinical evidence, a stance that is truly bizarre."[49]

In many respects Wilber and Grof stand at opposite ends of the spectrum. Grof is a man of clinical practice while Wilber is at his best as a theorist. Opposite the Apollonian thinker Wilber, who strives towards clarity in theory, stands the Dionysian doer Grof, who is primarily concerned with the therapeutic experience and does not shrink from using mind-altering substances in the process. Wilber and Grof are also mirror images of one another in terms of the importance they attach to the perinatal problem. Whereas Wilber appears to have studied literally everything in the field of psychology with the exception of Rank's birth theory, Grof appears to pin everything on this particular theory. As far as Grof is concerned, the fact that Wilber has changed his stage model to include a perinatal stage at the very start of the process of development is not enough.[50] Yet, according to Wilber, Grof is more open to his suggestion that it might be more appropriate to attribute memories of the perinatal period to the transpersonal soul than to the nascent personality.[51]

Another of Wilber's contemporary opponents is the philosopher Michael Washburn, the author of *The Ego and the Dynamic Ground* (1988), *Transpersonal Psychology in Psychoanalytic Perspective* (1994) and the recent *Embodied Spirituality in a Sacred World* (2003).[52] Washburn has been keen to formulate an alternative to Wilber's model that ties in explicitly not only with the depth psychology expounded by Freud and Jung but also with existentialist philosophy. One of his reasons for wanting to do so is that the spiral model is simpler than Wilber's ladder model in that it makes do with only two explanatory principles—the ego and the Ground (or Self), whereas Wilber insists that there need to be at least three categories—the body, the ego, and the Self.[53] In my opinion, in this instance the value of this criterion of simplicity, which is known in philosophy as Ockham's razor, is debatable. If we are to argue along these lines, materialism offers an even simpler explanation; then we need only be concerned with the single principle of matter. Clearly, in addition to meeting the requirement of simplicity, scientific theories also need to do justice to the complexity of the phenomenon that they seek to explain. And the reality of consciousness contains far more complexity than we are inclined to think.

Washburn and Wilber have already crossed swords in article form. In 1990 the *Journal of Humanistic Psychology* published an essay by Washburn entitled "Two Patterns of Transcendence" together with Wilber's reply to Washburn.[54] In 1996 *ReVision* published Washburn's article "The Pre/Trans Fallacy Reconsidered."[55] As a depth psychologist Washburn believes that the child lives in a state of unconscious union with the spiritual Self, which Washburn refers to as the "Ground." For the process of growing up to be able to occur, the Self must be repressed and pushed into the background. Yet, once a certain degree of identity has been consolidated, the repression can be released and the self-aware individual can return to the Self or Ground, this time consciously.

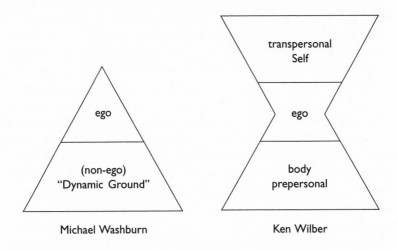

FIGURE 7.4.   Washburn versus Wilber

Washburn acknowledges that in formulating the pre/trans fallacy, Wilber has identified the most important theoretical question faced by transpersonal psychology, but he is not so sure that Wilber has come up with the right answer. For whereas Wilber relates the prepersonal and the transpersonal to two different aspects of the individual, Washburn suspects that the prepersonal and the transpersonal are two different expressions of the same "non-egoic potential." In this way Washburn hopes to be able to circumvent the pre/trans fallacy. Once the individual has emerged from the Ground in its prepersonal form, he then goes on to develop an ego, which enables him to return to the Ground in its transpersonal form. Thus, as far as Washburn is concerned, he is certainly not advocating regression to the prepersonal stages under the guise of spirituality.

Ironically enough, this is precisely the point of view that Wilber supported in his earliest work, in the phase he now refers to as Wilber 1. At that point he too suggested that there were only two main principles— ego and Mind (or Spirit), separated by a number of intermediary stages. However, it was only when Wilber abandoned this vision in favor of a vision involving at least three principles—body, ego, and Mind—in order to be more closely aligned with the perennial philosophy, that he finally had the impression that he was on the right track. Thus, essentially speaking, the controversy between Wilber and Washburn is the same as that between Wilber 1 and Wilber 2. In answer to Washburn's criticism Wilber can only repeat the criticism that he himself previously directed at his own work.[56]

Washburn's argument is based on the idea that the child is in contact with the Ground of existence, albeit a prepersonal expression of it that he calls the libido. This ambiguity in Washburn's definition of the Ground— which he sometimes conceives of as libido and sometimes as Spirit—is unacceptable as far as Wilber is concerned. In Wilber's opinion there can only be two options: either (1) the child is aware of Spirit and loses this awareness as it grows up, but can regain it as an adult by returning to this phase (hence the spiral model), or (2) the child is *not* aware of Spirit *and is therefore incapable of losing this awareness* as it grows—in which case spiritual development can no longer be conceived of as a return to an earlier phase. But, in Wilber's opinion, a child cannot be unconsciously one with the Ground.

Wilber considers it to be extremely unlikely that the child is in contact with the highest spiritual consciousness. Neither the Indian tradition nor the Tibetan tradition has ever claimed this to be the case. Only romantic depth psychologists attempt to maintain this point of view.[57]

Wilber's final objection to Washburn's theory is that Washburn suggests that repression of the Ground is the mechanism by means of which the normal process of development from child to adult is able to occur, while as far as Wilber is concerned development is propelled by a natural process of growth: "The prior and most important principle is that of growth, or self-actualization, or development, or evolution. That is primary. And then, no doubt about it, during the course of that growth and evolution, certain capacities and potentials can be repressed. But that is not the mechanism of development: that is something that can go wrong with it. Washburn, in particular, misunderstands this simplest of notions."[58]

Like Grof, Washburn also adopts a stance that is complementary to Wilber's position. Particularly in his early work Wilber based his vision primarily on Eastern philosophy and cognitive developmental psychology; Washburn, on the other hand, is more at home with Western mysticism and psychoanalysis. Certainly in *Transformations of Consciousness*, however, Wilber has also endeavored to take the insights of psychoanalysis into account in his model. Whereas Wilber has attempted to prompt a "revolution" in psychology—the term is used by British psychologist John Rowan in his book *The Transpersonal* (1992)[59]—by breaking away from the frame of reference developed by depth psychology, Washburn seems to be a counterrevolutionary thinker who wants to return to the cradle of Western depth psychology.

Thus while Grof and Washburn are both of the opinion that we lose contact with the reality of the spiritual dimension reality somewhere along the way—either when we leave the peaceful environment of the womb or during our early infancy—Wilber deliberately situates the spiritual dimension in the future: as far as he is concerned, the process of development is geared towards Spirit from the very beginning. Yet, having said this, Wilber's model also includes room for the idea that we did indeed lose contact with the spiritual dimension somewhere along the way, as will be clear from the following paragraphs, which discuss the metaphysical background to Wilber's model.

THE WILBER CONFERENCE IN SAN FRANCISCO

The *ReVision* trilogy devoted to Wilber's work led to a conference in San Francisco in January of 1997. The conference led to a book: *Ken Wilber in Dialogue*, which was published in 1998.[60] During the Wilber conference numerous points of criticism were leveled at Wilber's work, but certainly to my way of thinking, the main point of contention—the spiral model or the ladder model?—was scarcely addressed. Instead the various authors chose to focus on the following questions: (1) How should a discussion of transpersonal theory be conducted and, in particular, what part should criticism play in such a discussion?[61] (2) How should we actually conceive of the process of spiritual development? (3) Are there important differences between men and women in terms of spirituality? (4) How does Wilber see ecology and earthly spirituality? (5) Is Wilber sufficiently aware of the danger inherent in evolutionary theories? Aren't such theories bound to lead to a lack of appreciation of lower forms of consciousness? *Ken Wilber in Dialogue* has a somewhat different focus: (1) How accurate is Wilber's interpretation of the many sources he refers to in his work? (2) Are there any other paradigms (in addition to Wilber's paradigm) in the field of transpersonal theory? (3) How should transpersonal theory deal with the Other in the form of nature, women, indigenous cultures, and personal relationships? (4) What precisely do we mean by regression? (5) How should a spiritual discussion be conducted?[62]

Within the context of depth psychology development is visualized as a spiral from the Self to the ego and back again. The Self/unconscious is conceived of as a woman (the Great Mother) in relation to the masculine ego (the Hero) and the fact that the ego has separated itself from nature is generally said to be the cause of the current environmental crisis. Evolutionary theories that see this process of extrication as a positive development are often treated with suspicion because they place the ego and the corresponding mental faculties higher than nature, which is thought to contain the Self. Within the context of height psychology, however, development is thought of as a ladder that extends from the body and nature via the ego to the Self. The first of these two points of view associates the spiritual with the feminine and nature, from which the ego, which is conceived of as masculine, has separated itself. For this reason those working in these circles attach considerable value to feminist, ecological, and antimodern theories. Yet the second of these two points of view does not consider the feminine to be any more spiritual than the masculine. On the contrary, men and women both have to undergo the difficult process of development from prepersonal, body-bound consciousness via personal ego-consciousness to the transpersonal, spiritual consciousness of the Self. The fact that for men the emphasis in this process is often on will and effort while for women the emphasis is more likely to be on love and the sense of community does not alter this basic fact. The fact that the ego has succeeded in differentiating itself from nature is welcomed as an essential achievement, though to the same extent we may also regret the fact that in doing so the ego all too often dissociates itself from nature. Nevertheless, this latter phenomenon should never lead us to forget how important it is for the individual soul to differentiate itself from the biological aspect of nature. And finally, though it is important to keep an eye out for possible complications, this second point of view does not consider evolutionary theories to be dangerous per se. On the contrary, according to Wilber the idea of evolution enables us to renounce limited magical/mythical worldviews, with their inevitable ethnocentrism, in order to grow towards a liberal, humanistic, and pluralistic society, which can usher in a true spiritual wisdom culture of the future.

In my opinion all of these issues can be traced to a single more fundamental question: have we left the spiritual dimension behind us (as the depth psychologists claim) or is spirituality somewhere ahead of us (as height psychologists such as Wilber maintain)? Must we look back to the birth or to bodily emotions that have been repressed in order to be able to find the spiritual dimension, or ahead, to the Spirit that awaits us in the superconscious? In Wilber's vision we encounter the following paradox: in order to reencounter the spiritual dimension from which (also according to Wilber) we have become separated, we do not need to look back to the past but to continue along the path we set out on when we grew from child to adult. This paradox is resolved by the doctrine of involution, which claims that we descended from the Divine into matter, and through the process of evolution/development we are now finding our way back. Continuing this ascent will finally bring us back to the realm of Spirit that we once left. What distinguishes Wilber from most of his colleagues in the transpersonal field is his unequivocal espousal of the doctrine of involution. With this we enter the domain of esotericism and metaphysics. The following paragraphs cover this in more detail.

METAPHYSICAL RELIGION: THE DOMAIN OF SPIRIT

From his very first publication onwards Wilber has made no secret of the fact he allows himself to be guided by a metaphysical frame of reference in seeking to formulate theory. The foreword to his first book *The Spectrum of Consciousness* opens with the following quote from Fritjof Schuon: "There is no science of the soul without a metaphysical basis to it."[63] But how appropriate is it for Wilber to include metaphysical considerations in his argument? Doesn't this automatically disqualify him in the eyes of the scientific community as an unreliable interlocutor? Wilber might answer that it is better to be explicit about your own metaphysical assumptions than to embrace materialism under the guise of pure science, when materialism is ultimately also a metaphysical point of view. Wilber's plea for the rehabilitation of the interior dimension is certainly at odds with the prevailing materialist paradigm and shows far more affinity with spiritual and idealist philosophical movements. It is not without reason that Wilber has chosen the perennial philosophy, which attempts to formulate the insights of the spiritual traditions in intellectual terms, as his point of departure.

The perennial philosophy is said to be esoteric because it cannot be expounded in purely rational terms and requires a certain propensity for mysticism to be understood in its entirety. However, there are various schools in esotericism. Each world religion has its own esoteric or mystical core, and, in addition to this, there are also schools of thought developed by individual philosophers who have attempted to formulate this esoteric core in a way that makes it more comprehensible. The esoteric aspects of Wilber's model are based largely on the philosophy of Sri Aurobindo, an Indian thinker and visionary who succeeded in combining the insights of Eastern philosophy with the doctrine of evolution expounded in the West.[64] At the same time Wilber has also borrowed ideas from contemporary mystics, such as Adi Da Samraj, who have reformulated the universal body of thought in a highly individual manner.

THE PERENNIALISTS

In a certain sense Wilber can be said to be one of the school of so-called perennialists or traditionalists, which includes, among others, figures such as René Guénon, Ananda Coomaraswamy, Fritjof Schuon, and Huston Smith. It should be noted that this is not a tight-knit school of thought, but rather a group of like-minded authors, and also that Wilber has explored contemporary philosophy to a far greater extent than most of the traditionalists, who often abhor modern society. It was above all Huston Smith who sought to rehabilitate the age-old concept that reality should be conceived of as a series of layers in *Forgotten Truth* written in 1976. As we have seen, this idea also forms the backbone of Wilber's model.

In contrast to the majority of the traditionalists—and also in contrast to Huston Smith, who adopts an ambivalent position with regard to this point—Wilber is far more positive about modern Western culture, especially as far as the idea of evolution is concerned. For this reason he prefers to describe his own philosophy as "neo-perennial philosophy," in order to emphasize the fact that his reasoning differs from that of the traditionalists with regard to certain essential points.[65] While the other perennial authors tend to characterize the prescientific era as spiritual and modern society as unidimensional and materialistic, which rules out the possibility of evolution and suggests instead that degeneration has occurred, Wilber's criticism of contemporary culture is more subtle. Although he too has sharply criticized the superficiality of the materialist Western culture—which he graphically describes as flatland—he continues to maintain that the cultural history of humanity has shown steady but irreversible evolution. As far as Wilber is concerned, it is simply not true that in the past people in general were more spiritual than they are now—magical and mythical thought had the entire culture in its grip and individualism was not encouraged (except by those who deliberately set out in search of spirituality). It was only when Wilber realized that the traditional doctrine of the spheres could be used in support of the idea of evolution—in the sense that evolution can be conceived of as progression through the various planes of existence—that he saw the possibility of a truly contemporary synthesis of ancient wisdom and modern knowledge.

THE THEOSOPHICAL TRADITION

In view of the fact that the idea of the spheres of existence occupies such a crucial position in Wilber's work, it is legitimate to ask whether there are any other sources of information that might also throw a light on the subject. In this spirit I would like to refer to the theosophical tradition, which sought to introduce the idea of a perennial philosophy—which it described as the "ancient wisdom" or the "secret doctrine"—in the West as far back as 1875, well before Guénon and company were first heard of (around 1920).[66] Theosophy might be described as an early nineteenth-century, Western attempt to reformulate the perennial philosophy in more contemporary language. In doing so the theosophical authors tied in explicitly with the Western neoplatonic tradition partly expounded by Plotinus who is highly admired by Wilber. According to *The Key to Theosophy*, written by H. P. Blavatsky in 1889, the word *theosophy* dates from this period—approximately the third century A. D.[67]

It is immediately striking that the idea of evolution is a central theme in the theosophical literature. Not biological evolution, but an inner, spiritual evolution, which is said to occur in parallel to the evolution of the different life forms. In *The Secret Doctrine* (1888) H. P. Blavatsky presents a convincing alternative to Christian creationism and Darwinian evolution, which were the only two options in her day. In her eyes the doctrine of evolution was not wrong, as the theologians claimed, but incomplete, due to the fact that it overlooked the subjective component. Although I am not willing to stick my neck out in endorsing all of the statements she makes in her voluminous writing, she has the honor of being the first person to introduce this third way of thinking on a large scale in modern times.

Theosophical metaphysics is extremely comprehensive and shows a considerable amount of overlap with the ideas that Wilber presents in his books. It is a real goldmine of information, covering such concepts such as the inner makeup of the individual, the nature of the various spheres of existence, the process of life after death and reincarnation, the vast cosmic processes of involution and evolution, the various stages of spiritual development, and other subjects. Given that this is the case, we cannot afford to overlook theosophy as a source of information.[68] The fact that it is indeed often overlooked is explained historically by the fact that many of the traditionalist authors were opposed to theosophy—René Guénon even went as far as to refer to it as a "pseudo-religion." However, in *The Only Way*—a recent study of the views of René Guénon and Ananda Coomaraswamy published in 1997—William Quine, Jr., argues that, in fact, the perennialists and the theosophists are actually in agreement on the most important principles.[69] What is more, what follows can be seen as an attempt to show that the theosophical literature also proves its worth if we wish to explore the details of the "machinery of the Kosmos." And since three of Wilber's books—namely *The Spectrum of Consciousness*, *The Atman Project*, and *Up from Eden* (and also the collection of essays prompted by the recent Wilber conference, *Ken Wilber in Dialogue*)—are currently published by the American Theosophical publishers, Quest Books, a comparison between Wilber and theosophy seems to be more than justified. In my opinion the following subjects merit further investigation.

First, there is the question of the precise makeup of the inner world of the individual. In his most recent work, particularly in *The Eye of Spirit* (1997), *One Taste* (1999), and *Integral Psychology* (2000), Wilber sees the individual as a composite being made up of a physical body, a psychological ego, a spiritual soul, and a Divine Self. This is identical to the theosophical view of the individual, which sees the individual as being made up of a physical body, a psychological personality, a spiritual Ego, and a divine monad. The theosophical sources contain an unusually clear account of how the spiritual Ego (or soul) emerges from the monad and generates a personality and how the personality then incarnates in a physical body. Thus Theosophy traditionally starts at the top and works its way down, whereas the transpersonal literature starts at the bottom and works its way up—a transpersonal, higher Self is thought to exist above the personality, without the origin of this Self ever being clear. This tends to give rise to the false opinion that the individual needs to identify with this Self—which is impossible because only the Self is able to identify. The only thing the individual can do is to let go of the identification with the personality, and thus realize that he was *always* the Self. (And the same applies to the next stage of spiritual development, which leads from the spiritual Ego, or Self, to the monad.)[70]

A second point can throw light on the nature of consciousness and the process of development. Inspired by Hindu sources, the theosophical literature describes consciousness as having three different aspects: will, thought, and feeling (or, in Eastern terminology, *sat, chit, ananda*). Western psychology seems to be exclusively interested in the intellect, is reluctantly beginning to pay attention to emotion, and shows absolutely no interest in the will; a true integral psychology will need to honor all three aspects. This view of consciousness maintains that spirituality can be attained via the line of the will (*karma yoga*), the line of the intellect (*jnana yoga*), and the line of feeling (*bhakti yoga*). Theosophy even goes as far as to suggest that these are the three fundamental lines of development by means of which consciousness evolves.[71] In his recent work Wilber is fully aware of the countless dimensions within which development can occur, so it might be worth examining whether these countless dimensions can be reduced to a few core dimensions.

Third, it is possible to make an illuminating distinction between vertical and horizontal processes of development. The normal process of development occurs in a vertical direction from the body to the personality and from the soul to Spirit. In addition to this, individuals may differ in terms of the degree to which they have developed in a horizontal direction—some are physically stronger than others, some are intellectually stronger than others, some show more refined emotional development than others, and some show greater spiritual development than others. Thus it is possible to draw up relatively simple development profiles to indicate not only the degree of vertical development (the height of consciousness attained by the individual in question) but also the degree of horizontal development (the breadth of development within any one plane of existence). Or, to state it more clearly, just as people differ in terms of the size of their body and their physical strength, there are also individual differences in the emotional or astral body, the mental body, and the spiritual body.

Fourth, the theosophical view of reincarnation is similar to the view of reincarnation presented in Wilber's work, in the sense that both state that it is the soul that reincarnates and not the personality—a notion that can still occasionally be found in the New Age literature. However, Wilber is of the opinion that virtue and wisdom are the only qualities carried over to the next life and that concrete memories are not carried over. Yet according to theosophy the spiritual Self also has a mental aspect (in view of the fact consciousness itself has the three attributes referred to above). Why deny the possibility that the spiritual Self also has a mental aspect, as a repository of the memories that persist from one life to the next? It is said that the Buddha was able to look back over all of his previous lives to the time that he was still an animal being.

Fifth, there is a significant difference between the view of life after death presented in the theosophical literature and the view presented in the *Tibetan Book of the Dead* that Wilber subscribes to throughout his work. Wilber seems to assume that at the moment of death a person travels through the entire Chain of Being—from the dying body via the personality and the transpersonal soul to the Clear Light of Spirit and then subsequently back through the chain in reverse order—from Spirit via the soul and the personality into a new physical body. According to the *Tibetan Book of the Dead* this process takes no more than a few weeks at the most. Yet the theosophical literature describes the process of reincarnation differently, claiming that the individual does not ascend to the elevated level of Spirit immediately at the moment of dying, but between one life and the next rises to the highest regions of the mental plane, where the mental aspect of the Ego (known as *manas*) resides. Furthermore, the process is thought to take far longer—anything from a few hours to several centuries—than is suggested in the *Tibetan Book of the Dead*. The descent into the physical body, on the other hand, is said to take proportionally less time. One important result of this alternative view is that the amount of time spent in the hereafter can be extensive—the length of time being determined by the speed with which the individual being is able to let go of the personality in which it was clothed during the life that has just ended. If the individual is able to let go relatively rapidly, possibly because he has spent time meditating and has learnt not to be particularly identified with personal thoughts and feelings, the amount of time spent in the hereafter may be quite short—maybe even as short as is suggested in the *Tibetan Book of the Dead*. A being that is exclusively identified with the personal aspects of consciousness will spend far longer in the celestial realm. This alternative view of life after death might lead us to reconsider the extent to which the Tibetan view is universally applicable.

Sixth, the theosophical literature presents a clear overview of the various spheres, levels or planes of existence, from the physical plane to the world of the Divine. These planes are described independently of the process of descent and ascent through these spheres. Because Wilber has chosen to place a strong psychological emphasis on his presentation of the perennial philosophy, and is therefore more inclined to elaborate on the stages of development than on the spheres that provide the underpinning for this development, it is not always easy to see the correlation between spheres and stages in his reasoning. If we compare the theosophical model of the seven spheres with Wilber's model of development, we see among other things that there is no ontological basis in the form of a corresponding plane of existence for the psychic and existential stage stages in Wilber's model. Whereas the personal (physical, emotional, and mental) stages and the spiritual (subtle and causal) stages unfold within the context of a corresponding world, this is not the case for the psychic stage and the existential stage. Maybe it would be more accurate to make a distinction between primary stages, for which there is a parallel in the form of a separate plane of existence, and secondary stages, for which this is no such parallel (like there are spectral colors, such as red, yellow and blue, and nonspectral colors, such as brown, grey, and pink).

And last, Wilber stands out from the majority of his colleagues in the transpersonal world because he has no reservation in espousing the doctrine of involution (though he now prefers to speak of "involuntary givens"). Probably more than anything else, it is this that stands in the way of his vision being accepted by the scientific community, but in my opinion the doctrine of involution is an essential aspect of any complete metaphysical worldview. Like Aurobindo, Wilber uses the term *involution* to refer to the general movement from Spirit to matter; he sometimes relates this to the Big Bang that the physicists speak of, without elaborating any further. The theosophical literature describes at least four movements from Spirit to matter, only one of which can strictly be referred to as involution: (1) The process of creation that gives rise to the seven spheres, as the Divine orders primal matter into a series of worlds (this can be compared with the seven colors created by the refraction of white light); (2) The process by means of which these spheres are successively suffused with divine Life, from the highest sphere to the lowest, which is then followed by a change in direction as life begins to move upwards through the spheres in order to be able to return to its Source. *Only the first, descending part of this cycle can properly be referred to as "involution."* The second, ascending part of the cycle, which gives rise to

the various realms of nature—minerals, plants, animals and human beings—is referred to as "evolution"; (3) According to the theosophical literature once an animal has advanced to a certain stage of evolution, there is
an outpouring of divine Life, which creates a spiritual Ego or Self for the
first time. (Theosophy maintains that animals and plants do not have individual souls but are animated by a so-called group soul.) Only an individual spiritual Self is able to reincarnate, thus (contrary to popular Buddhist
teachings) theosophy rules out the possibility of reincarnation as an animal;
(4) And finally, there is the descending movement by means of which the
spiritual Ego creates a new personality for each incarnation, before connect-
ing itself to a new body.

The details from the theosophical literature outlined above may throw
more light on the esoteric background to Wilber's vision, which has been
largely unexplored thus far.

A WESTERN VEDANTA?

Is there a philosophy that genuinely allows scope for a consideration of
themes such as spiritual development, life after death, the existence of
other worlds, and related subjects? Any such philosophy would clearly
need to be a form of idealism. Wilber sees possible links in the German
idealism of Hegel, Fichte, and Schelling, who gave voice to similar insights just before flatland ideology struck and scientific materialism set in.
Wilber has also studied Eastern idealistic systems and in this context he
has occasionally used the term *Western Vedanta*.[72] Vedanta is the most
profound school of Indian philosophy. It claims that manifested reality is
ultimately illusory compared with Brahman—the One or Absolute—yet
at the same time Vedanta also recognizes the fact that this illusory or
relative reality—the Many—is not a homogenous phenomenon but consists of a multitude of layers or levels. In Vedantic philosophy human
consciousness is said to exist at all of these levels of reality and to be
capable, ultimately, of realizing its identity with Brahman. According to
Wilber these insights need to be reformulated in contemporary language.

The Dutch philosopher and theosophist, J. J. Poortman, Professor of
"metaphysics in the spirit of theosophy" at the University of Leiden from
1958 to 1967, formulated an idealistic philosophy that fully meets this
requirement.[73] He too, often described his system as a Western form of
Vedanta.[74] In his main work *Tweeërlei Subjectiviteit* (Twofold subjectivity)
(1929), he makes a distinction between the individual self or "infrasubject"
and the universal Self or "Suprasubject," in the same way that Vedanta

makes a distinction between Atman and Brahman. Poortman also considers manifested reality, which is made up of a series of spheres, to be ultimately illusory—or "as nothing," as he formulates it—but for us people extremely real—"nevertheless something." This paradox is such a primary paradox that Poortman refers to it as the "fundamental paradox."[75] He describes his metaphysical point of view as "realism within idealism."

Like Wilber, Poortman had great faith in the capacity of the human intellect to know reality in all of its facets. As far as he was concerned, in addition to grasping the reality that can be perceived by the senses, the individual was also capable of knowing the whole of manifested reality, in other words, all of the planes of existence from the material to the divine. As a result, he was positively disposed towards scientific research of any kind, and he was equally positive about phenomena that cannot readily be situated within the everyday worldview, such as paranormal phenomena. He even believed that in theory it was possible to elaborate a science of the hereafter, which would be charged with the task of studying the fate of the individual after death. He thought that investigations of the fate of the soul after death conducted by clairvoyants might be the main initial impulse in establishing such a science, even if it proved to be difficult to implement this approach in practice.

Poortman was of the opinion that the only insurmountable obstacle encountered by this highly advanced rationalism was the deliberate attempt to know one's own Self. Because as the subject the Self can never be completely reduced to an object, there is always a reality deep within the inner world of the individual that can only be experienced in a mystical way. The Self is always behind us as it were, so we never get to face it in a way that makes it possible for us to study it objectively. Nevertheless, the Self can be known by means of meditation—even if this is a fundamentally different method. Thus Poortman combined spirituality and rationality in such a way that mysticism and science are both given full scope. Similar ideas can also be found in Wilber's work. Remarkably enough, Poortman also had a clear sense of what Wilber has formulated as the pre/trans fallacy. Poortman used the terms *infrarational* and *suprarational,* and cautioned against confusing these two forms of irrationality.[76]

Poortman described his metaphysical point of view as a "noic monism" (from *nous,* mind) and as a "hylic pluralism" (from *hyle,* matter). Again, like Wilber, he was extremely sceptical about the kind of holism that is based on quantum physics, which seeks to suggest that modern physics had stumbled across the deepest Mystery. As we have seen, Wilber has also consistently rejected this idea, which nevertheless continues to thrive in alternative circles. According to Poortman, the deepest Mystery can only be encountered in the deepest depths of the human spirit, a reality that can never be penetrated by physics or any other kind of science. In this context Poortman often said that his deepest conviction was that, strictly speaking, there is only one miracle and that is the fact *that anything exists at all.* He refused to admit that there was more than one miracle. In his opinion there was a rational explanation for everything within the Many, yet the One was clearly beyond any rational explanation. In the experience of the One—the experience that Wilber refers to as "One Taste"—we touch the miracle that will never cease to exist, regardless of the degree to which we come to know reality. In fact, knowing this simply adds immeasurably to the miracle.

Plotinus, Poortman, and Wilber are all mystical philosophers who have a great deal of faith in the capacity of the intellect and who therefore attach a great deal of value to any form of scientific research. For this reason they oppose any movements which denounce rationalism under the guise of spirituality and seek salvation in the romanticism of holism. Plotinus, Poortman, and Wilber are all convinced that it is not rationalism that needs to be denounced, but materialism, which reduces the multidimensional Kosmos made up of matter, life, soul, and Spirit, to the unidimensional cosmos of visible matter. In their eyes, despite its popularity and despite the claims made by its supporters, holism is incapable of conquering materialism. On the contrary, holism actually sanctifies materialism by continuing to describe consciousness and spirituality in terms of quantum physics. Only genuine, deep holism is capable of conquering materialism once and for all, because it explicitly acknowledges the existence of worlds that transcend the physical. The existence of these worlds is, to use Huston Smith's phrase, a "forgotten truth," a truth that might have been completely lost in our culture, were it not for the fact that a handful of individuals have had the courage to draw our attention yet again to the message of the perennial philosophy.

EPILOGUE: THE MAP AND THE TERRITORY

Some people lay Wilber's books aside because they consider them to be purely theoretical and of little practical value when it comes to spiritual practice. Yet Wilber is the first to admit that ultimately it is the spiritual practice that counts, and not the studying of his numerous books. His model of consciousness is best conceived of as a cartography of the inner world—as a map that can help us to actually undertake the inner journey.

It is currently common to observe that the map is not the territory, in the sense that it is important not to confuse our theories regarding reality with reality itself. This often goes hand in hand with a rejection of any form of theory. But anyone who goes on holiday to an unknown country knows that a good map is an indispensable aid. It is true that a map is not the territory, but it is a useful means to help us orient ourselves within the territory it describes. In the same way, Wilber's model can help us to orient ourselves on our way through life.

Nevertheless, anyone who travels to a foreign country will often find that a map is not enough. They will also want a travel guide that describes the particularities of the country in question—places to stay, places worth visiting, the areas best avoided. Some of the passages in Wilber's oeuvre, particularly in his later work, are written more in this spirit. These passages describe the process of spiritual development itself. [77] One might go further still and decide to enlist the services of a native guide in the foreign country. In this sense we can study with a meditation teacher, who can guide us on our inner journey. And naturally, the more adventurous among us might also set out purely on the off chance simply to see where destiny leads. This too is possible when it comes to spirituality, in which case a reliable map of the territory will undoubtedly prove its worth.

Wilber's map of the inner world defines three regions—the prepersonal, the personal, and the transpersonal. He offers the following advice: avoid the prepersonal swamp as far as possible, how attractive it may appear. Traverse as much as possible of the extensive personal hill country that offers a glimpse of the transpersonal heights in the distance. Only once you have scaled the final peaks of the transpersonal heights will you be able to appreciate the breathtaking view. Whether or not we decide to undertake the journey is entirely up to us. But one way or another we have been presented with the map.

In charting the territory of the inner world, Wilber has been grateful to be able to draw on the information that other inner explorers have left behind in the past. He compares our relative ignorance of the inner world with the situation of the old explorers, who were determined to draw up maps of the exterior world regardless of the challenges they faced along the way. The theories that currently attempt to describe the inner world of the individual are as primitive as the early maps of the world—they too are full of gaps. Nevertheless, at the moment they are all we have and for the time being they will have to do: "We do indeed have the early maps of the interior New World left by these extraordinary pioneers. And relying on those maps—at least initially—is not a regressive yearning for yesteryear . . . but rather the only sensible course of action for a new breed of pioneers trying once again to plumb the depths that were utterly disqualified with the modern collapse [of the Kosmos]. Refine the maps, yes; redraw many of their outlines, surely; but thank the stars for the guts and glory of those who went before, and left a trail, clearly enough marked, for all those souls sensitive enough to follow."[78]

NOTES

INTRODUCTION

1. *The Eye of Spirit,* p. xi.

2. See, for example, his recent book *Boomeritis* (Shambhala, 2002).

3. See, for example, his book *One Taste: The Journals of Ken Wilber,* 1999.

4. A complete listing of Wilber's books can be found on page 311. His books have since been translated into German, Spanish, Japanese, Dutch, Italian, Chinese (Taiwanese), Polish, Danish, Portuguese, Korean, Russian, Greek, Czech, Swedish, French, Hindi, Swazi, and Latvian. There are also illegal editions in Indian and African dialects.

5. It should be noted that there are strong links between Random House and Shambhala in view of the fact that Random House has been distributing the titles published by Shambhala since the seventies.

6. In 1999 and 2000, Shambhala published a number of volumes of the *Collected Works of Ken Wilber*—a remarkable phenomenon given that Wilber is still alive and highly prolific as an author. The series currently runs to eight volumes and includes material not previously published. Since then, several monographs have appeared: *Integral Psychology, A Theory of Everything,* and the novel *Boomeritis.*

7. *The Atman Project (Het Atman project,* Servire, 1992) and *A Brief History of Everything (Een beknopte geschiedenis van alles,* Lemniscaat, 1997). I also edited the Dutch translation of *The Marriage of Sense and Soul (De integratie van wetenschap en religie,* Servire, 1998), and *Integral Psychology (Integrale Psychologie,* Ankh-Hermes, 2001).

8. Including a fax interview that I conducted with Wilber in 1995, published in Dutch in the transpersonal journal *PANTA* under the title "Bodhisattva's zullen aan politiek moeten gaan doen" (no. 11, Spring 1996). An English translation of the interview ("Bodhisattvas are going to have to become politicians") was included in *Eurotas News,* the newsletter of the European Transpersonal Association, which is published in Italy and sent to twelve European countries, in 1997. In 1998 a German translation of the interview was published in *Transpersonale Perspektiven.*

9. In the spring and autumn of 1997, I visited Wilber in Boulder, first to make his acquaintance and later to compile material for this book and to discuss his work with him in more depth. On 13 and 14 January 1997, I visited him following a conference devoted entirely to his work (held in San Francisco from 10 to 12 January) and spoke with him for nine hours. I visited him again from 8 to 11 November. On

that occasion the conversation was deliberately more structured, focusing primarily on his life and work.

10. See in this respect Wilber's article "Mind and the Heart of Emptiness," *The Quest*, Winter 1995. In this article Wilber states that he does not deliberately avoid publicity; he simply does not seek it, which in America is enough to make someone a controversial figure. He goes on to explain that in his own life he has found it impossible to combine the life of a public celebrity with that of a writer. This being the case, he has opted entirely and fundamentally for the latter.

11. Wilber 1 spans the years 1973 to 1978, the years during which Wilber wrote his first two books, *The Spectrum of Consciousness* and *No Boundary*. Wilber 2 marks the crucial years from 1979 to 1982, when Wilber radically revised certain basic concepts in his thinking. Wilber 3 stretches from 1983 to 1987, and Wilber 4 stretches from 1995 to the present. Between Wilber 3 and Wilber 4 there was a period of almost ten years during which personal circumstances prevented Wilber from writing. Chapters 2, 3, 4 and 6 discuss each of these four phases in more detail.

12. On the first occasion in "A More Integral Approach: A Response to the ReVision Authors," *ReVision*, Autumn 1996, p. 13. The same article is also included in *The Eye of Spirit*, 1997. In 1996 the editors of *ReVision* wanted to devote three entire issues of the journal to Wilber's work with a view to providing a platform for the criticism voiced in response to Wilber's work. Ironically enough, the journal itself was actually set up by Wilber and Jack Crittenden at the end of the seventies. In the mid eighties the journal came under different management and in recent years it has been strongly influenced by 'romantic Jungian' thinking. The tensions between Wilber and his critics are largely reflected by the differences between Wilber 1 and Wilber 2.

13. In *Integral Psychology*, which documents Wilber's most up-to-date viewpoint with regard to psychological and spiritual development.

14. See his article "The Neo-Perennial Philosophy," *The American Theosophist*, Autumn 1983 (reprinted in *The Quest*, Autumn 1992).

15. Quest Books, a theosophical publishing house established in Wheaton in the United States, published *The Spectrum of Consciousness* (1977), *The Atman Project* (1980), and the second edition of *Up from Eden* (1996). In 1998 Quest Books also brought out a collection of pieces entitled *Ken Wilber in Dialogue*—the conclusions drawn from the Wilber conference held in San Francisco in 1997.

16. A few years ago I wrote a book about the different planes of existence entitled *Zeven sferen* [Seven spheres] (Uitgeverij der Theosofische Vereniging in Nederland, Amsterdam, 1995).

CHAPTER I: WHO IS KEN WILBER?

1. In Wilber's case, the fact that his parents chose to call him "Ken" can be regarded as something of a foreshadowing. In many languages the root "k-n," "c-n," "g-n," or "j-n" signifies knowledge, as it does in the words *kennis* (Dutch), *Erkenntnis* (German), *knowledge* (English), *connaitre* (French), *conocer* (Spanish), *gnosis* (Greek), and *jnana* (Sanskrit). As things turned out, knowledge would come to be the essential theme of their son's life.

2. This was something that Wilber told me in person during a six-hour interview at his home in Boulder, Colorado, on 9 November 1997. The full transcript of this interview, entitled "Everyone is right: A Conversation with Ken Wilber on his Life and Books," runs to 104 pages. All of the other personal statements referred to in this chapter were made during the same interview.

3. Personal interview, 9 November 1997.

4. Ibid.

5. Ibid.

6. Ibid.

7. "Odyssey: a Personal Inquiry into Humanistic and Transpersonal Psychology," *Journal of Humanistic Psychology*, vol. 22, no. 1, p. 58.

8. Personal interview, 9 November 1997.

9. Ibid.

10. Ibid.

11. "Odyssey," p. 58.

12. Personal interview, 9 November 1997.

13. "Odyssey," p. 59.

14. Personal interview, 9 November 1997.

15. "Odyssey," pp. 59–60.

16. Personal interview, 9 November 1997.

17. "Odyssey," p. 67.

18. Personal interview, 9 November 1997.

19. Wilber makes this statement in a manuscript entitled *The Great Chain of Being*, which was written in 1987 but never published. I read it during my first stay at Wilber's home in January 1997.

20. Ibid.

21. "Mind and the Heart of Emptiness," *The Quest*, Winter 1995, p. 16.

22. Personal interview, 9 November 1997.

23. The biographical information about Wilber printed at the head of the "Odyssey" article, published in 1982, announced the planned manual of transpersonal psychology as follows: "a technical book . . . which is a sustained look at the traditional categories of psychology—conditioning, learning, dynamics, structure, development, motivation, pathology, diagnosis, therapy—in humanistic and transpersonal terms." In his relatively recent book *The Eye of Spirit* (1997) Wilber says of this several-year project: "Now I am calling it *Principles of Transpersonal Psychology*, but I deeply do not want to do this book, and wish somebody else would take the outline and run with it" (p. 339).

24. Personal interview, 9 November 1997.

25. "Bodhisattva's zullen aan politiek moeten gaan doen" ["Bodhisattvas are going to have to become politicians"], *PANTA*, Spring 1996, p. 15.

26. Ibid., p. 12.

27. Ibid., p. 13.

28. Ibid., p. 13.

29. Ibid., p. 14.

30. A passage from the fax interview not published in *PANTA*, but included in the English and German translations.

31. "A spirituality that transforms," *What is Enlightenment?*, no. 11, Winter 1997, pp. 29–30 (also occurs in *One Taste*, pp. 35–36).

32. The Sanskrit word *pandit* is often spelt *pundit* in English on account of the fact that 'u' is actually pronounced as a short 'a' in English.

33. "Mind and the Heart of Emptiness," p. 21.

34. Milarepa (1052–1135) was Tibet's most famous yogi and the founder of the Kagyupa lineage. Naropa (1016–1100) was an Indian yogi whose teachings reached Tibet via his devotee Marpa, where they formed the basis of the Kagyupa lineage. Longchempa (1308–1364), a Tibetan master and scholar in the Nyingmapa lineage, forged the teachings of the dzoghchen tradition into a unified whole. Dzogchen is the main teaching of the Nyingmapa school of Tibetan Buddhism, which maintains that the inherent purity of the essential nature of mind is always already present and simply needs to be realized. Plotinus (205–270) founded the philosophical system of Neoplatonism together with Ammonias Saccas (ca. 175–242). The *Enneads* compiled by his student Porphyrius (232–314) are the most famous of the writings he left behind.

35. C. Ingram, "The Pundit of Transpersonal Psychology," *Yoga Journal*, September/October 1987, p. 49.

36. Personal interview, 9 November 1997.

37. See, for example, *A Brief History of Everything*, pp. 219–40; *The Eye of Spirit*, pp. 281–301; and *One Taste*, pp. 273–76 and p. 302.

CHAPTER 2: A FLYING START

1. "Transpersonal psychology emerged in the sixties in response to a concern that the previous major models, the first three forces of Western psychology—behaviorism, psychoanalysis and humanistic psychology—had been limited in their recognition of the upper reaches of psychological development." Walsh and F. Vaughan, *Beyond Ego: Transpersonal Dimensions in Psychology*, Tarcher, 1980, p. 18. See also: Brant Cortright, *Psychotherapy and Spirit*, SUNY, 1997, for a detailed discussion of these four schools.

2. A. H. Maslow, *Toward a Psychology of Being*, Van Nostrand Reinhold, 1968, pp. iii–iv.

3. See G. Miller and R. Buckhout, *Psychology: The Science of Mental Life*, Harper and Row, 1973.

4. Miller and Buckhout venture to describe Piaget as "one of the greatest psychologists of all time" (*Psychology*, p. 354).

5. For the sake of brevity Wilber refers to Piaget's stages two, three, and four as *pre-op* (pre-operational) *conop* (concrete-operational), and *formop* (formal-operational) respectively.

6. Kohlberg's six stages of moral development can be further subdivided into three phases—*precon* (preconventional), *con* (conventional), and *postcon* (postconventional). To these Wilber then adds a fourth phase—the "post-postconventional" phase. The postconventional phase is that of the rational, autonomous individual with a sense of conscience; the post-postconventional phase is that of the transpersonal, spiritually aware individual.

7. In fact detailed research has since revealed that while Leibniz occasionally used the term *philosophia perennis*, it was first introduced by the sixteenth-century

Italian bishop Augustinus Steuchius (1497–1548) who wrote an essay entitled "Philosophia Perennis" in 1540 (W. Quinn, Jr., *The Only Way*, State University of New York, 1997, pp. 76–77).

8. A. Huxley, *The Perennial Philosophy*, Harper and Row, 1970, p. vii.

9. *Grace and Grit*, p. 79.

10. Wilber had already published an article bearing this title in the journal *Main Currents in Modern Thought*, November 1974, vol. 31, no. 2. A first version of this article was published in the journal *Human Dimensions* some months earlier in the summer of 1974.

11. "Psychologia Perennis: The Spectrum of Consciousness," *Journal of Transpersonal Psychology*, 1975, vol. 7, no. 2, pp. 105–06.

12. "Odyssey," pp. 61–66.

13. "Odyssey," p. 66.

14. "Odyssey," p. 65.

15. *The Spectrum of Consciousness*, p. 18.

16. In his later work Wilber no longer subscribes to and indeed deliberately distances himself from these comparisons between modern physics and mysticism. See also Chapter 4.

17. *The Spectrum of Consciousness*, pp. 125–27.

18. Not long after this Wilber presents a strong argument against this view in his book *Up from Eden* (1981). See also Chapter 3.

19. Again, very soon after this Wilber also refutes this notion in his book *The Atman Project* (1980). See also Chapter 3.

20. *The Spectrum of Consciousness*, p. 153.

21. *The Spectrum of Consciousness*, p. 153.

22. *The Spectrum of Consciousness*, p. 177.

23. *The Spectrum of Consciousness*, p. 309.

24. *The Spectrum of Consciousness*, p. 315. Here Wilber uses the expression "always already the case," frequently used by the American guru Adi Da Samraj and refers the reader to page 343 of the latter's autobiography, *The Knee of Listening*, 1973.

25. *No Boundary*, based on the diagram that features on pp. 9 and 10.

26. A reference to the book by Frithjof Schuon (*The Transcendent Unity of Religions*, Quest, 1984, originally published in French), also an exponent of the perennial philosophy.

27. *No Boundary*, pp. 3–4.

28. *No Boundary*, p. 11.

29. *No Boundary*, p. 106.

30. *No Boundary*, p. 137.

31. *No Boundary*, p. 145.

32. "Odyssey," p. 70.

33. "Odyssey," pp. 70–71.

CHAPTER 3: CRISIS AND REORIENTATION

1. See, for example, A. Stevens, *On Jung*, Penguin, 1991, p. 62.

2. See, for example, F. Vaughan, *The Inward Arc*, Shambhala, 1986.

3. Within the context of Wilber's work the expression "the Great Chain of Being" refers to the series of planes of existence ranging from the material to the Divine as identified by the perennial philosophy. The expression is sometimes also used to refer to the continuity of the evolutionary process, in which the various realms of nature form the individual links of the chain.

4. "Odyssey," pp. 72–73.

5. Though the term *subconscious* is often adopted in general usage, those working in the field of depth psychology prefer to use the term *unconscious*. However, the school of psychosynthesis, which is a kind of height psychology, deliberately subdivides the unconscious into a lower unconscious known as the *subconscious* and a higher unconscious known as the *superconscious*. Thus in this context the term *subconscious* serves to make a meaningful distinction.

6. At this point Wilber alters the meaning he had previously ascribed to the terms *involution* and *evolution*. Departing from the usage he had adopted in *The Spectrum of Consciousness*, he now refers to the movement from God to matter as involution and the movement from matter to God as evolution. Whereas he had initially adopted the usage coined by traditionalist Ananda Coomaraswamy, at this point he switches to the formulation suggested by Sri Aurobindo, whose work was to become an important source of inspiration for Wilber. For an account of the different meaning ascribed to the terms involution and evolution, see Wilber's foreword to the second edition of *The Spectrum of Consciousness*, which was published in 1993 (p. xviii).

7. H. Smith, *Forgotten Truth: The Primordial Tradition*, Harper, 1976. In this book Smith subscribes to the line of thinking expounded by the perennialist René Guénon, the author of *Les Etats Multiple de L'Etre*, and Arthur Lovejoy, the author of *The Great Chain of Being*, two of a limited number of studies on the layered nature of reality.

8. At the back of *The Atman Project* Wilber sets out as many as twenty-three developmental models taken from the world of Western developmental psychology or Eastern spirituality, showing how each of these models relates to his revised spectrum model. Here we come across names such as Sri Aurobindo, Stanislav Grof, Jane Loevinger, Lawrence Kohlberg, Erik Erikson, Jean Piaget, Erich Fromm, Abraham Maslow, Da Free John, John Welwood, and sources such as Buddhism and kundalini yoga.

9. In *Up from Eden*, the book that Wilber wrote virtually in tandem with *The Atman Project*, he makes the following important comment: "[The course of a human life] is presented as a circle, mostly because of its compact nature, but like any diagram it has its flaws. In particular, I warn the reader that this circular figure is not meant to imply that the lowest stage and the highest run directly into each other; they do not. . . . The levels themselves are 'vertically' hierarchical, and although ultimately they all issue from the Absolute, in the meantime they are intermediate stages of the return to that Absolute. . . . 'Rungs on a ladder, lowest to highest' will have to serve as our guiding spatial metaphor" (p. 11). Unfortunately, the circular design on the cover of the first edition of *The Atman Project* and the same circular motif that featured at the head of each chapter gave the distinct impression that development was conceived of as a cyclical process which returns to its point of departure, despite the fact that the entire content of the book repudiates this idea. Wilber now regards this as a very unfortunate choice (a statement he made during a personal interview conducted

9 November 1997). This suggestion was avoided in the second edition of *The Atman Project*, published in 1996.

10. *The Atman Project*, p. 3.

11. "Odyssey," pp. 85–86.

12. In contrast to what he had written in *No Boundary*, Wilber now sees the establishment of boundaries between the self and the outside world as a positive development, as a growth in consciousness, and no longer as a limiting factor that separates us and leads us away from our spiritual Self.

13. Wilber now sees the ability to express experience with the aid of language as an attainment that enriches our world of our experience with the addition of an extra dimension, rather than seeing the acquisition of language as a factor that clouds our view of reality, as he had suggested in *The Spectrum of Consciousness*. (Chapter VIII, which discusses the influence of language is entitled "The Great Filter.")

14. These phases largely correspond to the stages defined by Piaget as pre-operational (2–7 years), concrete-operational (7–12 years), and formal-operational (from 12 years). There is no equivalent for the stage of the mature ego in Piaget's work.

15. M. J. Meadow, "Spiritual and Transpersonal Aspects of Altered States of Consciousness: A Symposium Report," *Journal of Transpersonal Psychology*, vol. 11, no. 1, 1979, p. 68. This is an abridged report of the symposium "The Spiritual and/versus the Transpersonal" held during the annual convention of the American Psychological Association in Toronto in September 1978. Wilber took part in the symposium as a panel member and commented on the contributions made by the various speakers.

16. His phraseology here—including the frequent use of capital letters and terms such as *Radiance*—is very similar to that of the American guru Adi Da Samraj, who in the seventies went by the name of Bubba Free John and whose *The Paradox of Instruction* (1977) Wilber also cites as a source.

17. The term *astral* is borrowed from the occult literature and refers to the world that pervades the physical world and is next in line to the physical world in the series of spheres. Although the astral world cannot be perceived by the physical senses, it is understood to be perceptible to clairvoyants who are able to exercise a form of extra-sensory perception.

18. *The Atman Project*, p. 71

19. *The Atman Project*, p. 72.

20. *The Atman Project*, p. 74.

21. Though many have recently cast doubt on the existence of the Oedipus complex, Wilber has restored the validity of this central Freudian concept by giving it an ontological basis. Each individual has a physical body and can become too attached to existence at this level. Yet, given that there are several spheres of existence, there are also several complexes. By abstracting the general principle underlying all of these complexes, Wilber is able to see the Oedipus complex as an individual example of a general principle.

22. "Odyssey," p. 79.

23. "Odyssey," p. 79.

24. Wilber's vision of Jung is discussed in more detail in Chapter 7.

25. *Up from Eden*, p. 82.

26. Over the years Wilber has placed less and less emphasis on the paranormal aspects of what he calls the "psychic" stage. Whereas in his original model formulated

in 1978 two of the seven spheres were explicitly paranormal (see Fig. 3.5), in his later work he is more inclined to describe the psychic stage in terms of nature mysticism and/or as a stage that precedes spiritual development.

27. When it comes to comparing different models of spheres of existence or planes of consciousness, a great deal of precision is called for. The perennial philosophy states that there is a perfect correlation between the different levels of being within the individual and the different levels of reality. In other words, the physical body corresponds to physical reality, emotions are of the nature of the astral world, the faculty of thought relates to the mental world, and so on. In *The Atman Project* Wilber takes the four spheres (Body, Mind, Soul, and Spirit) suggested by Huston Smith and goes on to elaborate a highly refined model of developmental stages. Yet this undertaking is complicated by the fact that Wilber effectively translates Huston Smith's fourfold framework into a threefold framework based on the terms *gross, subtle,* and *causal.* This creates problems when it comes to defining the nature of the mental level of the personality. In his model of the seven planes of consciousness Wilber groups the physical body and the ego together as belonging to the lowest plane, which is then followed by two paranormal planes (the astral and the psychic, respectively), later grouped together as the "low-subtle." How does Wilber's low-subtle level relate to Smith's model? Is it supposed to correspond to the second sphere of the Mind, or to the third sphere of the Soul, as Wilber seems to suggest? In my opinion the two paranormal planes do not belong in a sevenfold model of the planes of consciousness, given that these paranormal planes are accessed by means of an expansion of the *senses,* rather than by means of the expansion of the *Self.* Both developments can be described within a sevenfold model. Most of us experience our senses to be confined to the reality of the physical world—we see other people's physical bodies but we are not able to see their inner thoughts and feelings. A clairvoyant, on the other hand, has expanded his or her senses to the extent that he or she is able to perceive the reality of the astral plane—the second plane in the series of seven spheres. So, in addition to seeing a person's physical body, a clairvoyant will also be able to see the emotional (or astral) vibration of the person's aura. This will provide the clairvoyant with information regarding the person's feelings, though he or she will not actually perceive the feelings themselves (see A. E. Powell, ed., *The Astral Body,* TPH, 1972/1927). A more advanced clairvoyant has expanded his or her senses to be able to perceive the reality of the mental world, which is the third in the series of seven spheres. The clairvoyant is now also able to perceive the mental vibration of a person's aura, and will pick up information regarding the person's thoughts (see A. E. Powell, ed., *The Mental Body,* TPH, 1967/1927). The ability to perceive the reality of the astral body and the reality of the mental body relates entirely to the second sphere of Smith's model (Mind), in that this kind of perception does not transcend the personal—it simply involves a refinement of the senses. The expansion of the Self is of a different nature, though it also encompasses seven levels. Initially, as Wilber describes, human awareness is entirely confined to the physical body. As the emotional body begins to develop, the center of the Self expands to encompass the second of the seven spheres—the astral or emotional plane. Then as the faculty of thought begins to develop the center shifts again, this time to the locus of the mental world—the third great sphere of existence. This development, which is still within the realm of the personal, also relates purely to the second sphere of Smith's model (Mind). In other words, personal development

and psychic or paranormal development are two *parallel* developments, each with its own mechanism and dynamic. The shift of the center of the Self to more expanded planes of consciousness is an entirely logical development as the faculties of the soul begin to awaken within the individual. Transpersonal development commences as the center of the Self moves to inhabit what Smith terms the realm of the Soul. Thus transpersonal development is indeed *a logical extension* of personal development as Wilber rightly claims, *without there being any need for any reference to paranormal abilities of whatever nature.* The suggestion that transpersonal development also proceeds through a number of characteristic phases leading eventually to the level of Spirit is also entirely in line with the tenets of the perennial philosophy. So it is clearly not necessary for these paranormal stages to be included in what purports to be a general model of human development, and which therefore, by definition, should only include 'normal' stages that every individual must go through, without it being possible for any of these stages to be omitted or bypassed.

28. Chapter 7 addresses the important question of the precise correlation between stages of development and spheres of existence in more detail. See also *Integral Psychology*, in which Wilber devotes several passages to this question of the correspondence between planes of consciousness and levels of reality (esp. p. 236–237).

29. *Up from Eden*, p. x.

30. Jean Gebser (1905–1973) was born in Poznan, Poland, and lived in Italy, France, and Spain before settling in Switzerland. He was concerned above all with the question of the evolution of human consciousness, which he saw as evolving through a number of recognizable stages throughout the course of history. He also anticipated the emergence of a new phase in the development of consciousness, which he called "integral consciousness." He believed that he saw the early signs of this new consciousness in modern developments in science and art.

31. *Up from Eden*, p. 179.

32. Western culture as a whole is now entering the second half of the evolutionary process, as it were. This also applies to the individual.

33. *Up from Eden*, p. 255.

34. While Buddhism does not actually recognize a God as such, philosophical movements within Mahayana Buddhism have developed certain notions regarding the Absolute that are reminiscent of a Trinity: the Nirmanakaya (or appearance body), the Sambhogakaya (or bliss body) and the Dharmakaya (or truth body). In the following quote Wilber uses these three terms to distinguish three different types of classical religious experience.

35. *Up from Eden*, pp. 78—79.

36. In terms of religion, the situation as it exists today might also be described in the following somewhat simpler manner. Broadly speaking there can be said to be three different types of religion: nature or body-religion, historical or mind-religion and mystical or soul-religion. In the *nature religions*—which include the primitive religions and (some parts of) Hinduism and Northern Buddhism—the body is considered to be central, and nature and the cosmos are regarded as being sacred. In the *historical religions*—which include Judaism, Christianity, Islam, and Southern Buddhism and Islam—the human personality, which is rooted in history and thinks rationally, is considered to be central. These historical religions are often at odds with the nature religions, which are thought to be inferior (and from the point of view of developmental

psychology this is actually the case). In the *mystical religions* the transpersonal Self is the central focus. In this case the divine is sought neither in nature nor in history but in the timeless present. Now that the historical religions are largely on the decline in Western culture, many people are reverting to the nature religions, but this is actually a regression to a previous stage of religious evolution. It would be far better to seek authentic forms of mysticism, in any of the traditional religions. Then, rather than being relinquished, the complexities of the personal level can be incorporated within a higher level of consciousness.

37. *Up from Eden*, p. 328.

38. "Odyssey," p. 80.

39. "Odyssey," p. 80.

40. "Odyssey," p. 81.

41. "Odyssey," p. 82.

42. "Odyssey," pp. 84—85.

43. This example is taken from H. Werner, *Comparative Psychology of Mental Development*, 1980, p. 8 (originally published as *Einführung in die Entwicklungspsychologie*, 1926).

CHAPTER 4: FURTHER REFINEMENTS

1. Those who dispute the existence of a self—a stance often prompted by Buddhist philosophy—usually argue that the self does not exist because it cannot be perceived either with the physical eye or with the introspective eye. However, it is immediately evident that this argument does not hold if we ask who it is that is in search of the self. It is of course the self. Those who contend that the self is simply a thought (which can therefore be perceived) are confusing the self with the self-image. During the course of its development the self forms all kinds of ideas about itself, each of which can indeed be perceived. Again in this instance the same question serves to reveal the reality of the self, for what is it that makes it possible for us to form these self-images, or at least watch them, if not the self?

2. *Eye to Eye*, p. 63.

3. *Eye to Eye*, pp. 201–02.

4. *Eye to Eye*, pp. 210–11.

5. *Eye to Eye*, p. 212.

6. Nevertheless, even as he wrote *The Atman Project*, Wilber was aware that his model simplified things: "I will simply present a working outline of some of the generally accepted stages of the development of the self sense, drawing freely from the major developmental schools in what might appear at times a rather indiscriminate fashion. Further, I will not absolutely distinguish the different lines of development, such as cognitive, moral, affective, conative, motivational, emotional, and intellectual, since whether any or all of these sequences are parallel, independent or equivalent, or whether they represent one source or many cannot yet be decided in all cases, and I wish from the start to avoid such intricate debate" (pp. 5–6).

7. *The Eye of Spirit* (1997), pp. 212–14.

8. *Eye to Eye*, pp. 267–91. This material is based on an earlier article entitled "Ontogenetic Development: Two Fundamental Patterns," *Journal of Transpersonal Psychology*, vol. 13, no. 1, 1981.

9. When this meeting between psychologists and Buddhists occurs within the context of modern cognitive psychology, which attempts to compare the human being with a computer, science and religion appear to find themselves on common ground in their denial of the existence of an essential self in the human being. This is a very unfortunate alliance, based on an extremely one-sided view of human consciousness.

10. *Eye to Eye*, p. 278.

11. Communicated to the author in person.

12. *Eye to Eye*, pp. 278–79.

13. In this respect the basic structures of consciousness appear to be the same as the "skandhas" referred to in Buddhist philosophy, the objective structures that are said to make up the human being. The teachings of Hinayana or early Buddhism claim that there is no self in the human being other than these skandhas—a notion that Wilber rejects, as do the teachings of Mahayana or later Buddhism. See also *Sex, Ecology, Spirituality*, 1995, pp. 691–708.

14. *Eye to Eye*, p. 284.

15. *Eye to Eye*, p. 282.

16. *Eye to Eye*, pp. 275–76.

17. *Eye to Eye*, pp. 290–91.

18. See F. Wiedemann, *Between Two Worlds*, Quest Books, 1986, which identifies three movements within the transpersonal field: a scientific movement (Capra, Bohm), a mystical movement (Wilber, Smith), and a process-oriented movement (Assagioli, Jean Houston).

19. The fact that a single perception—such as the sight of an orange, for example, in which impressions of color, fragrance, taste, and touch are collated to create a single image—is not processed in one part of the brain but in several parts of the brain at once—in other words, in the parts of the brain that regulate the perception of color, smell, taste, and touch—does not automatically mean that the *whole* orange can be found in *each* part of the brain.

20. Bohm and Pribram were awarded the Marilyn Ferguson Brain/Mind Bulletin prize for the "Greatest Breakthrough of the Century." Marilyn Ferguson is the author of *The Aquarian Conspiracy*, a book that is considered to be a seminal work in holistic circles.

21. "Physics, Mysticism, and the Holographic Paradigm: A Critical Appraisal" (pp. 157–86) and "Reflections on the New Age Paradigm: A Conversation with Ken Wilber" (pp. 249–94). Both chapters are also published in *Eye to Eye*.

22. *The Holographic Paradigm*, pp. 164–65.

23. *The Holographic Paradigm*, p. 166.

24. *The Holographic Paradigm*, p. 256.

25. *The Holographic Paradigm*, pp. 259–60.

26. The book does not include a chapter on Bohr because Niels Bohr's heirs were not willing for Wilber to publish passages selected from Bohr's work (communicated to the author in person).

27. *Quantum Questions*, p. 5.

28. *Quantum Questions*, p. 26.

29. *Quantum Questions*, p. 27.

30. *A Sociable God*, p. 76.

31. *A Sociable God,* p. 79.

32. *A Sociable God,* pp. 24–25.

33. *Eye to Eye,* p. 30.

34. *A Sociable God,* p. 119. See also the diagram in *The Holographic Paradigm,* p. 269.

35. *A Sociable God,* pp. 118–19.

36. See the essay "The Spectrum Model" (*Spiritual Choices,* pp. 237–64), which elaborates on the article "Legitimacy, Authenticity and Authority in the New Religions" published in *Eye to Eye* (pp. 247–66).

37. Wilber first described this distinction in *A Sociable God,* pp. 59–64.

38. *Spiritual Choices,* p. 251.

39. *Spiritual Choices,* pp. 255–59.

40. These chapters were based on articles that had already been published earlier: "The Developmental Spectrum and Psychopathology: Part I, Stages and Types of Pathology," *Journal of Transpersonal Psychology,* vol. 16, no. 1, 1984, pp. 75–118; and "The Developmental Spectrum and Psychopathology: Part II, Treatment Modalities," *Journal of Transpersonal Psychology,* vol. 16, no. 2, 1984, pp. 137–66.

41. *Transformations of Consciousness,* p. 8.

42. The subdivision of the spiritual Path into the stages of the Yogis, the Saints, and the Sages is taken from Da Free John. (Adi Da Samraj).

43. *Transformations of Consciousness,* pp. 102–04. Here Wilber presents a summary of his vision in language that is easily understandable for the layperson.

44. A. Lowen, *The Betrayal of the Body,* 1967.

45. A. Lowen, *Narcissism: Denial of the True Self,* 1983.

46. T. Moore, *Care of the Soul,* 1992, a book that reached the top of the best-seller lists in the United States.

47. T. Moore, *The Re-Enchantment of Everyday Life,* 1996. In this book the glorification of magical thinking assumes alarming proportions.

48. All of these human needs are recognized and ranked in relation to one another in Maslow's well-known hierarchy of needs. We start out in life dominated by physical needs (for food and safety), these are subsequently superseded by psychological needs (for belonging to a group and self-esteem), and finally—in some cases—these needs are superseded by spiritual needs (for self-realization and self-transcendence).

49. *Transformations of Consciousness,* p. 97.

50. *Transformations of Consciousness,* pp. 146–47.

51. *Transformations of Consciousness,* pp. 158–59.

CHAPTER 5: LOVE, DEATH, AND REBIRTH

1. Because this chapter is more personal than the previous chapters, I refer to Ken Wilber as "Ken" when I am portraying him as a partner and "Wilber" when I am referring to the writer and philosopher. As we will see, his wife changed her name from Terry to Treya at an important point in her life. From that point on I refer to her as Treya, in contrast to Wilber, who in looking back on this period in *Grace and Grit,* refers to her as Treya from the start.

2. *Grace and Grit,* p. 7.

3. *Grace and Grit,* p. 17.

4. *Grace and Grit,* p. 19.

5. *Grace and Grit*, pp. 49–50.

6. *Grace and Grit*, p. 58.

7. *Grace and Grit*, p. 58.

8. *Grace and Grit*, p. 65.

9. *Grace and Grit*, pp. 133–34.

10. *Grace and Grit*, p. 137.

11. *Grace and Grit*, pp. 140–41.

12. The expression "self-contraction" is used by the American guru Da Free John to describe the contracted condition of the I. In his opinion the myth of Narcissus illustrates the fundamental misconception of every religious seeker who looks outside himself for the Self that exists within him.

13. *Grace and Grit*, pp. 141–42.

14. Kalu Rinpoche died in 1989. He was considered to be the reincarnation of the Tibetan saint Milarepa. According to his followers he reincarnated again in 1990. The Dalai Lama confirmed the authenticity of the reincarnation in 1992.

15. *Grace and Grit*, p. 168.

16. *Grace and Grit*, pp. 212–13.

17. *Grace and Grit*, p. 218.

18. *Grace and Grit*, p. 246.

19. *Grace and Grit*, pp. 246–50.

20. Treya Killam Wilber, "Attitudes and Cancer: What Kind of Help Really Helps?" *Journal of Transpersonal Psychology*, vol. 20, no. 1, 1988, pp. 49–59.

21. I had an opportunity to look at this unpublished manuscript during my second meeting with Wilber in 1997. In it Wilber discusses themes such as narcissism and the New Age, death and rebirth in the Tibetan Buddhist tradition, modernism and postmodernism, psychotherapy and spirituality, and subjects such as tantra. Although it was never published in book form, some of the chapters have since appeared in a modified form as articles in various journals. Around the same time Wilber mentioned several books in progress, one of which is a book called *Odyssey: Birth and Death of a New Age*, covering "an account of my own journey, the highs and lows, interspersed with articles and essays not published before in book form" (*Yoga Journal*, September/October, 1987, p. 49). This book was never published; possibly *Odyssey* and *The Great Chain of Being* refer to the same project.

22. *Grace and Grit*, p. 261.

23. *Grace and Grit*, pp. 262–63.

24. *Grace and Grit*, p. 264.

25. *Grace and Grit*, pp. 266–68.

26. *Grace and Grit*, p. 268.

27. *Grace and Grit*, pp. 294–95.

28. *Grace and Grit*, p. 295

29. *Grace and Grit*, pp. 307–08.

30. *Grace and Grit*, pp. 310–11.

31. *Grace and Grit*, pp. 333–34.

32. *Grace and Grit*, p. 358.

33. *Grace and Grit*, p. 360.

34. "On Being a Support Person," *Journal of Transpersonal Psychology*, vol. 20, no. 2, pp. 141–59.

35. "On Being a Support Person," p. 159.

36. *Grace and Grit*, pp. 392–93.

37. "Death, Rebirth and Meditation," in G. Doore, ed., *What Survives?: Contemporary Explorations of Life After Death*, Tarcher, 1990, pp. 176–91.

38. *What Survives?* p. 176.

39. *What Survives?* p. 186.

40. *What Survives?* p. 188.

41. In his book *Een Ring van Licht*, 1983 (translated into English as *Exploring Reincarnation*, Arkana, 1990), which offers an extremely comprehensive overview of the different beliefs about reincarnation in both East and West, the Dutch author Hans ten Dam presents a very different picture. He bases his argument on the work of the parapsychologist Robert Crookall, who has published a number of books in which he has compiled evidence of life after death from clairvoyants, spiritualists, parapsychologist, and Theosophists. The ascent through the spheres immediately after death is depicted as a far more gradual process that can take a great deal longer than the Tibetans suggest. The experiences of the life just ended are processed during this gradual ascent, which does not continue to the highest level of existence but stops approximately halfway. In this view the moment of death is not considered to be particularly important—it is more likely to be compared with shrugging off an overcoat. Once the personality has been completely discarded, the soul catches a brief glimpse of the spiritual level, following which it redescends to the physical world. Again in contrast to the Tibetan version, the descent is said to occur relatively rapidly. The possibility of rebirth as anything other than a human being is excluded by these Western esoteric sources, though Buddhist authors are more inclined to entertain an element of doubt in this respect. Other than that, both agree that it is the soul that returns, not the personality. It may be the case that the Tibetan version only applies to people who have had considerable experience with meditation, as a result of which the process of ascent can occur far more rapidly.

42. *Grace and Grit*, p. 408.

43. With all due respect, in light of the view of the process of reincarnation referred to in note 41, such a meeting might be among the possibilities. Not a meeting with the personality through which Treya had expressed herself, but a meeting with a Treya as a recognizable individual who still exists within the spheres. Wilber relates reincarnation specifically to mystical experience, but the connection between these two themes is not necessarily as logical as he suggests.

44. *Grace and Grit*, p. 409.

CHAPTER 6: AN EVEN BROADER HORIZON

1. Wilber has recently summed up the key points of the planned *System, Self and Structure* in the form of the book *Integral Psychology*, which has also been published as part of volume 4 of the *Collected Works of Ken Wilber*.

2. There is now some doubt as to whether the book will ever be written. In *The Eye of Spirit* (1997) Wilber said of this long-term project: "Some readers will remember seeing references to *System, Self and Structure;* then something called *Patterns and Process in Consciousness;* and now I am calling it *Principles of Transpersonal Psychology;* but I deeply do not want to do this book, and wish somebody else would take the outline and run with it" (p. 339). A few pages further on he refers to "the transpersonal textbook that I have been not-writing for fifteen years" (p. 344).

3. Teilhard de Chardin had already used the term *noosphere* to refer to the realm of thought generated by humanity.

4. A complication with the concept of the holon is that it makes use of a spatial metaphor. In the series "atom, molecule, cell, organ, body" each successive link contains the one that precedes it. But the jump from the body to the more subjective aspects of one's being seems somewhat contrived. The series "atom, molecule, cell, organ, body, collection of bodies or group" would be more plausible. Also, it is not evident that all holons automatically possess a certain degree of consciousness—however rudimentary. An amoeba might be conscious, but is this also true of a sentence in a book? Wilber has refined his thoughts about holons after many discussions with Fred Kofman, who wrote the article "Holons, Heaps and Artifacts," (available at www.worldofkenwilber.com) in which he makes a distinction between sentient and nonsentient holons. One might ask: doesn't this invalidate the holon concept to explain consciousness itself?

5. From the verb *to emerge*—to appear, to become apparent. The word *emergent* does not actually explain anything. It simply indicates that new elements appear during the course of evolution, but does not offer clarification.

6. This statement deliberately disregards the possibility that the individual can survive the death of the body. Wilber does not consider it to be his task to convince people that this is the case. He simply attempts to clarify the spiritual dimension within the confines of our earthly existence. (Communicated to the author in person.)

7. *Sex, Ecology, Spirituality*, p. 107.

8. *Sex, Ecology, Spirituality*, p. 209.

9. *Sex, Ecology, Spirituality*, p. 253: "The great and rare mystics of the past (from Buddha to Christ, from al-Hallaj to Lady Tsogyal, from Hui-neng to Hildegard) were, in fact, ahead of their time, and are still ahead of ours. In other words, they are not figures of the past. They are figures of the future."

10. *Sex, Ecology, Spirituality*, p. 187.

11. The four quadrants can also be described as follows: the Upper-Left quadrant is the subjective, the Upper-Right quadrant is the objective, the Lower-Left quadrant is the intersubjective, and the Lower-Right quadrant is the interobjective. Readers are well advised to become familiar with these quadrants because they reappear in all of Wilber's recent works.

12. *The Eye of Spirit*, p. 373.

13. We will return to this aspect of Schumacher's thought in Chapter 7.

14. *A Guide for the Perplexed*, Harper (Perennial Library), 1977, pp. 62–120. (Chapters 6, 7, 8, and 9).

15. In describing how he hit upon the idea of the four quadrants in *A Brief History of Everything*, Wilber says: "I don't think this has been spotted before—perhaps because it was so stupidly simple; at any event it was news to me" (p. 73). However, *A Guide to the Perplexed* is listed in the bibliography of *Sex, Ecology, Spirituality*.

16. *A Guide for the Perplexed*, p. 62: "It has often been observed that for every one of us reality splits into two parts: Here am I; and there is everything else, the world, including you. We have also had occasion to observe another duality: there are visibilities and invisibilities or, we might say, outer appearances and inner experiences. . . . From these two pairs we obtain four 'combinations', which we can indicate thus: (1) I—inner; (2) The world (you)—inner; (3) I—outer and (4) The world (you)—outer. These are the *Four Fields of Knowledge*, each of which is of great interest and importance to every one of us."

17. It is important to make a distinction between descending spirituality and regression, which is also a movement of descent from Spirit to matter. Descending spirituality is in fact not so much descending as being *turned towards the world.* It ascends in the same way that ascending spirituality ascends in the sense that both forms of spirituality develop from the prepersonal via the personal to the transpersonal. The highest stage of descending spirituality is a sense of heartfelt concern for all that exists—a very *high* level of spirituality—certainly not a total relapse to the lowest level. Thus the end goal of descending spirituality is not the level of consciousness characteristic of the lowest level but a level of awareness that encompasses all of the levels of existence. When Wilber speaks of a "completely descended" worldview (i.e. flatland), he is not referring to the end goal of descending spirituality even though this may appear to be the implication. These two different versions of spirituality can also be characterised in the following way: the one looks towards the Light, the other looks at what the Light shines on. But both are approaching the Light step by step.

18. Undoubtedly a reference to *A Brief History of Time,* the best-selling book by physicist Stephen Hawking (who simply describes the physical cosmos and not the multidimensional Kosmos).

19. Communicated to the author in person.

20. *Brief History,* p. 82.

21. Although Wilber does not mention him here, Jung is clearly an important contemporary exponent of this idea of two opposing viewpoints, as is evident from his book *Psychological Types* (1921) in which he shows that introverts and extroverts have found it difficult to relate to one another in numerous fields in history.

22. *Brief History,* pp. 87–88.

23. *Brief History,* p. 200.

24. *Brief History,* p. 231.

25. *Brief History,* p. 240.

26. In the Netherlands there are three main political movements: progressive left, denominational center and conservative right. The third way that Wilber seeks in between liberal and conservative is not dissimilar to the attempts of the Dutch political party Democrats '66 to introduce social liberalism, though in the latter case there is no explicit acceptance of the spiritual dimension. For the last eight years, the Netherlands have had a third way government, including both progressive and conservation elements.

27. *The Eye of Spirit,* p. xvi.

28. *The Eye of Spirit,* pp. xvi–xvii.

29. *The Eye of Spirit,* p. xvii.

30. *The Eye of Spirit,* pp. 33–35.

31. *The Eye of Spirit,* pp. 72–73.

32. *The Eye of Spirit,* pp. 288–89.

33. *The Eye of Spirit,* p. 291.

34. In the essay "Eye to Eye," which he wrote in 1979, Wilber examined the extent to which science and religion shared common ground. At that stage he came to the conclusion that within a broader conception of science there was scope for natural science, the humanities, and spiritual science (see Chapter 4). In other words, not all religion was inherently unscientific. This was only true of forms of religion that were based on dogmatic statements or mythological ideas rather than on spiritual

experience. In Wilber's view only mystical religion is able to pass through the eye of the needle of the modern era; none of the other forms of religiosity are capable of doing so.

35. In the foreword to the third edition of *Eye to Eye* (Shambhala, 1996) Wilber indicates where he believes the solution to the mind/body problem is likely to be found: "What I would like to emphasize here is that, buried in the Western tradition—and in the Eastern—is a radical and compelling solution to these massive dualisms, a literal solution to the West's most intractable philosophical problems, from the absolute/relative to the mind/body dilemma. But this solution—appropriately known as "nondualism"—has an unbelievably awkward characteristic: namely, its utterly compelling answer cannot be captured in words. . . . " (p. xii). See also *Integral Psychology*, Chapter 14.

36. *The Marriage of Sense and Soul*, p. 142.

37. *The Marriage of Sense and Soul*, pp. 158–60.

38. *The Marriage of Sense and Soul*, p. 161.

39. *The Marriage of Sense and Soul*, p. 167.

40. *The Marriage of Sense and Soul*, p. 206.

41. *The Marriage of Sense and Soul*, p. 209.

42. *The Marriage of Sense and Soul*, p. 212.

43. *One Taste*, p. 80.

44. *One Taste*, p. 121.

45. *One Taste*, p. 121.

46. *One Taste*, p. 128.

47. *One Taste*, p. 138.

48. *One Taste*, p. 275.

49. *One Taste*, p. 302.

50. Wilber makes a distinction between *lucid dreaming*, in which one is active in the dream, and *pellucid dreaming*, in which one simply observes the dream.

51. *One Taste*, p. 341.

52. *One Taste*, p. 343.

53. *One Taste*, p. 318: "Based on my own experience, I can testify to the existence of constant consciousness and One Taste, both of them as prolonged and recurrent plateau experiences, sometimes lasting uninterruptedly 24–36 hours (although, in one case, constant consciousness persisted day and night for eleven days)."

54. *Collected Works*, vol. VIII, Introduction, and *A Theory of Everything*, Chapter 6 (with the exception of the last sentence).

55. *Collected Works*, vol. IV, pp. 423–647. *Integral Psychology* has since been published as a separate book.

56. *Collected Works*, vol. IV, p. ix.

57. Wilber compares the models of Huston Smith, Plotinus, Buddhism, Stan Grof, John Battista, kundalini yoga, the Great Chain of Being, James Mark Baldwin, Aurobindo, the Kabbalah, Vedanta, William Tiller, Leadbeater, Adi Da, Piaget, Commons and Richards, Kurt Fisher, Alexander, Pascual-Leone, Herb Koplowitz, Patricia Arlin, Gisela Labouvie-Vief, Jan Sinnot, Michael Basseches, Jane Loevinger, John Broughton, Sullivan, Grant and Grant, Jenny Wade, Michael Washburn, Erik Erikson, Neumann, Scheler, Karl Jaspers, Rudolf Steiner, Don Beck, Suzanne Cook-Greuter, Clare Graves, Robert Kegan, Kohlberg, Torbert, Blanchard-Fields, Kitchener and

King, Deirdre Kramer, William Perry, Turner and Powell, Cheryl Armon, Peck, Howe, Rawls, Piaget, Selman, Gilligan, Hazrat Inayat Khan, mahamudra meditation, Fowler, Underhill, Helminiak, Funk, Daniel Brown, Muhyddin Ibn 'Arabi, St. Palamas, classical yoga, highest tantra yoga, St Teresa, Chirban, St Dionysius, Patanjali, St Gregory of Nyssa, transcendental meditation, Fortune, Maslow, Chinen, Benack, Gardner, Melvin Miller, Habermas, Jean Houston, G. Heard, Lenski, Jean Gebser, A. Taylor, Jay Early, Robert Bellah, and Duane Elgin.

58. *Collected Works*, vol. IV, p. 638, chart 5c: "The self-related stages of morals and perspective."

59 *A Theory of Everything*, pp. 53–54.

60. See D. Beck and C. Cowan, *Spiral Dynamics: Managing Values, Leadership, and Change*, Blackwell, 1996.

61. The Spiral Dynamics literature also refers to a ninth stage which is related to the color coral. In *A Theory of Everything*, p. 146, Wilber expresses his assumption that the coral stage corresponds to the psychic stage of nature mysticism.

62 *Boomeritis: The Extraordinary Emergence of an Integral Culture and its Many Obstacles* was due to appear in 2001. In its rewritten form *Boomeritis: A Novel that Will Set You Free* was published in the Summer of 2002.

63. Wilber's reference to the work *French Philosophy in the Sixties* by Ferry and Renault is especially interesting. The authors of the work argue that the heroes of the extreme postmodernists (Lacan, Foucault, Bourdieu, Derrida) were all French philosophers who caricatured the insights of German philosophers (Freud, Nietzsche, Marx, and Heidegger respectively). The baby boomer generation then took the standpoints of these French philosophers to their extreme conclusions—despite the fact that the philosophers themselves often changed their minds about their extreme standpoints during the course of their lives (unpublished manuscript of *Boomeritis*, Chapter 5, note 10).

64. *A Theory of Everything*, p. 57.

65. *A Theory of Everything: An Integral Vision for Business, Politics, Science, Spirituality* was published at the end of 2000.

66. The political landscape in the United States is very different from the political landscape in the Netherlands (a typically "green" country). In the United States there is a two-party system of Republicans and Democrats, or conservatives and liberals—that could be described as "right" and 'left' in relation to one another. In the Netherlands the liberals are both right and conservative, while the left is occupied by the socialists—a movement that failed to get off the ground in the United States. Dutch politicians have also sought a "third way" for many decades—this was the manifesto of the d'66 party. Just why the Dutch liberal movement, which started out as a progressive, anti-religious party (in the Netherlands at any rate) should have changed into a conservative party that is right of centre is an interesting question, also in light of Wilber's attempt to chart all political options in relation to one another. In this book I have stuck to the American terminology in order to present Wilber's view.

67. In reference to this Wilber says: "Don't let the terminology of the quadrants confuse you—the political Left believes in Right-Hand causation, the political Right believes in Left-Hand causation; had I been thinking of political theory when I arranged the quadrants, I would probably have aligned them to match" (*A Theory of Everything*, p. 84).

68. *A Theory of Everything*, p. 88.

69. *A Theory of Everything*, p. 90.

70. J. Crittenden, B., Reynolds, F. Visser, and K. Crossen-Burroughs, *Kindred Visions: Ken Wilber and Other Leading Integral Thinkers*, Shambhala.

71. K. Wilber, Summary Statement, Integral Institute, 18 January 2000.

72. Summary Statement, Integral Institute.

73. *One Taste*, p. 79, 13 April 1997.

74. Communicated to the author in person.

75. "On the Release of Boomeritis, and the Completion of Volume 3 of the *Kosmos* Trilogy" (wilber.shambhala.com).

76. "On the Release of Boomeritis."

77. "Vom Wesen einer postmetaphysischen Spiritualität," *Transpersonale Psychologie und Psychotherapie*, vol. 2, 2001, pp. 33–48; also published simultaneously online under the title "On the Nature of a Post-Metaphysical Spirituality: Response to Habermas and Weiss" (wilber.shambhala.com).

78. Hans-Willi Weis, "Ken Wilbers Transpersonale Systemspekulation—eine kritische Auseinandersetzung", [The Speculative Reasoning behind Ken Wilber's Transpersonal System—A Critical Analysis], *Transpersonale Psychologie und Psychotherapie*, vol. 2, 2001, pp. 20–31.

79. See, for example, *The Marriage of Sense and Soul*, 1998, pp. 6–9, and *Integral Psychology*, 2000, pp. 5–12.

80. "On the Nature of a Post-Metaphysical Spirituality" (wilber.shambhala.com).

81. Volume 3 of the *Kosmos* trilogy now bears the working title of *Kosmic Karma and Creativity*. In this volume Wilber intends to show the many ways in which the past is operative in the present in all four quadrants.

82. Communicated to the author in person. Wilber expressed the main idea on which this next phase in his thinking is based in *The Marriage of Sense and Soul* (p. 183): "The material domains are not so much the lowest rung on the great hierarchy as they are the exterior forms of each and every rung on the hierarchy." On the basis of this idea Wilber hopes to be able to deconstruct the notion of higher spheres, with the physical world being the lowest sphere, into a view that is compatible with modern thought. However, Wilber has overlooked the fact that earlier representatives of the perennial philosophy also claimed that the different spheres interpenetrate one another completely (as Annie Besant said in *A Study in Consciousness*, 1904: "We are on all planes, at all times," p. 84. We will continue this discussion in Chapter 7.) Regardless of whether we speak of higher and lower spheres or of interior and exterior dimensions, we are simply using two different metaphors to describe the same reality, though in the four-quadrant model it might seem as if Wilber is advocating the idea of the quadrants as opposed to the idea of different levels.

83. See also my essay "Wilber and Metaphysics" (www.worldofkenwilber.com). Interestingly, In *Integral Psychology* Wilber emphatically denies that he neglects the ontological dimension: "This has led some critics to claim that I completely ignore planes of existence, but that is obviously incorrect." (p. 237) The reason for stressing the psychological over the ontological is merely pragmatic, it seems: "You can make essentially the same points using only the levels of consciousness." (p. 237)

84. Huston Smith, *Forgotten Truth: The Primordial Tradition*, 1976, Harper and Row, p. 17.

CHAPTER 7: KEN WILBER IN PERSPECTIVE

1. Two recent book-length postmodern critiques should be mentioned here: J. Ferrer's *Revisioning Transpersonal Theory* (SUNY, 2002) and Jeff Meyerhoff's *Bald Ambition* (submitted for publication).

2. *Forgotten Truth*, p. 37.

3. The expression "Piaget plus" was coined by Donald Rothberg during the opening of the Wilber conference in San Francisco in January of 1997.

4. See, for example, W. Lyons, *The Disappearance of Introspection*, MIT Press, 1986.

5. See, for example, H. Dreyfus, *Intentionality and Cognitive Science*, MIT Press, 1982.

6. See, for example, G. Graham, *Philosophy of Mind*, Blackwell, 1993, p. 93: "*Nothing* possesses intrinsic Intentionality. [This thesis] has been proposed by Patricia and Paul Churchland and Daniel Dennett, three of the most respected figures in recent philosophy of mind."

7. This is the opinion of Douglas Hofstadter, the author of the well known work *Gödel, Escher, Bach* (Basic Books, 1979), who, during the symposium on "The Nature of Intelligence" held at the Erasmus University in Rotterdam in 1987, was irritated enough to cry out: "But *we're* also machines!"

8. *Consciousness Explained*, Little, Brown and Co., 1991, p. 37: "It is not that I think I can give a knock-down proof that dualism, in all its forms, is false or incoherent, but that, given the way dualism wallows in mystery, *accepting dualism is giving up.*"

9. *Forgotten Truth*, p. 138: "Charges of begging the question can settle nothing here."

10. David Chalmers is the author of a number of works on the philosophy of mind including *The Conscious Mind*, Oxford University Press, 1996.

11. See also D. Chalmers, "Facing Up to the Problem of Consciousness," *Journal of Consciousness Studies*, vol. 2, no. 3, 1995, pp. 200–19. In this article Chalmers refers to all of the leading philosophers of mind of the day: Baars, Crick, Dennett, Edelman, Newell, and Penrose. None of them has an answer to the hard problem.

12. This does not come across as a very promising solution given that physical reality is said to be characterized by the fact that it is *not* conscious. But maybe it would be going too far to expect to find a spiritual worldview among the pages of *Scientific American*. Chalmers himself wants to have nothing to do with spiritual or mystical concepts of consciousness. In his article "Facing Up to the Problem of Consciousness" he says explicitly: "There is nothing particularly spiritual or mystical about this theory—its overall shape is like that of a physical theory."

13. See K. Wilber, "An Integral Theory of Consciousness," *Journal of Consciousness Studies*, vol. 4, no. 1, February 1997, in which Wilber integrates the findings of as many as twelve different psychological schools of thought. This article is also featured in *The Eye of Spirit*, pp. 270–74).

14. See Chapter 14 of *Integral Psychology*.

15. *Forgotten Truth*, p. 17.

16. Personal interview, 9 November 1997.

17. E. F. Schumacher, *A Guide for the Perplexed*, Harper, 1977. Schumacher is described as a "Buddhist economist" on account of the fact that he attempts to combine spirituality and economy. His most well-known work is *Small is Beautiful: Economics as if People Mattered* (1973). Schumacher was firmly convinced of the truth of the perennial philosophy.

18. *A Guide for the Perplexed*, p. 18.

19. *A Guide for the Perplexed*, pp. 22–23.

20. *A Guide for the Perplexed*, p. 23.

21. *A Guide for the Perplexed*, p. 24.

22. *A Guide for the Perplexed*, p. 32.

23. *A Guide for the Perplexed*, p. 18.

24. See, for example, J. H. Flavell, *Cognitive Development*, Prentice Hall, 1985.

25. *Cognitive Development*, pp. 84–85.

26. *Cognitive Development*, pp. 84–117.

27. G. B. Matthews, *Philosophy of the Young Child* (1980), *Dialogues with Children* (1992), *The Philosophy of Childhood* (1994), and *The Philosopher's Child* (1998).

28. *The Philosophy of Childhood*, pp. 19–20.

29. *Sex, Ecology, Spirituality*, p. 221.

30. *The Great Chain of Being* (unpublished manuscript).

31. The discipline of philosophy of development is currently being pursued in the Netherlands by the Department of Philosophical and Historical Pedagogics of the Catholic University of Nijmegen, headed by Professor Wouter van Haaften. One of the publications produced by this group, *Ontwikkelingsfilosofie* (Coutinho, 1986), was recently completely revised and reissued in English under the title *Philosophy of Development* (Kluwer Academic Publishers, 1997).

32. *Philosophy of Development*, pp. 39–41.

33. *Philosophy of Development*, p. 18.

34. J. F. Lyotard, *The Postmodern Condition*, p. 84 (translation of *La condition postmoderne*, 1979). Quoted in *Philosophy of Development*, p. 255.

35. Personal interview. 9 November 1997.

36. *Philosophy of Development*, p. 257.

37. B. W. Scotton, A. B. Chinen, and J. R. Battista, ed., *Textbook of Transpersonal Psychiatry and Psychology*, Basic Books, 1996.

38. See also my essay "Transpersonal Psychology at a Crossroad," published on the Internet at www.worldofkenwilber.com.

39. *Grace and Grit*, p. 181; *A Brief History of Everything*, p. 214.

40. *A Brief History of Everything*, p. 216.

41. See, for example, R. Bly, *Iron John*, 1990; C. P. Estes, *Women Who Run with the Wolves*, 1992.

42. K. Wilber, "Paths Beyond Ego in the Coming Decades," in R. Walsh and F. Vaughan, *Paths Beyond Ego*, Tarcher, 1993, p. 262.

43. Roberto Assagioli (1888–1974) wrote only two books: *Psychosynthesis* (1965) and *The Act of Will* (1974)—very little compared with Freud and Jung. However, the extent of his oeuvre is inversely proportional to its theoretical importance. A collection of essays entitled *Lo sviluppo transpersonale* [Transpersonal Development] was published posthumously in 1988. Assagioli worked in close collaboration with the theosophist Alice Bailey. Her ideas are clearly recognizable in the system of psychosynthesis.

44. S. Grof, "Ken Wilber's Spectrum Psychology: Observations from Clinical Consciousness Research," *ReVision*, vol. 19, no. 1, Summer 1996, p. 12.

45. Grof, "Ken Wilber's Spectrum Psychology," p. 22.

46. Grof, "Ken Wilber's Spectrum Psychology," p. 22.

47. K. Wilber, "A More Integral Approach: A Response to the ReVision Authors," *ReVision*, vol. 19, no. 2, Fall 1996, p. 18; *The Eye of Spirit*, p. 174. Wilber responds to his critics in this article, but because of the length of his response the

ReVision version is abridged. *The Eye of Spirit* contains the complete text of his response spread over various chapters.

48. "A More Integral Approach," p. 18; *The Eye of Spirit*, p. 175.

49. *The Eye of Spirit*, pp. 184–85.

50. See, for example, *A Brief History of Everything*, p. 155, Fig. 10–1, in which Wilber defines perinatal pathology as pathology that stems back to the zero or 'F–0' stage of development.

51. K. Wilber, "Afterword," *ReVision*, vol. 19, no. 2, Fall 1996, p. 46.

52. All titles are published by State University of New York Press.

53. See, for example, M. Washburn, "Linearity, Theoretical Economy and the Pre/Trans Fallacy," *ReVision*, vol. 19, no. 2, p. 36.

54. M. Washburn, "Two Patterns of Transcendence," *Journal of Humanistic Psychology*, vol. 30, no. 3, Summer 1990, pp. 84–112. The same issue also includes Wilber's response, "Two Patterns of Transcendence: A Reply to Washburn," pp. 113–36.

55. M. Washburn, "The Pre/Trans Fallacy Reconsidered," *ReVision*, vol. 19, no. 1, Summer 1996, pp. 2–10.

56. *The Eye of Spirit*, Chapter 6: "The Recaptured God: The Retro-Romantic Agenda and its Fatal Flaws," pp. 139–64.

57. *The Eye of Spirit*, pp. 360–61: "Not even the Tibetans (nor the Hindus, for that matter) believe that the child is fully realized or fully in touch with Atman, and that Atman is lost as one grows up."

58. "Bodhisattvas zullen aan politiek moeten gaan doen" ["Bodhisattvas are going to have to become politicians"], PANTA, Spring 1996, pp. 14–15.

59. J. Rowan, *The Transpersonal*, Routledge, 1993, p. 95.

60. D. Rothberg and S. Kelly (eds.), *Ken Wilber in Dialogue: Conversations with Leading Transpersonal Thinkers*, Quest Books, 1998. The collection of essays includes contributions by Donald Rothberg, Roger Walsh, Michael Washburn, Michael Murphy, Stanislav Grof, Sean Kelly, Joseph Goldstein, Jack Kornfield, Michelle McDonald-Smith, Michael Zimmerman, Peggy Wright, Jürgen Kremer, Jeanne Achterberg, Robert McDermott, Kaisa Puhakka, and Ken Wilber. The pieces by Murphy and Puhakka (who attended the conference) were written specially for the collection.

61. During the Wilber conference some of those present regretted the fact that the discussions occasionally assumed the nature of a fight in which there were winners and losers. Wouldn't it be better, they said, to pursue the debate within the context of another metaphor such as that of a dance? But to my way of thinking there is a danger of complacency in this approach. During a heated theoretical discussion it is always clear that truth is at stake; the sense of urgency is not as clear if the discussion is perceived as a dance. Maybe the metaphor of a tournament would be better in this context: during a tennis match the players can fight to the death and still appreciate the game. But halfway through the match neither player is likely to stop and say: "After all, it's only a game . . ."

62. *Ken Wilber in Dialogue*, pp. 15–22.

63. *The Spectrum of Consciousness*, p. 11.

64. See, for example, *The Eye of Spirit*, p. 327; *One Taste*, pp. 293–98.

65. *The Eye of Spirit*, p. 63. Wilber sees Sri Aurobindo, Hegel, Adi Da, Schelling, Teilhard de Chardin, and Radakrishnan as all belonging to this neo-perennial school. See also the article "The Neo-Perennial Philosophy," first published in *The American*

Theosophist, Fall 1983, and subsequently reprinted in the Theosophical magazine *The Quest*, Autumn 1992.

66. Wilber is not entirely accurate when he writes: "The West has been—at least since the seventeenth century—almost completely bereft of even the least conception of the perennial philosophy." (*Journal of Transpersonal Psychology*, vol. 7, no. 2, p. 130). The theosophical movement was extremely popular in the twenties and did a great deal to popularize the ideas of the perennial philosophy.

67. H. P. Blavatsky, *The Key to Theosophy*, Theosophical University Press, 1889/1946, pp. 1–2.

68. The summaries of the work of A. Besant and C. W. Leadbeater compiled by A. E. Powell in the twenties—*The Etheric Double* (1925), *The Astral Body* (1926), *The Mental Body* (1927), *The Causal Body* (1928), and *The Solar System* (1930)—are also very informative in this respect.

69. W. Quine, Jr., *The Only Way*, State University of New York Press, 1997.

70. In *One Taste* Wilber suggests that the personality, the soul, and the Self should all be conceived of as lines of development that can exist relatively independently of one another (see in particular Fig. 7 on p. 294). This might explain why some enlightened individuals have a strong ego, in the sense that they have a powerful personality. In my opinion, however, in this notion the link between the human and the Divine is broken. In the sequence body / personality / Ego / monad, on the other hand, there is a single uninterrupted line from matter to spirit. Differences between enlightened individuals might also be explained by the fact that vertical development towards the spiritual planes of existence can coexist with various degrees of horizontal development within the personal planes of existence. For instance, one enlightened individual might have a great deal of physical strength, while another might have more highly developed mental abilities; yet this personal development is quite independent of the degree of spiritual development that both have attained.

71. See, for example, I. K. Taimni, *A Way to Self-Discovery*, Quest Books, 1970.

72. *Sex, Ecology, Spirituality*, pp. 356–62 and 643–45.

73. Among other things J. J. Poortman (1896–1970) wrote *Tweeërlei subjectiviteit* [Twofold subjectivity] (1929), *Ochèma* (1954/1967) [translated into English as *Vehicles of Consciousness* (1978)], and *De grondparadox* [The fundamental paradox] (1961). A collection of essays *Raakvlakken tussen oosterse en westerse filosofie* [Common ground between Eastern and Western philosophy] was published posthumously in 1976.

74. See, for example, "De vruchtbaarheid van de vedanta voor westers-wijsgerige probleemstellingen" [The fruitfulness of Vedanta in defining Western philosophical problems], *De grondparadox*, Van Gorcum, 1961, pp. 324–32.

75. That this is a true paradox, or apparent contradiction, is evident from the fact that there are two possible ways of looking at it: from the point of view of the universal Self mundane reality is illusory, yet from the point of view of the individual self mundane reality is undeniably real.

76. *De grondparadox*, p. 18. The infrarational is everything that has not yet been explained, but which is in principle ultimately explicable. The suprarational is that which can never be explained.

77. The discipline of so-called contemplative psychology, which is currently being pursued in the Netherlands by Dr. Han de Wit, and is inspired by the work of Chögyam

Trungpa, is more specifically concerned with the problems encountered during spiritual practice. See his books *Contemplatieve psychologie* [Contemplative psychology] (1987) and *De verborgen bloei* [The hidden flowering] (1993).

78. *Sex, Ecology, Spirituality*, pp. 421–22

BIBLIOGRAPHY

BOOKS BY KEN WILBER

1977   *The spectrum of Consciousness,* Quest Books.

1979   *No Boundary: Eastern and Western Approaches to Personal Growth,* Center Publications.

1980   *The Atman Project: A Transpersonal View of Human Development,* Quest Books.

1981   *Up from Eden: A Transpersonal View of Human Evolution,* Anchor/Doubleday.

1982   *The Holographic Paradigm and Other Paradoxes: Exploring the Leading Edge of Science,* Shambhala.

1983   *A Sociable God: A Brief Introduction to a Transcendental Sociology,* McGraw-Hill.

1983   *Eye to Eye: The Quest for the New Paradigm,* Anchor/Doubleday.

1984   *Quantum Questions: Mystical Writings of the World's Great Physicists,* Shambhala.

1986   *Transformations of Consciousness: Conventional and Contemplative Perspectives on Development,* Shambhala (co-edited with Jack Engler and Daniel Brown).

1987   *The Great Chain of Being: A Modern Introduction to the Perennial Philosophy and the World's Great Mystical Traditions* (unpublished manuscript)

1987   *Spiritual Choices: The Problem of Recognizing Authentic Paths to Inner Transformation,* Paragon House (co-edited with Dick Anthony and Bruce Ecker).

1991   *Grace and Grit: Spirituality and Healing in the Life of Treya Killam Wilber,* Shambhala.

1995   *Sex, Ecology, Spirituality* (Kosmos-trilogy, vol. 1), Shambhala.

1996   *A Brief History of Everything,* Shambhala.

1997   *The Eye of Spirit: An Integral Vision for a World Gone Slightly Mad,* Shambhala.

1998   *The Marriage of Sense and Soul: Integrating Science and Religion,* Random House.

1999   *One Taste: The Journals of Ken Wilber,* Shambhala.

1999   *Boomeritis: The Extraordiary Emergence of an Integral Culture and its Many Obstacles* (unpublished manuscript, rewritten as novel and published in 2002).

2000   *Integral Psychology: Conscioiusness, Spirit, Psychology, Therapy,* Shambhala

2000   *A Theory of Everything: An Integral Vision for Business, Politics, Science and Spirituality,* Shambhala.

2002   *Boomeritis: A Novel that Will Set You Free,* Shambhala.

COMPLETE BIBLIOGRAPHY OF KEN WILBER

A special thanks to Robert Fisher, Leslie McKay, and Brad Reynolds for helping me compile this bibliography.

1974

"The Spectrum of Consciousness," *Human Dimensions,* Summer.
"The Spectrum of Consciousness," *Main Currents in Modern Thought,* vol. 31, nr. 2, November/December.

1975

"Psychologia Perennis: The Spectrum of Consciousness," *Journal of Transpersonal Psychology,* vol. 7, nr. 2.
"The Perennial Psychology," *Human Dimensions,* vol. 4, nr 2.
"The Ultimate State of Consciousness," *Journal of Altered States of Consciousness,* vol. 2, nr. 3.

1976

"The Eternal Moment," *Science of Mind,* June.

1977

The Spectrum of Consciousness, Wheaton, Ill., The Theosophical Publishing House.

1978

"Spectrum Psychology, Part I: Transpersonal Developmental Psychology," *ReVision,* vol. 1, nr. 1.
"Spectrum Psychology, Part II: The Transpersonal Dynamic of Evolution," *ReVision,* vol. 1, nr. 2.
"Spectrum Psychology, Part III: Microgeny and the Tibetan Book of the Dead," *ReVision,* vol. 1, nr. 3/4.
"On Dreaming: The Other Side of You," *Foundation for Human Understanding,* vol. 1, nr. 1.
"Projection," *Foundation for Human Understanding,* vol. 1, nr. 2.
"A Working Synthesis of Transactional Analysis and Gestalt Therapy," in *Psychotherapy: Theory, Research and Practice,* vol. 15, nr. 1.
"Where It Was, I Shall Become," in Walsh and Shapiro (ed.), *Beyond Health and Normality: An Exploration of Extreme Well-Being,* New York, Van Nostrand Reinhold.

1979

No Boundary: Eastern and Western Approaches to Personal Growth, Los Angeles, Center Publications.
"A Developmental View of Consciousness," *Journal of Transpersonal Psychology*, vol. 11, nr. 1.
"Eye to Eye: Science and Transpersonal Psychology," *ReVision*, vol. 2, nr. 1.
"Spectrum Psychology, Part IV: Into the Transpersonal," *ReVision*, vol. 2, nr. 1.
"Physics, Mysticism and the New Holographic Paradigm: A Critical Appraisal," *ReVision*, vol. 2, nr. 2.
"Development and Transcendence," *The American Theosophist*, May.
"Heroes and Cults," *Vision Mound*, vol. 2, nr. 6.
"The Master-Student Relationship," *Foundation for Human Understanding*, vol. 2, nr. 1.
"Are the Chakra's Real?" in J. White (ed.), *Kundalini, Evolution and Enlightenment*, New York, Doubleday.
"Psychologia Perennis," in J. Welwood (ed.), *The Meeting of the Ways*, New York, Schocken.
"On Ego Strength and Egolessness," in J. Welwood (ed.), *The Meeting of the Ways*, New York, Schocken.
"Discussion of Symposium Presentations," in "Spiritual and Transpersonal Aspects of Altered States of Consciousness," *Journal of Transpersonal Psychology*, vol. 11, nr. 1.

1980

The Atman Project: A Transpersonal View of Human Development, Wheaton, Ill., The Theosophical Publishing House.
"The Pre/Trans Fallacy," *ReVision*, vol. 3, nr. 2.
"On Heroes and Cults," "Foreword" in Da Free John, *Scientific Proof of the Existence of God Will Soon Be Announced by the White House!*, Middletown, Cal., Dawn Horse Press (reprint of 1979).
"Who am I? Eastern and Western Approaches to Personal Growth," *Inner Paths*, March/April.

1981

Up from Eden: A Transpersonal View of Human Evolution, Garden City, New York, Anchor/Doubleday.
"Ontogenetic Development: Two Fundamental Patterns," *Journal of Transpersonal Psychology*, vol. 13, nr. 1.
"Republicans, Democrats and Mystics," *Association for Humanistic Psychology Newsletter*, November.
"The Physicist and the Mystic—Is a Dialogue Between Them Possible?" *ReVision* vol. 4, nr. 1.
"Reflections on the New Age Paradigm," *ReVision*, vol. 4, nr. 1.

1982

The Holographic Paradigm and Other Paradoxes: Exploring the Leading Edge of Science, Boulder, Shambhala.
"Odyssey: A Personal Inquiry into Humanistic and Transpersonal Psychology," *Journal of Humanistic Psychology*, vol. 22, nr. 1.

"Up from Eden: Ken Wilber Cracks Open the Creation/Evolution Debate: A New Age Interview with Ken Wilber," *New Age*, April (interview by Rich Ingrasci).
"The Problem of Proof," *ReVision*, Spring, vol. 5, nr. 1, pp. 80–100.

1983

A Sociable God: A Brief Introduction to a Transcendental Sociology, New York, McGraw-Hill.
Eye to Eye: The Quest for the New Paradigm, New York, Anchor/Doubleday.
"Kierkegaard's Passion," *ReVision*, vol. 6, nr. 1.
"The Neo-Perennial Philosophy," *The American Theosophist*, special fall issue.
"Reply to Critics," (an unpublished response to a paper by Dick Anthony called "The New Hegelians"), published as "Sociocultural Evolution" in *Collected Works of Ken Wilber*, vol. 4, 1999.

1984

Quantum Questions: Mystical Writings of the World's Great Physicists, Boulder, Shambhala (New Science Library).
A Sociable God: Towards a New Understanding of Religion, Boulder, Shambhala (New Science Library, reprint of 1983).
"The Developmental Spectrum and Psychopathology, Part I: Stages and Types of Pathology," *Journal of Transpersonal Psychology*, vol. 16, nr. 1.
"The Developmental Spectrum and Psychopathology, Part II: Treatment Modalities," *Journal of Transpersonal Psychology*, vol. 16, nr. 2.
"Sheldrake's Theory of Morphogenesis," *Journal of Humanistic Psychology*, vol. 24, nr. 2.
"Of Shadows and Symbols: Physics and Mysticism," *ReVision*, vol. 7, nr. 1.
"What is Transpersonal Psychology?" *The Laughing Man*, vol. 5, nr. 2.
"God, Evolution and the Spectrum of Consciousness: An Interview with Ken Wilber," by John White, *Science of Mind*, part 1, January, part 2, February.
"In Praise of the Ego: An Uncommon Buddhist Sermon," *The Middle Way*.

1985

"On Heroes and Cults," *The Laughing Man*, vol. 6, nr. 1 (reprint of article of 1979).
"The Dawn Horse Testament: A Brief Appreciation," promotional praise for *The Dawn Horse Testament* of Da Free John.

1986

Transformations of Consciousness: Conventional and Contemplative Perspectives on Development, Boston, Shambhala (co-edited with Jack Engler and Daniel Brown).

1987

Spiritual Choices: The Problem of Recognizing Authentic Paths to Inner Transformation, New York, Paragon House (co-editied with Dick Anthony and Bruce Ecker).
The Great Chain of Being: A Modern Introduction to the Perennial Philosophy and the World's Great Mystical Traditions (not published; some chapters have appeared as magazine articles).

"The Pundit of Transpersonal Psychology," *Yoga Journal*, nr. 76, September/October (interview by Catherine Ingram).

1988

"On Being a Support Person," *Journal of Transpersonal Psychology*, vol. 20, nr. 2.
"There Is No New Age: Baby Boomers, Narcissism and the 60's," *Vajradattu Sun*.
"Do We Make Ourselves Sick?" *New Age Journal*, September/October. 1989.

1989

"Two Humanistic Psychologies?: A Response," *Journal of Humanistic Psychology*, vol. 29, nr. 2.
"Let's Nuke the Transpersonalists: A Response to Albert Ellis," *Journal of Counseling and Development*, vol. 67, nr. 6.
"God is so Damn Boring: A Response to Kirk Schneider," *Journal of Humanistic Psychology*, vol. 29, nr. 4.
"Reply to Schneider," *Journal of Humanistic Psychology*, vol. 29, nr. 4.
"Love Story," *New Age Journal*, July/August.
"Foreword," in G. Feuerstein, *Yoga: The Technology of Ecstasy*, Los Angeles, J. P. Tarcher.
"Foreword," in L. Hixon, *Coming Home: The Experience of Enlightenment in Sacred Traditions*, Tarcher.
"Do We Make Ourselves Sick?" *New Age Journal*, September/October.
"Paradigm Wars: An Interview with Ken Wilber," *The Quest*, Spring.

1990

Eye to Eye: The Quest for the New Paradigm, Boston, Shambhala (2nd edition, with new chapter on art "In the Eye of the Artist: Art and the Perennial Philosophy").
"Two Patterns of Transcendence: A Reply to Washburn," *Journal of Humanistic Psychology*, vol. 30, nr. 3.
"Death, Rebirth and Meditation," in G. Doore (ed.), *What Survives?: Contemporary Explorations of Life after Death*, Los Angeles, J. P. Tarcher.
"In the Eye of the Artist: Art and the Perennial Philosophy," in A. Grey, *Sacred Mirrors: The Visionary Art of Alex Grey*, Inner Traditions.

1991

Grace and Grit: Spirituality and Healing in the Life of Treya Killam Wilber, Boston, Shambhala.
"Sex, Gender and Transcendence," *The Quest*, Summer.
"Gender Wars: A Continuing Conversation on Ken Wilber's 'Sex, Gender and Transcendence,'" *The Quest*, Fall.
"Taking Responsibility for Your Shadow," in C. Zweig and J. Abrams, *Meeting the Shadow: The Hidden Power of the Dark Side of Human Nature*, Los Angeles, J. P. Tarcher (A New Consciousness Reader).
"Foreword," in J. E. Nelson, *Healing the Split: Madness or Transcendence?: A New Understanding of the Crisis and Treatment of the Mentally Ill*, Los Angeles, J. P. Tarcher.

1992

"There are no Others to Save," in E. and D. Shapiro (ed.), *The Way Ahead: A Visionary Perspective for the New Millennium*, Element.

"Two Modes of Knowing," *Mind Field*, Summer.
"The Neo-Perennial Philosophy," *The Quest*, Fall (reprint of 1983 article).
Foreword in Chagdud Tulka, *Lord of the Dance, The Autobiography of a Tibetan Lama*, Padma Publishing.

1993

The Spectrum of Consciousness, Wheaton, Ill., The Theosophical Publishing House (2nd edition, with new foreword).
"The Great Chain of Being," *Journal of Humanistic Psychology*, vol. 33, nr. 3.
"Psychologia Perennis: The Spectrum of Consciousness," "The Spectrum of Transpersonal Development," "The Pre/Trans Fallacy," "The Spectrum of Pathologies," "The Spectrum of Therapies," "Eye to Eye: Science and Transpersonal Psychology," "The Great Chain of Being," "Paths Beyond Ego in the Coming Decade," in R. Walsh and F. Vaughan, *Paths Beyond Ego: The Transpersonal Vision*, Los Angeles, J. P. Tarcher (A New Consciousness Reader).
"Paths Beyond Ego in the Coming Decade," *ReVision*, Spring, vol. 15, nr. 4.

1994

"Foreword," in J. E. Nelson, *Healing the Split: Madness or Transcendence?: A New Understanding of the Crisis and Treatment of the Mentally Ill*, Albany, State University of New York Press (2nd edition, with foreword by Michael Washburn).
"Stages of Meditation: An Interview with Ken Wilber," *The Quest*, Spring.

1995

Sex, Ecology, Spirituality: The Spirit of Evolution, Boston, Shambhala (*Kosmos* trilogy, vol. 1).
"An Informal Overview of Transpersonal Studies," *Journal of Transpersonal Psychology*, vol. 27, nr. 2.
"Mind and the Heart of Emptiness: Reflections on Intellect and the Spiritual Path," *The Quest*, Winter.
"A Message to Eurotas," *Eurotas News*, nr. 2, Spring.
"The World According to Wilber," interview by David Guy, *New Age Journal*, July/August.
"Don't Blame Men for the Patriarchy: A Conversation with Ken Wilber," *New Age Journal*, July/August.
Foreword in F. Vaughan, *Shadows of the Sacred: Seeing Through Spiritual Illusions*, Quest Books.

1996

A Brief History of Everything, Boston, Shambhala.
The Atman Project: A Transpersonal View of Human Development, Wheaton, Ill., The Theosophical Publishing House (2nd edition, with new foreword).
Up from Eden: A Transpersonal View of Human Evolution, Wheaton, Ill., The Theosophical Publishing House (2d edition, with new foreword).
Eye to Eye: The Quest for the New Paradigm, Boston, (3rd edition, with new foreword).
"Transpersonal Art and Literary Theory," *Journal of Transpersonal Psychology*, vol. 28, nr. 1.

"A More Integral Approach: A Response to the *ReVision* Authors," and "Afterword" *ReVision*, vol. 19, nr. 2 (Wilber's response to critical contributions in nrs. 18(4) and 19(1)).

"How Big is Our Umbrella?" *Noetic Sciences Review*, winter.

"Big Map: The Kosmos According to Ken Wilber," *Shambhala Sun*, September (interview by R. Kornman).

"Bodhisattva's zullen aan politiek moeten gaan doen" [Boddhisattvas will have to become politicians], PANTA, nr. 11, Spring (interview by Frank Visser).

"Foreword," in B. W. Scotton, A. B. Chinen, and J. R. Battista (ed.), *Textbook of Transpersonal Psychiatry and Psychology*, New York, Basic Books.

"How Shall We See Art?" in M. R. Severens, e.a., *Andrew Wyeth: America's Painter*, New York, Hudson Hill Press.

1997

The Eye of Spirit: An Integral Vision for a World Gone Slightly Mad, Boston, Shambhala.

"Transpersonal Hot Spots: Reflections on the New Editions of *Up from Eden, The Atman Project* and *Eye to Eye*," *Journal of Humanistic Psychology*, vol. 37, nr. 4.

"An Integral Theory of Consciousness," *The Journal of Consciousness Studies*, vol. 4, nr. 1.

"A Spirituality that Transforms," *What is Enlightenment?* nr. 12, Fall/Winter.

"To See a World: Art and the I of the Beholder" (essay for an exhibition by Anselm Kiefer, a contemporary German painter).

"Bodhisattvas are Going to Have to Become Politicians," *Eurotas News: Newsletter of the European Transpersonal Association*, nr. 4 (interview by Frank Visser).

"Everyone is Right: A Conversation with Ken Wilber on his Life and Books," (unpublished interview by Frank Visser.)

"Foreword," in David Deida, *The Way of the Superior Man : A Spiritual Guide to Mastering the Challenges of Women, Work, and Sexual Desire*, Plexus.

"Foreword," in S. Boorstein, *Clinical Studies in Transpersonal Psychotherapy*, State University of New York Press.

1998

The Marriage of Sense and Soul: Integrating Science and Religion, New York, Random House.

"Up Close and Transpersonal," *Utne Reader*, August (interview with Mark Matousek).

"A More Integral Approach", in D. Rothberg and S. Kelly, *Ken Wilber in Dialogue: Conversations with Leading Transpersonal Thinkers*, Wheaton, Quest Books (reprint of 1996).

"Foreword," in A. Grey, *The Mission of Art*, Boston, Shambhala.

"Foreword," in *Talks with Ramana Maharshi*, Inner Directions.

"A Ticket to Athens," *Pathways*, (interview by Richard Young).

"Egoless Means More," *Shambhala Sun*, July.

"So Who Are You?" *Shambhala Sun*, September.

"The Irony and the Ecstacy," *Shambhala Sun*, November.

'Response to Jorge Ferrer's "Speak Now or Forever Hold Your Peace: A Review Essay of Ken Wilber's *The Marriage of Sense and Soul*," ' *Journal of Transpersonal Psychology*, vol. 30, nr. 1.

1999

One Taste: The Journals of Ken Wilber, Boston, Shambhala.
Collected Works of Ken Wilber, Boston, Shambhala.
—vol. I: The Spectrum of Consciousness / No Boundary.
—vol. II: Up from Eden / The Atman Project.
—vol. III: A Sociable God / Eye to Eye.
—vol. IV: Integral Psychology / Transformations of Consciousness / Selected Essays.
"An Approach to Integral Psychology," Journal of Transpersonal Psychology, vol. 31, nr. 2.
Boomeritis: The Extraordinary Emergence of an Integral Culture and Its Many Obstacles,
    (unpublished manuscript, rewritten as novel and published in 2002).
"Constant Consciousness," Shambhala Sun, January.
"The Denial of the Universal," Shambhala Sun, March.
"Is it Only Rock and Roll?" Shambhala Sun, May.
"Liberalism and Religion: We Should Talk," Shambhala Sun, July.

2000

Integral Psychology: Consciousness, Spirit, Psychology, Therapy, Boston, Shambhala.
Collected Works of Ken Wilber, Boston, Shambhala.
—vol. V: Grace and Grit.
—vol. VI: Sex, Ecology, Spirituality.
—vol. VII: A Brief History of Everything / The Eye of Spirit.
—vol. VIII: The Marriage of Sense and Soul / One Taste.
A Theory of Everything: An Integral Vision for Business, Politics, Science and Spirituality,
    Boston, Shambhala.
No Boundary: Eastern and Western Approaches to Personal Growth, Boston, Shambhala
    (2nd edition, with new foreword).
A Brief History of Everything, Boston, Shambhala (2nd edition, with new foreword).
One Taste: Daily Reflections on Integral Spirituality, Boston, Shambhala (2nd edition).
Eye to Eye: The Quest for the New Paradigm, Boston, Shambhala (4th edition).
Grace and Grit: Spirituality and Healing in the Life and Death of Treya Killam Wilber,
    Boston, Shambhala (2nd edition).
"Foreword," in J. Marion, Putting on the Mind of Christ, Hampton Roads Publishing
    Company.
"Foreword," in M. J. Ryan (ed.), The Fabric of the Future: Women Visionaries of Today
    Illuminate the Path to Tomorrow, Berkeley, Conari Press.
"Foreword" in A. S. Dalal (ed.), A Greater Psychology: An Introduction to the Psychologi-
    cal Thought of Sri Aurobindo, Tarcher/Putnam.
"Foreword," in Ph. Rubinov-Jacobson, Drinking Lightning: Art, Creativity, and Trans-
    formation, Boston, Shambhala.
"Integral Transformative Practice: In This World or Out of It?" What is Enlighten-
    ment? Fall/Winter.
"The Terror of Tomorrow: A Response to Bill Joy" (wilber.shambhala.com).
"Announcing the Formation of Integral Institute" (wilber.shambhala.com).
"On Critics, Integral Institute, My Recent Writing, and Other Matters of Little
    Consequence: A Shambhala Interview with Ken Wilber" (wilber.shambhala.com).
"Waves, Streams, States and Self: A Summary of My Psychological Model (Or, Outline
    of An Integral Psychology)" (wilber.shambhala.com)

"Waves, Streams, States and Self: Further Considerations for an Integral Theory of Consciousness," *Journal of Consciousness Studies*, vol. 7, nrs. 11–12, November/December.

2001

"Do Critics Misrepresent My Position? A Test Case from a Recent Academic Journal" (wilber.shambhala.com).
"On the Nature of a Post-Metaphysical Spirituality: Response to Habermas and Weiss" (wilber.shambhala.com), interview by Frank Visser and Edith Zundel.
"Prologue To Boomeritis, The Novel" (wilber.shambhala.com)
"Introduction To 'The Deconstruction of the World Trade Center'" (wilber.shambhala.com).
"The Deconstruction of the World Trade Center: A Date That Will Live in a Sliding Chain of Signifiers" (wilber.shambhala.com)
"To See a World: Some Technical Points" (www.worldofkenwilber.com)
"Some Thoughts on Samuel P. Huntington's The Clash of Civilizations" (www.worldofkenwilber.com)
"Speaking of Everything," interview by Jordan Gruber, Enlightenment.Com (also on CD).

2002

Boomeritis: A Novel that Will Set You Free, Boston, Shambhala.
"Interview with Ken Wilber: On the Release of Boomeritis, and the Completion of Volume 3 of the Kosmos Trilogy" (wilber.shambhala.com)
"Endnotes to Boomeritis" (wilber.shambhala.com)
"Sidebars to Boomeritis" (wilber.shambhala.com):
  A: "Who Ate Captain Cook? Integral Historiography in a Postmodern Age"
  B: "The Many Names of the Levels of Consciousness"
  C: "Orange and Green: Levels or Cousins?"
  D: "Childhood Spirituality"
  E: "The Genius Descartes Gets a Postmodern Drubbing"
  F: "Participatory Samsara: The Green-Meme Approach to the Mystery of the Divine"
  G: "States and Stages"
  H: "Boomeritis Buddhism"
Excerpts from the *Kosmos* trilogy (wilber.shambhala.com)
  A: "An Integral Age at the Leading Edge"
  B: "The Many Ways We Touch: Three Principles Helpful for Any Interpretive Approach"
"Foreword," in A. Cohen, *Living Enlightenment: A Call for Evolution Beyond Ego*, Moksha Press.
"Foreword," in D. Deida, *Finding God Through Sex: A Spiritual Guide to Ecstatic Loving and Deep Passion for Men and Women*, Plexus.
"Foreword," in W. Teasdale, *A Monk in the World: Cultivating a Spiritual Life*, New World Library.
"Foreword," in F. Visser, *Ken Wilber: Thought as Passion*, State University of New York Press.
"The Guru and the Pandit: The Evolution of Enlightenment, Andrew Cohen and Ken Wilber in Dialogue," *What is Enlightenment?* Spring/Summer, p. 38–49, 136–143.
"The Guru and the Pandit: Breaking the Rules, Andrew Cohen and Ken Wilber in Dialogue," *What is Enlightenment?* Fall/Winter, p. 39–49.

"Foreword," in M. Schlitz and T. Hyman, *Integral Medicine: A Noetic Reader* (submitted for publication).
"Foreword," in S. Harguindey, *Spirit and Politics* (submitted for publication).

2003

Excerpts from the *Kosmos* Trilogy, (www.integralinstitute.org)
 C: The Ways We Are in This Together: Intersubjectivity and Interobjectivity in the Holonic Kosmos
 D: Zone #2: The Outsides of the Interiors
 E: The Gathering of the Zones
 F: Integral Post-Metaphysics
 G: A Comprehensive Theory of Subtle Energies

2004

Collected Works of Ken Wilber, Boston, Shambhala.
—vol. IX: *Boomeritis / Sidebars / Endnotes.*
—vol. X: *A Theory of Everything / Essays / Interviews / Forewords.*
—vol. XI: *Kosmic Karma and Creativity.*

INDEX